AMERICAN GENERALSHIP

Other Books by Edgar F. Puryear Jr.

19 Stars
Stars in Flight
George S. Brown

AMERICAN GENERALSHIP

Character is Everything:
The Art of Command

Edgar F. Puryear Jr.

PRESIDIO

This book is dedicated to the millions of soldiers, sailors, airmen, and marines who, along with their spouses and families, devoted themselves to a life of selfless service to God and country. It is their commitment and sense of duty that has kept our nation, and the rest of the western world, free from the many threats democracy has faced in our country's history.

Copyright © 2000 by Edgar F. Puryear Jr.

Published by Presidio Press, Inc.
505 B San Marin Drive, Suite 300
Novato, CA 94945-1340

Library of Congress Cataloging-in-Publication Data

Puryear, Edgar F., 1930–
    American generalship : character is everything: the art of command / Edgar F. Puryear.
      p. cm.
    ISBN 0-89141-658-7
    1. Command of troops. 2. Generals—United States. 3. Leadership. 4. Character. I. Title.

UB210 .P77 2000
355.3'31'0973—dc

                    99-048919

Printed in the United States of America

Contents

Acknowledgments

In writing this book, I have been assisted by too many people to mention them all, particularly each of the more than 100 generals and admirals whom I interviewed over the last thirty-five years. These men are the epitome of character, whose selfless service to God and country has made others admire them, follow them, and believe in them. These exceptional men have never stopped serving, and unlike any other profession I know, have a never-ending commitment to the development of subsequent generations of young men and women who have chosen military service as their career. To each of these officers, we all owe a huge debt of gratitude.

No author could have received better support from a publisher than the support I received from Presidio Press. Colonel Robert V. Kane, USA (Ret.), the founder of Presidio Press, read the early drafts of the manuscript three times, and with each draft taught me more and more about what skilled and intelligent editing can contribute to organization and to enlightening prose. I was also fortunate to have received meaningful editorial assistance from Richard Kane and E. J. McCarthy of Presidio Press. During the process of publishing the manuscript, copyeditor Barbara Feller-Roth made many sound suggestions for improving the book for which I am most appreciative.

My youngest son, A. A. "Cotton" Puryear, provided exceptional computer skills and journalistic ability. His ideas and suggestions were invaluable and I owe much to him for the quality of the prose and the organization of the chapters. I cannot thank Deborah Foster enough for her patience, speed, and efficiency in typing many drafts of the manuscript. Helen M. Slaven gave meaningful assistance in typing letters and interviews, as well as relieving me of routine matters that allowed me time to focus my attention on this book. The contribution of my second eldest son Edgar F. "Chip" Puryear III, has been significant. He is a fine scholar and his research in tracking down reliable leads was vitally important. My son S. B. "Colt" Puryear was of assistance as an example of an exceptional soldier with his experiences in the trenches. I appreciate the extensive editorial assistance of Jinnie B. Mason whose attention to detail and foundation in grammar has provided a much more polished version for the scrutiny of the copy editor.

I appreciate the association with the National Defense University Foundation and the Presidents of the National Defense University, Lt. Gen. Ervin J. Rokke, USAF, (Ret.), president from 1994 to 1997; and Lt. Gen. Richard A. Chilcoat, president from 1997 to present.

I owe a special debt of gratitude to Gen. Robert W. Porter Jr., USA (Ret.), who, to my good fortune, chose to retire in my home county of Madison, Virginia. He has been a living example of a man of character, an embodiment of Duty, Honor, Country, and an inspiration to me and my entire family. I want to especially express my gratitude to Brig. Gen. Philip J. Erdle, USAF (Ret.), for the opportunity to share ideas, for his contagious enthusiasm, his character, his belief in this endeavor, but most of all, for his friendship over the last forty-plus years.

Last, but certainly not least, I want to thank my wife, Agnes G. Puryear, for years of patience and support during the countless hours of research, traveling, and writing of the manuscript.

Introduction

T his study of leadership represents thirty-five years of research on how one leads successfully in the U.S. military. Over this period of time, I have had personal interviews with more than a hundred officers of four-star rank, and interviews or personal correspondence with more than a thousand officers of the rank of brigadier general and higher. In addition, I have sent and received more than ten thousand letters and consulted many diaries and hundreds of autobiographies, biographies, memoirs, and military histories.

In 1971 I wrote a book entitled *Nineteen Stars: A Study in Military Character and Leadership,* a comparative study of the leadership of four of the most outstanding American generals of World War II, of what made them good leaders and how they led. For this comparative study I selected General of the Army George C. Marshall, chief of staff of the U.S. Army from 1939 to 1945; General of the Army Douglas MacArthur, commander in chief in the Far East, General of the Army Dwight D. Eisenhower, supreme commander of Allied forces for the invasions of North Africa, Sicily, and Europe—the greatest invasion in the history of warfare; and Gen. George S. Patton, Jr., commander of the U.S. Army I and II Corps in North Africa, the Seventh Army in Sicily, and the Third Army in Europe.

The reasons for the selection of these four personalities is too obvious to deserve more than a cursory mention. Marshall, MacArthur, and Eisenhower held the most responsible military positions of World War II, and Patton was the best-known combat general of the war. The title of the manuscript reflects the total number of stars, nineteen, earned by these four great leaders. *Nineteen Stars* is still in print, having had numerous reprints, and is still in demand by individuals interested in military leadership.

Since the publication of *Nineteen Stars*, I have given hundreds of talks on leadership to military and civilian audiences. During these presentations, I have been asked frequently to say more about recent U.S. military leaders. These inquiries have encouraged me to write a sequel to *Nineteen Stars*, to bring the leadership study up-to-date by interviewing or researching military leaders for the period from World War II through 1999. My personal one-on-one interviews, with more than a hundred four-star generals and admirals, include chairmen of the Joint Chiefs of Staff, army commanders of World War II, commanders of various army commands and air force units, chiefs of staff of the army and air force, commandants of the Marine Corps, and chiefs of naval operations. The research also includes interviews and correspondence with more than a thousand officers of the rank brigadier general, and higher, and correspondence with more than ten thousand people who served with, under, and above the generals. All this in an effort to answer the question of how one becomes a successful leader in the American military.

Since *Nineteen Stars* was published, hundreds of new books have appeared on American military leaders, including autobiographies, memoirs, biographies, and military histories. In addition, I have had access to many diaries and the letters and speeches of the key generals, all of which have provided considerable new resource material.

World War II, the Cold War and post–Cold War, and the wars in Korea, Vietnam, and Iraq offered great challenges for American military leadership. Upon the quality of this leadership rests the freedom of the United States and the world. In a Pentagon office in 1946 after World War II was over, Winston Churchill spoke informally to a group of thirty of the most outstanding U.S. Army and Army Air Force leaders of the war. With his chair tilted back, his feet propped up on the desk, and a glass of brandy in one hand and a big black cigar in the other hand, he told this group that he had believed that the United States had the materiel and manpower to swing the fate of the war to the side of the Allies, but he was truly amazed that we produced such superior military leadership.

The United States during World War II and the postwar period has had a wealth of brilliant military leaders who devoted their lives to serving God and country. When war was forced upon America, we were ready to provide military leadership unequaled anywhere in the world. This book provides readers with the thoughts and insights of these generals on how leadership has won our wars and preserved freedom for the West.

One of the purposes of this volume is to determine how these leaders developed and obtained their insights on how to lead successfully. The comment is often made that leaders are born, not made. If they are all born that way, what is the value of this book? The statement "born, not made," if taken literally, would mean that at birth one's ability to be a leader is already decided, that upbringing and environment have no role in the development of an individual. If the statement is interpreted less strictly, it might mean that a person is born with certain qualities that offer the potential, in a nurturing environment, for successful leadership.

I interviewed twenty of the thirty generals who were in the office with Churchill in 1946. One of the members of this group was General of the Army Dwight Eisenhower, who during a discussion of leadership with me commented on the statement that leaders are born, not made. "I think," he said, "that there is something to the expression 'born to command' or 'born to lead.' But there are many people who have the potential for leadership, just as there are probably many people born with the potential to be great artists that never have the opportunity or the training for the full development of their talents. I think leadership is a product of native ability plus environment. By environment, I mean training and the opportunity to exercise leadership."

I interviewed Eisenhower's American army field commander, General of the Army Omar N. Bradley. His answer to the born leader question was, "I would say some are born. A person can be born with certain qualities of leadership: good physique, good mental capacity, curiosity, and the desire to know. When you go to pick out the best pup in a litter of bird dogs, you pick out the pup even though he is only six weeks old. He is curious, going around looking into things, and that kind of dog usually turns out to be the best dog.

"But there are qualities one can improve on; a thorough knowledge of your profession is the first requirement of leadership, and that certainly has to be acquired. Observing others is important—trying to determine what makes them stand out. That's why I think we can learn a lot by studying past leaders. Studying Lee, other Civil War leaders, Jackson, Lincoln. Trying to see what made them great."

The question was put somewhat differently to Gen. Anthony C. McAuliffe: "Do you think the ability to handle masses of men is something a young man can train himself to do?" McAuliffe, author of the most famous one-word speech of World War II ("Nuts," in reply to a German order to surrender when his men were surrounded at Bastogne), said, "I think that's a God given gift you are born with. People like General MacArthur, General Patton, Field Marshal Montgomery were actors in addition to being leaders. They had a sort of flair that had a great effect on masses of men." McAuliffe said that the decisiveness of leadership was a quality a man could develop, but "you can improve it only to an extent; you have to be born with a large measure of it." McAuliffe gave a qualification, however. "After character, knowledge is most important. Knowledge builds confidence and decisiveness. When you know your business thoroughly, I think you are encouraged to be bold and decisive in action. That has been typical of General MacArthur and General Patton. I think their broad knowledge of the military profession contributed greatly to their boldness in decision and their success as leaders."

One of the strongest supporters of the born leader thesis was the commander of the VII Corps in World War II, Gen. J. Lawton Collins, who was chief of staff of the U.S. Army from 1949 to 1953. He said: "Only a limited number of people combine the necessary qualities of character, integrity, intelligence, and a willingness to work, which leads to a knowledge of their profession, to become our successful leaders. There are God-given talents we inherit from our forebears." Still he does not believe that one is limited at birth: "There are, however, techniques of leadership that anybody can learn if given a modicum of intelligence and a willingness to work."

Another successful corps commander of World War II, Gen. Wade H. Haislip, reflected: "One thing that disturbed me when I started out in this business was the old theory that leaders are born, not made. When I started studying, I tried to break down that theory; and I developed what I consider the basic elements with which anybody could be successful if they stuck to it."

General Eisenhower was reported to have said of his World War II air commander, Gen. Carl "Tooey" Spaatz: "He was the only general I had who never made a mistake."

I also asked General Spaatz about the "why" of successful leadership. "I think leaders just happen to grow up," he said. "I think you must be born with certain characteristics, but it's more a case of what takes place after you are born that decides whether or not you are going to be a leader."

General Mark W. Clark, commander of the Fifth Army in the invasion of Italy in World War II, concluded, "I would say that most leaders are made. A fellow that comes from a long line of ancestors with determination and courage has no doubt inherited some leadership qualities. I have seen many times in combat where somebody who is small and meek was given the opportunity and had leadership you never before realized he had, and he becomes a Medal of Honor winner. There are some qualities you inherit that make you a good leader; but many who don't have these qualities develop them when opportunity knocks."

General Lucian K. Truscott, respectively a division, a corps, and an army commander in World War II, said, "I suppose men are born with traits that can be cultivated in the direction of leadership. But there is also no doubt that leadership can be cultivated. The idea of any man being born an army commander or being born to be a theatre commander, such as General Eisenhower, just isn't so. The characteristics of leadership, any leadership, necessarily have to include a certain decisiveness, a certain confidence. In most cases you will find that decisiveness and confidence come from knowledge based on studies and training. The fundamental thing is your basic knowledge, the development of your mind, and your ability to apply this knowledge as you go along your military career."

General William H. Simpson, who led the Ninth Army in World War II, believed, "Everyone is not a born leader. Leadership can be learned. I wish somebody had told me that when I was young. The successful handling of men requires the application of certain qualities of leadership. There are few natural leaders, very few."

General Albert C. Wedemeyer, senior American commander in China during the latter part of World War II, replied to the comment that leaders are born, not made: "No, I don't agree with that. I think there are some men who have a better chance of developing into leaders. This is primarily because of their interest in the activities that lead to leadership. I think most genius is the result of hard work; and any young man, if he has guts and stick-to-itiveness, can make good in life, if given an average body and mind. It's up to the individual, but there must be a spark, a continuing curiosity."

The comments of the above officers, all of whom achieved great distinction as successful wartime commanders, offer a sample of the thinking of American military leaders. The strongest supporters of the born leader thesis believe that there are certain qualities you must be born with, but even these characteristics must be developed. There are others who have concluded that anyone can be a leader by working at it. All emphasized the role of education, experience, study, and environment in developing leaders. The post–World War II generals all concurred that leaders are not born but are developed, but they pointed out that there are certain qualities that an individual is born with that are important in leadership development.

The study of great captains and the classical writers on war will always be necessary in the development of military leaders, for wars will always be won by men and women. Weapons may change, but human nature will not. The United States will always need trained military leaders for wars. "Only the dead," said Plato, "have seen the end of war." Is war the normal condition of mankind? It would seem so; thus we need to study military leadership. We have been fortunate in past wars; we have had time to prepare. But modern warfare will not permit long preparation time. A great nation responsible for the world's freedom must be prepared for instant war. No longer can we depend upon nations such as Great Britain and France to hold off the enemy while we spend several years deciding whether to enter the conflict and, if so, have the luxury of leisurely preparation for war. In the future, we may be hit first.

While researching this book, I received comments to the effect that the subject of my inquiry was not leadership but generalship, or that a particular personality was not a leader but a staff officer. Others commented that the topic being researched was not leadership but command. Still others said it was administration or management. There is no need to argue semantics. This book is a discussion of generals, why they became top generals and how they ran the show after achieving their high positions of military responsibility. The word used here to encompass how they ran the show is *leadership*.

In comparing the leadership of the officers in this study, it became clear that they possessed certain qualities that were essential to their success. I do not contend that a study of these qualities will guarantee the reader the same greatness achieved by these generals; however, it will certainly, at a minimum, make the average man better. It is a great mistake to make no conscious effort at leadership training. It should not just be the by-product of other forms of training. Services of all nations publish material listing rules of thumb on how to lead men, but listing rules is not enough. The qualities for successful leadership need to be given life and meaning.

The literature on military leadership is in agreement that there are some qualities absolutely necessary for successful leadership: selflessness; the willingness to accept the responsibility to be involved in decision making; possessing and developing the quality of "feel" and sixth sense in decision making; an aversion to " yes men;" officers who grew and developed through a life of reading; having careers that developed through mentors, particularly being close to men making decisions; understanding the importance of consideration and concern for troops; and realizing that the ability to delegate determines how far one will go in the American military. The greatest of all is character, which is everything in leadership. It permeates throughout all the qualities essential for leadership success. This book has as its purpose the objective of giving life and meaning to what character is. It cannot really be defined. It must be described. And that is what this book endeavors to do.

The qualities of leadership need to be given meaning so they can become alive through the personalities of well-known and proven leaders. If this were not true, it should be enough to list all the necessary qualities and expect a person reading them to become a great leader. The qualities necessary for success require more than just a listing. What is necessary is a description of leadership and the qualities for success. That was the objective of *Nineteen Stars* and now of *American Generalship: Character Is Everything.* Neither book claims to have *the* answer to success as a military leader, but they do have *an* answer.

There is a consensus among the leaders I have interviewed on the essential qualities for successful American military leadership: establishing a pattern. The generals who had the key leadership responsibilities in World War II, the Korean War, the Vietnam War, and the war with Iraq all support the others' insights on successful leadership.

Chapter 1: Selflessness

I had been accustomed throughout my life to classify all public servants into one or the other of two general categories: one, the men who were thinking what they could do for their job; the other, the men who were thinking what the job could do for them.
—Henry L. Stimson, Secretary of War, 1909–11;
Secretary of State, 1928–32; Secretary of War, 1939–45

There are many qualities that combine to make a leader successful. Among the most important are professional knowledge, decision, humanity, equity, courage, consideration, delegation, loyalty, selflessness, and character. From all my research, however, it is clear that there is absolutely nothing as important in successful leadership as character. Many great generals, such as George Washington, Robert E. Lee, George C. Marshall are remembered not only as great leaders but as men whose character predominated.

There are many comments and discussions in this book that focus on the quality of character. One was made by Henry L. Stimson, secretary of war from 1939 to 1945, who commented: "General Marshall's leadership takes its authority directly from his great strength of character."

There were many other references to Marshall's character. Prime Minister Winston Churchill said Marshall was "a man of singular eminence and character." In a letter to Marshall on V-E Day, Churchill wrote: "I have waited to answer your message until the stir was somewhat less, because I wished to tell you what pride it has been to me to receive such words of friendship and approval from you. We certainly have seen and felt together a great deal of the hard inside working of this terrific war, and there is no one whose good opinion at the end of the struggle I value more than yours.

"It has not fallen to your lot to command the great armies. You have had to create them, organize them, and inspire them. Under your guiding hand the mighty and valiant formations, which have swept across France and Germany, were brought into being and perfected in an amazingly short space of time. Not only were the fighting troops and their complicated ancillaries created, but, to an extent that seems almost incredible to me, the supply of commanders capable of maneuvering the vast organisms of modern armies and groups of armies and of moving these with unsurpassed celerity were also found wherever they were needed; apart from this and in the sphere of major strategy, you have been the mainspring of that marvelous organization, the Combined Chiefs of Staff, whose conduct and relationship will ever be a model for the planning and supervision of Allied and Combined operations.

"There has grown in my breast through all these years of mental exertion a respect and admiration for your character and massive strength which has been a real comfort to your fellow toilers, of whom I hope it will always be recorded that I was one."[1]

President Woodrow Wilson, in a speech to the University of North Carolina, said of Robert E. Lee: "[His achievements] are in the memory not only of every soldier, but of every lover of high and gifted men who likes to see achievements which proceed from character to see those things done which are not done with the selfish purpose of self-aggrandizement, but in order to serve a country, and prove worthy of a cause. These are the things which make the name of this great man not only prominent but in some regard unapproachable in the history of our country."

General Ulysses S. Grant, who led the Union army to victory, in his *Memoirs* reflected on Lee's character, and his own as well, at the surrender of Appomattox: "What General Lee's feelings were I do not know. As he was a man of much dignity, with an impassable face, it was impossible to say whether he felt inwardly glad that the court had finally come, or felt sad over the result, and was too manly to show it. Whatever his feelings, they were entirely concealed from my observation: but my own feelings, which had been quite jubilant on the receipt of his letter, were sad and depressed. I felt like anything rather than rejoicing at the downfall of a foe who had fought so long and valiantly, and had suffered so much for a cause, though that cause was, I believe, one of the worst for which a people ever fought, and for one which there was the least excuse. I do not question, however, the sincerity of the great mass of those who were opposed to us."[2]

The Reverend J. William Jones, D.D., who was Lee's chaplain in the Civil War and his minister after the war, wrote: "I have been the daily witness to those beautiful traits of character which made him seem even grander in peace than in war."

Lee received many accolades from scholars. In the translation of Homer's *Iliad* by British scholar Philip Stanhope Worsley, Fellow of Corpus Christi College, Oxford, England, the dedication was to General Robert E. Lee. Worsley wrote: "You will allow me, in dedicating this work to you, that Lee . . . is the hero, like Hector in the *Iliad*, . . . and some of the grandest passages in the poem come to me when I remember his lofty character. . . ."

The two most prominent and successful generals for the Union in the Civil War were Ulysses S. Grant and William Tecumseh Sherman. When Grant was singled out by Lincoln to be his top general, he was called to Washington to receive his promotion from Lincoln. Sherman, knowing what Washington was like, wrote to his brother Sen. John Sherman: "Give Grant all the support you can. He is subject to the disgusting but dangerous process of being lionized. . . . Grant is as good a leader as we can find. He has honesty, simplicity of character, singleness of purpose, and no hopes to usurp civil power. His character, more than his genius, will reconcile armies and attach the people."[3]

The most significant scholarly writing on Lee was the definitive biography written by Dr. Douglas Southhall Freeman. It illustrated Lee's impact upon Marshall. Dr. Freeman had a great deal of research material left over after completing the Lee biography, and he used that resource material to write the three-volume work entitled *Lee's Lieutenants*. Freeman published an article at that time (during World War II) entitled "General Lee and General Marshall," which read in part: "At this stage of the war, two items of General Lee's equipment as a commander that are most important in our leadership were his ability to guess well, and his sound judgment. I believe General George C. Marshall, Army Chief of Staff, is showing exactly the same thorough, detached judgment General Lee showed. The nation can afford to gamble on the gamble General Marshall is taking because behind the gamble is great intellect, sound judgment, and magnificent character."[4]

Mrs. Marshall was moved by the article and said in her book *Together:* "I sent this article in my next letter to George, as General Lee was one of the two men he admired most in our history, the other being Benjamin Franklin. General Lee he esteemed for his character and ability as a soldier, Benjamin Franklin for his common sense and understanding of human nature."[5]

General of the Army Dwight (Ike) D. Eisenhower was the embodiment of character. In 1941 he was advising his only living son, John, on what he should do after graduating from high school. Ike elaborated upon this in his book *At Ease: Stories I Tell My Friends:*

John must have wondered why I stayed in the Army at all. To give him the less gloomy side of the picture, I said that my Army experience had been wonderfully interesting and it had brought me into contact with men of ability, honor, and a sense of high dedication to their country.

Later, Ike asked his son:

"Obviously, John, from what Uncle Ed says, you've made up your mind to try to enter West Point."

"Yes, that's right."

I asked him about his reasons. The substance of his answer was: "It's because of what you told me the other evening. When you talked about the satisfaction you had in an Army career, and the pride you had in being associated with men of character, my mind was made up right then." He added, "If I can say the same thing when I've finished my Army career, I'll care no more about promotions than you did."[6]

These comments emphasize the importance of character. What then is character? What role does character play in successful leadership?

To some, success is the only common denominator applicable to eminent commanders because success signifies leadership and creates conscience. But George Washington lost many battles before the final victory, and the majority of his men did not lose confidence in him. Lee was a commander on the losing side, but his name is synonymous with leadership. Why? Both were men of character.

Leadership is really the unconscious expression of the character and personality of the leader. Eisenhower told me: "Character in many ways is everything in leadership. It is made up of many things, but I would say character is really integrity. When you delegate something to a subordinate, for example, it is absolutely your responsibility, and he must understand this. You as a leader must take complete responsibility for what that subordinate does."[7]

To General Bradley, character meant "dependability, integrity, the characteristic of never knowingly doing anything wrong, that you would never cheat anyone, that you would give everybody a fair deal. Character is sort of an all-inclusive thing. If a man has character, everyone has confidence in him. Soldiers must have confidence in their leader."[8]

General Mark Clark, commander in Italy in World War II, remarked about the qualities necessary for successful leadership: "I would put character at the top of the list. If you want to select an officer for your command, you want one who is confident of his abilities, who is loyal and who has got good character. It is the man of good character that I am going to seek out. There are a lot of people who know the 'smart' way of getting things done, but they also ride roughshod over people that they are supposed to be working with. I don't want that."[9]

"Character," said Lucian K. Truscott, a corps and army commander in World War II, "as we used to say when I was in elementary school, is what you are. Reputation is what others think you are. The reason that some fail to climb the ladder of success, or of leadership if you want to call it that, is that there is a difference between reputation and character. The two do not always coincide. A man may be considered to have sterling character. Opportunity might come to that man; but if he has the reputation for something he is not, he may fail that opportunity. I think character is the foundation of successful leadership."[10]

To Gen. Carl Spaatz, first chief of staff of the air force and air commander in Europe during World War II, character is a strong will. "You can't be wishy-washy as a military leader," he commented. "You must be able to size up the situation and make a decision. Indecisiveness is weakness of character. You must be able to have confidence in what a leader tells you."[11]

General J. Lawton Collins, chief of staff of the army during the Korean War, stated, "I would place character as the absolutely number one requirement in leadership. By character, I mean primarily integrity. A man whose superiors and, even more important, whose subordinates can depend upon that leader taking action based on honesty and judgment. If he does not base his actions on honor, he is worthless as a leader."[12]

General William H. Simpson, an army commander in World War II, believed that "there are many qualities that go into a man of 'sterling' character. I don't know how to break it down. A man of high character has integrity, he is honest, he is reliable, he is straightforward in dealing with people. He is loyal to his family, his friends, his superiors."[13]

"I get accused all the time," said Gen. Jacob Devers, an army group commander in World War II, "of using the word integrity when I mean character and character when I mean integrity. I think character is everything in leadership. It is what we try to build in all our young officers. It means the truth to me. That's the only way I can put it. To stand up and tell the truth and not be in the gray area."[14]

The personal meaning of character to Gen. Albert Wedemeyer, the army's senior general in China in World War II, is "an officer who stands up under fire, who has the courage to defend his convictions, not arrogantly, not stubbornly, but intelligently. Someone who does not believe he knows all the answers, who will listen to others with different experiences and different knowledge. It means a deep sense of loyalty. Unless an officer has character, nothing he can do can cause his men to love and respect him."[15]

"Character plays a tremendous role in leadership," said Gen. Anthony McAuliffe. "It's a combination of many things—personality, clean living, presence. I just don't know; it's a very difficult word to describe because, as everyone knows, leaders come in all shapes and sizes and all sorts of personalities. I don't suppose I ever knew two men whom I knew well who differed as much as General MacArthur and General Patton, yet both were tremendous leaders of mass armies, both were men of great character."[16]

In any group larger than two, one can seldom find unanimous agreement on a point. As reflected in these comments from military officers who achieved the highest pinnacle of leadership, there is unanimous concurrence that character is the foundation of military leadership. The belief in the importance of character in leadership was also unanimous among more than a thousand other brigadier generals and higher with whom the author talked and corresponded. But agreement on what the word means is not unanimous. Actually, character defies definition; it must be described.

Secretary of War Henry L. Stimson made the comment to Marshall at a surprise birthday function: "You are one of the most selfless public officials whom I have ever known." Commented Paul Hoffman, who served at the Economic Cooperation Administration: "I have never known anyone who in my opinion was as completely selfless as George Marshall in the handling of any problem." (Hoffman was the administratior who supervised the Marshall Plan, which saved Europe from communism in the post–World War II period).

This selflessness was and is a vital part of the character of our military leaders. Eisenhower emphasized character, and his career illustrates its role in successful leadership. He reflected in his book *At Ease:* "Washington was my hero. . . . The qualities that excited my admiration were Washington's stamina and patience in adversity, first, and then his indomitable courage, daring and capacity for self-sacrifice."

Self-sacrifice, or selflessness, was a quality Ike possessed; when General Marshall recognized this, it was a turning point in Ike's career. Ike told me, "One thing that General Marshall despised more than anything else was anyone thinking rank—looking out for himself. One day we were talking about something, and he told me about a man who came in to see him and towards whom he had been favorably disposed. This man came in and told Marshall all the reasons why he needed to be promoted. It was just absolutely necessary, and Marshall was almost livid. 'I told the man,' Marshall said, 'now look, the men that get promoted in this war are going to be the people that are in command and carry the burdens. . . . The staff isn't going to get promoted at all.'

"Suddenly Marshall turned to me and said, 'Now you are a case. I happen to know General Joyce tried to get you as a division commander. General Krueger told me that he would be glad to give you a corps at any time. Well, that's just too bad. You are a brigadier, and you are going to stay a brigadier and that's that.' Eisenhower replied, 'General, you are making a mistake. I don't give a damn about your promotion and your power to promote me. You brought me in here for a job. I didn't ask you whether I liked it or didn't like it. I'm trying to do my duty.' I got up to leave his office. Something just happened to make me look around and I saw a faint smile on General Marshall's face. I had the grace to smile myself. I knew I had made an ass of myself.

"You know from that day on he started promoting me. Well, not that day, within ten days. He had written the request for the promotion to major general to the Senate himself. He said the operations division as he had set it up in the United States Army was not truly a staff position. He said I was a commander since I was making deployments, etc. This was his rationalization. It wasn't too long after that that he decided to send me to England, and when he sent me there he gave me another star and then another."[17]

A later conversation between Marshall and Eisenhower sheds some light on significant characteristics of both men. On June 12, 1944, six days after the invasion of Europe, Marshall, along with General of the Air Force Henry H. "Hap" Arnold and Adm. Ernest King, chief of naval operations, came over to see him. Marshall remarked, "Eisenhower, you've chosen all these commanders or accepted those we sent from Washington. What's the principal quality you look for? Without even thinking I said 'selflessness.' After I thought of it I realized that that man himself gave me that idea. This was the greatest quality of all. Going back to that commotion in his office and my reactions, General Marshall made up his mind that here was a guy that was not thinking about his own possibilities of promotion in the work he was trying to do. I think that the selflessness quality was one of those thoughts that was not really an original thought but my subconscious brought it out. I probably would have finished the war as the operations officer of the War Department if it hadn't been for that conversation with General Marshall."[18]

Selflessness was the hallmark of Ike's entire life. His diary from his tour in the Philippines under General MacArthur reveals that the experience was not pleasant. Ike and MacArthur were certainly not close; there was no real camaraderie between them.

Ike spent four months in the States during his four-year tour in the Philippines. He did not have to return there from the States, and he certainly had friends who could have had him reassigned, but duty and selflessness pulled him back to the Philippines. He never gave up hope that he could work with MacArthur, and he realized that the mission was an important one.

Certainly Ike's concept of duty, of service before self, was illustrated while he was stationed in the Philippines when he turned down several lucrative job opportunities in civilian life and private industry. He refused to accept corporate directorships and turned down "deals" and endorsements.

Honor and integrity are vital qualities in decision making. In his diary Ike wrote of an incident that further reflects his selflessness when he turned down a handsome sum of money on June 20, 1942: "The president of the Philippines visited me at 10:00 A.M. today. His purpose was to tender to me an honorarium for services rendered during the period I was acting as General MacArthur's chief of staff in Manila, where he [MacArthur] went as military adviser to the Philippine government.

"President Quezon brought with him to my office a draft of a citation, which he had written to accompany the presentation to me of the honorarium.

"I carefully explained to the president that I deeply appreciated his thought and was grateful for his expressions of gratitude, but that it was inadvisable and even impossible for me to accept a material reward for the services performed. I explained that while I understood this to be unquestionably legal, and that the president's motives were of the highest, the danger of misapprehension or misunderstanding on the part of some individual might operate to destroy whatever usefulness I may have to the allied cause in the present war. My government has entrusted me with important tasks, carrying grave responsibility."[19]

Quezon accepted his explanations and stated that "the matter was ended once and for all," with a written commendation in place of the honorarium. Ike stated: "Such a citation would be of great and more value to my family than any amount of money. . . . [Quezon] obviously accepted my decision without resentment and without loss of face—this latter point was one that had given me tremendous concern. To refuse a gift from anyone raised in the Far East, especially if a point of ethics has to be pled, is quite apt to develop into a serious personal matter."[20]

Ike's father died in March 1942, but his sense of duty, even in this traumatic time, was overwhelming. Because of the pressures of his duties as the deputy of operations in Washington, he was not able to attend the funeral. "I have felt terribly," he wrote in his diary on March 11, 1942, "I should like so much to be with my mother these few days. But we're at war. And war is not soft; it has no time to indulge even the deepest and most sacred emotions. She has been the inspiration for dad's life and true helpmate in every sense of the word. I'm quitting work now, 7:30 P.M., I haven't the heart to go on tonight." The following day he wrote about his father, "His word has been his bond and accepted as such; his sterling honesty, his insistence upon the immediate payment of all debts, his pride in his independence earned him a reputation that has profited all of us boys."[21]

After Ike's performance as the D-day Allied commander, and army chief of staff, his country and the world continued to call on him for leadership. The key national defense issue during the early 1950s was the containment of communism, so Eisenhower was assigned to be NATO commander. General MacArthur's firing by President Truman was a disturbing distraction during this time. Ike's thoughts again turned to the importance of selflessness. He commented in his diary on April 27, 1951: "In the United States the 'great debate,' which is nothing more than a heterogeneous collection of personal, partisan, and private quarrels, still rages. For most it has now been simplified (oversimplified I mean) into a Truman-MacArthur struggle. How tragic that, at this critical stage in world history, we should be torn apart by human selfishness. We should, by all means, continue to debate seriously the various means and methods open to us for waging effective war against communism. There is much room for instructive discussion and argument, but we have not a minute to waste, nor any right to weaken ourselves, in the wicked business of attempting to satisfy personal ambition.

"As far as I know, every senior officer in this headquarters would like to be somewhere else. Every man here is serving because of an overpowering sense of duty and of urgency in human affairs. It is too bad that they have to combat daily the pessimism and discouragement born of a realization that in London, Washington, and Paris, unworthy men either guide our destinies or are fighting bitter battles in the hope of getting an opportunity to guide our destinies.

"If ever we needed moral and intellectual integrity, now is that time. I thank God (and I mean it) for the few who still hold the respect of the masses. For my family and for America, the only real passions of my life, I shall continue to work as effectively and optimistically as I have the strength to do. But I desperately wish that there could be now established in places of influence in the free world new, young, and virile civil and military leaders devoted only to their respective countries, to decency, and to security."[22]

Eisenhower's concept of duty was not just to serve as a military officer. It carried over to consider accepting a draft as a presidential candidate at the same time that he was head of NATO forces. On October 25, 1951, a contingent met with him to encourage him to run for president. He reflected upon this conference, "I do not want to be president of the United States, and I want no other political office or political connection of any kind. I am now on a job in which success is of the most tremendous importance to the future of the United States."[23]

He also gave emphasis to the selflessness involved in his sense of duty: "I entered upon this post (as SHAPE [Supreme Headquarters Allied Powers Europe] commander) only from a sense of duty—I certainly had to sacrifice much in the way of personal convenience, advantage, and congenial constructive work when I left New York. I will never leave this post for any other kind of governmental task except in response to a clear call to duty. I will not be a participant in any movement that attempts to secure for me a nomination because I believe that the presidency is something that should never be sought, just as I believe, of course, that it could never be refused.

What future circumstances could convince me that I had a duty to enter the political arena, I am not prepared to say. I simply do not know what they could be. I merely admit that, as of now, I would consider the nomination of which they speak, if accomplished without any direct or indirect assistance or connivance on my part, to place upon me a transcendent duty."[24]

The tragedy of the suicide of Secretary of Defense Jim Forrestal, a truly selfless public servant, was a major challenge. "I talked with Jim Forrestal," Eisenhower said, "more often than with anyone else about these things because of his very great honesty of purpose and his dedication to public service. Moreover, he was so personally concerned with the dangers that our nation was incurring that he wanted to talk about these things. Some of my associates in the service and in other governmental or civil positions have been equal to Jim Forrestal in selflessness, but few have had his insatiable desire to learn and then to apply his knowledge for the public good. So we explored and searched together to see if we could define an appropriate course in language clear enough to be specific and general enough to be applicable over a period of time."[25]

Ike very much resented anyone who was not selfless. As president he reflected, "In the case of the governor of Hawaii, there are two principal candidates who are themselves seeking the job. Each has developed a 'pressure group' to support his claims. Such an approach to a public service position violates every instinct I have. To seek such a post is, to me, clear evidence of unsuitability. I feel that anyone who can, without great personal sacrifice, come to Washington to accept an important governmental post is not fit to hold that post. This, of course, is not true in some of the more technical and professional positions, and it is unfair to assume that everyone should share my feelings in the matter when high positions are involved. But just the same, my respect and admiration for any individual who turns out to be a seeker after a political post diminishes almost to the vanishing point."[26]

He added, "All of these would jump at the chance to get a job that a successful businessman has to sacrifice very much to take. Reasonable sacrifices are, of course, to be expected; in fact the government can scarcely afford to allow anyone to occupy an important post unless he did have to sacrifice very materially in order to take it. But it is the carrying of the practice to the extreme that will eventually damage us badly, unless we get some logical breaks in the Senate in the handling of these cases."[27]

EISENHOWER'S REFLECTIONS ON THE PRESIDENCY
When Mamie and I came to the White House, we probably had a fairly good understanding of what living in it would be. The prominent military positions I had occupied for some years had given me some experience that definitely, even though faintly, resembles that through which a president is compelled to live. This was especially true when I was abroad commanding at SHAEF in World War II and later as commander at SHAPE. In both those positions, I led a fairly lonely life, the first time living only with my aides, and the second time with Mamie at Marnes-la-Coquette. We could not visit in restaurants, theaters, or other public places with the same freedom that is enjoyed by the ordinary citizen; problems of security, of protocol, and of autographing were always with us. The finding of time necessary for health and recreation was always difficult.

We knew all of these difficulties would be multiplied in White House existence, but at least we were psychologically prepared for them.[28]

General George Washington's career as commander during the Revolution illustrated selflessness quite early for our military officers, and it developed an example to be followed by all of the top military officers for the next two hundred years. Many of his men had no muskets and learned to drill with broomsticks. Many were without shoes, and blankets were scarce, food was inadequate, and enlistment tenures were inconsistent. Washington bared his thoughts and concerns to his friend Joseph Reed in a letter dated January 14, 1776: "The reflection on my situation and that of this Army produces many an unhappy hour when all around me are wrapped in sleep. Few people know the predicament we are in on a thousand accounts; still I believe if any disaster happens to these lines, from what cause it flows. I have often thought how much happier I should have been if, instead of accepting a command under such circumstances, I had taken my musket on my shoulder and entered the ranks, or if I could have justified the measure to posterity and my own conscience, had retired to the back country and lived in a wigwam. If I should be able to rise superior to these and many other difficulties which might be enumerated, I shall most religiously believe that the finger of Providence is in it, to blind the eyes of our enemies; for surely if we get well through this month, it must be for want of their knowing the disadvantages we labor under. . . ."[29]

Fortunately for our country, Washington didn't go to live in a wigwam or enter the ranks but selflessly led our country to victory. Perhaps his most significant act of selflessness was his rejection of a monarchy. There were many who wanted to anoint him as a king in our newly formed United States, but he refused, thereby leading to what is the world's greatest republic.

This refusal of royal power, which he might well have achieved, demonstrated the primacy of selflessness in Washington's being. As the single indispensable man for victory in the Revolution, he could refuse "the crown." In doing so, he certified to his contemporaries and posterity that character, not greed, was the thrust of his great life.

At the end of the war, Washington saw another great test of his character. On March 15, 1783, some of his officers, led by General Gates, met to consider military action to secure pay for the army. "The issue was civilian versus military control of the new government."[30] So precarious was the situation that "Washington's own command . . . was in danger. The army felt that his 'delicacy carried to an extreme' had made him stand in the way of their achieving their just dues."[31] This was one of the most dangerous moments in American history. For the only time in the entire history of the United States, civilian rule was seriously threatened by the military. Had this devious threat succeeded, our history as a nation may well have taken a very different road.

But here again, Washington provided the crucial difference: his leadership, backed by his indomitable character. Made aware of an officers' meeting by Alexander Hamilton, Washington decided to attend. When he appeared, "the faces of his gathered officers made it clear that the surprise was not a pleasant one. For the first time since he had won the love of the army, he saw facing him resentment and anger."[32] He gave a short speech respectfully requesting that the officers resist the temptation to take military action. He told them: "Let me entreat you, gentlemen, on your part, not to take any measures which, viewed in the calm light of reason, will lessen the dignity and sully the glory you have hitherto maintained."[33]

But even these moving words spoken by their hero could not sway them. At the end of his written speech, however, he used "a device of reading a letter, and captured his audience with an emotional and impromptu remark."[34] He reached into his pocket and produced a letter from a member of Congress explaining the dire financial condition of the nation and the Congress's efforts to compensate the army. But "something seemed to go wrong. The General seemed confused; he stared at the paper helplessly. The officers leaned forward, their hearts contracting with anxiety. He then reached into his waistcoat pocket and produced a pair of glasses."[35]

His men were stunned to see him use glasses to read the crabbed writing. "Gentlemen," he said apologetically, "you will permit me to put on my spectacles, for I have not only grown gray but almost blind in the service of my country."[36]

This poignant admission gripped his audience: This simple statement achieved what he had been unable to accomplish. The officers were instantly in tears, and from behind the shining drops their eyes looked with love at the commander who had led them so far and long. Washington quickly finished reading the congressman's letter; he knew that the battle was won. With his instinctive sense of the dramatic, he avoided any anticlimax and walked out of the hall.

Once again, Washington had saved the country from tyranny. First, he rescued America from the tyranny of the British crown. Next, by refusing the crown himself, he spared the country from enduring another monarchy. Finally, through his "spectacle speech," he protected the young republic from a military insurrection. In all three instances, his character, specifically his selfless disregard for personal power, salvaged his country from peril.[37]

Washington's career as commander of our revolutionary forces was one of constant adversity. I believe that this influenced General Marshall in a speech he delivered to the first graduating officer candidate school (OCS) class of World War II at Fort Benning. "The truly great leader overcomes all difficulties, and campaigns and battles are nothing but a long series of difficulties to overcome. The lack of equipment, the lack of food, the lack of this or that are only excuses. The real leader displays his qualities in triumph over adversity, however great it may be."

Selflessness was certainly part of Marshall's character, and the epitome of this was never illustrated more sharply than by his actions during discussions of who would lead the Allied invasion force.

Early in 1942, President Roosevelt and Prime Minister Churchill agreed that the supreme commander of the Allied invasion would be a British officer. As the war developed, however, it became obvious that there would be a preponderance of American troops and materiel in the invasion force. This presented an awkward political position for both Roosevelt and Churchill. Should the commander be British, Roosevelt would have to inform the American people that a foreigner would command an invasion force having a majority of American soldiers. On the other hand, Winston Churchill would find it politically difficult to explain to the British people that an American would be commanding a European invasion. Churchill relieved Roosevelt from this embarrassing situation by voluntarily saying that the commander should be an American.

The selection of the supreme commander, a matter of vital interest to everyone, required a long and indecisive two years. After it was agreed that it would be an American, Roosevelt failed to name him for eighteen months, during which time Churchill pressed frequently for a decision. At Teheran in 1943, Stalin asked preemptorily, "Who will command Overlord?" The president replied that he had not yet decided. Stalin declared his preference for General Marshall as supreme commander and tried to pressure Roosevelt into a decision by saying it was clear to him that until a supreme commander was named, he could not consider the Allies sincere about invading Europe. Stalin was desperate for a second front, but Roosevelt would not be pressured.

Marshall was, indeed, the primary American contender for the role. On July 31, 1942, Churchill sent a wire to Roosevelt stating, "It would be agreeable to us if General Marshall were designated for Supreme Command of Roundup." On August 10, 1943, in a letter to Roosevelt, Secretary of War Stimson gave his position on the selection of the D-day commander: "Finally, I believe that the time has come when we must put our most commanding soldier in charge of this critical operation at this critical time. You are more fortunate than was Mr. Lincoln or Mr. Wilson in the ease with which that selection can be made. Mr. Lincoln had to fumble through a process of trial and error with dreadful losses until he was able to discover the right choice. Mr. Wilson had to choose a man who was virtually unknown to the American people and to the foreign armies which he was to serve. General Marshall already has a towering eminence of reputation as a tried soldier and as a broadminded and skillful administrator. This was shown by the suggestion of him on the part of the British for this very post a year and one-half ago. I believe that he is the man who most surely can now, by his character and skill, furnish the military leadership which is necessary to bring our two nations together in confident joint action in this great operation. No one knows better than I the loss and the problems of organization and worldwide strategy centered in Washington which such a solution would cause. I see no other alternative to which we can turn in the great effort which confronts us."[38]

On August 22, 1943, Stimson and Roosevelt discussed the matter. Stimson said Roosevelt told him that "Churchill had voluntarily come to him and offered to accept Marshall for the Overlord operation. This, the President said, relieved him of the embarrassment of being obliged to ask for it. He also discussed with me Marshall's successor [as chief of staff], mentioning Eisenhower."[39]

Marshall was clearly Roosevelt's number one choice for the position. In November 1943, while Roosevelt was visiting North Africa, he talked with General Eisenhower. "Ike," the president said, "you and I know who was the Chief of Staff during the last years of the Civil War but practically no one else knows the names of the field generals. Grant, of course, and Lee, and Jackson, Sherman, Sheridan, and the others—every schoolboy knows them. I hate to think that fifty years from now practically nobody will know who George

Marshall was. That is one of the reasons why I want George to have the big Command—he is entitled to establish his place in history as a great General."[40]

As it became clear that the Allies would soon have to name the D-day commander, rumors began to spread in Washington about Marshall. When the news leaked that he was going to leave to take command of the invasion, it created a furor of discussion. Three senior members of the military affairs committee, Senators Warren R. Austin, Styles Bridges, and John Gurney, protested that Marshall was too important to Congress to leave Washington. "They told me," Stimson said, "how much they relied on him not only individually, but how they were able to carry controversial matters through with their colleagues if they could say that the measure in question had the approval of Marshall."[41] The senators were concerned that there was an ouster movement, aided and abetted by enemies who wanted to remove Marshall from the position of chief of staff because his influence was great with the president and the Joint and Combined Chiefs of Staff.

The *Washington Times Herald* even carried an article on the "rumor," maintaining that General Marshall was going to be taken away from Washington and sent abroad because he had attacked the president. On September 28, 1943, another story accused the president of a plot to get Marshall out by "kicking him upstairs" and putting General Summerville in as chief of staff. Roosevelt was doing this, so the story went, to enable Summerville to use the patronage of his position for Roosevelt's 1944 presidential campaign.

General Pershing too was opposed to General Marshall's leaving the position of chief of staff. In a letter to Roosevelt, Pershing said that it "would be a fundamental and very grave error in our military policy" for Marshall to be transferred. Roosevelt replied to the Allied Expeditionary Force (AEF) commander of World War I that he wanted General Marshall to be the Pershing of World War II.

Admiral Leahy, Gen. Henry H. "Hap" Arnold, and Adm. Ernest King had all gone to Roosevelt, individually and privately, to urge the president to keep General Marshall in Washington. All three believed Marshall to be too important to the harmony of the Joint and Combined Chiefs organizations to be spared. All the service chiefs recognized him as the dominant figure, particularly in deciding upon and implementing joint strategic decisions. He was vital to service unity in these decisions. He was, according to Arnold and King, the acknowledged leader in the Joint Chiefs of Staff.

King told President Roosevelt, "We have the winning combination here in Washington, why break it up?" Arnold stated that no one else could have Marshall's "extraordinary sense of the requirements of global war, his knowledge of land, sea and air logistics, his balanced judgment as to the importance of one theater or one ally or one arm of the service as opposed to another."[42]

An editorial in the unofficial organ of the services, *The Army and Navy Journal*, said that to remove General Marshall as chief of staff "would shock the Army, the Congress, and the nation at large."

Finally, Secretary Stimson took a strong position on the subject. "I can make a statement," he said at a press conference on September 30, 1943, "about some of the reports that have come out. . . . I am in a position to say with absolute confidence that whatever duties General Marshall may hereafter be called upon to perform will be decided by the President in a spirit of entire confidence in General Marshall and with the sole purpose of placing this superbly able officer in the United States Army in the position where he can render the best service towards a successful conclusion of this war."

Often a man performs a responsible job in such a brilliant manner that he makes it look easy. This was the way General Marshall performed as army chief of staff. The result was that sometimes his outstanding job was taken for granted. Certainly the rumors about his transfer gave emphasis and public recognition to the brilliant work that General Marshall was accomplishing.

At the Cairo Conference in December 1943, Roosevelt announced his decision: Gen. Dwight D. Eisenhower was going to be supreme commander. Roosevelt made the decision in favor of Eisenhower over Marshall in spite of the impassioned advice of two of his closest advisers, Harry Hopkins and Secretary Stimson, both of whom wanted Marshall in the job. Stalin and Churchill also had made known their preference for Marshall.

Why then was Eisenhower selected and not Marshall? Part of the answer lies in Marshall's selflessness. Had he indicated at any time his preference for the job as supreme commander, he would have had the position. At Cairo in December 1943, before the decision was finally made, the president called him to his villa. In writing about this meeting when he was asked about the supreme commander position, Marshall replied, "I recalled saying that I would not attempt to estimate my capabilities; the President would have to do that; I merely wished to make clear that whatever the decision, I would go along with it wholeheartedly, that the issue was too great for any personal feeling to be considered. I did not discuss the pros and cons of the matter. If I recall, the President stated in completing our conversation, 'I feel I could not sleep at night with you out of the country.'"[43]

Secretary Stimson recorded Roosevelt's account of this conversation. "The President brought the subject [of supreme commander] up in a rather noncommittal way and asked Marshall what he wanted, or what he thought ought to be done. Marshall, as usual, dug his feet in and said it was not for him to say what should be done. But then, he added, on one subject he would give his opinion and that was that if he, Marshall, went to Overlord, the President should not leave the position of Chief of Staff open but should put Eisenhower there as full Chief of Staff [they were considering putting in Eisenhower as acting chief of staff], that any other course would not be fair to Eisenhower or to the Staff."[44] This was another act of Marshall's selflessness; it would make Ike his superior, because chief of staff is the senior position regardless of date of rank.

Then the president announced his decision. He told Marshall, "I've been thinking this matter over and have decided that I will keep you as Chief of Staff and put Eisenhower in as head of Overlord."[45] Marshall accepted the president's decision without displaying any emotion. He discussed the meeting with John J. McCloy, an assistant secretary of war, who observed that Marshall did not "seem as if he were a very greatly disappointed man." But Stimson averred, "I think I know better. I know [what] his deepest ambition in his heart is and it was to command the invasion into France. It was simply his matchless power of self-sacrifice and self-control that gave the other impression."[46]

After the decision was made, by mutual consent further discussion of Marshall's commandership of Overlord was dropped in conversations between Stimson and Marshall. Stimson's comment on Marshall's reaction to the decision was that he showed "his usual bigness about the whole damn thing."

Marshall's success and the respect all had for him was strongly rooted in his character. The president, the secretary of war, and the Congress were all forces influencing the chief of staff's conduct of the war; but in America the final authority is the people. The pulse of American public opinion was gauged in part by the press; a reporter could sometimes ask questions that citizens could not ask directly. After the Japanese invaded the Philippines, things went badly for the American forces there. An underground feeling of doubt began to develop in some quarters toward General Marshall. "One of his friends," wrote a member of the army's public relations staff in 1942, "who was head of the Washington Bureau of a large Midwest newspaper came to my home one evening and told me of the dissatisfaction which was spreading with regard to General Marshall's fitness for leadership."[47] Reporters asked that Marshall hold a press conference; but at the time, the policy of the War Department was for Secretary of War Stimson to hold all press conferences—an arrangement more than satisfactory to Marshall.

A few days after the suggestion of a Marshall press conference, Secretary Stimson had to leave Washington on an inspection of the Panama Canal and its defenses. Instead of canceling the scheduled War Department press conference, however, Marshall was persuaded to conduct it.

General Marshall told the Washington press corps that he realized they had many questions to ask about the conduct of the war and requested that they individually state all their questions at the beginning. Then he would attempt to answer them together. Marshall listened attentively to the questions, then told them he was going to be quite frank.

"Marshall spoke for more than thirty minutes, giving an account of practically everything that had happened up to that time, telling of the various efforts that been made to send supplies to our forces on Bataan. He told of the purchase of ships and the provision in advance of insurance funds for families of the ships' crews engaged in the attempts. He told, as much as he could safely disclose, the extent of the disasters we had suffered which had prevented the carrying out of plans long ago drawn up to meet such an eventuality."[48]

Marshall's conduct of the press conference was masterful. He won the day with the press for the rest of World War II because of his honest and frank statements. He took the press into his confidence and won the doubters to support him. The rumbling comments of dissatisfaction with his ability ceased entirely. A member of the army public relations staff said, "General Marshall exhibited a magnetism I had never seen before."

Throughout the rest of the war, Marshall held press conferences once or twice a week. He habitually asked for all questions first, then would answer each question in turn, giving his reply directly to the correspondent who had asked the question. His memory for facts and names was phenomenal. He was not only frank but trusting. He indicated which facts were classified, trusting the reporters not to violate his confidence; they never did. Had he not won the confidence of the press and maintained it throughout the war, he could not have been as effective in his leadership.

Only once during the war was Marshall's rapport with Congress threatened. At the urging of the U.S. Navy, President Roosevelt was considering promoting Marshall to field marshal and King to the position of admiral of the fleet. The first time that Stimson heard of this maneuver was on February 16, 1943, when navy secretary Knox mentioned the proposal to him. "When I got back to the Department," Stimson said, "I told Marshall of this because it contained a request from the President that I should go to the Hill and talk with the Chairmen of the two committees on Military Affairs. Marshall was dead against any such promotion. . . . He said that it really came from the lower admirals in the Navy Department forcing this upon King and Knox and upon the President."

General Marshall had a reason for his opposition to the promotion. He was afraid it would destroy all his influence with Congress and the people because he would appear to be self-seeking. His selflessness was part of his character and vital to his leadership. This promotion would present an obstacle to accomplishing his primary mission of winning the war. Stimson remarked of Marshall's position on the promotion, "It was a wonderfully unselfish thing for Marshall to do. . . ."[49]

Because of Marshall's opposition, Stimson sent a memorandum that same day to President Roosevelt stating, "I have talked the matter over with Marshall and he feels, so far as he is concerned, his promotion would be harmful rather than helpful, particularly with reference to his relations with Congress and the reaction of the American people. He feels very strongly on the subject, and I am inclined to agree with him."[50] Several days later Stimson discussed the matter with President Roosevelt who decided to drop it. The issue was later reopened, however, and eventually President Roosevelt and Congress decided at the end of the war to award the five-star rank over General Marshall's opposition.

In January 1942, one of the most difficult problems facing Secretary Stimson and General Marshall was the selection of an American general for assignment to China. It would be an extremely challenging job because the Chinese were in rapid retreat from the Japanese onslaught. The American general would be even more taxed because his command would include Chinese troops as well as American, and he would have to deal with a corrupt political system. One of the first officers considered was Lt. Gen. Hugh Drum. Stimson wrote that Drum "took the position. . . . He did not think the role in China which I had offered him was big enough for his capabilities."[51]

Stimson discussed Drum's position that evening with Marshall. The next day the situation came to a head. "The afternoon," wrote Stimson, "was taken with the wretched Drum affair. . . . I received a letter from Drum, who had evidently been scared at the effects of his recalcitrance with reference to his going to China and had written in this letter to me that he would do anything I wanted him to do."

Stimson showed the letter to Marshall, who saw it as additional evidence of General Drum's "unfitness and thought that it indicated mainly that he was trying to protect himself against criticism for virtually declining to go."[52]

Any officer who seemed to Marshall to be anxious to select an assignment to suit his own personal preference was in trouble. "General William N. Haskell came in to see me," Stimson wrote in his diary early in 1941, "in regard to his detail in the next eight months before he finally retires. I am fond of Haskell . . . but when I spoke to Marshall about it I found that Haskell had very much irritated Marshall by his choosiness in regard to his future." Marshall had excellent rapport with Stimson, but he refused to give Haskell special consideration for the simple reason he had asked for it.[53]

There were two significant periods in the history of the air force from the 1920s throughout the 1970s that illustrate the selflessness and truly superb character of air officers in their fight for airpower and readiness. These key leaders were General of the Air Force Henry H. "Hap" Arnold; the first chief of staff of the separate air force, Gen. Carl A. "Tooey" Spaatz; and the second general, David C. Jones, chief of staff from 1974 to 1978 and then chairman of the Joint Chiefs from 1978 to 1982. These men over five decades were completely selfless and willing to sacrifice their personal careers in the interest of developing the airpower that helped preserve the West's freedom. On numerous occasions, they did what they knew was right for the development of airpower, often to the detriment of their careers. Arnold and Spaatz were important in the 1920s in developing airpower. But that history is not complete without the perspective offered by Billy Mitchell's selfless contribution to air force leadership.[54]

Mitchell's first interest in aviation was perhaps reflected in an analysis of military ballooning. Long a member of the signal corps, which had the responsibility within the army for aviation, Mitchell did not begin pilot training until the fall of 1916 during off-duty hours at his own expense. In January 1917 the War Department decided to send him as an aeronautical observer to Europe. This opportunity and the experience gained developed Mitchell's knowledge of aviation, causing General Pershing to promote him to full colonel and give him a combat command in the Allied Expeditionary Force.

Pershing saw Mitchell as a man of great fighting ability with a flair for combat leadership. He was, de facto, the commander of American aviation forces. Pershing was so pleased with him that he recommended his promotion to brigadier general. In December 1918, Mitchell was returned to the United States as director of military aeronautics, but after the war it was disbanded as the army reorganized.

Mitchell's World War I experience and growth caused him to develop a vision for airpower. He could see the important role that aviation would play in the next war and was dedicated to preparing our country for it. To Mitchell, aerial warfare was as important as ground and naval warfare, and he believed there ought to be a separate air force.

The immediate post–World War I accomplishment for which Mitchell is perhaps most remembered was his insistence that airplanes were capable of sinking naval vessels. He proved this, much to the irritation of the navy, by sinking the ex-German battleship *Ostfriesland* on July 22, 1921, and the battleship USS *Alabama* (an overage target ship) in August.

After the end of the war, Mitchell was often in the headlines. Both friends and enemies acknowledged his dedication to the cause and his stature as an expert. Not all agreed with him, however, on the importance of airpower, and only a handful had his unique vision and enthusiasm. There were many ups and downs for Mitchell during the postwar period. These finally culminated in a showdown.

On September 5, 1925, an incident occurred that was a major turning point in the establishment of a separate air force. Mitchell held a press conference, the impact of which will never be forgotten in air force history. Although I will not detail the court-martial trial that resulted, I will cover the key issues because of their impact on the future of airpower, a separate air force, and its air leaders.

On September 1 and 3, 1925, two tragedies occurred involving navy aviators. On September 1, 1925, Comdr. John Rodgers and his crew of four were reported missing in the Pacific Ocean on a flight from San Francisco to Honolulu. Considerable publicity was given to the allegation that the airplane's fuel was insufficient for the headwinds encountered. Mitchell, assigned at that time in San Antonio, went on the radio on September 2, calling Rodgers and his crew "martyrs."

On September 3, with Rodgers and his crew still missing, the *Shenandoah,* a lighter-than-air craft, ran into a squall: Its commander and fourteen crew members fell to their deaths. The grief over this loss was aggravated by a rumor that the commander had objected to the flight because of adverse weather but had been ordered to proceed. The situation was made worse by the lack of concern over the deaths by the secretary of the navy. He said publicly, trying to minimize the two tragedies, that it was proof of our country's safety from invading airpower. Such a callous comment did not sit well with the proponents of airpower and the families of those who died.

These tragedies ended Billy Mitchell's public silence. On September 5, he called a press conference in San Antonio that surfaced a controversy that had been building between Mitchell and his superiors for years. He charged that these "terrible accidents . . . are the direct results of incompetence, criminal negligence, and almost treasonable administration of the national defense by the War and Navy Departments."

There was no doubt that Mitchell had set the stage for either a court-martial or a reprimand. His charges were too grave to be ignored. Those who knew him believed that he wanted the court-martial, to win support for his fight to replace the archaic air policy with a progressive and farsighted one. He believed that if he were to be dismissed from the service, he would have a better opportunity to advance aviation than if he were in uniform.

A mere reprimand would not have accomplished one of Mitchell's objectives—to force a congressional investigation. A reprimand attached to his record would not answer his public charge that military aviation was in the hands of "stupid" superiors who "knew nothing about flying" and who, as he put it, risked the lives of airmen as "pawns" in foolish and ill-timed ventures.

A court-martial would afford Mitchell an opportunity to prove his charges or be drummed out of the army. At a trial, he could rely on the due process of law, including his own evidence and witnesses, and the right to cross-examine the government's witnesses. It would thus bring the controversy to a head. President Calvin Coolidge decided to charge Colonel Mitchell with conduct prejudicial to good order and military discipline, insubordination, and utterances contemptuous of his superiors.

The court-martial record is composed of seven thick volumes. Although there had been more than twenty investigations of the air service since the end of World War I, the public had paid little attention. This time the audience was the whole country; this time they did pay attention.

The key issues debated were (1) whether there should be a unified air service—that is, a separate air force; (2) whether the development and progress of aviation had been retarded by conservatism in the army and navy; (3) whether there was any discrimination in pay and promotion against officers of the army air service; and finally (4) what importance and role aviation should have in fighting on land and sea.

In his defense, Mitchell pointed out, "In the Army, we have no air force, none whatever, either in materiel (that means airplanes and equipment), in personnel (pilots, observers, gunners, mechanics) or in operations (that is, method of using it) . . . and that the aircraft we have are worn out, they are dangerous, they are incapable of performing any functions of a modern air force."

The inadequacy of men and materiel was, as Mitchell put it, because "air matters are entrusted to the Army and Navy, which are handled and governed and dominated by non-flying officers. They not only know next to nothing about aviation, but regard it merely as an auxiliary of their present activities and not as a main force in the nation's military equipment. Their testimony regarding air matters is almost worthless—sometimes more serious than this. . . . The voice of the air is smothered before it is heard."

He added that instead of having aviation needs explained by admirals and generals who knew what aviation was about, they were "selected on the principle of 'Tag, you're it; go and talk to Congress about aviation.'"

Mitchell was particularly bitter about the army's system of recruiting and training mechanics, "which was so poorly done [that] it amounts to training these men with the pilots' lives." He prophetically argued not only for a modernized separate air force but for reorganization of the War and Navy Departments into a department of defense with the army, navy, and air force as subdivisions.

Countercharges were made by Mitchell's supporters that the court-martial was the latest step taken by the general staff in its efforts to get Mitchell, and that years before the court-martial, Mitchell had been warned that if he did not stop his efforts for the air force, he would be forced out of the service.

The army chief of staff, Major General Hines, strongly opposed the separate air force that Mitchell advocated. To him, an air service was an essential element of an army or a navy, tied to the ground or to a ship. The navy's position was that a unified air service would remove the type of command needed in time of battle and the uniform training in time of peace.

Mitchell's attack received mixed reactions; some of his fellow officers resented the accusations he made of incompetence, negligence, and treason. It was upsetting to those who believed that the motives of Mitchell's superiors were beyond suspicion and had the best possible provisions for our nation's security at heart.

News commentators were more than unkind. A *New York Times* editorial stated scathingly that "Colonel Mitchell is plainly 'asking for it,' and he ought to get it, even if he is still under the delusion that it will add to his glory and induce sensible men to hold him in respect." The same editorial commented that his statement would break "the back of what reputation he had left."

Said one news commentator in the September 7, 1925, issue of the *New York Times:* "He has not altogether pleased some of his best friends by the tactics he is pursuing. They feel he is hurting his own cause by making what they regard as reckless and inaccurate statements."

Mitchell's San Antonio manifesto startled the whole country as he dared the lightning to strike him. The army could not let his challenge go unanswered because the effect on army morale would be disastrous.

Mitchell, however, had a strong following of officers who believed in his cause, such as two officers who testified during the trial and were to become the most important air leaders of World War II— Hap Arnold and Tooey Spaatz. Both were warned not to testify, for doing so might hurt or end their careers; neither was intimidated.

At the trial, Arnold's testimony confirmed the contention that members of the army and navy had given false or misleading information to Congress. Arnold stated that his superiors had given misleading information on such matters as how current the aircraft of foreign powers were and the organizational structure of the foreign services as separate and distinct air forces.

Mitchell reflected on this episode: "Fighting from my side of the barricade was an officer whose convictions and courage may help to bring our Air Force to its required strength before the next war comes upon us. He was Major H. H. Arnold, one of my boys, fearless before his bigoted superiors."

After the court-martial, which resulted in Mitchell's conviction, Arnold did not want to give up the fight. He wrote in his memoirs, "The first ones to try to keep the battle going were Maj. Herbert Dargue and myself. After such long service in Washington, we had many friends in Congress and in the press. We continued going out to Billy's house in Middleburg, and also over to Capitol Hill, and writing letters to keep up the fight.

"At once the boom was lowered with a bang. After all the trouble with Billy Mitchell—and the case unpopularly closed—there was no thought of allowing small fry to keep it going. It was understood now that President Coolidge himself had been the prime accuser. We were both called on the carpet to answer for our 'irregular' correspondence relative to changes in Air Service status. Dargue got off with a reprimand. I was, as the press announced, 'exiled.'"

The issue that brought about his exile arose a year after the court-martial when a news release, highly complimentary of the air corps but critical of the army general staff, was circulated surreptitiously. "It was traced," said Ira Eaker, "to Arnold by the army inspector general. He had used a government typewriter and paper and was charged with misappropriating public property in a project inimical to the army. The inspector general recommended Arnold's court-martial, but instead, at General Patrick's intercession, he was relieved of duty on the air staff, banished from Washington, and assigned command of one air squadron at Fort Riley, Kansas, a cavalry post."

Captain Eaker told me that when he was an assistant executive to Maj. Gen. Mason Patrick, he was present during these difficult times. "Arnold carried out his functions and duties for Patrick," Eaker said of the exile incident. "Patrick thought he was a bright, able officer and was completely satisfied with the work he was doing for him. Then, aside from [Arnold's] official duties to Patrick, all of his extracurricular activities were devoted to helping Mitchell—which we all thought was right . . . and we were doing the same thing. . . . I think Arnold always felt that Patrick had been severe with him."

In a statement to the press, Patrick said that the issue was the distribution of circulars urging support for legislation and that the endeavors by these officers were "without his knowledge and through mistaken zeal." In response to allegations that a number of air officers were implicated, Patrick said, "The investigation disclosed the fact that only two officers in this office were concerned in an attempt to influence legislation in what I regard as an objectionable manner. Both of them will be reprimanded, and one of them [Arnold], no longer wanted in my office, will be sent to another station."

Certainly the attitude of some of his fellow officers had much to do with Arnold's reaction. After reporting to Fort Riley, "When the children were in bed in our new quarters," Arnold recalled, "Bee and I started the uncomfortable walk to General Booth's house, the post commander, for our first official call. The house was all lit up. As we were admitted, we saw that the commanding general was having a card party. The living room was full of people. We stood there, and General Booth looked across the room and apparently recognized me. He rose and came toward us. Then he held out his hand and put the other on my shoulder. . . . 'Arnold,' he said cordially, 'I'm glad to see you. I'm proud to have you in this command.' And then, so that everybody could hear, he added, 'I know why you're here, my boy. And as long as you're here you can write and say any damned thing you want. All I ask is that you let me see it first!'"

General Summerville, who became Arnold's boss after the exile, sent a wire to the commandant at Fort Leavenworth inquiring whether an additional officer could be accommodated in the next class at Command and Staff School. The reply came back, "Yes, who is he?" Arnold's name was submitted. The answer came back that they didn't want him, but if he did come he would naturally be accepted.

"In a private letter to General Fechet," said Arnold, "the commandant at Leavenworth wrote that if I came to Leavenworth as a student I would be 'crucified.' However, I was determined to go. I remembered that the commandant of the school had served on the court that had tried Billy Mitchell, which probably had something to do with his feelings. In spite of the lack of cordiality in his letter, I found the course there of great value. I didn't get into many difficulties, and I did not find the going very tough.

"Naturally, I did not agree with many of the school's concepts relative to the employment of aircraft and I thought the course, as far as the air army was concerned, could and should be modernized."

Arnold graduated twenty-sixth in a class of eighty-eight.

A few years later, Arnold said, "When Gen. E. L. King, who had been my commanding officer at Leavenworth, arrived for . . . maneuvers in 1931, he surprised me by saying he appreciated very much the paper I had submitted when I left Leavenworth, outlining my ideas of the proper instruction in air operations at the school. He also congratulated me on the way I had handled my job as G-4. This, from the man who had said he would crucify me if I went there, made me feel good."

The other key officer, along with Arnold, testifying at the Billy Mitchell court-martial trial was Carl Spaatz. Spaatz had been worried that he might be reassigned because he had stood up to General Patrick over an earlier dispute, but he underestimated the latter's regard for him. On June 18, 1925, he was ordered to report for duty in the office of the chief of the air staff in Washington, D.C. It was to be an important assignment for his personal development and his career.

Six months after his assignment to Washington, he was involved in Billy Mitchell's fight for airpower. Spaatz decided to testify, although he was warned by his superiors that it might jeopardize his career.

The attorney for the defense asked Spaatz, "Would you tell the court the condition of the equipment at the present time that the air service is supplied with?"

Spaatz responded, "The equipment in the air service has reached a condition where it is very difficult to figure out how we're going to continue to fly. . . . The bulk of equipment in the air service is very obsolescent or obsolete."

As the testimony continued, Spaatz was asked, "What percent of the aircraft on hand were available for the pursuit mission with fighter aircraft?"

He replied, "None of those that we have on hand—I would not care to go to war with any of them on hand. They are a very hard maintenance job to start with and have been in use for approximately three years. I think the greater portion of them have been to the depot at least once for repairs and reissued to the units," As for the shortage of aircraft, Spaatz estimated that the shortage came to 355 airplanes.

Next came an inquiry into the availability of personnel. Spaatz stated that they were short 660 officers in tactical units: 85 officers short in Hawaii, 55 for the Philippines, and 54 for Panama.

Mitchell's council was aggressive and tenacious, and in questioning Spaatz's attorney went for the army's jugular: "Are the officers of the general staff qualified by training or experience to lay down principles for military aviation?" Spaatz at first was not permitted to answer because of the challenge to higher authority. After strenuous objection and a lengthy discussion, Spaatz was permitted to continue and responded: "With the exception of Maj. M. F. Harmon and Maj. C. G. Brant, no officers of the general staff have had air service training [but were still placed] in command of tactical units of the air service."

As the trial proceeded, Spaatz received encouragement from his friends in the air service. Captain Frank O. D. Hunter wired him on November 10, 1925, "That a boy." From a man named Pickering came, "Congratulations on your testimony and nerve. Best to Mitchell. Can I help?"

I discussed this matter in several interviews with General Spaatz to put it in perspective. Spaatz commented: "I think the basic factor was the old one that goes down to history: resistance to change. When you're well drilled and trained in your profession, you don't like something to come along that makes you have to learn all over again, and the older you are in your profession, the more you resist change. The old order has to give way to new order, then the appropriations to the old order become decreased, their advantages lessened, and the career and rank go to the new order. Essentially it's a psychological mass prejudice against change on the part of the military, and I think that's been true enough through history."

Spaatz said later in life, "I testified for Billy Mitchell against the general staff position, and they never did anything to me. They can't do anything to you. When you're under oath, you have to tell them the truth when you answer their questions."

Another critical period in the development of airpower began in the 1950s with the B-70 program and the need for moving forward with a new strategic bomber. It is best told through Gen. David C. Jones, who with selflessness was willing to sacrifice his career to stand up for airpower, even temporarily losing a promotion to brigadier general. "In the 1950s," reflected Jones, "as a lieutenant colonel, I was aide to General Curtis E. LeMay while he was commander in chief of Strategic Air Command. During this assignment I gained a clear understanding of the need for strategic airpower. Later, when I was on the air staff while LeMay was air force chief, he asked me to develop a staff study on the need for the B-70, a new supersonic strategic bomber. I briefed Secretary of Defense McNamara on the study and thought we had convinced him of the need. We were surprised shortly thereafter when he canceled the program.

"A major controversy ensued with strong disagreements voiced in the Congress on the wisdom of the cancellation. The House Armed Services Committee, headed by the all-powerful Carl Vinson, asked me to give his committee the same briefing I had given to Secretary McNamara. The briefing resulted in the committee writing into the appropriations bill that the air force was ordered, required, directed, and mandated to spend $491 million in the next fiscal year on the development of the B-70.

"Despite objections from Secretary McNamara, the Defense Appropriations Subcommittee of the Senate insisted that the same briefing be given to them. Harold Brown, head of research and development for the department, got with me to modify the briefing. Harold Brown and I had many arguments over issues in the briefing, but I gained a great deal of respect for his brilliancy and integrity. We finally came up with a briefing we could both accept. When Brown took it to McNamara for approval, he ran into a buzz saw. McNamara changed the briefing, making many changes in the margins that were somewhat illegible. Furthermore, the charts were not changed so there were discrepancies between the charts and the text. By the time I got the briefing script, I was overdue on the Hill.

"Normally an entourage consisting of senior officers is present during such briefings. This time I was accompanied by only one person, a very reluctant assistant secretary of the air force, Brock McMillan. As the hearing started, Senator Robertson, chairman of the subcommittee, first expressed some irritation with our being late and then stated that Colonel Jones 'is to give us the same briefing he gave to the House Armed Services Committee. Is that correct?' He heard two answers. One from me saying 'no' and one from assistant secretary of the air force McMillan saying 'yes.'

"When Chairman Robertson was told that Mr. McNamara had changed the briefing, he was very mad and closed the hearing without receiving the briefing. Cooler heads prevailed and McNamara went to Capitol Hill to give Robertson a copy of the original script. Subsequently, the issue was solved by President Kennedy taking Carl Vinson for a walk in the Rose Garden. An agreement was made to cancel the B-70, but to prepare a new study on a more advanced bomber, which led to the B-1.

"The initial guidance was to study the need for an advanced strategic manned aircraft, ASMA. We soon changed it to advanced manned strategic aircraft, AMSA. It would not do to have the new aircraft referred to as one who could not get air because of a respiratory disease."[55]

Jones was informed before this hearing started that he had been selected to be promoted to brigadier general, but his name was taken off the list after it left the air force; one can safely assume that his name was removed by McNamara. Jones could have said "yes" and saved his promotion to brigadier general, but his character and belief in the future of airpower wouldn't permit it. Although he lost that one star, his character finally earned him three more. It did not end his career as it might have, and he went on to become chief of staff of the air force and chairman of the Joint Chiefs.

Secretary Harold Brown recently stated that the two officers who gave him the most trouble when he was head of research and development in the McNamara days were young O-6s, Col. David Jones and navy captain Ike Kidd. Brown said that the same officers were the two candidates to become chairman in 1978. It is ironic that two such mavericks would end up in top leadership positions within the Defense Department.

When Jones became air force chief of staff, the B-1 was well along in its development program. However, the ax fell again when President Carter canceled the program. Controversy reigned. Key leaders in Congress wanted to fight the decision. Their strategy was to force the spending of large sums to procure two more aircraft. If the air force joined them, it is likely that the two aircraft would be built, but the possibility of having a complete program was small.

The vice chief of staff of the air force at the time was Gen. William McBride, who vividly remembered the reaction to the announcement that the B-1 was to be canceled. "The day of the decision on the B-70, General Guy Harrison, head of the Office of Information, burst into my office with the word that the president was going to announce in fifteen minutes the cancellation of the B-70. I called David on the squawk box to report this action. David could not believe it. But he is an organized guy mentally and he said, 'Find out exactly what the president says on this action and then prepare comments for the press. We will be asked by many as to our reaction and what we are going to do about it.' It became apparent that over the next few days we would be asked time and time again as to what we planned to do. Would we fight the president's decision? Would we resign? Would we accept the decision? In the emotion of the time, a couple of senior officers said, 'Damnit, I'll be happy to give in my papers.' Clear heads would have been much more useful.

"After discussions with many people, including major commanders, Dave made the decision that it would not make sense to fight the decision. The best we could have achieved was authority to build two more aircraft. The administration would not support a program of eighty aircraft. Dave said, 'I have worked harder on this aircraft than anyone, but now that the decision has been made, I will give it my support.'"[56]

General Jones received a letter from Sen. John C. Stennis, chairman of the Senate Armed Services Committee, asking for his views on the decision. In his answer, General Jones stated: "I believe our security interests will be best served by continuing to modernize our strategic forces, including the manned bomber leg of the Triad. . . . So long as the B-1 program remains shrouded in uncertainty, consuming funds without adding to capability and diverting attention from our broader strategic needs, I am convinced that it will be more difficult to focus our collective energies on the many critical issues pertaining to our strategic forces in the days ahead."

In an interview with General Jones, I asked if he had given thought to resigning to protest the president's decision. He responded: "No, I never contemplated it. We in the military would do a great disservice to this country if we ever ended up with a military where a single decision on a single weapons system meant a difference between life and death. Once the president made a decision, I did not think it appropriate for our service to try to undermine the decision."

Whereas Jones was extensively involved with the controversy over the B-1 weapons system for the air force during his tenure as chief of staff, Gen. Edward C. Meyer had an equally alarming concern as chief of staff of the army about the entire U.S. Army. Meyer had been selected by President Carter over many other more senior generals to become chief of staff in June 1979. In this capacity, he testified before the personnel subcommittee of the House Armed Services Committee on May 7, 1980. General Meyer was asked by Congressman Hopkins: "I went to Fort Knox and visited with the general down there, and had a great day and so forth. I spent time with some of the enlisted personnel. . . . We really got down to what it is all about, and I asked if the all-volunteer service was working. Without exception, all of them said 'no' and many of them were getting out. They said that what you are getting today are your street-wise kids who know how to sell drugs, and were selling them. In fact, they were selling drugs right then at Fort Knox. If that is what we have for the defense of this country we are in very deep trouble. That is how I personally feel about it. I want to correct that, and I want you to help me do that."

General Meyer's response may not have been "the shot heard around the world," as at Lexington to start our Revolutionary War in 1776, but clearly his comments had an impact and received considerable attention. His response to Congressman Hopkins was: "I would merely say in defense of the 80 percent of the great young soldiers out there from your district and Mr. Nichol's district and from others that if you were to view them in our forward deployed areas, such as Berlin, Europe or Panama, where they are fully manned and equipped, you would find a different situation. But it is spotty and those situations you describe do exist. It is in essence what I call a hollow army in the United States today because we have not been able to provide the NCOs and manpower to fill it with both the quantity and the quality we need, and this bill begins to do that. . . ."

Not only did Meyer's response receive attention within the administration, but shortly thereafter, on December 5, 1980, Meyer was asked to appear on what was then the number one morning news program on television, ABC's *Good Morning America*. The moderator was David Hartman, and here is how the conversation progressed:

Hartman: "General Meyer, good morning. Welcome. Nice to have you with us."

General Meyer: "Good morning. Thank you very much. I'm very happy to be here."

Hartman: "Not too long ago, you said that the United States had what you called a hollow army. And it has been reported that six of our ten combat divisions really aren't combat ready. That's frightening. I think it would be to most people across the country. What do you mean by hollow army? And do you stand by your statement?"

General Meyer: "Sure. As I spoke to a 'hollow army,' I was talking about the fact that, in an effort to maintain our forces overseas in a ready status, it was necessary for us to have to draw down on our noncommissioned officers and our soldiers here in the States. So as a result of keeping that army up-to-date as far as equipment and manpower in our forward deployed areas in Europe, in Korea, in Panama, in Alaska . . . we've had to draw down on the forces here in the United States. And therefore, we have companies and platoons that have not been up to strength, and we're short noncommissioned officers out there to be able to train them."

I discussed this matter with Meyer in the context of the challenges that other military leaders have had. He made it clear that he followed the appropriate understanding of civilian authority: "I went through that lots of times [meaning fighting for the army's needs], but the highlight occurred when I told Congress we had a 'hollow army.' There was an attack on the army. Fortunately, I told this privately to both the president and Secretary of Defense Brown, so they had known my view on it, but a lot of people didn't. One of my superiors asked me to withdraw my statement. I said no I wouldn't, and I went back to the office and wrote my resignation. I didn't have to turn it in, because suddenly it came to them, we really do have a country in which we have a responsibility. We don't take our oath of allegiance to the president, we take our oath of allegiance to the Constitution. That means we have an equal responsibility to Congress and the president."[57]

Later, on February 25, 1983, Meyer appeared before the Senate Armed Services Committee to testify on the fiscal year 1984 Department of Defense budget request. In his opening statement to the committee, he commented, "I got into a bit of trouble for saying we had a hollow army. All I can say is that the $153 billion that the Congress has given us in the past three years has permitted us to take steps to provide a solid base on which to build the army of the future."

Committee chairman Tower responded, "May I say, General, you did not get into trouble with this committee. You got our attention."

Virginia senator John W. Warner then commented: "The point I wish to make is that if we have cured the hollow army concept in a two-year period and if we are compelled to take cuts now, would it not be more advisable to take those in terms of active personnel strength rather than modernization, recognizing that most of your procurement programs are five to ten years in duration?"

The bottom line in all of this is, did General Meyer's straightforward and honest approach work? I specifically asked him about this and he responded, "It had an impact both within and without the army. It was a signal to those inside the army that the top leadership was aware of the problem and willing to address the problems with which they were concerned. Externally, it was a signal that leaders have a responsibility to speak freely, both within the Department of Defense and to members of Congress when asked about the real challenges they are facing."[58]

The army over the next several years was provided much of the funds needed to improve on training and readiness shortcomings. This is another example of the importance of character in our military leaders. Meyer spoke up before Congress, but not before he had informed the president and secretary of defense that he was going to do so. He would not back down from his position, and he felt strongly enough about how important a position it was that he prepared his resignation and was willing to put the welfare of the army ahead of his own personal welfare.

There is a moral to the events described with the defense of Billy Mitchell by Arnold and Spaatz: They selflessly put their careers on the line. But later in life both Arnold and Spaatz made the comment that Mitchell should have remained in the service and fought within the system for airpower. That is exactly what Arnold and Spaatz did.

At the time that Arnold was exiled to Fort Riley, he was offered the presidency of Pan American Airways, the civilian commercial airline, but he rejected it, stating, "I couldn't very well quit the service under fire." I asked General Spaatz about it, and he informed me that it was so and that at the same time he was offered the vice presidency of Pan American.

When President Carter decided against the continued development of the B-1, many people told General Jones that he should resign in protest. But he didn't, like Arnold and Spaatz; he stayed in and fought within the system—and ultimately won. Similarly, Gen. George S. Brown, Jones's predecessor as air force chief, was chairman of the Joint Chiefs of Staff when the B-1 was rejected, and some told him he should have resigned as chairman.

General Brown's sense of humor flashed one day while he was appearing before Congress. One congressman changed the train of thought from the main line of questioning and asked, "By the way, General Brown, you're a senior air force general. Carter has decided to cancel the B-1. Why don't you resign from the air force?" Brown, less than diplomatically, said, "I certainly could, but it would have about as much effect on this country as your resigning from the Congress."

Our country has been blessed with having brilliant military leaders ready when it became necessary to defend our freedom and the freedom of the world in time of war. They were selfess men who devoted their lives to serving their country and stood ready when crises arose. In many respects, the entire military is selfless, as are their families. They put up with low pay, slow promotions, frequent moves, long family separations, and periods of inadequate funding for training and supply resources; sometimes they have to put up with bureaucratic stupidity and self-seeking politicians, often suffering a lack of recognition and appreciation, indeed, sometimes the hostility of the population. On occasions, their families have tolerated poor medical care, and they suffered and sacrificed as their children were uprooted from their friends and schools when they were required to move to a new duty station.

One of the most meaningful interviews I ever had was with the widow of General Spaatz, the first chief of staff of a separate air force. She reflected on an occasion when her oldest daughter, packing to leave for her second year of college, made the comment, "Mom, do you realize this is the first time in my life where I will be going to the same school two years in a row?"[59]

The greatest act of selflessness on the part of these men was the willingness to give their lives in defending our country in time of war, and in time of peace to put their careers on the line to fight for what they believed needed to be done to maintain readiness for future conflicts.

Notes

1. Cited in Katherine Tupper Marshall, *Together* (New York: Tupper and Love, Inc., 1946), 250.

2. U. S. Grant, *Personal Memoirs, Volume II* (New York: Charles L. Webster & Company, 1886), 489.

3. B. H. Liddell Hart, *Sherman: The Genius of the Civil War* (London: Eyre and Spottiswoode, 1933), 240.

4. Marshall, *Together*, 135.

5. Ibid., 135.

6. Dwight D. Eisenhower, *At Ease: Stories I Tell My Friends* (New York: Doubleday & Company, Inc., 1967), 241.

7. Personal interview with General of the Army Dwight D. Eisenhower and Edgar F. Puryear, Jr., May 2, 1963.

8. Personal interview with General of the Army Omar N. Bradley and Edgar F. Puryear, Jr., February 15, 1963.

9. Personal interview with Gen. Mark Clark, USA (Ret.), and Edgar F. Puryear, Jr., December 20, 1962.

10. Personal interview with Gen. Lucian K. Truscott, USA (Ret.), and Edgar F. Puryear, Jr., September 11, 1962.

11. Personal interview with Gen. Carl Spaatz, USAF (Ret.), and Edgar F. Puryear, Jr., September 12, 1962.

12. Personal interview with Gen. J. Lawton Collins, USA (Ret.), and Edgar F. Puryear, Jr., September 20, 1962.

13. Personal interview with Gen. William H. Simpson, USA (Ret.), and Edgar F. Puryear, Jr., September 20, 1962.

14. Personal interview with Gen. Jacob Devers, USA (Ret.), and Edgar F. Puryear, Jr., September 12, 1962.

15. Personal interview with Gen. Albert Wedemeyer, USA (Ret.), and Edgar F. Puryear, Jr., September 28, 1962.

16. Personal interview with Gen. Anthony McAuliffe, USA (Ret.), and Edgar F. Puryear, Jr., September 10, 1962.

17. Eisenhower, *At Ease*, 244, and personal interview.

18. Eisenhower interview.

19. Robert H. Ferrell, ed., *The Eisenhower Diaries* (New York: W. W. Norton Company, 1981), 63.

20. Ibid.

21. Ibid., 50–51.

22. Ibid., 192–93.

23. Ibid., 204.

24. Ibid.

25. Ibid., 210.

26. Ibid., 220.

27. Ibid.

28. Ibid., 267.

29. Douglas Southall Freeman, *George Washington, Volume V* (New York: Charles Scribner's Sons, 1952), 7.

30. William Safire, ed., *Lend Me Your Ears* (New York: W. W. Norton and Company, 1992), 91.

31. James T. Flexner, *Washington: The Indispensable Man* (Boston: Little Brown and Company, 1969), 171.

32. Ibid., 174; Safire, *Lend Me Your Ears,* 91–94.

33. Flexner, 171.

34. Ibid.

35. Ibid.

36. Ibid.

37. Ibid.

38. Letter from Secretary of War Henry L. Stimson to President Franklin Delano Roosevelt, dated August 10, 1943.

39. Stimson diary, August 22, 1947.

40. Robert Sherwood, *Roosevelt and Hopkins* (New York: Harper and Brothers, 1948), 770.

41. Stimson diary, September 15, 1943.

42. Sherwood, *Roosevelt and Hopkins,* 759.

43. Ibid., 803.

44. Stimson diary, December 17, 1943.

45. Ibid.

46. Ibid.

47. Letter from Maj. Gen. Ward H. Maris, USA (Ret.), to Edgar F. Puryear, Jr., dated September 10, 1962.

48. Ibid.

49. Stimson diary, February 16, 1943.

50. Stimson letter to President Roosevelt, February 16, 1943.

51. Stimson diary, January 13, 1942.

52. Ibid.

53. Stimson diary, January 14, 1942.

54. The following discussion is summarized from a more extensive discussion in *Stars in Flight: A Study in Air Force Character and Leadership* (Novato, Calif.: Presidio Press, 1981), 38–59.

55. Personal interview with Gen. David C. Jones, USAF (Ret.), and Edgar F. Puryear, Jr., January 20, 1998.

56. Personal interview with Gen. William V. McBride, USAF (Ret.), and Edgar F. Puryear, Jr., March 20, 1978.

57. Personal interview with Gen. Edward C. Meyer, USA (Ret.), and Edgar F. Puryear, Jr., July 14, 1997.

58. Ibid.

59. Personal interview with Mrs. Carl Spaatz and Edgar F. Puryear, Jr., February 11, 1976.

Chapter 2: Decision: The Essence of Leadership

Making decisions is of the essence in leadership.
—General of the Army Dwight D. Eisenhower

In my discussion with General Eisenhower he commented, "I have pondered the question of leadership quite a bit, and I think I can come back to take as my starting point the statement that Napoleon is reputed to have made: 'Genius in leadership is the ability to do an average thing when everyone around you is going crazy and [is] at least hysterical.'

"When you come right down to it, leadership is, of course, being exerted all the time in the capacity of boosting morale, confidence and all that, but leadership is most noticeable when tough decisions finally have to be made. This is the time when you get conflicting advice and urgent advice of every kind. Now this is the kind of leadership that's often concealed from the public. . . . But making decisions is of the essence in leadership—that is, handling large problems whether or not you are at war or at peace. When you make these decisions it is not done with any reaching for the dramatic. It is almost everyday and commonplace. You reach a conclusion based upon the facts as you see them, the evaluations of the several factors as you see them, the relationship of one fact to another, and, above all, your convictions as to the capacity of different individuals to fit into these different places. You come to a decision after you've taken all these things into consideration. Then you decide and say, 'That's what we'll do.'"[1]

The position of command is a lonely one. At no time does a leader feel loneliness more deeply than when having to make a critical, high-level decision dealing with life and death, success or failure, victory or defeat. It is an overwhelming responsibility that few people desire and for which considerably fewer people are qualified. But making decisions is part of leadership; in time of war the general who does not have the strength to make decisions and the judgment to be right a large percentage of the time does not remain long in a position of high command. Generals are human and are subject to the strains and stresses of the mind just as lesser beings. Their mistakes can be counted in deaths and destruction, a responsibility that no sane person takes lightly.

The generals in time of war were faced daily with innumerable difficult and grave decisions. There are two points of caution, however, that need special emphasis. First, wartime commanders have to make critical decisions, but seldom were these decisions based upon the kind of information that a historian presently has available for evaluation. A commander must act upon the facts available at decision time. Second, to one who has never been involved with making high-level decisions, the process looks easy. Those in lower echelons are mostly ignorant of the complexity of the commander's problems and become impatient when they receive a late or an unclear decision. It is easy to criticize but hard to do better if placed at a similar level of responsibility.

There is a third factor in high command decision making. Normally, a wartime commander can select his key staff members, probably the most competent people he knows: dedicated and strong professionals. One cannot take the advice of such people lightly. When they are all opposed to a top general's conclusion, the decision-making process becomes far more difficult.

The greatest decision faced by General Eisenhower during World War II was the place, day, and hour of the Allied invasion of the European continent, as well as sending airborne divisions into the Cherbourg peninsula preliminary to the invasion. These divisions would secure our landings in both the British and American sectors. According to Ike's chief of staff, Gen. Walter Bedell Smith, the reasons were "compelling. Behind the landing area stretched the low ground the Germans had flooded. A few roads crossed the marshy, mile-wide strip, but unless airborne troops were put down on the firm ground behind to seize the road heads and engage the defenders, the narrow causeways across the marshes could be raked by enemy fire. Our troops would take heavy casualties forcing their way inland from the beaches."[2]

The senior air adviser on Eisenhower's staff, British air chief marshal Leigh-Mallory, was opposed to the airborne drop because he believed that it would result in the useless slaughter of fine divisions. He contended that the strong antiaircraft defenses of Cherbourg and the small drop area would result in losing 75 percent or higher of the gliders and 50 percent of the paratroopers, causing thousands of men to die. The mission, in his opinion, would fail because of these excessive losses.

On May 30, 1944, Leigh-Mallory came to Eisenhower to make one final protest against carrying out the operation. As he presented his case, these were the thoughts that went on in Eisenhower's mind: "To protect him [Leigh-Mallory], in case his advice was disregarded, I instructed the air commander to put his recommendations in a letter and informed him he would have my answer within a few hours. I took the problem to no one else. Professional advice and counsel could do no more.

"I went to my tent alone and sat down to think. Over and over I reviewed each step. . . . I realized, of course, that if I deliberately disregarded the advice of my technical expert on the subject, and his predictions should prove accurate, then I would carry to my grave the unbearable burden of a conscience justly accusing me of the stupid, blind sacrifice of thousands in the flower of our youth. Outweighing any personal burden, however, was the possibility that if he were right, the effect of the disaster would be far more than local: it would be likely to spread to the entire force."[3]

In considering what should be done, Ike weighed these factors:

1. He was convinced that the operation was vital to the success of the assault.

2. Without the Utah Beach landing to get the base of the Cotentin Peninsula immediately, the entire operation was too risky to attempt.

3. In his own judgment, he just didn't believe that the Germans would inflict such heavy losses.

Ike called Leigh-Mallory and told him that the attack would go on as planned. History proved Ike to be correct. The losses to the airborne elements in the first drop were less than 2 percent, and less than 10 percent for the whole operation. Navy captain Harry Butcher, Ike's aide, cited in his book that "in typical British sport fashion," air chief marshal Leigh-Mallory admitted he was wrong and stated quite frankly: "It is sometimes difficult in this life to admit that one is wrong, but he has never had a greater pleasure in doing so than on this occasion. Leigh-Mallory congratulated General Ike on the wisdom of his command decisions."[4]

There was another incident similar to this. Although the Allies were collecting forces after the abortive Ardennes counteroffensive, Eisenhower wanted to extend their effective campaigns west of the Rhine. He believed that a large portion of Hitler's power should have been destroyed before storming the river barrier. Field marshal Sir Alan Brooke was opposed to this strategy because it would disperse Allied forces and divert divisions from Montgomery's northern crossing of the Rhine aimed at the Ruhr. Brooke had very strong feelings about the matter, but Ike stuck to his decision. Several weeks later Brooke said to Eisenhower, "You were completely right, and I am sorry if my fear of dispersed effort added to your burdens. Thank God you stuck by your guns!"[5]

The discussions that decided the time and place of the Second Front in World War II, Ike's most difficult decision, were conducted for more than two years. When he was named supreme commander, the place, France, had been decided upon. The staff planners had selected May 1944 as the date of the invasion. This date was to be Eisenhower's first change. He concluded that he would need to increase the number of assault divisions from three to five. To accomplish the personnel and logistic changes (particularly the need for additional landing craft) meant a postponement from May to June. The month's delay was significant because good spring weather would be advantageous for offensive operations.

The critical aspect was the weather. When Eisenhower had to decide on "go" or "no go" in North Africa, weather then was a problem. The weather issue in Sicily was worse. The decision had been made that the Allies would invade, but the evening before, the wind—instead of dying as predicted—increased to forty miles an hour. This would cause high waves, which not only could make many soldiers seasick but could make the landing hazardous. Nor was the news encouraging for the 82d Airborne Division, which planned to drop into the midst of the enemy. General George Marshall wired, wanting to know, "Is the attack on or off?" Ike said to himself, "My reaction was that I wish I knew!"[6] But the decision was his to make. Again he was alone, and again he calculated the risks. If he were to call off the invasion now, there would be many isolated catastrophes among the units that, because of their particular mission, departed early. These forces, should they receive too late the message to return, would be slaughtered. The element of surprise, upon which they were counting heavily, would be lost. Outside, Ike gauged the wind once more, went into his office, and ordered: "It's on. There's a high wind, but I think we'll have good news tomorrow."

As the evening wore on, however, the wind velocity increased. During the lonely and desperate hours of waiting, Ike fingered his lucky coins. "There was nothing we could do but pray, desperately."[7]

Because the Normandy invasion required the right combination of moon, tide, and time of sunrise, the target date for the attack would be on June 5, 6, or 7. The decision for which of these days would depend upon the weather. Ike said of the situation: "If none of the three days should prove satisfactory from the standpoint of weather, consequences would ensue that were almost terrifying to contemplate. Secrecy would be lost. Assault troops would be unloaded and crowded back into assembly areas enclosed in barbed wire, where their original places would already have been taken by those to follow in subsequent waves. Complicated movement tables would be scrapped. Morale would drop. A wait of at least fourteen days, possibly twenty-eight, would be necessary—a sort of suspended animation involving more than 2,000,000 men! The good-weather period available for major campaigning would become still shorter and the enemy's defenses would become still stronger."[8]

It was tentatively decided that the invasion would be launched on June 5. The final decision meeting was held at 0400 on June 4, even though some of the forward elements had already embarked. The weather was bad; there were low clouds and high winds and waves, all of which indicated a hazardous landing. Air support would be impossible and naval gunfire inaccurate. General Eisenhower consulted his key advisers: Admiral Ramsay was neutral from the naval side, Montgomery said "go," and air marshal Tedder said "no go." But they could only advise. The final decision was Eisenhower's. He decided to postpone the attack.[9]

The staff met again the next morning. The weather outlook for June 6 was good but would probably last only about thirty-six hours. General Smith, Ike's chief of staff, described the scene on the morning of June 5:

> All the commanders were there when General Eisenhower arrived, trim in his tailored battle jacket, his face tense with the gravity of the decision which lay before him. Field Marshal Montgomery wore his usual baggy corduroy trousers and sweat-shirt. Admiral Ramsay and his chief of staff were immaculate in navy blue and gold.
>
> The meteorologists were brought in at once. There was the ghost of a smile on the tired face of Group Captain Stagg, the tall Scot.
>
> "I think we have found a gleam of hope for you, sir," he said to General Eisenhower, and we all listened expectantly. "The mass of weather fronts coming in from the Atlantic is moving faster than we anticipated," the chief meteorologist said, and he went on to promise reasonable weather for twenty-four hours. Ike's advisers then started firing rapid questions at the weatherman. When they had finished asking questions there was silence which lasted for a full five minutes while General Eisenhower sat on a sofa before the bookcase which filled the end of the room. I never realized before the loneliness and iso-lation of a Commander at a time when such a momentous de-cision has to be taken, with full knowledge that failure or suc-cess rests on his judgment alone. He sat there quietly, not getting up to pace with quick strides as he often does. He was tense, weighing every consideration of weather as he had been briefed to do during the dry runs since April, and weighing with them those other imponderables.
>
> Finally he looked up, and the tension was gone from his face. He said briskly, "Well, we'll go!"[10]

It is history that it went well, but what goes on in a commander's mind after such a monumental decision? Ike said of the occasion in his memoirs, "Again I had to endure the interminable wait that al-ways intervenes between the final decision of the high command and

the earliest possible determination of success or failure in such ventures."[11]

In spite of all the people around him during, before, and after
decisions, it is easy to see why Ike wrote to a friend during the war,
"The worst part of high military command is the loneliness. . . ."

Some of the greatest decision-making challenges for any American commander in chief were those that were faced by President
Harry S. Truman. At the time of Roosevelt's death, Truman had been
vice president for eighty-three days. He had not been to Europe since
his service there as an army captain in World War I; he had never
been invited into the War Room in the West Wing of the White
House that daily kept the president informed of the war's progress;
he had not been invited to or briefed on the Yalta Conference; he
was not aware of the confrontation between the United States and
the Union of Soviet Socialist Republics (USSR) over Poland; he knew
nothing of the development of the atomic bomb; and he never had
a day of college.

In the first month after being sworn in as president, Truman was
presented with an awesome number of critical decisions that had
to be given immediate attention: the decision to drop the atomic
bomb; how to handle the occupation of a defeated Germany; to
encourage the Soviet Union to declare war against Japan, and what
should be done about the Soviet Union's establishing a puppet
Communist regime in Warsaw. It is no wonder that Truman ap-
propriately entitled the first volume of his memoirs *Year of Decisions*.
In the preface to this book, he wrote: "The presidency of the
United States carries with it a responsibility so personal as to be
without parallel.

"Very few are ever authorized to speak for the President. No one
can make decisions for him. No one can know all the processes and
stages of his thinking in making important decisions. Even those closest to him, even members of his immediate family, never know all
the reasons why he does certain things and why he comes to certain
conclusions. To be President of the United States is to be lonely, very
lonely at times of great decisions."[12]

Dean Acheson, then an assistant secretary of state, responded to
a friend's question about Truman's leadership. "[He] . . . is straight-

forward, decisive, simple, entirely honest."[13] All of these qualities were indicators of Truman as a man of character, so vital and essential in decision making.

Averell Harriman, U.S. ambassador to the Soviet Union during World War II, had worked closely overall with Roosevelt and his administration for almost fourteen years. Contrasting the two, he said of Truman, "You could go into his office with a question and come out with a decision from him more swiftly than any man I have ever known."[14]

Critics have accused President Truman of making a "snap decision" on the use of the atomic bomb, but it was not. He commented: "My own knowledge of these developments had come only after I became President, when Secretary Stimson had given me the full story. He told me at the time the project was nearing completion and that a bomb could be expected within another four months. It was his suggestion, too, that I had them set up a committee of top men and had asked them to study with great care the implications the new weapon might have for us."[15]

The committee was headed by Secretary of War Stimson. Truman wrote: "It was their recommendation that the bomb be used against the enemy as soon as it could be done. They recommended further that it should be used without specific warning and against a target that would clearly show its devastating strength. I had realized, of course, that an atomic bomb explosion would inflict damage and casualties beyond imagination. On the other hand, the scientific advisors on the committee reported, 'We can propose no technical demonstration likely to bring an end to the war; we see no acceptable alternative to direct military use.' It was their conclusion that no technical demonstration they might propose, such as over a deserted island, would be likely to bring the war to an end. It had to be used against an enemy target.

"The final decision of when and where to use the atomic bomb was up to me. Let there be no mistake about it. I regarded the bomb as a military weapon and never had any doubt that it should be used. The top military advisors to the President recommended its use, and when I talked to Churchill, he unhesitatingly told me that he favored the use of the atomic bomb if it might aid the end of the war."[16]

There were times, however, when Truman completely put aside the counsel of his closest advisers when he made decisions. In 1948, a key challenge for the United States was the establishment of the independent Zionist state of Israel. Great Britain was financially and militarily bankrupt after World War II and had to give up many areas of the world in which she had a sphere of influence, such as Palestine. Responsibility for this troubled land passed to the United Nations and finally to the United States.

Truman was sympathetic to the plight of the Jews, particularly when he considered the horrors of the Holocaust and its many survivors who wanted to settle in Palestine. Truman was sensitive to this desire for humanitarian reasons and believed they were entitled to a homeland of their own.

His most important advisers were opposed to the establishment of the state of Israel: Secretary of State George C. Marshall and his undersecretary, Robert Lovett; Secretary of Defense James V. Forrestal, George F. Kennan, and Charles E. "Chip" Bohlen, Truman's key State Department advisers and Soviet expert; and Dean Acheson. They believed that Israel posed a significant risk for U.S. national security, particularly with our dependence on Arab oil. Recognition of Israel would be offensive to the Arab world and probably would provoke a war between Israel and the Arab countries. The United States might have to send troops to assist them, and this would probably push the Arabs into the Soviet camp.

Truman almost always followed the advice of his foreign policy advisers, but when the British mandate was to end on May 15, 1948, he decided that the United States would recognize Israel.

One biographer wrote of the main conference on this issue:

> General Marshall was indignant. He thought that Truman was buckling under the political pressure, an unpardonable sin to the old general. At a meeting at Blair House on May 12, he listened with rising anger to Clark Clifford make the case for recognition. He was furious that Clifford, whom Marshall regarded as a political operator, was even allowed into the meeting to discuss such a sensitive national security issue. Clifford recalled uneasily watching the color rise in Marshall's pink face.

"In the first place, I don't even know why this man is here," Marshall said to Truman, gesturing at Clifford. The old general was harsher than anyone in the room had ever heard him be. "If you follow Clifford's advance," he coldly told Truman, "and in the election I were to vote, I would vote against you." From a man Truman regarded as the "greatest living American," this was bitter medicine.[17]

Robert Lovett said during the meeting that he thought Truman was being "so politically transparent as to defeat its purpose." Forrest C. Pogue's definitive biography of Marshall adds further insight into the decision-making process: "As Marshall listened to the discussion, he saw honesty in Lovett's charge that Clifford's was a political approach—recognition of a new state because there were enough Jews in the United States to make recognition a good ploy in an American election. He said it would damage the presidential office. Perhaps Clifford's manner upset the Secretary, because he retorted in what Clifford supposedly termed 'a righteous God-damned Baptist tone' that this matter was not to be settled on the basis of politics and that if domestic politics were not involved Clifford would not be at the conference. He suggested that they take another look at the matter after May 16. Truman, quickly seeing that the meeting was getting out of hand, said he was inclined to agree with Marshall but they should sleep on the matter.

"Jewish leaders were soon aware of the substance of the May 12 meeting in the White House, and fresh pressures were applied to Truman. Chiam Weizmann wrote an eloquent appeal on May 13 that moved the President. The next day, he called Clifford and told him to arrange for recognition that afternoon."[18]

Lovett's position was that it was the president's decision and would be implemented without hesitation. He was concerned, however, that Marshall might resign over the incident, so he discussed it with him. Marshall's response was that he recognized that he "was duty-bound to his chief; having argued and lost, they must now carry out the President's orders." Several of Marshall's friends urged him to resign, but he did not, telling them that the president had a right to make a decision and it was Marshall's duty to implement it. The decision-making process over the recognition of Israel certainly illustrates Truman's character in making the decision and that of Marshall, who so strongly opposed recognition, selflessly carrying out the commander in chief's decision, the good soldier to the end.

As chief of staff of the army from 1939 to 1945, Marshall had to make more key decisions than any other single individual. What process did he follow in making decisions? Was there a methodology to his decision making? Yes, and there is no better model.

Marshall relied upon a group of talented officers to assist him with the many decisions he was required to make. He established a body he named "the Secretariat" to assist him in his decision making.

When Marshall became chief in 1939, prior to World War II, and thereafter during the war, "Studies calling for decision by the Chief or one of the deputies were prepared in the appropriate divisions of the General Staff," commented then Maj. J. Lawton Collins. Collins was a member of the Secretariat and went on to become chief of staff of the army from 1949 to 1953. "Action papers based on these studies were routed through the office of Colonel Ward, who allocated them to one of his assistants for presentation to one of the deputies, or directly to the Chief. Each of us on the Secretariat was assigned from five to ten papers every day. While I was there we had no special assignments of subjects. We reviewed our papers, checked them for obvious errors, and any loose ends or unclear points, which we believed would raise questions by the Chief, or Deputy. We then 'briefed' a deputy, or the Chief, on each of the completed papers."[19]

There are many books published on decision making, but none surpassed Marshall's simple methodology. It was followed successfully by the best officers under his tutelage. Many of them, in the later years of their careers, became top generals. "General Marshall required that all staff papers, no matter how complicated the subject, be reduced to two pages or less," Collins wrote. "The format was fairly rigid: first, a statement of the problem; next, factors bearing on the problem, pro and con; a brief discussion, if necessary; conclusions; and finally, and most importantly, recommended action. 'Tabs,' which could be attached to the basic papers but only briefly noted therein, would cover aspects of the subject requiring more detailed background, discussion, or explanation. The file on a very involved subject might be an inch or more thick, but the material calling for a decision had to be reduced to not more than two pages. This forced careful analysis by the staff, and led to definitive recommendations."[20]

Collins further recalled: "We on the Secretariat made our presentations orally, using the minimum of notes, restricting ourselves to the key points of each paper. We had to be prepared to answer any questions from the Chief or Deputy, or to elaborate on any point they wished amplified. Papers requiring a letter from the Chief of Staff or a major decision affecting policy would always be presented to the Chief. General Marshall had known each member during our prior service and respected our judgment. We were encouraged to express any disagreement we might have with the proposed recommendations, or make any other suggestions that we felt worthwhile."[21]

Walter Bedell Smith, Eisenhower's chief of staff in Europe, was another influential Marshall protégé. He came to the attention of then Maj. Omar Bradley, the head of the Infantry School's Weapons Department, who was impressed with Smith's "absolutely brilliant and analytical mind." Marshall observed Smith making a class presentation and commented to Bradley, "There is a man who would make a wonderful instructor."[22]

In 1939, Bradley was the assistant secretary on Marshall's staff. He remembered Smith from Benning days and suggested to Marshall that he bring Smith on board to handle the chief's correspondence. In no time, Smith became indispensable to Marshall. He knew how to express Marshall's ideas in writing.

The chief of staff could not ignore the inevitable political matters while dealing so closely with Franklin Roosevelt. The president insisted on retaining many decisions in his hands but had to be prevented from interfering in purely military matters. This presented real challenges for Marshall, because Roosevelt was indecisive and vacillated. His White House military assistant was Maj. Gen. Edwin "Pa" Watson. Bedell Smith was assigned to "handle" Watson, a task at which he was remarkably successful. The diplomatic Smith was able to minimize political interference between the White House and the War Department.

Smith's biographer commented, "The ability to make decisions and the self-assuredness to criticize Marshall, scarce commodities in the War Department, distinguished officers on the rise." General Eisenhower commented that Marshall said to him, "The Department is filled with able men who analyze well, but feel compelled always to bring [problems] to me for a final solution. I must have assistants who will solve their own problems and tell me what they have done."[23]

Marshall instructed Bradley, "Unless I hear all the arguments for or against an action I am about to take, I don't know whether or not I'm right."[24] Marshall insisted that his staff make decisions even though they were in conflict with him. They had to be able to support their positions, however. Thus, Marshall created an atmosphere for independent thinking.

General Henry H. "Hap" Arnold commanded the U.S. Army Air Force, a position subordinate to Marshall. At its peak, the air corps included some 2,400,000 men and women and 80,000 aircraft. Arnold was a dynamic decision maker. Major General Howard C. Davidson reflected: "I had a good chance to observe General Arnold, for I worked with him as Nineteenth Bombardment Group Commander at March Field and later as executive officer to Chief of the Air Corps when Arnold was assistant chief. Arnold was quick to make a decision; some of them were wrong, but most of them were right, because Arnold was constantly seeking information on people and subjects concerning the Air Corps. Even at social gatherings, such as cocktail parties and dinners, he was picking everyone's brain. If a bush pilot came to Washington from Alaska, Arnold would invite him around and entertain him while he found out all he could about Alaska."[25]

Arnold's thirst for information was insatiable and valuable to his decision making. He had an army attaché in Berlin before World War II give talks to the air staff. He used every possible opportunity to have American manufacturers visit Europe to study aircraft production there. He asked to be briefed by Charles Lindbergh, after his trip to Germany, on the capability of the Luftwaffe. He included members of the army general staff and the secretary of war in these briefings. He wanted the "Lone Eagle" to tell the story to the wide audience of what he had seen in Germany to corroborate the concern that Arnold had about the buildup of the German air force.

General Davidson also commented that in the process of leading and making decisions, "Arnold was very impatient and short-tempered. His impatience helped him to get things done quickly, and, fortunately, he could not remember four hours later what had made him angry. He was too impatient to read long-winded reports, and as an executive officer I would have the staff summarize in about one page what they had expressed in many pages."[26]

Sticking with the Decision

When George Marshall became secretary of state in 1947 during the Cold War, he was again in a position to make many critical decisions. In spring 1948, George F. Kennan, in charge of the plans staff, recommended to the secretary a conciliatory gesture to be made to the Soviet Union concerning the Marshall Plan. Word was sent to the Soviets to invite them to talk over their problems. The recommendation was quickly accepted but unfortunately exploited by the Soviets, who interpreted it as an invitation for a high-level conference. This created a furor among the Allies, who were upset because the meeting had not been coordinated with them. They demanded an explanation, believing that the United States was negotiating behind their backs. Said Kennan:

> I can recall [an] episode that endeared him [General Marshall] to me beyond all others.
>
> I was appalled at what I had done. For two evenings, I walked the streets of Foxhall Village, trying to think out the course of events and to discover where our error had lain. On the third day, I went in to the general to render my accounting. He was absorbed in a pile of papers.
>
> "General," I said, "I know that a man should try to learn from his mistakes, and not weep over them. I have spent two days, now, trying to figure out what it was that we did wrong. For the life of me, I cannot see it. I think we were right, and that the

critics are wrong. But where there is so much criticism, there must be some fault somewhere."

General Marshall put down his papers, turned ponderously in his chair, and fixed his eyes on me penetratingly over the rims of his glasses. I trembled inwardly for what was coming.

"Kennan," he said, "when we went into North Africa, in 1942, and the landings were initially successful, for three days we were geniuses in the eyes of the press. Then that business with Darlan began and for another three weeks we were nothing but the greatest dopes.

"The decision you are talking about had my approval; it was discussed in the Cabinet; it was approved by the President.

"The only trouble with you is that you don't have the wisdom and the perspicacity of a columnist. Now get out of here!"[27]

Criticism goes with the territory for responsible leaders. When significant decisions are made, there may be a great deal of criticism from the "all-knowing press."

It was clear to Eisenhower that once a decision is made, one sticks with it. In reflecting upon one of his British generals as Allied commander, Gen. Harold R. L. C. Alexander, on June 11, 1943, Ike commented: "He has a winning personality, wide experience in war, an ability to get along with people, and sound tactical conceptions. He is self-effacing and energetic. The only possible doubt that could be raised with respect to his qualifications is a suspected unsureness in dealing with certain of his subordinates. At times it seems that he alters his own plans and ideas merely to meet an objection or a suggestion of a subordinate, so as to avoid direct command methods."[28]

Often General Eisenhower, when others weakened on a decision made, would go out to inspect the situation. When the British were leery about one plan, Ike wrote in his diary on July 1, 1943: "The ground force detailed for the attack was the First British Division, under General Clutterbuck. He was not favorably impressed by the prospects. He made a personal visit to me to lay out the difficulties and feared that he would have a great number of his men slaughtered. Even General Alexander was greatly impressed by the most unfavorable reactions upon the Husky operation, if we should encounter a repulse in Pantelleria.

"Because of these fears and doubts, I engaged to make a personal reconnaissance of the place, by the sea, two or three days before D-day. My reconnaissance, made in company of Admiral Cunningham, convinced me that the landing would be an easy affair and resistance would be light, and I directed definitely that the plans go ahead as ordered. Actually, the place surrendered before the leading assault boats got to the shore, and the defending commander later stated that he did not even know an infantry attack was intended for that day. We captured over eleven thousand troops."[29]

Similarly, with the invasion at Salerno, Ike wrote, "Doubts were frequently expressed in this headquarters as to the wisdom of going on with Avalanche. I felt that the possible results were so great that, even with the meager allotments in landing craft, . . . we should go ahead. I so informed the combined chiefs of staff."[30]

Marshall also was cool and detached as a decision maker. Dean Rusk, then serving as an assistant secretary of state, reflected: "Whenever his advisers disagreed about policy, we couldn't see Marshall alone; he insisted that all parties to a dispute be present. During the Roosevelt administration, FDR's advisers often threatened to resign, hoping to win a presidential vote of confidence or pressure him on a policy matter. Marshall regarded that behavior as blackmail and wouldn't allow it at State. After he became Secretary of State, a senior officer of the department suggested a change of policy, then added that if Marshall didn't adopt the change, he—the officer—would have lost his usefulness and would have to resign.

"Mr. So-and-So, whether you or I work for the U.S. government has nothing to do with the merits of this question," Marshall retorted promptly. "So let's remove the irrelevancy. I accept your resignation, effective immediately. Now that this matter is resolved, if you wish to spend a few minutes discussing the issues with me, I'll hear your views. After this story got around, nobody pulled a 'New Deal resignation' on George Marshall."[31]

Another insight into decision making by Eisenhower comes from an entry of December 10, 1942: "Through all this, I am learning many things: (1) that waiting for other people to produce is one of the hardest things a commander has to do; (2) that in the higher positions of modern army, navy, and air force, rich organizational experience and an orderly, logical mind are absolutely essential to success. The flashy, publicity-seeking type of adventurer can grab the headlines and be a hero in the eyes of the public, but he simply can't deliver the goods in high command. On the other hand, the slow, methodical, ritualistic person is absolutely valueless in a key position. There must be a fine balance—that is [one in] such a position must have an inexhaustible fund of nervous energy. He is called upon day and night to absorb the disappointments, the discouragement, and doubts of his subordinates and to force them on to accomplishments, which they regard as impossible."[32]

Intuition

Although many decisions are made with input from staff and commanders, some leaders are so able and experienced that their intuition contributes greatly to decision making. Being courageous to act upon intuition is also a test of the character of leaders, such as Gen. Douglas MacArthur during the Korean War.

In June 1950, North Korean troops invaded South Korea against little opposition, but forces began to stop them by establishing a stable line of defense around Pusan in the south of the peninsula. The United States successfully petitioned the United Nations to defend South Korea, and MacArthur was selected as commander of the United Nations forces. He wanted to conduct a turning movement into the flank and rear of the enemy by an amphibious operation to cut off its supply line from Communist China and encircle the enemy forces south of Seoul at Inchon, twenty miles west of Seoul, and the second-largest port in South Korea. Timing of the operation was critical because of the tides; it had to be held in the middle of September. In his memoirs, MacArthur reflected: "This meant that the staging for the landing at Inchon would have to be accomplished more rapidly than that of any other large amphibious operation in modern warfare."[33]

MacArthur stood alone in the decision to land at Inchon. He reflected in his *Reminiscences:* "My plan was opposed by powerful military influences in Washington. . . . The Chairman of the Joint Chiefs of Staff, General Omar Bradley, was of the opinion that such amphibious operations were obsolete—that there would never be another successful movement of that sort. . . . The Joint Chiefs of Staff wired me that [they] . . . were coming to Tokyo to discuss the matter with me. It was evident immediately upon their arrival that the actual purpose of their trip was not so much to discuss as to dissuade. The Chief of Naval Operations, Admiral Forrest Sherman, stated in his presentation at the meeting, 'If every possible geopolitcal and naval handicap were listed—Inchon had 'em all.'"

After all the chiefs had made their discouraging recommendations, MacArthur reflected, "I could feel the tension rising in the room." He summarized his thoughts, telling the group: "The enemy, I am convinced, has failed to prepare Inchon properly for defense. The very argument you have made as to the unpracticabilities involved will tend to ensure for me the element of surprise. . . . Surprise is the most vital element for success in war. . . . The Navy's objections as to tides, hydrography, terrain and physical handicaps are indeed substantial and pertinent. But they are not insuperable. . . . I seem to have more confidence in the Navy than the Navy has in itself."[34]

But MacArthur was confident of his decision and not intimidated even by such powerful opposition, and the operation went forward. He relied upon his planning and intuition, and the operation was an immense success. It is considered one of the most brilliant strategic decisions ever made in the history of warfare and a classic case for the education of our present and future generals.

Politics in Military Decisions

Early in his career in the Philippines, working for MacArthur, Eisenhower learned the lesson that politics can interfere with sound military decision making. Because of the army's extremely limited funds, army advisers during the period from 1936 to 1938 wanted to supply the Philippine army with Enfield rifles at the lowest possible cost. It should have been a simple thing to accomplish, because the United States considered the rifle to be obsolete. Eisenhower commented in his diary on January 20, 1936: "When the request was received in Washington, it was apparently looked upon as one involving major policy and was referred to the President for a decision. We are at a loss to determine exactly what the question of policy may be, whether it involves domestic policies or whether it is supposed to have somewhat of an international tinge."[35]

Eisenhower continued: "Was the President concerned about the pacifist group, a revolt against the central government, would the Filipinos in a crisis turn against the United States government and be accused of arming them at American expense, would it affect the U.S. relationship with Japan, would Congress see it as a violation of its attempt at an arms embargo and propose new utility legislation?" He went on to comment on that date, "All these questions upon analysis failed to furnish any satisfactory explanation of what seems to us to be a short-sighted policy on the part of the administration."[36]

But Ike as a soldier summed up the reality of politics: "We must never forget that every question is settled in Washington today based on getting votes next November. To decide this matter completely in our favor would gain no votes, while to disapprove the request and give the matter some publicity might be considered as a vote-getting proposition among the pacifists and other misguided elements of the American society."[37]

He closed his thoughts on that day with a clear understanding that every American soldier must understand: that when a decision is made by a senior person, "our attitude . . . should be that we have given our best professional advice on the subject and that no matter what decision is rendered, we stand ready."[38] This is the code, the guideline, indeed the mandate of our military professionals.

During World War II, not all of Eisenhower's political difficulties— and there were many for the commander—were with the British; some were with American politicians. He was surprised to learn in July 1942 that the United States ambassador to Great Britain wired Washington suggesting that he be allowed to establish a committee to select targets of strategic bombing. Ike immediately stepped up and, without causing any friction, kept the ambassador away from the target selection business.[39]

General William C. Westmoreland, as commander of U.S. forces in Vietnam, was not as fortunate as Eisenhower. He had hoped that bombing North Vietnam would boost the morale of the South Vietnamese and help bring about an end to the war. But as he reflected in his memoirs: "It had no apparent effect on the will of the North Vietnamese to continue the fight . . . particularly in [the] irresolute way Washington dictated that the campaign proceed."[40] In his book, he commented critically on interference in his decision making, stating: "Instead of round-the-clock, thousand-plane raids, Washington authorized only two to four raids a week and those by only a few dozen planes at a time. . . . Interference from Washington seriously hampered the campaign. President Johnson allegedly boasted on one occasion that 'they can't even bomb an outhouse without my approval.' Washington's timidity was an outgrowth of the advice of well-intentioned but naive officials, and of its effect on a President so politically oriented that he tried to please everybody rather than bite the bullet and make the hard decisions. . . .

"Those officials and some White House and State Department advisors appeared to scorn professional military advisors in a seeming belief that presumably superior Ivy League intellects could devise some political hocus-pocus or legerdemain without using force to destroy his war-making capability."[41]

Westmoreland's patience with the interference finally ended. "Almost all B-52 targets were in the hinterland," he reflected, "usually far from any populated area, and usually consisted of troop concentrations or base camps. During the early months, Washington scrutinized every proposed target to the point of absurdity. When Clark Clifford, a member of the President's Foreign Intelligence Advisory Board, was visiting Saigon in 1965, I was particularly piqued over refusal to allow a proposed strike, presumably because somebody in Washington thought he spotted a thatched-roof shed of some kind in the aerial photograph of the target, which, presumably, indicated habitation. I asked Clifford to take back word that if Washington had no more confidence in me than exemplified by that case, somebody should come up with another commander. Interference eased after that."[42]

One of the most critical decisions before the Joint Chiefs during Gen. George Brown's tenure as chairman of the Joint Chiefs of Staff was consideration by the administration of a new Panama Canal treaty, the transfer of ownership of the canal to Panama. This scenario is an excellent illustration of the appropriate relationship between our military and the president. The security of the United States was tied closely to any treaty that provided for loss of sovereignty by the United States over the Panama Canal and the Canal Zone. Such a decision would have international consequences, particularly on United States' influence in the Central America area. The U.S. Navy depends on the canal because passage through it was critical in providing security in exchanging forces from one ocean to another.

Those who wanted to relinquish sovereignty over the canal argued that we had unjustly taken this territory from Panama and that we would be able to placate Third World countries upon which we were increasingly dependent for raw materials.

On September 26, 1977, Brown testified at hearings by the House committee on international relations. The essence of his remarks was that the important need of the United States was the canal's use, not its ownership. He felt, and spoke for the Joint Chiefs, that our armed forces had to have access to the canal both in war and in peace, and that its security had to be continually assured. He saw that our capability to defend the canal depended on cooperation between the United States and Panama, which the new treaty covered.

The media criticized Brown and the service chiefs for their being forced to endorse the treaty or lose their jobs. In response to such allegations, Brown said to the House committee: "Mr. Chairman, the charge has been made by one or more columnists and several individuals around the country that the Joint Chiefs of Staff and I particularly support these treaties because the Commander in Chief has made a decision. As Secretary Brown [Secretary of Defense Harold Brown] has stated, the only appropriate way for us to fail to be supportive of a decision is to leave active duty and then take an adversary position.

"But there is another fact of life. The rules of the game quite clearly provide that we will testify before Congress and in response to interrogation will respond fully and factually to every question. This I have done for many years.

"I testified before this committee, if you will recall, on the issue of the proposed withdrawal of the U.S. ground combat forces in Korea, and the public record will show that the Joint Chiefs of Staff did not support that proposed action in January. We addressed a memorandum to the Secretary of Defense and in turn to the President, which stated that three provisions should be accounted for: (1) that we should withdraw our forces in such a manner that the military balance was retained or not disturbed; (2) that there should be a public pledge to the continued mutual security treaty with the Republic of Korea; and (3) that we remain a Pacific power. These were accepted, and at that point the Joint Chiefs of Staff supported the proposed program and have worked diligently to plan for that to occur over four or five years.

"Similarly, and it will come as no surprise, we did not share the judgment on the B-1. We thought the B-1 should go into production, and so recommended, but that judgment went against us.

"So it is not right to say that the Joint Chiefs of Staff are supportive of the President in all cases. The public record is quite clear in testimony before Congress, particularly on the Panama Canal Treaty issue. I have personally worked hard for four years to achieve these treaties. And we have had General Dolvin as a member of the negotiating delegation. We have worked out in detail, that is, the Joint Chiefs of Staff and the U.S. Commander of the Southern Command, the so-called waters and land issues, that is, what land and waters we could give up from the Canal Zone that were no longer required for defense or operation of the Canal."

An active-duty army officer and the top commander in Korea, Maj. Gen. John Singlaub, had openly criticized the Carter administration's decision on withdrawing U.S. military forces from Korea and was chastised personally by the president. Senator John Glenn, at hearings on the canal issue, questioned Brown at length. He reminded Brown that the Singlaub incident was still remembered by Congress and that four retired chiefs of naval operations had taken exception to the treaty. Yet he saw senior people on active duty, such as Brown, in favor of the administration's position and wondered as to their motivation and their possible inability to speak out.

Brown answered: "I would just like to make a comment on the Singlaub affair. I don't propose that it be reopened here, but I think it only fair to say since it has been mentioned, . . . you are absolutely right in how they understand it. But they really misunderstand it. They fail to recognize one fundamental thing that we cannot have in a military organization if we are to have a disciplined military force responsive to proper authority. This is, that once a decision is made, you support it or you get out and contest it. You don't stay on active duty and contest it. That is where I draw the line."

How One Develops as a Decision Maker

In response to the question of how one develops as a decision maker, Gen. David C. Jones, then chairman of the Joint Chiefs of Staff, reflected: "I had, and still do have, an insatiable appetite—indeed, a great thirst—for information through reading, watching, listening. For example, when I took over Second Air Force, there were the beginnings of racial problems. I concentrated on the issue. I probably read eight books on it, read everything I could get my hands on the subject. I also talked and discussed extensively with black airmen. . . . The most important thing in leadership is decision making, and one of the most important aspects of that is deciding what people you put in what jobs. It's important that you observe people in their jobs and get a good feel for how well they do.

"You need in your leaders someone who is willing to make decisions. Your poorest leaders are those who are indecisive. Sometimes a bad decision is better than no decision.

"As you come up through the system, decisions are quite narrow. As a squadron commander, for example, there are few really big decisions. Maybe you will have to relieve your operations officers, or take some course of action against one of the people in your command that will hurt his career, but you do so because he has done something wrong, and corrective action needs to be taken. But, most of your decisions are small ones."[43]

I asked Gen. Norman Schwarzkopf, "What happens if you're working for a terrible leader?"

He said: "That's a wonderful opportunity because while you can obviously learn from good leaders, you also learn from bad leaders. You say, 'I think if I ever get the chance, I'll try that.' You see a bad leader and you say, 'I'll never do that.' I think that throughout my early years in the army, I learned that probably the worst leader was one who wouldn't make a decision—I mean, who would just agonize over it, would never make a decision. A bad decision, at least, causes action to occur within an organization, and the organization itself can take a bad decision and turn around and make a good one. But when you get no decision at all, then the whole organization just kind of sits there."

I then asked him, "What was your methodology?"

He responded: "Basically, you get your mission, you do your analysis on your mission, you give your guidance to your staff. I used to demand a minimum of three courses of action on every major decision. Then when they would come in, I would require them to brief me [on] the three courses of action. . . . We would look at the advantages and disadvantages of each of those courses of action. When they got to that point—briefing me on the options—then it became my job to make a decision. I might send them back to the drawing board saying that's not good enough, I need more information on course of action one, two, or three. Many times I would pick, say, option 2A, which would be a modification of the two, but there comes a time when you must make that decision. I have always felt that one of my strengths was a willingness to make the decision and then pursue that. Even if it's a bad decision, if you pursue your decision to fruition, you accomplish your mission. This comes back to what I've already said, that I would never undertake any task expecting to fail. Once I made the decision, as far as I was concerned, it was going to work. That doesn't mean you don't go back and revisit your decision if things aren't going well. You certainly need to look carefully, as the decision is being implemented, to see if anything goes wrong. Then you say let's go back and look at this thing again. But I think probably one of the principal characteristics of a good leader is someone who is willing to make a decision."

What went on in General Schwarzkopf's mind when making decisions? "I didn't sleep very well in the Gulf, even after the plan was locked in concrete. Every night I would lie in bed and say, What have I forgotten? What have we missed? Is there something more we can do? And I would go back out and look at the maps again. I think it takes that kind of driving of yourself as a commander if you care about soldiers."

When asked about the concepts of "feel" and "sixth sense," his response was, "I think I had that. On many occasions I made decisions based upon intuition. But it is an intuition that is tempered by experience and judgment. It is not a guess. I just intuitively know what the right thing to do is, and it comes from years of training, from years of experience."[44]

General Schwarzkopf's comment emphasizes the statement that General Eisenhower made about loneliness in the career of a general. General Colin Powell, chairman of the Joint Chiefs, remarked in a speech:

> Command is lonely, I said, and that was not just a romantic cliche. Sharing a problem with the boss, in this corps, would not be seen as weakness or failure, but as a sign of mutual confidence. On the other hand, they did not have to buck every decision up to me. "I have a wide zone of indifference," I said. "I don't care if you hold reveille at five-thirty or five forty-five A.M. And don't ask me to decide."
>
> I explained my idea of loyalty. "When we were debating an issue, loyalty means giving me your honest opinion, whether you think I'll like it or not. Disagreement, at this stage, stimulates me. But once a decision has been made, the debate ends. From that point on, loyalty means executing the decision as if it were your own."
>
> This particular emperor expected to be told when he was naked. He did not care to freeze to death in his own ignorance. "If you think something is wrong, speak up," I told them. "I'd rather hear about it sooner than later. Bad news isn't wine. It doesn't improve with age." I would not jump in too early if they could still handle a problem. But I did not want to find out when it was too late for me to make a difference. "And if you screw up," I advised, "just vow to do better next time. I don't hold grudges. I don't keep book.
>
> "I will give you clear guidance as to what I want," I continued. "If it's not clear, ask me. If after a second or third expla-

nation you still don't get it, there may be something wrong with
my transmitter, not your receiver. I won't assume you are deaf
or stupid." The worst thing was for subordinates to labor in ig-
norance in order to conceal their confusion and wind up doing the wrong thing. "If you ever leave my office and don't understand what I want, just march right back in and ask," I said.

    I told them that I would fight for everything they needed to
perform the mission. "If we don't have it in Frankfurt, I'll go
to USAREUR [U.S. Army Europe]. If they don't have it, I'll go
to Washington. But I will back you all the way."[45]

What was Powell's approach to decision making? In an interview
I discussed decision making with him. "My talents, if I have any—
and you will decide whether you think this is correct or not—that is,
my talents in terms of what I am able to do are solving problems and
leading people. I can organize people and I can motivate people and
I can solve problems. I can think to whatever level I have to, strate-
gically or otherwise, but leadership is fundamentally solving problems, at a strategic or personal level."
He reflected in his memoirs:

    My daily life in the West Wing amounted to constant deci-
    sion-making and then passing along my recommendations, is-
    sues ranging from where best to hold a summit in New York to
    helping craft nuclear disarmament treaties at the summit. By
    now, I had developed a decision-making philosophy. Put sim-
    ply, it is to dig up all the information you can, then go with your
    instincts. We all have a certain intuition, and the older we get,
    the more we trust it. When I am faced with a decision—pick-
    ing somebody for a post, or choosing a course of action—I
    dredge up every scrap of knowledge I can. I call in people, I
    phone them. I read whatever I can get my hands on. I use my
    intellect to inform my instinct. I then use my instinct to test all
    this data. "Hey, instinct, does this sound right? Does it smell
    right, feel right, fit right?"
        However, we do not have the luxury of collecting informa-
    tion indefinitely. At some point, before we can have every pos-

sible fact in hand, we have to decide. The key is not to make quick decisions. I have a timing formula, P-40 to 70, in which P stands for probability of success and the numbers indicate the percentage of information acquired. I don't act if I have only enough information to give me less than a 40 percent chance of being right. And I don't wait until I have enough facts to be 100 percent sure of being right, because by then it is almost always too late. I go with my gut feeling when I have acquired information somewhere in the range of 40 to 70 percent.[46]

In his memoirs, chairman of the Joint Chiefs of Staff, Adm. William J. Crowe, Jr., provided some excellent insight into what goes into effective decision making: "In retrospect, the most significant human quality the Gulf demanded was flexibility of mind. We put some individuals in command there who had very fine records and were highly regarded but who turned out to be rigid and dogmatic. . . . Reality demands that a commander evaluate each situation on its own terms and adjust for it. He must have officers who are capable of that, who are willing to do things differently from the way they have been taught. It worries me that our system often fails to tell us if we have people with that quality. The only way to find out is to put them under pressure and observe. Often the kind of individual who does well in situations that require flexibility and innovativeness does not do well in the normal lockstep procedures of the peacetime service, and he or she gets winnowed out along the way.

"That thought disturbed me deeply at the time and still does. Breeding open-minded commanders is a high priority, yet we often seem to fall short in this regard. So much in service life even militates against it. But not having them is an invitation to disaster. . . . Struggling with this problem during the Gulf crisis convinced me that flexibility of thought was our single most crucial need."[47]

Crowe's earlier career provided insight into another essential of decision making. When the time came for Captain Crowe to be considered for promotion to admiral, there were fourteen hundred captains in the running for thirty admiral openings. Fortunately for Crowe, the navy, and our country, the chief of naval operations, Adm. Elmo Zumwalt, was influencing the navy to promote "mavericks and dissidents." Crowe commented: "The single most difficult problem in selecting top leadership in the military is how to insure that an individual who succeeds in the promotion process will have the independence of thought needed for high command. Zumwalt himself was the first I ever saw who achieved high rank and also managed to preserve a highly idiosyncratic cast of mind. In every military organization, some mavericks do survive. but their numbers are extremely small. The great problem is to structure the organization so those people get promoted. Zumwalt tried to attack the problem institutionally. He was the CNO, and the CNO spends a large chunk of his time selecting flag officers, but he does convene promotion boards, and he lays down guidelines for them to follow. Though the boards themselves are statutorily independent, the CNO is still able to influence the general promotion policy. But the CNO's guidelines do have some influence and Zumwalt tried to alter those values faster. He promulgated guidelines that said in essence, 'I want some iconoclasts.' He'd say, 'Last year we didn't have a single one of those kinds of people! This year I want two! Don't give me all these peas in a pod.' As a result, a number of people who were outside the traditional patterns were selected, including myself."[48]

I asked General Powell what his most important decisions were as chairman of the Joint Chiefs. He responded, "I will mention one or two, but I have to caution you, I resist all interviewer attempts for me to do the 'best, most, worst, first, last' thing, because I think that throws you out of context. But, so as not to give you a complete dive on the question, the one thing that I remember is not so much Desert Storm, because there was a buildup up to that. There wasn't much deciding when it finally came; we knew it was going to happen. Panama was a much more trenchant and pressing decision for me because it came so suddenly. Within a period of twelve hours, we went from a quiet Saturday evening to a decision to invade a country."

Powell related how, on the weekend of December 17–18, 1989, a member of Noriega's Panamanian Defense Force (PDF) shot a United States Marine in Panama. Four officers in civilian clothes drove into Panama City for dinner and were stopped by a PDF roadblock. When the soldiers attempted to yank the Americans from the car, the driver hit the gas to get away. The PDF soldiers fired at them, and a Marine lieutenant, Robert Poz, was shot and killed. Shortly thereafter, as the weekend went on, matters grew worse. The PDF arrested a navy lieutenant and his wife who had witnessed the shooting, and the lieutenant was beaten up and threatened with death. His wife was forced to stand against the wall and was molested by PDF soldiers so badly that she passed out.

Powell held a meeting with the Joint Chiefs: Carl Vuono, army; Larry Welch, air force; Carl Trost, navy; and Al Gray, Marine Corps. The chairman took the position that these actions by the PDF could not be overlooked. After a discussion, the Joint Chiefs unanimously accepted the plan of Gen. Max Thurman, commander of U.S. Southern Command, headquartered in Panama, for invading Panama and overthrowing Noriega's revolutionary government and reinstating the democratically elected government of Panama.

On Sunday afternoon December 17, 1989, Powell went to President Bush's private quarters in the White House to brief him. Also present was Secretary of Defense Dick Cheney, Secretary of State Jim Baker, and Brent Scowcroft, Bush's national security adviser. Powell commented: "I started off with our prime objective: we were going to eliminate Noriega and the PDF. If that succeeded, we could be running the country until we could establish a civilian government and a new security force. Since this plan went well beyond 'getting Noriega' I paused to make sure this point had sunk in, with all its implications.

"George Bush sat like a patron on a barstool observing the brawl, while his advisors went hard at it. Brent Scowcroft's manner had an irritating edge that took getting used to, but his intelligence was obvious and his intent admirable. He wanted to leave the President with no comfortable illusions. 'There are going to be casualties. People are going to die,' Scowcroft said. The President nodded, and let the debate roll on."

Powell pointed out the reasons why we should intervene—that Noriega was trafficking in drugs, had killed a U.S. Marine, was threatening our rights to the canal, and held contempt for democracy.

"The questions continued, thick and fast, until it started to look as if we were drifting away from the decision at hand. But then Bush, after everyone had had his say, gripped the arms of his chair and rose. 'Okay, let's do it," he said. 'The hell with it.'"[49]

Just as with Eisenhower and other generals who had the responsibility for life and death decisions, Powell had anxious and lonely moments: "The last night before the invasion, sitting alone in the dark in the back seat of my car on the drive home, I felt full of foreboding. I was going to be involved in conducting a war, one that I had urged, one that was going to spill blood. Had I been right? Had my advice been sound? What if the icy weather in the States hampered the airlift? How would we then support troops already in Panama? What would our casualties be? How many civilians might lose their lives in the fighting? Was it all worth it? I went to bed gnawed by self-doubt.

"When I got to the Pentagon early on Tuesday morning, December 19, I found that my Joint Staff, under its director, Lieutenant General Mike Carns, and Max Thurman's SOUTHCOM staff in Panama were on top of things. Army Lieutenant General Howard Graves was skillfully merging our military plans with State and NSC political and diplomatic efforts. All loose ends were being tied up. We were 'good to go.' My confidence came surging back. My worries vanished and I entered the calm before the storm."[50]

What conclusions, then, does one draw from the foregoing reflections and comments from generals in the performance of their leadership responsibilities? In the military, making decisions involves life and death. It is lonely and particularly requires toughness when there is opposition to a leader's conclusion from competent people whose opinions are respected. There is the anxious period of waiting for things to start and then for the expectation of the outcome.

President Truman was astute enough, as are most top leaders, to seek advice from able people as he went through the decision-making process. The methodology used by Marshall, as outlined by General Collins, is as appropriate today as it was in the 1940s. Although one must obtain all the information possible in formulating the decision, often there is too little time. Experience and knowledge are obviously important, but intuition is a factor. MacArthur, Grant, Patton, Bradley, Eisenhower, and others possessed it. But as Acheson commented, the "capacity for decision . . . is God's rarest gift of mind to man."

But it is a quality that can be developed. General Eisenhower, when I asked "How does one develop as a decision maker?" responded, "Be around people making decisions" and "books."

Being around people making decisions is developed in chapter 6, on mentorship. Ike's comment on books are developed further in chapter 5, on the importance of reading.

Notes

1. Personal interview with General of the Army Dwight D. Eisenhower and Edgar F. Puryear, Jr., May 2, 1963.

2. Walter B. Smith, *Eisenhower's Six Great Decisions* (New York: Longmans, Green, 1956), 35.

3. Dwight D. Eisenhower, *Crusade in Europe* (New York: Doubleday and Company, Inc. 1948), 246–47.

4. Harry C. Butcher, *My Three Years with Eisenhower* (New York: Simon and Schuster, 1946), 570.

5.Smith, *Eisenhower's Six Great Decisions,* 19–20.

6. Eisenhower, *Crusade in Europe,* 172.

7. Ibid., 172.

8. Ibid., 239.

9. Ibid., 249.

10. Smith, *Eisenhower's Six Great Decisions,* 53–55.

11. Eisenhower, *Crusade in Europe,* 251.

12. Harry S. Truman, *Year of Decisions* (Garden City, N.Y.: Doubleday & Company, Inc., 1955), ix.

13. Walter Isaacson and Evan Thomas, *The Wise Men* (New York: Simon and Schuster, 1986), 255.

14. Ibid., 256.

15. Truman, *Year of Decisions,* 419.

16. Ibid.

17. Isaacson and Thomas, *The Wise Men,* 452.

18. Forrest C. Pogue, *Statesman 1945–1959* (New York: Viking Penguin, Inc., 1987), 371.

19. J. Lawton Collins, *Lightning Joe: An Autobiography* (Baton Rouge and London: Louisiana State University Press, 1979), 96.

20. Ibid.

21. Ibid., 96–97.

22. Omar N. Bradley and Clay Blair, *A General's Life* (New York: Simon and Schuster, 1983), 69.

23. Eisenhower, *Crusade in Europe,* 21–22.

24. Personal interview with General of the Army Omar N. Bradley and Edgar F. Puryear, Jr., February 15, 1963.

25. Letter from Maj. Gen. Howard Davidson, USAF (Ret.), to Edgar F. Puryear, Jr., dated July 19, 1979.

26. Ibid.

27. George F. Kennan, *Memoirs 1925–1950* (Boston: Little, Brown, 1967), 346–47.

28. Robert H. Ferrell, ed., *The Eisenhower Diaries* (New York: W. W. Norton & Company, 1981), 272.

29. Ibid., 29.

30. Ibid., 99.

31. Dean Rusk, *As I Saw It* (New York: I. B. Taurus & Co., Ltd., 1991), 112–13.

32. Ferrell, *The Eisenhower Diaries,* 84.

33. Douglas MacArthur, *Reminiscences* (New York: McGraw-Hill, 1964), 348–51.

34. Ibid.

35. Ferrell, *The Eisenhower Diaries,* 13.

36. Ibid., 14.

37. Ibid.

38. Ibid., 14–15.

39. Butcher, *My Three Years with Eisenhower,* 35.

40. William C. Westmoreland, *A Soldier Reports* (New York: Doubleday & Company, Inc., 1976), 119.

41. Ibid., 120.

42. Ibid., 137.

43. Personal interview with Gen. David C. Jones, USAF (Ret.), with Edgar F. Puryear, Jr., January 10, 1997.

44. Personal interview with Gen. H. Norman Schwarzkopf and Edgar F. Puryear, Jr., October 27, 1995.

45. Colin L. Powell, *My American Journey* (New York: Random House, 1995), 320–21.

46. Ibid., 393.

47. William J. Crowe, Jr., *The Line of Fire* (New York: Simon & Schuster, 1993), 210.

48. Ibid., 86–87.

49. Powell, *My American Journey,* 423–25.

50. Ibid., 427.

Chapter 3: "Feel" or "Sixth Sense" in Decision Making

Although I am convinced after interviewing more than a hundred four-star generals that there is a pattern of successful leadership in the American military, some people do not agree. But even the strongest opponents of the thesis concede that all truly great military leaders have a "feel" or "sixth sense."

Contact with the troops played a role in Eisenhower's decision making. Just before he was to transfer from the Mediterranean area to London to assume his duties as supreme commander of the Allied invasion of Europe, he became uneasy over the Anzio project. He was disturbed to hear that his plan for concentrating air force headquarters in Caserta was to be dropped. "To me this decision," General Eisenhower commented, "seemed to imply a lack of understanding of the situation and of the duties of the highest commander in the field: regardless of preoccupation with multitudinous problems of great import, he must never lose touch with the 'feel' of his troops. He can and should delegate tactical responsibility and avoid interference in the authority of his selected subordinates, but he must maintain the closest kind of factual and spiritual contact with them or, in a vast critical campaign, he will fail. This contact requires frequent visits to the troops themselves."[1]

Eisenhower did not spend all of his time with his senior commanders and his staff; he visited the soldiers in his command frequently. In fall 1944, he went to the front to talk with several hundred men of the 29th Infantry Division. He spoke to them on a muddy, slippery hillside. After he had finished talking, he turned to go back to his jeep but slipped and fell on his back and became covered with mud. The soldiers he had been talking with could not refrain from laughing, but this did not upset him. "From the shout of laughter that went up," he reflected, "I am quite sure that no other meeting I had with soldiers during the war was a greater success than that one."[2]

Once Eisenhower's headquarters for SHAEF was set up, it was his policy to devote about a third of his time to visiting the troops. When he did so, he ordered that no parades or formal inspections would be held, because he wanted training to continue as usual. His visits were normally made without press coverage. He spent little time with the brass, concentrating his attention on the soldiers and their food and quarters.

When a unit inspection was scheduled, the standard procedure was to have the men in open ranks formation. Eisenhower would walk along, at a moderate pace, up one line and down the other. After every dozen men, he would stop and talk with one of the soldiers. The conversation with the soldier would usually go like this:

General Eisenhower: "What did you do in civilian life?"

Soldier: "I'm a farmer, sir."

General Eisenhower: "Fine, so am I. What did you raise?"

Soldier: "Wheat."

General Eisenhower: "Good. How many bushels did you get to the acre?"

Soldier: "Oh, about thirty-five bushels, when we had a good year."

General Eisenhower: "You did? Well, when the war is over I'm coming to you for a job."

Then he would normally close by saying to the soldier, "Do me a favor, will you? Go and finish this war fast, so I can go fishing."

His jeep had a loudspeaker that he would use with groups of soldiers. He generally emphasized their importance in the war by saying, "You are the men who will win this war." He told them it was a privilege to be their commander. "A commander," he would say, "meets to talk to his men to inspire them. With me it's the other way around. I get inspired by you."

Once, visiting the front when the Allies were getting ready to cross the Rhine, Eisenhower encountered a soldier walking along the bank of the river. The man looked very depressed. Eisenhower asked, "How are you feeling, son?" "General," the soldier replied, "I'm awful nervous. I was wounded two months ago and just got back from the hospital yesterday. I don't feel so good."

"Well," Eisenhower said, "you and I are a good pair then, because I'm nervous, too. But we've planned this attack for a long time, and we've got all the planes, the guns, and airborne troops we can use to smash the Germans. Maybe if we just walk along together to the river, we'll be good for each other."[3]

There was a pattern as well as a purpose to Eisenhower's visits. Lieutenant General Alvan C. Gillem, Jr., the commander of the XIII Corps during the Battle of the Bulge, decided that after the crisis was over he would get away for a day or so to relax. He went to Paris, checked into the Ritz Hotel, and after dinner that night went to the Follies. He returned to the hotel at about one in the morning. As he entered his room, he received a call to return to his headquarters immediately. After a hazardous flight and an equally bad jeep ride, he arrived at his command post and hastened to the mess hall. "As I arrived, General Eisenhower and several staff officers emerged [from having lunch]. I reported and stated my regrets at not being present to meet him when he arrived. He informed me, with a broad smile, that his visit was unexpected and that, as a matter of fact, it was better to inspect a Headquarters when the Commander was away, for if it could not function under such circumstances it was not efficient. He further stated he was eminently satisfied and that he would not return, that he had obtained the viewpoint he wanted and that he regretted he must leave. He congratulated me on my command and expressed his pleasure at what he had seen of the conduct of the Corps during the recent battle. We shook hands and he departed. That was the last time I heard from him or his Headquarters until the final days on the Elbe River."[4]

"The importance of such visits by the high command," Eisenhower stated, "including, at times, the highest officials of government, can scarcely be overestimated in terms of their value to a soldier's morale. The soldier has a sense of gratification whenever he sees very high rank in his particular vicinity. . . ."

Eisenhower had a style of visiting with the men that developed an informal and friendly rapport. It was impossible for him to visit all the men in his command; but when he talked with individual soldiers or small groups of them, it established a closeness with those men, who in turn told their story to others. In this way, the word spread among thousands of men. The stories were exaggerated as they were spread, but the account always described Eisenhower as personal and human. It disturbed him when he read a story about his visit in the newspaper. If the men concluded that he was doing it for publicity, he would lose his effectiveness.

But Eisenhower could not always keep his actions out of the newspapers. Once during the drive through Paris in January 1945, he performed an unintentional act of showmanship that reached millions of American soldiers through a story in the military journal *Stars and Stripes:*

> At SHAEF last week, an appeal was made to headquarters men for contribution of type O blood, needed immediately at the front.
>
> A couple of days later, volunteers were lined up in the dispensary. No one paid much attention at first as an officer walked into the room. He lay down in a litter and a nurse bustled over to wrap a tourniquet around his arm.
>
> A soldier on the next litter looked over idly, looked back, then did an astonished double take. The guy next to him was General Eisenhower.
>
> "It was just like any other GI," said T/4 Conrad J. Segrin, one of the dispensary's medics. "He wasn't a special case at all. Ike came in, they took his blood, he got a cup of coffee and he left. Just like that."
>
> There was a private in the waiting line who saw the Supreme Commander on his way out. He turned to the man beside him and said, "Hey, that'd be the blood to get. Maybe I could make General with it."
>
> Ike overheard him, turned around and grinned. "If you do, he said, "I hope you don't inherit my bad disposition."

As the momentum of preparation built up before a big battle, so did Eisenhower's visits and those of his senior commanders. In the four months before the invasion of Europe, from February 1 to June

1, 1944, Eisenhower visited twenty-six divisions, twenty-four airfields, warships, and numerous depots, shops, hospitals, and other important installations. The visiting schedules of Generals Bradley, Montgomery, Spaatz, and Tedder followed his example. Their visits were squeezed in among countless conferences and staff meetings during a period when the top generals were overwhelmed with work, but they always made time to see the men.

Eisenhower's friends urged him to give up or at least to curtail his visits with soldiers. They told him he could at best hit only a small percentage of the total and was wearing himself out without accomplishing anything. He did not agree with or follow this well-meaning advice. "In the first place," he said, "I felt I gained accurate impressions of [the men's] state of mind. I talked to them about anything and everything . . . so long as I could get the soldier to talk to me in return. This, I felt, would encourage men to talk with their superiors, and this habit promotes efficiency." He believed that if men were aware that they could talk to the "brass," they would not be afraid to talk with their lieutenant. He hoped his example would encourage the junior officers to seek information from his men. "There is," Eisenhower said, "among the mass of individuals who carry the rifles in war, a great amount of ingenuity and initiative. If men can naturally and without restraint talk to their officers, the products of their resourcefulness become available to all." One of his favorite questions was to ask a soldier if his squad or platoon had found any new trick or gadget that improved their fighting in combat. The overall effect of this was to promote "mutual confidence, a feeling of partnership that is the essence of esprit de corps."[5]

In December 1944, because certain decisions relative to Allied unity had been made in favor of the British, Eisenhower found that some American soldiers were saying that "Eisenhower is the best general the British have." This bothered him. Shortly after this comment started, he paid a visit to the front. After his visit, Wes Gallagher, correspondent for the Associated Press, sent a note to Captain Butcher that stated in part: "Thought you might like to know that Ike's recent trips to the front, coupled with the recent U.S. activity, appear to have completely silenced that 'best general in the British Army' business."[6]

From the time he became commanding general of the European theater of operations in spring 1942 until he returned to the United States after the war in Europe was over in spring 1945, Eisenhower was never late for an appointment to review the troops. He just did not believe in keeping the men waiting.

In May 1945, Sen. Homer Capehart was traveling with Eisenhower inspecting a unit. They were walking through an American army camp in Paris to their aircraft, and as they walked the word spread among the soldiers that Ike was there. Huge crowds gathered, making passage difficult. The supreme commander spoke briefly to every fourth or fifth man. The soldier would then turn around and tell the others excitedly what was said. One commented, "GI sure stands for General Ike." As Senator Capehart observed this, he said, "I hope that fellow never decides to run against me in my state. He's got what it takes. I can see now why the GIs worship him. He speaks their language; he isn't high hat like you expect from brass, and he knows their problems and they know it."[7]

Eisenhower also made a point to visit the wounded in hospitals, where he would ask each soldier his name, shake his hand, and ask him how and where he was wounded and when he hoped to return to duty. It was necessary in World War II to set aside some hospitals and camp facilities for soldiers who were suffering from self-inflicted wounds, real or put-on hysteria, psychoneuroses, and deliberately contracted venereal disease. General Eisenhower believed: "It is profitable for a commander to visit these places, to talk with individuals, to understand something of the bewilderment, the fear, the defeatism that affect men who are essentially afraid of life, though believing they are afraid of death. An astonishing number of these individuals react instantly and favorably to a single word of encouragement. More than one has said to me immediately upon discovering another's interest in him, 'General, get me out of here; I want to go back to my outfit.' Harshness normally intensifies the disease, but understanding can do much to cure it and in my opinion, if applied in time, can largely prevent it."[8]

Eisenhower recorded in his memoirs a major reason for his attention to the troops: "Soldiers like to see the men who are directing operations. They properly resent any indication of neglect or indifference to them on the part of their commanders and invariably interpret a visit, even a brief one, as evidence of the commander's concern for them. Diffidence or modesty must never blind the commander to his duty of showing himself to his men, of speaking to them, of mingling with them to the extent of physical limitation. It pays big dividends in terms of morale, and morale, given rough equality in other things, is supreme on the battlefield."[9]

On one of Eisenhower's trips he traveled from Paris to Cherbourg, north up the coast to Antwerp, then back to his command post. While motoring to an old French port near Antwerp, he noticed a group of men boarding a ship. He stopped to talk to a few of them and learned that they were going home on rotation. Within five minutes, some four hundred men surrounded him. He told them that he hoped they would find their friends well and happy, that they should have a good time, get a good rest, and come back to him ready to do another big job. Then he noticed a captain who he was told had been wounded five times. He asked the man where he wanted to go when he returned. The captain replied, "To my old outfit, sir." General Eisenhower liked his attitude and spirit. The supreme commander's car hadn't moved fifty yards from the place where he had talked with the men when he turned to Gen. Ben Lear, who was with him, and said in a deeply concerned voice: "Lear, that captain has had five chances. Will you please see that he doesn't take any more of them."[10]

Part of "feel" is a special gift to sense instinctively when something is wrong. As chief of staff, Gen. George Marshall made frequent inspection trips. Said Mrs. Marshall, "Although he made his inspections at such a pace that officers found difficulty in keeping up with him, he missed little, very little indeed." Once, while watching him inspect troops at Fort Knox, she noticed that he went quickly through two lines of men, then paused to talk for several minutes with a soldier in the rear line.

"I asked why he had picked out that particular soldier," Mrs. Marshall wrote, "and he replied, 'I caught the man's eye and I knew something was wrong. I wanted to find out what.'"

"Did you find out?" she asked.

"Yes," he answered, "everything was wrong. The man ought never to have been drafted. He was over-age, had a large family, and was in no physical condition for active service. He was a good soldier, too, wanted to do his part, and I had to question him for some time before I could get at his trouble. The Draft Board made a slip-up on that fellow." Arrangements were made that very day to send the soldier back to his family.[11]

General Curtis LeMay, as a combat air commander in World War II, started the policy of "select crews" to lead each mission. In an interview with him, I asked how he picked them. He replied, "I tried to pick the best crews I had. Don't ask me how I did this. I don't know how I did it. I could walk down the line before a mission and say to myself, 'this guy is going to get shot down,' go further down and again say, 'this guy is going to get shot down,' and sure enough they'd get shot down. I got superstitious about it and I tried not to think about it anymore."[12]

"One day during the latter part of the Sicilian Campaign," wrote General Patton's World War II aide, Col. Charles R. Codman, the boss "was suddenly called upon, or felt he was, to make a critical decision. It was one of those decisions where if you guess right others get the credit and if you guess wrong you and you alone get the blame. Well, he was right and it wasn't a guess, either, but that sixth sense made up of intuition and conviction which goes to make a grand chief."[13]

"Patton," said Omar Bradley, "had that sense. I remember when Third Army was going up the Rhine to Cologne and turned right to flank the people who were holding up the American Seventh Army on our right. Patton went for about two days, meeting only token resistance, then he suddenly stopped. Some members of my staff said, 'Why doesn't he keep going?' 'He senses something,' I said, 'that we can't sense because we don't have all the information.' The next day three German divisions hit him. But he had stopped to prepare for them; he bounced them off, and then he moved forward again."[14]

Is this feel or sixth sense a quality a man is born with? Patton, who called this sense "military reaction," wrote to his son at West Point on June 6, 1944: "What success I have had results from the fact that I have always been certain that my military reactions were correct. Many people do not agree with me; they are wrong. The unerring jury of history, written long after both of us are dead, will prove me correct.

"Note that I speak of 'military reactions.' No one is born with them any more than anyone is born with measles. You can be born with a soul capable of correct military reactions or a body capable of having big muscles, but both qualities must be developed by hard work. . . ."[15]

"My theory," General Bradley said regarding his feel in decision making, "is that you collect information, little bits of it, and it goes into your brain like feeding information into a 1401 IBM calculator. It's stored in there, but you are not conscious of it. You hear some of it over the phone, you see some of it on the map, in what you read, in briefings. It is all stored in your mind, then suddenly you are faced with a decision. You don't go back and pick up each one of the pieces of information, but you run over the main items that are involved and the answer comes out like when you push the button on an IBM machine. You have stored up this knowledge as it comes in and when you are suddenly faced in battle with a situation needing a decision, you can give it. When people would call me on the phone and give me a situation I would push a button, and I would have an answer right then. You can't go back and pore over the maps for two or three days."[16]

There is more to feel than solving a problem that comes up at the moment. It also involves intuition. "Maybe there is such a thing as intuition," J. Lawton Collins remarked in a discussion of the quality of feel, "but I don't believe it is really intuition. I think it is a quality based on sufficient intelligence to make a careful evaluation of the situation—to know where the trouble spots are likely to develop. All good commanders that I knew had that faculty. They could antici- pate where there would likely be trouble and they went there. They went there to be sure that they could do something about that trou- ble as it developed. If there is such a thing as intuition it is based first of all on knowledge, knowing the tools you have available. You have got to know your business. You know your business by working hard and studying as a younger man."[17]

General William H. Simpson expressed a similar conclusion when he stated that this feel "comes from several things. One is your back-

ground of training. As I look back on my long career and the first
eight or ten years of basic work that I did, seven long weary years of
which I was a second lieutenant, I realize it gave me a background
of knowledge and experience that helped me understand situations
that came up. I think it prepared me for anticipating things that
might occur."[18]

General Lucian K. Truscott thought that "knowledge is the basis
for feel. Your training, your study, your knowledge of men, your understanding of the capability of what they can do for themselves,
their physical limitations, their reaction to discipline. It requires an
interest in people."[19]

General Wade Haislip said the same thing. "I think feel is the result of education, of thoroughly knowing your profession. When I
was over in Ireland in 1944 with a corps, we were waiting and training for the invasion of Europe. I was to be in the second echelon to
cross, so I had from July 9 to August 1 to observe the fighting. I got
permission, while my men were training, to go to Italy on a sight-see-
ing trip. This was of the utmost value to me, and I saw there was nothing mysterious about it. It was exactly what I had been studying all
my life. So when my corps got into action, nothing changed; we did
exactly what we had been doing in all of our maneuvers and command post exercises. The only difference I knew was that people
were shooting at us."[20]

General Anthony McAuliffe's comments were no different. "A
combat leader has to be something of a psychologist, both in the
mass training of men and in the handling of his subordinate commanders. Some do better with a pat on the back while others need
a kick on the backside. I think this is something a man learns over
the years as he serves in the military. It requires an understanding
of men. Experience has a great deal to do with it. You meet many
people in your military career and you learn to measure people."[21]

This feel, sixth sense, military reaction, or whatever one chooses
to call it is not limited to battlefield situations. Omar Bradley said:
"George Marshall was a great character. He had great foresight. He
had imagination. It's hard to define imagination. It is the faculty of
foreseeing what is going to happen as a result of certain things. In
battle you call it the feel of the battle, a sixth sense."[22]

Tooey Spaatz had it. Robert A. Lovett, assistant secretary of war for air, Spaatz's close friend and confidant and an unusually keen and accurate observer, felt that Spaatz had an instinct for strategy that generally proved to be correct. Spaatz was not a systematic planner but allowed his intuition to guide him to correct decisions. One of his staff officers, Brig. Gen. Laurence S. Kuter, said: "A staff study was anathema to General Spaatz. The staff studies were made, but Tooey would want to be told immediately what the conclusions were, what the options were, what the recommendations were, and who should do it. . . . He did not read the whole staff study. He wanted the conclusions, the results, the options and little more."[23]

General George S. Brown had it. His career had been operational until he was assigned to Air Force System Command—the scientific part of the air force—just before he became chief of staff in 1973. One of his generals, Maj. Gen. Jerry Cook, commented to me: "Despite his high confidence level, Brown was not arrogant. When General Brown got to Systems Command, the first thing he did was to assure people that he did not know their business, that he was there to be their commander and a channel to handle their business when they had run out of clout. But I do not know your business, he would say. In fact, I'm ashamed to be here and not know your business. He was very humble about it.

"But he used that as a strength. When the experts would come in to brief him, he would very often say, 'Now, I can't quarrel with any of the engineering details or the specifications you're talking about or production data or timing. But I can quarrel with the feel I have of the way you're telling me these things.' He would sometimes say, 'There's just something wrong about that,' picking out obvious mismatches. For instance, where he observed a conflict as when a man with 'clout' on a configuration control board had a conflicting interest in engineering, Brown would jump on it in a flash. But when he did pick up on something like that, he would always give the briefer a chance to correct it right there. He'd let the man build himself up after being caught."[24]

Lieutenant General L. K. Truscott, Jr., was a corps commander in the invasion of Italy under Gen. Mark Clark. In his memoir Truscott made an interesting observation writing about "feel": "Clark had been an able staff officer, and he was an unusually able executive and administrator. However, he lacked Alexander's training and experience in high command, his first major command having been Salerno—a rough lesson. When Clark visited my Command Post, he usually arrived with an entourage including correspondents and photographers. His public relations officer required all press dispatches, even from Anzio, to include the phrase 'Lieutenant General Mark W. Clark's Fifth Army.' His concern for personal publicity was his greatest weakness. I have sometimes thought it may have prevented him from acquiring that 'feel of battle' that marks all top-flight battle leaders, though extensive publicity did not seem to have that effect on Patton and Montgomery. Few men had greater personal charm than Clark, and no superior commander ever made greater efforts to support subordinates in their tasks. I cannot recall that Clark ever disapproved of any request I made, and he was always untiring in his efforts to immediately expedite any logistical or tactical problem."[25]

Is "feel" a God-given talent? I asked Gen. Edward C. "Shy" Meyer, former army chief of staff. He replied: "It is a combination. I believe it is principle developed. God gives you a lot of things—brains, genes, hair or not [he was balding]; you get all kinds of gifts. Some people develop these capabilities, some don't. One way of developing these capabilities is by observing others. It has been the opportunity to develop these capabilities that has permitted the great leaders to be successful in top leadership positions."[26]

I made the same inquiry of Gen. John M. Shalikashvili, former chairman of the Joint Chiefs of Staff. He responded: "I don't know where it comes from, but I do feel that I have a feeling in the pit of my stomach when things are right, or they're not right, even when most people around advise me otherwise. I have no idea, but do I think that I always had it? No. I think partly it comes from confidence: After you've done things often enough, you've been around the block long enough, you develop that sense. I was never aware of it when I was a lieutenant. You know, no matter what the majors say, I know what's right. It was different then. Now I have a feeling [that] the only way I can tell you is it comes from confidence."[27]

It is clear from my interviews that commanders' visits to the troops are vital to the "feel" in decision making. Concerning the invasion by the United States to recapture the Philippines, Lt. Gen. Robert Eichelberger, Eighth Army commander, in the Far East in the war against Japan, reflected: "MacArthur was restless in Manila anyhow. Except for one April trip to the Marakina Valley, twenty miles northeast of the capital, where Krueger's GIs were battling thirty thousand entrenched Japanese, he hadn't left the city since the arrival of his family, and he said he wanted 'a feel' of the combat to the south. On June 3rd, he and several members of his staff boarded the *Boise* for what Eichelberger called a 'grand tour' of Eighth Army battlefields, and at the end, participation in the Brunei Bay landing. He would be away twelve days."[28]

When Eichelberger took over the Eighth Army, he began to inspect immediately, and what he found was alarming: "The troops were deplorable. They wore long dirty beards. Their clothing was in rags. Their shoes were uncared for, or worn out. They were receiving far less than adequate rations and there was little discipline or military courtesy. . . . When Martin and I visited a regimental combat team to observe what was supposed to be an attack, it was found that the regimental post was four and a half miles behind the front line. The regimental commander and his staff went forward from this location rarely, if ever.

"Troops were scattered along a trail toward the front line in small groups, engaged in eating [and] sleeping during the time they were supposed to be in an attack. At the front there were portions of two companies, aggregating 150 men.

"Outside of the 150 men in the foxholes in the front lines, the remainder of the 2000 men in the combat area could not have been even considered a reserve—since three or four hours would have been required to organize and move them on any tactical mission."[29]

As the invasion proceeded, Eichelberger, to improve this deplorable display of lack of discipline and organization, described how he covered the vast territory he was responsible for: "By late April I had become one of the Orient's busiest air commuters. The Eighth Army was waging war in many places, and, like a faithful commercial traveler, I tried to visit them all. The airplane was a magic carpet for me. I could rise early, be in the air by seven, take off for a conference with GHQ in Manila, and be back at my desk for a staff conference before sundown. The frequent confusions and contradictions of field reports have always bothered commanders who must make strategic decisions. Because of the airplane, I could whisk out over the green mountains of Leyte, land on Zamboanga, Cebu, Negros—or, later, on one or two of a dozen makeshift grass strips on Mindanao—and investigate the field situation for myself. In the spring of 1945, during a ninety-day period, I was in the air seventy days."[30]

General Ridgway, who prevented defeat in Korea, considered visiting the troops a vital part of his success as a leader and decision maker. "If the commander relies on his staff, he's lost. You've got to have the most intimate relations with your staff, above all with your chief of staff. But your commander has got to go down direct to his principal commanders. He's got to be out there with the troops and there he gets the feel and checks his own impressions and what he sees and hears firsthand along with what the staff reports to him. But there are some commanders who have relied and placed overreliance on their staffs to the point where they get their reports really thirdhand (certainly secondhand instead of firsthand, which most of the time you can get). In a unit the size of a division, there's no reason for such reliance. There's rarely more than one crisis erupting at one time, and the commander can, with rare exceptions, anticipate it. So he should be there before it happens and then he's in the best possible position not to trespass on the sphere of the subordinate at all but to help him in every way possible. To foresee his needs before he asks for them."[31]

"I don't believe I ever made a major decision in combat," Ridgway confirmed, "unless I was present on the spot right at the moment of action or I had previously consulted the commander to whom I was going to entrust this mission and acquainted him with it and gotten his prior acquiescence. In other words he thought it was okay, thought it could be done. Now when you do that and you combine that with the fact that the commander doesn't ask his troops to do anything that he hasn't done himself, then you don't get this challenge."[32]

When Ridgway was the division commander of the 82d Airborne Division in the invasion of France, he made these visits in a small airplane. "I asked Mike, my pilot, if he could go down there as I made

my reconnaissance by air, so we went down. We could pass notes back
and forth to each other in this little light plane, so we decided to
duck in under the telephone wires and we landed on the street in
that little town. Then, by the grace of God, we got out the same way.
So I contacted the engineer patrol that was examining the bridge to
see if the demolition charges on this bridge were disconnected. Then
we landed in various other places [such as] dry streambeds, and
maybe get in at the very last shred of light. You couldn't have any
lighted field to land on up there. But he was a great pilot."[33]

General Ridgway was active in visiting the troops as commander
of the Eighth Army in Korea in 1950. Colonel Harold K. Johnson,
then a regimental commander, who went on to become army chief
of staff from 1964 to 1968, commented: "A great change happened
when General Ridgway came in and he promptly began to hold commanders' conferences and visit us. We had commanders down
through company commanders attending. General Ridgway talked
to us and turned us around by the sheer force of his own personality and made changes. He really did. He made many checks in person to see that the turnaround happened. He was impatient and
wouldn't tolerate slowness. He physically moved himself and his aides
with him and lived in our command post. He even ate in our mess,
coming morning and night to the main headquarters. He was out
visiting all during the daylight hours. He went to bed quite early, and
left early. I learned from this and tried to visit and pick up what was
going on. I followed General Ridgway around to discover what he
was telling people. This proved very useful and helpful, particularly
so I could describe in briefings about things to other commanders."[34]

General Collins, a corps commander in World War II, commented
in his autobiography: "Ridgway and I were much closer to our own
troops and had far more accurate knowledge of conditions than
Montgomery, who placed too much faith in the daily reports of
'phantom' observers, junior British staff officers, whom he placed
at our headquarters."

When David C. Jones was air force chief of staff, he made many
inspection trips. His aide-de-camp, then Lt. Col. Robert H. Baxter,
traveled with him. He described Jones's methodology: "He had a set
procedure when he inspected a base. I think he was absolutely un-

canny. He developed the technique or knack for it. He would know a great deal about a base before he went there. The staff would prepare a lot of background papers on both the base and any issues or problems that might be there, like if there were environmental complaints, if the air force was trying to acquire more property, current issues, as well as just what the mission issues were. He had a group of people, Generals Abbot Greenleaf and Currie, programmers, who were very good at preparing him. He just walked through the base and at the end of the day he'd start talking about what can be moved, to cut here and there. Inevitably, there would be some reaction from the base, but that just always seemed to work.

"We were at March Air Force Base one time and [he] made some observations out loud. I turned to him and said, 'How do you know that? How do you walk the streets around the base and come up with such an accurate assessment just by looking at it?' He said to me, 'Well, it comes with experience. If you poke your nose in enough nooks and crannies, you finally get a feel for it.'

"He was trying to consolidate, for instance, twenty-four-hour work centers where there is a great deal of redundancy. He wanted to put different functions in different locations to improve efficiency. This was a time when we were shifting around in the air force to consolidate and save money.

"I just never ceased to be amazed at the feel that he seemed to have for a base as we inspected it. That was one of the more controversial things about him to many people; he was always squeezing a lot more into a base than what people thought could be done or should be done. He frequently increased the loading of the facility. Sometimes he'd just consolidate what was on the base already in a more efficient manner, but frequently just looking for places to bring additional functions on so as to eventually work it all around to where you'd have another base that you could close."[35]

The ability to have a feel for things is also important in your relationship with your seniors. "When I was aide to General LeMay," Jones commented, "I was able from the first day to understand his body language. I knew when he was in deep thought on a big subject and I made sure he was left alone, or when he was bored to death it was the time to bring something to his attention. Timing was so important."[36]

Jones also had this feel in dealing with the bureaucracy. The former commander of Tactical Air Command, Gen. W. L. Creech, commented: "Dave Jones is a very political person. I mean that in a very laudatory sense in that he's very much tuned into the feelings of others, both individually and collectively. He understands biases, prejudices, how they form, where they exist. He is a master at assessing all those cross currents of opinions and the way they will flow as the result of a decision. When he decides that something needs to be done, he has the courage to proceed even though it may not be a popular decision. My own perspective on watching him in operation [is that] he never did things just to tweak the tail of the bureaucracy. He just did what he thought was right; if that wasn't what the rest of the people thought needed to be done, it didn't bother him. He had his own vision of what needed to be done and he did that. I think it's important to note that it wasn't because he didn't care, because he does care. And it wasn't because he didn't understand, because he did understand. But he just pressed on."[37]

General Schwarzkopf provided a truly remarkable example of "feel" in an experience he had in the Vietnam War with one of the Vietnamese officers, Col. Ngo Quang Truong, who Schwarzkopf said did not look like the military genius he was. Schwarzkopf described him as five feet seven, in his midforties, skinny, with hunched shoulders, a head that looked too big for his body, and a pinched face; he was not handsome and almost always had a cigarette hanging from his lips. "Yet he was revered by his officers and troops—and feared by those North Vietnamese commanders."

An incident occurred where the North Vietnamese regiments that had been defeated in the Ia Drang Valley were kept from escaping and going into Cambodia. Colonel Truong was selected by the South Vietnamese Army chief of staff to prevent this, and Schwarzkopf was selected by Truong to be his American adviser. "It was fascinating to watch him operate," said Schwarzkopf. "As we marched, he would stop to study the map, and every once in a while he'd indicate a position on the map and say, 'I want you to fire ar-

tillery here.'" Schwarzkopf was skeptical at first but called in the bar-
rages. When the troops reached the areas, they would find bodies.
Simply by visualizing the terrain and drawing on his experience fighting the enemy for fifteen years, Truong showed an uncanny ability
to predict what they were going to do.

That night he laid out his battle plan, telling them, "At dawn send
out one battalion and put it here, on our left, as a blocking force between the ridge and the river. Around eight o'clock tomorrow morning, they would make a big enemy contact. Then send another battalion here, to our right. They will make contact around eleven
o'clock, so have artillery ready to fire into this area in front of us."
Then he said, "We will attack with our third and fourth battalion
down toward the river. The enemy will then be trapped with the river
to his back."[38]

Schwarzkopf reflected, "I'd never heard anything like this at West
Point. I was thinking, What's all this about eight o'clock and eleven
o'clock? How can he schedule a battle that way? But I also recognized
the outline of his plan: Truong had reinvented the tactics Hannibal
had used in 217 B.C., when he enveloped and annihilated the Roman legions on the banks of Lake Trasimene."

Schwarzkopf said that Truong issued his attack orders, then sat
smoking his cigarettes and studying the map, going over the plan
again and again late into the night, visualizing every step of the battle. Then at dawn they sent out the 3d Battalion. They got into position and at eight o'clock they called and reported heavy contact.
Truong sent the 5th Battalion to the right. At eleven o'clock they reported heavy contact. As Truong had predicted, in the jungle below
them, the enemy had run into the 3d Battalion. Truong had antici-
pated this and had boxed them in. He looked at Schwarzkopf and
said, "Fire your artillery." They shelled the area below us for a half
hour. Then he ordered his two remaining battalions to attack down
the hill; there was a lot of shooting as we followed them in. Then
Truong announced, "Okay. We'll stop." He picked a clearing, and
they sat down with his staff and had lunch. Halfway through the meal,
Schwarzkopf said that Truong put down his rice bowl and issued
some commands on the radio. He proceeded to order his men to
search the battlefield for weapons, saying, "We killed many enemy,

and the ones we didn't kill threw down their weapons and ran away." In amazement Schwarzkopf reflected, "Now, he hadn't seen a damn thing! All the action had been hidden by jungle. But we stayed in that clearing for the remainder of the day, and his troops brought in armful after armful of weapons and piled them in front of us. I was excited—we'd scored a decisive victory! But Truong just sat, smoking his cigarettes."

General Schwarzkopf was a believer in visiting the troops. As a lieutenant colonel in Vietnam, he was given command of a battalion in the field. He met with the outgoing battalion commander, who had been described as "an unprepossessing older guy, medium-sized, thin, with a receding chin." Schwarzkopf expected a two- to three-hour discussion of the battalion but instead was told only that the outfit had lousy morale and a lousy mission. "Good luck to you," said the outgoing commander. With that, he shook his hand and walked out.

Schwarzkopf wanted to learn what was going on, so he proceeded to headquarters. The battalion executive officer saluted and said, "Sir, we're prepared to give you your briefings."

"I don't want briefings now. I want to visit the companies."

"Sir?"

"I want to visit the companies. Don't we have a command-and-control helicopter?"

"Sir, we do, but Major Lee has it." Major Will Lee was the operations staff officer. "As a matter of fact, sir, he has the helicopter all the time."

"What do you mean? Isn't that a command-and-control helicopter for the battalion commander? Get it back here right now."

There was a stunned silence in the operations center. "Sir, may I talk to you for a minute outside?" said the exec. We stepped out and he explained, "I know this is unusual, but the chopper isn't here because your predecessor never went out in the field."

It required half an hour for the helicopter to return. Schwarzkopf went inside to wait and discovered that there was no place in the operations center for the battalion commander—no desk, no chair, nothing. He went back to his little cabin desperately trying to figure out what he should do next, asking himself, "How does this outfit function? Who's in charge?" Finally the helicopter landed. He walked back into the operations center and overheard someone say, "What the hell did you guys call me in for? I've got work to do out there." It was Major Lee, who as it turned out was an enthusiastic veteran officer, eager to follow orders, who had simply been trying to hold the operation together in the absence of any real leadership. Said Schwarzkopf, "When I introduced myself and told him I wanted to go out in the field, he exclaimed, 'That's great, sir! Let's go! Which company do you want to see first?'"

What Schwarzkopf found were deplorable conditions. The company camps were in disarray; men were sloppily dressed and had no foxholes; and the machine guns had no ammunition and were rusting. He reflected, "I knew I had to put an end to this carelessness before men started dying. I took the company commander aside, the guy who had been wearing red shorts. 'Things are going to start changing around here, Captain, right now. *Right now.* My inclination is to relieve you of your command, but I can't do that because apparently this is the way you've been allowed to operate. But I'm telling you: you know what to do and it had better happen. First, when you stop someplace, you will put out security, and I mean *good* security. Second, I want every portable radio out of the field. Third, I want every weapon in this outfit cleaned, and I'd better never come in again and find anybody without a weapon. Ever! In his hand! With clean ammunition! Fourth, I want every man, starting with you, shaved, cleaned up, and in proper uniform. With a helmet! And fifth, there is no way these men can go on ambush patrol tonight and stay awake, because they're all awake now."

Schwarzkopf returned to his headquarters to the mess hall, where there was a long line—troops standing in the rain. He took his place at the end of the line, which caused a mess sergeant to trot over to him: "Sir, you don't have to stand in line. We've got a special section for officers."

Schwarzkopf responded: "Sergeant, if my troops have to stand in line out here in the rain, I'll stand here, too." The troops stared at him. But they started talking to him and for the first time he felt encouraged. "You the new battalion commander?" asked one. "You gonna make a lot of changes?" asked another. A third added, "This is the first time we've ever talked to our battalion commander. It's good to talk to you, sir." The line moved along, and once he got inside he discovered that the officers didn't even have the same dinner hour as the men. They waited until the troops were done, then sat down and got served. He sent for the exec and told him that from now on all officers would eat with the troops.[39]

General Shy Meyer reflected on the role of visiting and developing the "feel" while visiting: "In my experience in Korea and Vietnam, and as chief of staff of the army, I visited unexpectedly, without alerting people in the posts, camps, and stations. About a half an hour out, I would call in and say we're on our way—I didn't want them to get all spruced up for me. You need to have an on-the-ground feel for what's going on, whether it's in a supply depot, a tactical unit, or an R&D element. Regardless of what it is, there are things going on where people work that you must understand the basic rationale for it if you're going to be able to make good judgments about how their work contributes to the overall good of the organization. So the need to get on-the-ground observations, the need to go out and visit the troops, is vital in obtaining 'feel' or 'sixth sense.'"[40]

Showmanship

Showmanship is one of the techniques that often permits you to reach the lowest level of your command. General Patton wrote to his cadet son at West Point, "Be particularly spooney [well groomed], so spooney that you not only get by but attract attention. Why do you suppose I pay so much attention to being well dressed? Have your clothes well pressed; when I was boning [working to achieve cadet rank] I always had one uniform that I never sat down in."

Patton was the beau ideal in his military dress. It was a vital part of all leaders, and Patton used it to reach his troops; it was important in getting the "feel." As a general officer he wore a magnificently tailored, form-fitting battle jacket with brass buttons. Above the left pocket were four rows of campaign ribbons and decorations, and on each shoulder and shirt collar were pinned oversized general's stars.

His trousers were whipcord riding breeches. He wore high-topped cavalry boots, shined to a mirrorlike finish, and spurs. Around his waist was a hand-carved leather belt with a gleaming brass buckle. On each hip rested an ivory-handled pistol ornamented with general's stars. In his hand he carried a riding crop. His helmet was polished to a lustrous finish. The impression you get the first time you see him is *boom!* There is no doubt that his appearance in uniform attracted attention. His dress seemed to say, I'm Patton—the best damn general in this or any other army.

When a town was captured, Patton was among the first to enter even though there was danger of sniper bullets and delayed bombs. After an amphibious invasion, he would leap into the surf before his landing barge was grounded and wade ashore amid zinging bullets, artillery shells, and mortar fire, yelling encouraging remarks to the men. He waded across many a river as his army moved over France and Germany. He even practiced to perfection his facial expressions. Once his sister Nita asked him, "Why do you look so mean and ornery in your pictures?" Patton laughed and replied, "That's my war face."

One cold, rainy afternoon during the war, Patton came upon a group of men at work repairing a tank that had been hit by enemy fire. The tank, because of the heavy movement of traffic forward toward the line of battle, had pulled about ten yards off the road. Seeing this, Patton ordered his driver to stop. He jumped out of his jeep, went over to the disabled tank, and crawled underneath it. The two mechanics, busy working on the necessary repairs, were awestruck to see the shiny silver stars of a general in the mud. Patton, according to the assistant division commander whose area he was touring at the time, remained under the tank for twenty-five minutes. When he returned to his jeep, he was covered with mud and grease. His aide asked, "Sir, what was wrong?" Patton replied, "I don't know, but I'm sure that the word will spread throughout the division that I was on my belly in the mud repairing the tank."[41]

Sometimes the effectiveness of Patton's showmanship was based on simplicity. In Berlin, just after the war was over, Patton and Marshal Zhukov were representing their respective countries at the dedication of a Russian war memorial. Zhukov's uniform blouse was completely covered with medals on both sides. By contrast, General Patton wore only a few campaign ribbons. An observer of the ceremony commented: "Patton, looking so neat and trim, was more lethal than even the big Russian tanks."[42]

Patton's showmanship as a general was not new to him or to colleagues in the military leadership rank. As a cavalryman in the twenties, he was known as "Horse George" because of his antics in polo and riding. One friend said of his relationship with Patton, "We always seemed to be charging." When Patton took command of the 2d Armored Division, he designed a special green uniform for tank personnel that earned him the nicknames "Green Hornet" and "Flash Gordon." Others found such names as Buck Rogers, Man from Mars, and Iron Pants fitting for his personality. This earned him another name as a combat army commander, "Old Blood and Guts." To him such names were indicative of successful showmanship. He considered such notoriety vital to leadership style. With a command of hundreds of thousands of men, Patton necessarily had to exert his leadership from a distance, and flamboyance helped to spread the image he wanted his men to see.

Major General Reinhart, commander of the 65th Infantry Division, wrote of his action under Patton in Germany. He said that the advance "was extremely rapid and was in the nature of a pursuit. Our flanks were seldom secure and we were threatened by envelopment . . . so much so that my three-infantry regimental commanders once in a group protested informally to me that they did not like our situation. 'We have been riding all the way up here with our shirttails out' [meaning their exposed flanks] was the way they expressed it." Reinhart asked them if they did not believe that if worse came to worst and they were surrounded, "Georgie" would be on the way to pull them out. "This idea," said General Reinhart, "seemed to satisfy them completely and I never heard another word about it from any of them."[43] These officers had never met Patton, but they knew his reputation. Loud and colorful even from a distance, he was able to create an aura of personal leadership.

Eisenhower noted that Patton's showmanship "was a shell that was worn constantly and carefully." Everything Patton did had a purpose. He believed that a leader, in order to make himself known in the lower echelons, should exhibit an individualism calculated to cause men to talk about him. His soldiers knew him as a personality, and he assiduously preserved the image. He told Maj. Gen. Robert C. Macon in North Africa in 1943, "During training I wore two ivory-handled revolvers. They called me 'Two Gun Patton.' Well, when I came ashore here, I was not going to let them down. I wore the damn two guns."[44]

Those who were close to Patton saw that he was an actor. He could turn his showmanship on or off as the situation required. For the dedication of a cemetery, for a speech of praise to his officers and men, or for biting criticism of a unit that performed poorly, he had different but appropriate acts. He was not, however, insincere. Nor did his showmanship seem awkward; though admittedly a costume, it was a tailored and well-fitted one.

Patton's rationale for the role of showmanship and acting was developed and put into perspective in an article entitled "Success in War," published in the *Infantry Journal* in 1931.

> After a discussion of the traits of successful leadership [self-confidence, enthusiasm, abnegation of self, loyalty, and courage], Patton concluded: "courage, moral and physical, is almost a synonym of all the foregoing traits. It fosters the resolution to combat and cherishes the ability to assume responsibility, be it successes or failures. . . . But as with the biblical candle, these traits are no military value if concealed.
>
> A man of difficult manner will never inspire confidence. A cold reserve cannot beget enthusiasm, and so with the others there must be an outward and visible sign of the inward and spiritual grace.
>
> It then appears that the leader must be an actor, and such is the fact. But with him . . . he is unconvincing unless he lives the part.[45]

Can this be learned? Patton thought so. "Can men then acquire and demonstrate these characteristics? The answer is they have—they can. 'As a man thinketh, so is he.' The fixed determination to acquire it, to conquer or perish with honor is the secret of success in war."[46]

* * *

There was much about Douglas MacArthur that made others susceptible to hero worship. He was handsome, dashing, and oratorically brilliant. He had an incredible veneer of showmanship although he was at the same time a recluse. He was rarely seen by the troops, and his style of showmanship when he did visit surrounded him with a mystical aura.

The crux of his showmanship was a distinctive simplicity. Throughout all of World War II, he was usually seen in a plain khaki uniform with an open-necked shirt and sharply pressed pleated trousers. He wore no medals, only his general's stars and his rakish hat with the gold braid on the bill. Other than this, his only accoutrements were a corncob pipe and a bamboo swagger stick. On other occasions, he smoked cigarettes in an up-tilt position with a long black cigarette holder, and he swung a curved-handled brown cane.

There was a certain drama to MacArthur's actions that made him stand out. His performance at the Japanese surrender on board the USS *Missouri* was characteristic. It occurred on Sunday morning September 2, 1945. The Japanese delegation of diplomats and military officers arrived at 8:55. Awaiting them were the representatives from the United States, Britain, China, Holland, France, and the Soviet Union. The eleven members of the Japanese delegation were dressed in morning coats or heavily medaled dress military uniforms. A few minutes after everyone was in a place, MacArthur came out from his cabin. He was dressed in the type of khaki uniform he had worn throughout the war, with an open, tieless collar, no medals, and his field marshal cap at the usual rakish angle. As he read his preliminary remarks, he stood erect, but his hands were shaky as he read from his prepared text. Then there was complete silence as the surrender was signed. By 9:08, only thirteen minutes after the ceremony officially began, it was all over.

The signing by MacArthur was reminiscent of presidential practice. He used five pens, one of them his own. He signed "Doug" with the first, "las" with the second, "MacArthur" with the third. For his second signature, he used two pens. Thus, he could provide his friends with a pen that had played a significant role in history. One of the pens went to the museum at his beloved West Point.

At this surrender, MacArthur was responsible for an unparalleled act of showmanship. The Bataan death march of the Allied soldiers after the surrender of Corregidor was one of the saddest, most cruel incidents of World War II. The treatment of Allied soldiers by the Japanese on this march resulted in many deaths; the time in the prisoner-of-war camps rivaled it but was longer in duration. MacArthur wrote in his memoirs: "Prisoners had begun dribbling out of the Japanese camps almost as soon as the landings in Japan were made, and among the first of those liberated were General Wainwright and General A. E. Percival. They had been held in Mukden in Manchuria and had been flown back to Manila. I immediately directed that they be brought to Japan for the surrender ceremonies on the Missouri. I was just sitting down to dinner when my aide brought me the word that they had arrived. I rose and started for the lobby, but before I could reach it, the door swung open and there was Wainwright. He was haggard and aged. His uniform hung in the folds on his fleshless form. He walked with difficulty and with the help of a cane. His eyes were sunken and there were pits in his cheeks. His hair was snow white and his skin looked like old shoe leather. He made a brave effort to smile as I took him in my arms, but when he tried to talk his voice wouldn't call."[47]

As the surrender of the Japanese was signed on the battleship *Missouri* on September 2, 1945, standing behind MacArthur were Generals Wainwright and Percival. The recognition was even more meaningful for Wainwright, who lived in mental agony throughout his entire time as a prisoner of war and who, after the war, if he survived, would be court-martialed for surrendering the American forces in the Philippines. But nothing stopped MacArthur's having him present at the surrender.

When he went to Japan as conqueror in 1945, MacArthur traveled in a gleaming, silvery C-54. When he landed at the Atsugi airport, a band began to play as the ramp was let down. He was the first person to emerge from the door of the aircraft, named *Bataan*. He took several steps down the ramp, puffing on his corncob pipe. Then he paused dramatically. He was the first Caucasian in Japan's history to take control of the country. After he had gazed out for a few minutes, he continued down the ramp, warmly shaking hands with old friends in the advance party.

When the American delegation arrived at the U.S. Embassy, MacArthur commanded, "General Eichelberger, have our country's flag unfurled, and in Tokyo's sun let it wave in its full glory as a symbol of hope for the oppressed and as a harbinger of victory for the right." The flag raised was the one that flew over the Capitol in Washington, D.C., on December 7, 1941.

All of the four-star generals I interviewed concurred that top leaders have a "feel" or "sixth sense." Eisenhower's comment that a leader "must never lose touch with the feel of his troops" focuses and sums up "feel." He also said that "contact requires frequent visits to the troops," that "the importance of visits by the high command can scarcely be overestimated in terms of a soldier's morale," that the "soldier has a sense of gratification whenever he sees very high rank in the vicinity," that "visits improve efficiency when men are encouraged to speak to their supervisors," that "visiting encourages junior officers to seek information from their men," that "among the mass of individuals who carry rifles in war there is a great amount of ingenuity and initiative," that the visit is "evidence of the commander's concern for them," that visits are "a part of the basic equipment of a commander," and that "attention to the individual is the key to success."

Yes, gifted military leaders throughout history had that feel or sixth sense, but is it a God-given talent or can it be developed? This study establishes that it can be developed. Patton summed it up: Military reaction, which he said no one is born with, "must be developed by hard work." Bradley said his experiences were "stored" in his mind, and when suddenly faced with a decision he would "push a button and . . . would have an answer right then." Collins said feel is "based first of all on knowledge" and is "developed by working hard and studying as a younger man."

Simpson said background and experience helped him to understand situations that would come up. Truscott said that "knowledge is the basis of feel" and "requires an interest in people." Haislip said feel is the result of education, of thoroughly knowing your profession. McAuliffe said, "A man learns over the years he serves," that "[feel] requires an understanding of men" and "experience has a great deal to do with it."

Brown became a commander of Systems Command but was not an engineer or a scientist. At one of his meetings he told a briefing officer he couldn't quarrel with the engineering details but could quarrel with the "feel" he had for what he was being told.

Shalikashvili said he had a "feeling in the pit of my stomach when things are right, or they're not right, which comes from confidence after you have done things often enough"—again experience.

But visiting the troops is key. Ridgway stated that a comander has "got to be out there with the troops and there he gets the feel," that it is important to see his troops' needs before the men ask for them, and that as an adviser and army commander he never made a decision in combat unless he "was present on the spot right at the moment of action."

Jones went visiting and said his observations came from experience, that if you poke your nose in enough nooks you finally get a feel for things, and that he could read body language.

Showmanship is a part of the visiting and obtaining the feel you need to reach your men. Patton said a leader should be "spooney" [well groomed] and "attract attention." He certainly practiced this, with his ivory-handled pistols; his oversized stars on his shining helmet, collar, and shoulders; his riding boots; and the riding crop in his hand. He said that his traits were of no military value if concealed and that "as a man thinketh, so he is." He needed to reach his 500,000 soldiers with his showmanship, and he did.

Eisenhower had to reach more than a million and a half troops. When inspecting he wore his overseas cap, cut-off jacket named the "Ike jacket," which became standard army issue, and riding breeches, boots, and riding crop. Ike's smile was natural and was worth two divisions. All these top generals had their own style of showmanship and their own way of reaching out to their troops, but they all had it and practiced it.

Notes

1. Dwight D. Eisenhower, *Crusade in Europe* (New York: Doubleday & Company, Inc., 1948), 213–14.

2. Ibid., 313–14.

3. Ibid., 389.

4. Letter from Lt. Gen. Alvan C. Gillem, Jr., USA (Ret.), to Edgar F. Puryear, Jr., August 19, 1963.

5. Eisenhower, *Crusade in Europe*, 314.

6. Harry C. Butcher, *My Three Years with Eisenhower* (New York: Simon and Schuster), p. 723

7. Ibid., 854.

8. Eisenhower, *Crusade in Europe*, 455.

9. Ibid., 238.

10. Letter from Gen. Ben Lear, USA (Ret.), to Edgar F. Puryear, Jr., August 17, 1943.

11. Katherine Tupper Marshall, *Together* (New York: Tupper and Low, Inc., 1946), 176.

12. Personal interview with Gen. Curtis E. LeMay, USAF (Ret.), and Edgar F. Puryear, Jr., November 17, 1976.

13. Charles R. Codman, *Drive* (Boston: Little, Brown 1957), 124.

14. Personal interview with General of the Army Omar N. Bradley and Edgar F. Puryear, Jr., February 15, 1963.

15. Letter from Gen. George S. Patton, Jr., to his son, cadet George S. Patton II, dated June 6, 1944.

16. Bradley interview.

17. Personal interview with Gen. J. Lawton Collins, USA (Ret.), September 20, 1962.

18. Personal interview with Gen. William H. Simpson, USA (Ret.), September 20, 1962.

19. Personal interview with Gen. Lucian K. Truscott, USA (Ret.), and Edgar F. Puryear, Jr., September 11, 1962.

20. Personal interview with Gen. Wade Haislip, USA (Ret.), and Edgar F. Puryear, Jr., September 14, 1962.

21. Personal interview with Gen. Anthony McAuliffe, USA (Ret.), and Edgar F. Puryear, Jr., September 10, 1962.

22. Bradley interview.

23. Personal interview with Gen. Carl Spaatz and Edgar F. Puryear, Jr., September 12, 1962.

24. Personal interview with Maj. Gen. Jerry Cook, USAF (Ret.), and Edgar F. Puryear, Jr., July 22, 1980.

25. L. K. Truscott, *Command Missions* (New York: E. P. Dutton and Company, Inc., 1954), 547.

26. Personal interview with Gen. Edward C. Meyer, USA (Ret.), and Edgar F. Puryear, Jr. July 14, 1997

27. Personal interview with General John M. Shalikashvili, USA (Ret.), and Edgar F. Puryear, Jr., June 4, 1997.

28. Robert L. Eichelberger, *Our Jungle Road to Tokyo* (New York: The Viking Press, 1950), 43.

29. Ibid., 25.

30. Ibid.

31. Interview with Gen. Matthew Ridgway, USA (Ret.), and Lt. Col. John M. Beair, November 24, 1971.

32. Ibid.

33. Ibid.

34. Ibid.

35. Personal interview with Col. Robert H. Baxter, USAF, and Edgar F. Puryear, Jr., April 19, 1979.

36. Personal interview with Gen. David C. Jones, USAF (Ret.), and Edgar F. Puryear, Jr., January 28, 1998.

37. Personal interview with Gen. Wilbur L. Creech, USAF (Ret.), and Edgar F. Puryear, Jr., June 15, 1979.

38. H. Norman Schwarzkopf, *It Doesn't Take a Hero* (New York: Bantam Books, 1992), 123

39. Ibid.

40. Meyer interview.

41. Personal interview with Brig. Gen. Don C. Faith and Edgar F. Puryear, Jr., September 12, 1962.

42. The observer was Brig. Gen. John L. Whitelaw, USA (Ret.), assistant division commander of the 17th Airborne Division.

43. Letter from Maj. Gen. Stanley E. Reinhart, USA (Ret.), to Edgar F. Puryear, Jr., October 24, 1962.

44. Letter from Maj. Gen. Robert C. Macon, USA (Ret.), to Edgar F. Puryear, Jr., dated October 8, 1962.

45. Joseph I. Greene, ed., *Infantry Journal* (New York: Doubleday, Doran & Company, Inc., 1943), 264.

46. Ibid.

47. Douglas MacArthur, *Reminiscences* (New York: McGraw-Hill, 1964), 271–72.

Chapter 4: Aversion to "Yes Men": Having the Character to Challenge

In 1940, Gen. George C. Marshall assigned Maj. Omar N. Bradley as assistant secretary of the general staff, a job that included briefing Marshall on decision papers. After a few weeks on the job, Marshall called Bradley and his assistants into his office. "Gentlemen," he said, "I'm disappointed in you. You haven't disagreed with a single decision I've made." Bradley replied, "General, that's only because there has been no cause for disagreement. When we differ with you on a decision, sir, we'll tell you."[1] This incident focuses on one of the most important aspects of decision making—the assurance that you don't have on your staff any "yes men."

Not being a "yes man" was a turning point for Marshall in his own career. His initial assignment in Europe in World War I was on the staff of Maj. Gen. William L. Sibert, the 1st Division commander.

As the several divisions were training, Pershing made frequent inspection trips to evaluate their progress. In September 1917, he announced, with little notice, that he, along with the president of France, Raymond Poincaré, was going to review Sibert's division. Indeed, the order for the review came extremely late in the afternoon before it was to be held. The division's troops were spread over an area some thirty square miles, an all-night march from Houdelcourt, France, where the review and inspection were to be held. Captain Marshall was put in charge of the arrangements for the review, but because of the short notice he had to select the site for the inspection late in the evening. In the dark, he could not see that the ground chosen was on a hillside torn up by constant troop drilling, ankle deep in mud. Most of the personnel in the division had had no previous military experience and only a month of training. As a result the review went badly. General Pershing, reflected Marshall, "just gave everybody hell," stating that the division didn't show much evidence of any training, had made poor use of its time, and failed to follow directives. To Marshall, this seemed terribly unfair, particularly when Pershing "was very severe, with General Sibert [the division commander] in front of the officers."[2] Pershing then proceeded to interrogate Sibert on matters that Marshall had been handling. General Sibert was unaware of these, because he had arrived only two days before this review. Pershing curtly dismissed Sibert and asked him to leave. Marshall's reaction, as reported by his biographer Forrest Pogue, was to be expected:

> Marshall, stung at the manifest injustice, tossed aside the caution that a junior officer could be expected to feel on such an occasion. He decided that, whatever the cost to him, he had to explain some things. He began to talk. Pershing, in no mood to listen, shrugged his shoulders and turned away. Marshall, "mad all over," put his hand on the general's arm.
>
> "General Pershing," he said, "there's something to be said here and I think I should say it because I've been here longest."
>
> Pershing stopped. "What have you got to say?"
>
> Exactly what the irate captain had to say was not recorded and afterward he could not remember. An associate of these days has said that in anger Marshall talked very fast and overwhelmed his adversary with "a torrent of the facts." Marshall himself recalled that he "had an inspired moment" and that his fellow officers standing by "were horrified." When he finished General Pershing remained calm. He walked away, saying to Marshall, "You must appreciate the troubles we have."
>
> Marshall, aware that he had "gotten into it up to my neck," gave no quarter. "Yes, General," he replied, "but we have them every day and they have to be solved before night."
>
> Then General Pershing was gone and tempers cooled. General Sibert was sorry that Marshall had got into such hot water for his sake. Some of Marshall's friends were sure he was finished and "would be fired right off." Marshall himself had no regrets. To those who tendered sympathy he said, "All I can see

is that I might get field duty instead of staff duty, and certainly that would be a great success."

No retribution came. On the contrary, thereafter when Pershing visited the division he would often take Marshall aside and ask him how things were going. In the months following, it was clear that the general's respect and liking grew. Pershing—Marshall was to discover—was always willing to listen to honest criticism and to an extraordinary degree was able to detach himself from it. "You could talk to him as if you were discussing someone in the next country. He never held it against you for an instant. I never saw another commander I could do that with. . . . It was one of his great strengths that he could listen to things."[3]

So, far from being fired, Marshall rose to the rank of full colonel within a year, ultimately becoming Pershing's operations officer before the end of the war. After the war, Pershing became chief of staff of the army, and Marshall served with him for four years as his aide and executive officer. The normal tour as an aide in those days was only two years.

A similar incident occurred when General Marshall was serving as deputy chief of staff of the army under Gen. Malin Craig. On November 14, 1938, Roosevelt called a conference with members of his cabinet and military advisers, proposing a program to build 10,000 combat aircraft. Marshall thought initially that the aircraft were for the U.S. military, but as the meeting developed he realized that the president's intention was to send them to Britain and France to aid in their war with Germany. The military personnel present at the briefing did not think much of this, and Marshall was surprised that no one challenged Roosevelt's idea. Roosevelt asked for comments and, turning to Marshall, inquired, "Don't you think so, George?" Marshall looked him in the eye and responded, "I am sorry, Mr. President, but I don't agree with you at all."[4]

One observer who was present said of the incident, "A startled expression crossed Roosevelt's face. He seemed about to ask why and then thought better of it, and the meeting broke up. Afterward the others . . . came up to him one by one to shake his hand." Secretary of the Treasury Henry Morgenthau, in particular, told Marshall, "Well, it's been nice knowing you." Like the rest of them, Morgenthau thought that Marshall, with his outspokenness, had just ruined his career and that his tour in Washington would be over.[5]

But it wasn't over. In 1939, Roosevelt decided to select Marshall as chief of staff of the army, a jump from one star to four stars. He accepted, but in doing so he again made it clear that he was not going to be a "yes man." Marshall recalled: "I saw the President in his study when he told me. It was an interesting interview. I told him I wanted the right to say what I think and it would often be unpleasing. 'Is that all right?' He said, 'Yes.' I said, 'You said "yes" pleasantly, but this may be unpleasant.'"[6] Rather than firing Marshall for standing up for what he thought, Roosevelt realized, knowing the incredible difficulties facing the country, that he could not afford or desire a "yes man."

Marshall required the same candor of his staff and commanders. During World War II, it was standard procedure for division commanders to receive a briefing before sailing with their units for combat. This briefing included a talk from General Marshall. "I had expected," one division commander wrote of the briefing, "to be counseled and advised as to his standards for combat readiness. Instead, he devoted the entire time to excoriating the type of officer who gives answers he thinks the chief wants to hear rather than the hard facts. He was in a bad mood because of some specific incident. He strongly impressed those of us who were present with the importance of an officer having the moral courage to report facts, unpleasant as they may be, to the ears of the commander, rather than trying to keep bad news from him."[7]

A specific example of Marshall's expectations was provided when he was visiting in Europe in 1944. He stopped on an inspection trip at Herrlen, Holland, which at the time was the headquarters for the 30th Division, commanded by Maj. Gen. Charles H. Corlett. Because some units of the division were prepared and others were not, Corlett was concerned. Replacements for the divisions then in action presented a major problem to army commanders, so Marshall asked Corlett if it would help to send replacements over by regiments to be incorporated into divisions already in Europe. Corlett immediately answered in the affirmative. Marshall gave him a stern look and said, "Corlett, you are not giving me this answer just because I am Chief of Staff, are you?" Corlett blew up at the implication that he was a "yes man" and left little doubt in Marshall's mind that he had been given a straight answer. Almost a fanatic in his antipathy toward "yes men," Marshall insisted that the officer responsible for a study attend the briefing when his paper or staff report was presented. He admonished all who were present to speak out regardless of the presence of their immediate superiors.[8]

As chief of staff, Marshall initially had run-ins with Congress. One of these was in fall 1941 when he took steps to purge the army of "over the hill" and incompetent officers. He briefed Secretary Stimson of his actions at a war council meeting on September 15, 1941. Stimson's reaction to the proposal was, "I anticipate trouble."

It was not long in coming. Stimson commented in his diary, "We had scarcely finished our meeting when Senator Tom Connally of Texas . . . bounded in with his hair standing up on end and full of anger and resentment because two Texas Generals of the National Guard had been retired and sent back from active duty."[9] Marshall had retired one of these generals because of age and the other for incompetence. He refused to reconsider either decision or be intimidated by political pressure. It was this kind of strength, courage, and honesty that progressively won for him the confidence of the members of Congress.

General Joseph T. McNarney, U.S. Air Force, who was given the serial number 1A when the Army Air Force became separated from the army to stand on its own as a separate service, told me of his first meeting with General Marshall: "I was serving on the general staff in Washington in the War Plans Division just before we got into the war, and at that time I was a lieutenant colonel. I was made chief of the Plans Division under the Joint Plans Division, which was then making joint war plans with the navy. One day, General Marshall sent down for some information on the plans we were working on, but my boss was not there, so I went up. This was the first time I had ever seen General Marshall and the first time he had ever seen me. We got into a little argument. I went back to my office to get some more of the information to prove my point, along with a map I needed; I put the map on the floor to show him my point, and we had another little argument about it.

"I was a brash young man, I guess, but I didn't back off. General Marshall kept asking me questions, and I finally got a little bit irked. I said, 'My God, man, you can't do that!' He then dismissed me. I walked out of his office, and his secretary, who was an officer from the Class of 1914, tapped me on the shoulder and said, 'Don't worry about that. That's what the old man does every time. He was just feeling you out.'"

Marshall must have been favorably impressed. McNarney rose from the rank of lieutenant colonel to four-star general during World War II under Marshall.

McNarney went on to say of General Marshall: "He disliked the 'yes man.' He wouldn't have anything to do with the 'yes man.' If anybody agreed with him the first time, he would look upon him with some suspicion. Of course, it didn't necessarily always mean that, because maybe agreeing with him on that was the proper thing to do. But to come in and agree with him right away, he didn't like that. He was not a 'yes man,' and he didn't like that in people under him. He wanted frank expression of your views."[10]

Marshall did not change when he was secretary of state. On January 21, 1947, as the new secretary, he asked Dean Acheson, then an assistant secretary, to serve as the equivalent of chief of staff for the State Department. Acheson's reflections on the incident provides insight into Marshall's expectations from those who served on his staff: "Smiling inwardly at the shock which lay in store for the department, I explained that the arrangement could not work just as he outlined, and then I hastily assured him that I understood what he wanted. Was there anything else?

"There was. I have recalled it often because General Marshall's words were so typical of him. 'I shall expect of you,' he said, 'the most complete frankness, particularly about myself. I have no feelings except those I reserve for Mrs. Marshall.' With that he left me. The General's statement about his lack of sensitivity was soon to be put to the test."[11]

Douglas MacArthur was selected by President Herbert Hoover to be army chief of staff. With the Depression, times were hard and finances limited. In spite of MacArthur's efforts, the budget for the army was consistently cut during his tenure.

The cuts were bad enough, but one of the most serious challenges came from the pacifist-isolationist group in Congress that wanted to cut drastically the size of the officer corps of the regular army, a devastating move to U.S. national security. A bill was proposed to put many officers on forced furlough and halve the pay of those remaining. To head this off, MacArthur, in testimony before the House Military Affairs Committee, stated: "The foundation of our National Defense system is the Regular Army, and the foundation of the Regular Army is the officer. He is the soul of the system. If you have to cut everything out of the National Defense Act, the last element should be the officer corps. If you had to discharge every soldier, if you had to do away with everything else, I would still professionally advise you to keep those 12,000 officers. They are the mainsprings of the whole mechanism; each one of them would be worth a thousand men at the beginning of the war. They are the only ones who can take this heterogeneous mass and make it a homogeneous group."[12]

MacArthur was persuasive in his argument, and the offensive bill was tabled. The executive branch then moved to reduce the regular army budget greatly.

The secretary of war was George Dern, former governor of Utah and a successful businessman before joining Roosevelt's cabinet. He was knowledgeable on national defense matters and was disturbed about these proposed cuts. At a private meeting with the president were Dern; MacArthur and his assistant chief of staff, Gen. Hugh Drum; and the chief of engineers, Gen. Lytle Brown. The meeting did not go well. The men informed the president that Germany and Italy were arming rapidly and Japan was invading Manchuria and China, so cutting the military appropriation so much would be a fatal mistake.

Secretary Dern, a soft-spoken man, received biting comments from President Roosevelt, clearly intimidating him. But such was not the case with MacArthur, who reflected on the discussion in his memoirs: "I felt it my duty to take up the cudgels. The country's safety was at stake, and I said so bluntly. The President turned the full vials of his sarcasm upon me. He was a scorcher when he was aroused. The tension began to boil over. For the third and last time in my life, that paralyzing nausea began to creep over me. In my emotional exhaustion I spoke recklessly and said something to the general effect that when we lost the next war, and an American boy, lying in the mud with an enemy bayonet through his belly and an enemy foot on his dying throat, spat out his last curse, I wanted the name to not be MacArthur, but Roosevelt. The President grew livid. 'You must not talk that way to the President!' he roared. He was, of course, right, and I knew it almost before the words had left my mouth. I said that I was sorry and apologized. But I felt my Army career was at an end. I told him he had my resignation as Chief of Staff. As I reached the door his voice came with a cool detachment which so reflected his extraordinary self-control, 'Don't be foolish, Douglas; you and the budget must get together on this.'

"Dern had shortly reached my side and I could hear his gleeful tones, 'You've saved the Army.' But I just vomited on the steps of the White House.

"Neither the President nor I ever spoke of the meeting, but from that time on he was on our side. He sent for me frequently and often asked my comments on his social programs, but almost never again on military affairs. One evening, during dinner, curiosity and perhaps some measure of pique prompted me to ask him, 'Why is it, Mr. President, that you frequently inquire my opinion regarding the social reforms under consideration, matters about which I am currently no authority, but pay little attention to my views on the military?' His reply took all the wind out of my sails. He said, 'Douglas, I don't bring these questions up for your advice but for your reactions. To me, you are the symbol of the conscience of the American people.'"[13]

Again, we have an example of an officer whose strength of character was such that he refused to be a "yes man." Instead of being fired, MacArthur became a valuable asset to his commander in chief.

Although some would challenge it, others have argued that MacArthur did not appreciate "yes men" as commanders of U.S. forces in the Far East during World War II. One individual said of him, "MacArthur cannot stand to take advice. It is his greatest defect that he has to do everything alone." Some would say he was so brilliant and intuitive that he didn't need advice. This was not true. Along this same line of criticism, accusations were made about MacArthur that his staff during World War II was filled with "yes men." Nor was this true. He sought and received advice from his staff on all major decisions, and he insisted upon honest opinions. He quickly got rid of anyone who seemed to insincerely or fawningly agree with him.

Much has been made by the media and certain historians that MacArthur and the navy did not get along during World War II. Actually, under MacArthur's leadership, interservice rivalry was kept to a minimum. Admiral "Bull" Halsey, so named because of his tenacious and outspoken personality, was charmed by the eloquence and logic of MacArthur. Halsey reflected: "The over-all strategy of the whole area was in MacArthur's hands; the Joint Chiefs of Staff had put tactical command of the Solomons sub-area in mine. Although this arrangement was sensible and satisfactory, it had the curious effect of giving me two 'hats' in the same echelon. My original hat was under Nimitz, who controlled my troops, ships, and supplies; now I had another hat under MacArthur, who controlled my strategy.

"To discuss plans for New Georgia with him, I requested an appointment at his headquarters, which were then in Brisbane, Australia, and I flew across from Noumea early in April. I had never met the General before, but we had one tenuous connection: my father had been a friend of his father's in the Philippines more than forty years back. Five minutes after I reported, I felt as if we were lifelong friends. I have seldom seen a man who makes a quicker, stronger, more favorable impression. He was then sixty-three years old, but he could have passed as fifty. His hair was jet black; his eyes were clear; his carriage was erect. If he had been wearing civilian clothes, I still would have known at once that he was a soldier.

"The respect that I had for him that afternoon grew steadily during the war and continues to grow as I watch his masterly administration of surrendered Japan. I can recall no flaw in our relationship. We had arguments, but they always ended pleasantly. Not once did he, my superior officer, ever force his decisions upon me. On the few occasions when I disagreed with him, I told him so, and we discussed the issue until one of us changed his mind. My mental picture poses him against the background of these discussions; heels pacing his office, almost wearing a groove between his large, bare desk and the portrait of George Washington that faced it; his corncob pipe in his hand (I rarely saw him smoke it); and he is making his points in a diction I have never heard surpassed."[14]

It was necessary, however, to be very persuasive to convince MacArthur. On one occasion, he had a meeting with Halsey concerning a jurisdictional issue between MacArthur's "turf" and that of the navy. Halsey wrote of this session:

> When he had finished, he pointed his pipe stem at me and demanded. "Am I not right, Bill?"
>
> Tom Kinkaid, Mick, Felix, and I answered with one voice, "NO, Sir!"
>
> MacArthur smiled and said pleasantly "Well if so many fine gentlemen disagree with me, we'd better examine the proposition once more. Bill, what's your opinion?"
>
> "General," I said, "I disagree with you entirely. Not only that, but I'm going one step further and tell you that if you stick to this order of yours, you'll be hampering the war effort!"
>
> His staff gasped. I imagine they never expected to hear those terms this side of the Judgment Throne, if then. I told him that the command of Manus didn't matter a whit to me. What did matter was the quick construction of the base. Kenney or an Australian or an enlisted cavalryman could boss it for all I cared, as long as it was ready to handle the fleet when we moved up New Guinea and on toward the Philippines.
>
> The argument had begun at 1700. By 1800 when we broke up, I thought I had won him around, but next morning at 1000 he asked us to come back to his office. (He kept unusual hours from 1000 until 1400, and from 1600 until 2100 or later.) It seemed that during the night he had become mad all over again, and again was dead set on restricting the work. We went through the same arguments as the afternoon before, almost word for word, and at the end of an hour we reached the same

conclusion: the work would proceed. I was about to tell him good-by and fly back to Noumea when he suddenly asked if we would return at 1700. I'll be damned if we didn't run the course a third time! This time, though, it was really final. He gave me a charming smile and said, "You win, Bill!" and to General Sutherland, "Dick, go ahead with the job."[15]

A superb example of character and leadership in dealing with a wartime ally, particularly in an aversion to being a "yes man," was Gen. Joseph W. Stilwell. There were few on active duty in the U.S. Army who were as accomplished in Asian affairs and fluent in the Chinese language as Stilwell when Pearl Harbor was bombed on December 7, 1941. He spoke and read Chinese fluently and knew Chinese psychology and government. In addition, he was an extremely able soldier. When we entered World War II, General Marshall chose him for a third tour in China to become chief of staff to Chiang Kai-shek, the Chinese nationalist leader. Stilwell's first mission in 1942 was the unsuccessful attempt to try to stop the Japanese army's advance through Burma. The loss of Burma cut off the Burma road, an important link between China and her western Allies. Chiang gave Stilwell command of the Chinese Fifth and Sixth Armies, a frustrating command. The Chinese wouldn't attack, and Chiang, whose Chinese generals were "yes men," was constantly undermining Stilwell's authority.

After the Japanese defeated the Chinese and Allies in Burma, Stilwell had to save the U.S. Army and Chinese army personnel for whom he was responsible. When the railroad became inoperative, they had to walk out of Burma, suffering incredible hardships—disease, the difficulties of the jungle, enemy soldiers, wild animals, hunger, and exhaustion. They made it through, thanks to the tenacity, leadership, and character of Stilwell.

Stilwell believed that Chinese soldiers needed only proper training and leadership to be effective fighters. When he took over, he found that the soldiers were starved, sickly, and underequipped. Most individual Chinese officers were able and honest; it was the top brass who caused the problem, because corruption was part of the way things were run.

The United States was sending millions of dollars to Chiang in weapons and credit. President Roosevelt and General Marshall consistently backed Stilwell in his differences with Chiang. Roosevelt and Marshall believed that Stilwell's leadership would provide an effective Chinese army, so much so that Roosevelt proposed that Stilwell be given command of the entire Chinese army. But because Stilwell refused to be a "yes man," Chiang was indignant and insisted on his recall. Finally, in October 1944, Stilwell returned to the United States. This was unfortunate, because Stilwell understood the minds of the Chinese soldiers and could generate a spark in them that most of the Chinese generals could not. History established that his retreat through the Burmese jungle and leading a Chinese army to the capture of Mykikyana was a brilliant example of tactical planning and execution.

What caused the difficulty between Chiang and Stilwell was Stilwell's refusal to be a "yes man." Chiang was a dictator and was surrounded by "yes men," as most dictators are. Stilwell wrote in his diary, "In all fairness, it must have been a severe strain on him [Chiang Kai-shek] to put a foreigner in command of regular Chinese troops in action at all. It had never been done before, and he was trying it on short acquaintance with a man he knew little about. Even though, as I found out later, he had ways of effectively circumscribing the authority he apparently delegated without restrictions, the face of the Chinese high command was severely affected and it put an extra burden on me to gain their confidence." Chiang constantly interfered, even though he was 1,600 miles from the front, and repeatedly sent instructions on what Stilwell was to do "based on fragmentary information, and a cockeyed conception of tactics. He thinks he knows . . . everything, and wobbles this way and then [changes] his mind at every change in action . . . He [consistently interferes with my] authority . . . The army and division commanders are vitally interested in doing what they think he wants them to do. Why should they obey me?"

Stilwell's character was illustrated with a comment he wrote on April 1, 1942: "Chiang Kai-Shek has been boss so long and has so many 'yes men' around him that he has the idea he is infallible on any subject. . . . My only concern is to tell him the truth and go about my business. If I can't get by that way, the hell with it: it is patently impossible for me to compete with the swarms of parasites and syco- phants that surround him."

In a letter to his wife dated June 7, 1942, from Chungking, Stil- well wrote, "I made a report to the Big Boy [Chiang]. I told him the whole truth, and it was like kicking an old lady in the stomach. How- ever, as far as I can find out, no one else dares tell him the truth, so it's up to me all the more. . . . I pay no attention to them all—just go ahead and let nature take its course."

There are times that when an officer speaks up, he is "put down" and is better off for it. For example, after George Marshall retired as chief of staff of the U.S. Army in October 1945, General Eisen- hower succeeded him in that position. J. Lawton Collins had learned that Ike was going to appoint him to a new job, that of chief of army information. Collins was upset, so he went to Ike to "head off the as- signment." Collins described the interview with Eisenhower in his memoirs: "The general greeted me with a friendly grin, but his ex- pressive face changed to a frown as I fired my opening gun. 'I've been hearing rumors that you are considering recommending me to be Chief of Information of the War Department, but I would like you to know that I don't want any part of it.' I paused for a moment as his smile quickly became a scowl, then added: 'I thought my métier was commanding troops.'

"Ike growled at me, 'Joe, what have you been doing for the past two years?' I beat a hasty retreat. Next day, December 16, 1945, or- ders were issued appointing me Chief of Information of the War De- partment."[16]

Ike knew what he was doing. Collins was a man of character, straightforward and open. The army was being subjected to much criticism from the media and Congress in the handling of the re- duction of the military and of the occupation of Germany. Collins developed excellent relations with much of the press because of his candor, but at times he lost patience. Ike sent Collins to Europe to do something about the bad press.

A reporter asked Collins if he thought that the American people were aware of the complexity of the occupation, and he replied with firm frankness, as told in his own words:

"No," and when asked, "Why not?" I said, "because you fellows spend most of your time concentrating on scandal instead of the important aspects of the cold war being fought between the Russian and Allied Forces of occupation."

My statement was reported by all the wire services and understandably raised the ire of American reporters in Germany. They were waiting for me with sharpened pencils when I went to Berlin. There, on August 19, 1946, I was the guest of the Berlin Press Club at an unusual dinner. Attendance was limited to club members, myself, and one aide. After a pleasant round of cocktails and an excellent meal, I was subjected to an attack by Kendal Foss, Chairman of the Correspondents Association of Berlin, and others, who made the point that as long as there was scandalous conduct among the officers and men in our occupation forces, it would be reported by the press. I agreed that it should be, but stuck to my guns that the scandal reports were far out of balance with the general character of the Army's performance, and overshadowed the real problems of the occupation.

Finally one man spoke up and said he agreed with me to some extent, but that I should talk to the city editors at home. He said he had been sending reports for months on our difficulties with the Russians without any response. Then he wired a story on pregnant nurses and immediately received a reply, "Send us more of the same."

I wound up the discussion by saying that the whole object of my trip was to emphasize to our commanders that they would get no better reports from the press than their performance deserved, to which the reporters chorused "Amen!" It may have been wishful thinking, but I felt my give-and-take exchange with the Berlin press had a salutary effect on them and our officer corps.[17]

This assignment, and Collins's success in the position, was significant in his ultimate success. "In retrospect," he said, "much as I objected to my assignment as Chief of Information, if I had deliberately chosen a position in which to school myself to be Army Chief of Staff,

I could not possibly have picked a better one. It gave me insight to the problems of congressional, public, and army information relations that I could not have gotten any other way.

"As Chief of Information, I saw Eisenhower almost daily and we came to know one another on a more personal basis, which probably accounted for his telling me one day, in the autumn of 1947, that he wished to make me his Deputy. This came out of the blue. I said, of course, that I would be delighted, but wondered if we might not think too much alike on most matters, and if he wouldn't be better served by someone less outspoken—a remark that Ike simply waved aside. So, on September 1, 1947, I became Deputy Chief of Staff of the Army. As Deputy, I relieved the Chief of most of the routine business of his office."[18]

Later in 1947, Collins was appointed to succeed Eisenhower as army chief of staff. After being informed that he had been designated as the next chief, Collins called Gen. Wade Haislip on the phone and said, "Wade, I've been informed I am to be the next chief of staff of the army, and I'd like you to be my deputy. Will you take the job?" Haislip responded, "Why do you want me? You and I haven't agreed on anything in thirty years." Collins replied, "That's exactly why I want you."[19]

Collins did not want a "yes man." No outstanding leader does.

But one should not disagree just for the sake of showing you are not a "yes man." I asked Lt. Gen. James Doolittle if it were correct that General Eisenhower did not want him as his air commander in the North African campaign early in World War II. Doolittle confirmed that statement, saying that, at a staff conference, Eisenhower had given a briefing on his ideas for the plans for a forthcoming invasion of North Africa and then asked for the views of the group that was present. "Patton told him what he would do, and then Eisenhower called upon me...," said Doolittle. "Ike responded, 'The first thing we will do is capture the airfields.' I should have said, 'Yes, General Eisenhower, that's the first thing we have to do after the group troops are ashore—secure the airfields.'

"It was so obvious," said Doolittle. "I then did as stupid a thing as could be done. I continued to talk and said, 'General, the airfields will be of no value to us until we have supplies, the oil, the gas, the bombs, the ammunition, the supporting men, the food, and the facilities to take care of them.' This was all true. But it wasn't what I should have said. What I was doing was pointing out to my superior that he didn't know what he was talking about. I should have merely said, instead of what I did say, General Eisenhower, you are quite right. The first things that we must have are the airfields, and after that, with all possible expedition, get in the supplies to accomplish this."

"I watched Eisenhower's face as I spoke; I could have chewed my tongue off because I knew what I had done. But it was too late. It took me a year to overcome that. I am not suggesting that you become a 'yes man.' What I am suggesting is what you should not do is to imply that your superior is a little stupid for not having mentioned these things all at the same time. I do not believe in being a 'yes man.' I do believe in using tact in getting ideas over."[20]

When I asked what the relationship of a commander with his people should be during the decision-making process, General Spaatz, the first chief of staff of a separate air force, responded, "I certainly wanted to have the respect of the people around me, but I didn't want them to have any fear. I always encouraged all members of my staff and the commanders to feel free to discuss anything with me they wanted to. And I always liked to have at least one man on staff who disagreed with the others. To have a real good 'no man.' He had to be a pretty smart, talkative individual."

When asked the purpose of the "no man," Spaatz answered, "To challenge before the decision is made. But all this has to take place before the decision is made. That is the difference between what I call a successful commander and an unsuccessful commander. If there's no challenge before the decision, and after the decision is made the challenge comes up, then there is indecisiveness, which in military operations can end in disaster."[21]

General Nathan F. Twining, air force chief of staff from 1952 to 1956 and the first air force officer to be selected as chairman of the Joint Chiefs of Staff, expressed the "no man" concept, suggesting that the decision maker has to be tough and have a thick skin. He commented in a similar vein: "Another thing about leadership is that you should say what you think. Nobody can be so great that they don't have to listen to others. Some people think they are, and that's where they get into trouble. Sure, they can be geniuses on the piano or violin or a specialty like that, but that's not leadership; that's personal accomplishment. In leadership, you have got to have the ability to sit back and listen to your staff or an individual who briefs you—men who can speak with authority. You have got to have the courage to sit down and listen, have them say what they think is right, no matter how sore you might get at them. You also need a commander who will come in and tell you off when he thinks you are wrong. I have had that happen to me many times, and it's been helpful to me. It sure takes the ego out of you, too."[22]

General Bruce K. Holloway, U.S. Air Force, felt the same way about the "no man" who Spaatz and Doolittle referred to. Holloway had a remarkable career: flying fighters in combat with the Flying Tigers in China early in World War II; becoming an ace by shooting down thirteen Japanese planes; serving on the staff as director of operational requirements, responsible for a vital role in the development of many air force aircraft and missile systems; and capping a brilliant career as the first nonlongtime Strategic Air Command (SAC) officer to be its commander. In an interview with me, Holloway addressed the issue of the "yes man" when he answered my question, "As a commander, what do you look for in the leadership of your subordinates?" Said Holloway: "Primarily getting results. I didn't like anyone who had a slight degree of being a 'yes man,' nor anyone that took exception to my views just to back up a reputation or a belief that they had to do that to assert their character. There were some of those around who were too much of a 'no man.' They are in the minority, but I avoided them like the plague, too.

Well, I guess what you might say I was looking for was somebody who had a combination of experience and intellectual integrity. By intellectual integrity I mean someone who will disagree with me when they really disagree in substance but who will immediately agree with me if he does agree with me rather than think, Well, I have got to make an appearance of disagreeing whether I do or not, or be a devil's advocate. There are a few of those around."[23]

* * *

Holloway particularly named a major general who would disagree with him whether he actually did or not. Holloway commented that this man irritated many people that way: "I would never have hired that general, if I had any option in it, for that very reason. There are a few people like him that are tremendously endowed otherwise, who are going to disagree. You might bring them around and they might be loyal and probably would be if you sat them down. You have got to talk real straight to these guys. After you have discussed it and they still argue, I would say, 'Either do it like I tell you or I'll get somebody else who will.'

"I would very cheerfully put up with the somewhat less than genius level of intellect of judgment if I thought the guy was honest with himself and with me and tried his damnedest to do what I wanted to do after the decision was made, but who still would tell me if he disagreed. I would rather have somebody like that than a supergenius who had some kind of a thwarted ego that usually comes out of being a superhigh intelligence level. I just don't like them. I would prefer to have some guy who is well balanced in his attitudes. If you find them, well, boy, you've got a gold mine. And I had gotten several gold mines during my career. I think that's why I did as well as I did. I know it is. No individual is so smart that he does well on his jobs all on his own. He just isn't. And the people that think they are rarely get there."[24]

General Edwin W. Rawlings had the unique responsibility of commanding air materiel command for eight years immediately after the air force became a separate service. During that period of time, he made decisions on spending $96 billion. He commented: "A leader must create the best atmosphere in a command for decision making. All my effort when I was running air materiel command was to seek out and assign the good people I could get for the particular key jobs I had. If you work at it hard enough, naturally you get the best ones for the best slots. Then it becomes easier to get a good one to replace him when he has to leave, because one of the qualities of a good leader is that he is always training someone to follow him, so it begins to snowball.

"There are all sorts of ways of doing it. I did it with a monthly review of our operation with my commanders and key staff members. We would look at all of our problems, and each top man was given the opportunity to express his philosophy, his attitude, and to keep everybody abreast of the facts of the problem he had to deal with at that particular period of time. Generally, people are a lot better than we think they are, so the responsibility of the top man, I think, is to create an atmosphere where they can use their full horsepower. Part of that is knowing the problems the top man is dealing with, what factors surround these problems, what is the top man's personal philosophy. By that, I don't mean 'yes men.'

"One of the grave hazards of command is that too many people will tell you what they think you want to hear. So you have to work very hard to create an atmosphere in which they are willing to disagree with you. This is not easy. If you take decisive action, they are apt to think you will hold it against them if they disagree. My philosophy was one of wanting everybody to say what he thinks, because none of us is smart enough to think about everything. Somebody will have an idea or a thought that, if we knew it, might change our course. Now, once you make the decision, that's something else. You expect everybody to carry out the decision, and if they don't, you're in trouble. But if you have created this atmosphere to draw out a lot more people's ideas, they are more likely to be happy, for if they aren't happy, they aren't going to work as well."[25]

General David C. Jones, air force chief of staff from 1974 to 1978, tried hard to establish an atmosphere receptive to speaking up. Major General Henry J. Meade, then air force chaplain, reflected: "I recall watching David Jones conduct many, many of our commanders' conferences. It's a credit to his staff that they were not timid of him, nor was the senior leadership timid of him. They would let the chief know what they thought. General Jones never lost his cool. He never, never showed irritation. . . . I recall there was one period of time when the matter of fringe benefits was under attack. General Jones, acting as a devil's advocate, challenged his senior officers to justify certain of these benefits. He was trying to solicit the strongest arguments in defending these benefits. At no time did General Jones ever lose his cool, ever show irritation, ever show impatience. He was the master of holding himself under control. I never saw him, at any time in the four years, get ruffled. I think that's remarkable for a guy. And certainly at a time when you need a cool head, that's a powerful feature of a man's conduct and behavior, don't you suppose?"[26]

General Charles Gabriel, air force chief of staff from 1982 to 1986, was also adverse to "yes men": "You want to do the best job for the air force; you don't want 'yes men' on your staff. But you also need to be careful how you say 'no' when you disagree with somebody. You need people who are giving you their utmost. You also get a feeling about your people—their background, their experience, their judgment. You sort out who has the strongest case. You don't worry about who is on your side and who isn't.

"I want to particularly emphasize that the worst thing that can happen in the relationship between a commander and his staff is for [the men] to be afraid to say something for fear of being wrong. Many commanders have denied themselves the proper information because of cutting down a staff member for his input."[27]

General Larry Welch, who succeeded General Gabriel as air force chief of staff, had the same outlook: "There's a great problem when you hear only things that people think you want to hear, but you can recognize that instantly. And those were not the people we picked for the air staff, and I've watched this over a number of years. We just don't pick these men. The only way that you can get 'yes men' on the air staff is for you to turn them into 'yes men,' that is, for you to not tolerate differences of opinion or for you to reward the 'yes man' instead of the 'no man.' I haven't seen any tendency for chiefs to tolerate 'yes men,' of all the chiefs I've known. That's just not air force. That's just not the way we are."[28]

When Lieutenant Colonel Schwarzkopf volunteered for a second tour in Vietnam to serve as a battalion commander, he already exhibited strong character and leadership. He was certainly not a "yes man" as a combat leader. He related an experience illustrative of the unit he had recently joined: "The next day I was awakened with the news that a dawn patrol had shot a Vietcong sneaking through the wire along our perimeter. On his body they'd found detailed sketches of LZ Bayonet—the sort of reconnaissance needed for one of the Vietcong's most devastating tactics, called a sapper attack."[29]

This brought to Schwarzkopf's attention the terrible lack of preparedness of the unit he had inherited. His brigade commander, Col. Joe Clemons, a national hero and winner of the Distinguished Service Cross in the battle of Pork Chop Hill during the Korean War, came to visit and inspect Schwarzkopf's unit. He was horrified to find bunkers caved in, gaps in the barbed wire surrounding the camp so the enemy could easily go through, and the Claymore mines rusted and turned around so that if they went off they would throw the shrapnel inward, killing and maiming American soldiers.

After seeing the sad condition, Clemons turned to Schwarzkopf. "This is a disgrace. I've never seen anything this bad in all my years in the army." Schwarzkopf, of course, agreed with his commander: "We walked the whole perimeter, and the colonel berated me the entire way. I knew he was right: if there had been a sniper attack the night before, a great many of my men would have died.

"As soon as he left, I rounded up the officers and NCOs and we spent the entire day making sure sandbags got filled, foxholes dug, and Claymores replaced so we could defend the camp. We extended the perimeter to take in the operations center and my cabin, although I had decided that eventually both would be moved down into the base. Clemons' reproaches kept echoing in my mind. I decided I couldn't work with a commander who doubted my competence. I called and asked if we could meet. He received me at his headquarters that evening but did not offer me a seat.

"'Sir, you had every reason to be angry at what you found at my unit today,' I said. 'But I want you to know that I was angry, too. I was as shocked as you at the state of that perimeter. And I recognize I was at fault not to have inspected it as soon as I took command.'

"Clemons locked eyes with me as I spoke and didn't say a word. I took a breath and continued. 'I don't know what you know about my unit. But on the basis of two days' experience, I can tell you I've probably inherited the worst battalion in the United States Army. I know what's wrong and I will fix it, but that can't happen overnight. And it won't do any good for you to chew my ass off every time you come around. You'll just slow me down.'

"He didn't say anything, just kept staring at me with his icy blue eyes. Finally he said, 'Colonel Schwarzkopf, I want to tell you that

I've inherited the worst *brigade* in the United States Army. I'm willing to believe you know what needs to be done. Now let's do it together.' There was no smiling or backslapping—we were both under the gun."[30]

Schwarzkopf had another experience in Vietnam that illustrates a price that some pay for not being a "yes man." It also emphasizes the need for tact when poor leadership is encountered. One day an assistant division commander flew in to inform Schwarzkopf that his unit wasn't killing enough Vietcong. This man's career had been in the Army Corps of Engineers and he really didn't understand combat, not having served his time in the trenches. He made a decision that showed no grasp of the infantry combat situation. Schwarzkopf, realizing this, informed him it wouldn't work, and gave him reasons. "This made the general furious. 'Well, that just sounds like a leadership problem to me! Obviously you need to exercise firmer control over the men in this battalion.'

"Stung, I was on the brink of saying, 'General, I'm sorry, but I cannot obey your order.'

"Luckily, Joe Clemons stepped in and said, 'Sir, Schwarzkopf's analysis is absolutely correct. What you're suggesting would not be a wise course of action.' The general stormed out of the bunker too angry to speak.

"If Clemons hadn't interposed himself, my career might have ended on the spot. The general was just vindictive enough to say, 'That's insubordination. Since you refuse to follow my orders, you are relieved of your command.' Instead, Clemons took the heat. It was the right thing to do—a commander sticks up for his subordinates when they're right—yet it required tremendous moral courage."[31]

General Schwarzkopf expressed to me his attitude toward "yes men": "I would bring along with me, or would seek to have serving under me, people who were not intimidated by me. When you're a general, when you're six foot four, when you weigh two hundred and fifty pounds, and when you're as enthusiastic as I am about everything and you want so much to succeed, and you do not want to fail, you can intimidate a lot of people. Some people would crumble in front of me, and the guys that I want around me are the guys who wouldn't crumble. Guys that would say, wait a minute, sir, you're out in left field on this, or you're wrong on this, or I don't agree with you on this, or I think you're doing the wrong thing. I wouldn't always agree with them, but the point is that the people I wanted around me were the people who, if they thought I was making a mistake, or if they thought I was doing something wrong, would not hesitate to tell me that. You've got to have that. The absolute worst thing in the world you can have around you is a bunch of 'yes men.'"[32]

I had the opportunity to discuss in great depth the concept of "yes men" with Adm. William J. Crowe, Jr., chairman of the Joint Chiefs of Staff from 1979 to 1983. I inquired of him about the value of candid input. He responded: "I'm human. Sometimes a 'no man' really upsets me. You have something you want to do and here comes some wise son of a bitch and tells you that's a dumb idea. That gets under your skin. But those are the kind of guys who really matter. But it is so hard to fill out a good fitness report on an abrasive guy.

"But I did run into several people who were not 'yes men' who just cut their own throats. They got so enamored with being disagreers that they didn't give a great deal of thought to how they disagreed. There are ways to let people know you are not aboard and that you think you have a better idea without just totally pushing them off a cliff. That's an art.

"The secretary of defense will depend on your advice and if he's smart will depend a lot on your advice; he'll always seek it. But if you go in there and tell him he's wrong every time he asks a question, you lose your credibility. He doesn't have to seek your advice; then pretty soon he's going to say I don't know why I want to talk to Crowe about this, he's a disagreeable son of a bitch. The secretary of defense can cut the chairman right out of the problem.

"When dealing with the secretary, you . . . agree with him on most things that don't matter one way or another and when you have something that matters, you've got to step up. That doesn't come naturally. You have to work at that. You have to work at getting your guts up to speak up."[33]

Just as with Marshall, Eisenhower, and MacArthur, Crowe thought his career might have come to an end with his candidness. In my interview with him he commented, "Admiral Haywood had a vice commander by the name of Bob Long. I'm a great admirer of Bob Long. I did not know him before my assignment to the office of the chief of naval operations. He was a nuclear submariner. He had been there about a week and had called me up and started telling me something about my business and I really stood up to him. His executive assistant came down, a friend of mine, and said Bob Long doesn't like that—nobody talks to Bob Long that way. I said to myself, Well, that's the end of that. I thought I was finished. It didn't turn out to be the end at all."

I discussed the "yes man" concept with Gen. Colin Powell and his standing up earlier in his career to his then superior officer Maj. Gen. John W. Hudachek, his division commander of the 4th Infantry Division at Fort Carson in Colorado, to which Powell was assigned as assistant division commander. Powell agreed with me on the importance of not being a "yes man." The scenario is well developed in his book *My American Journey:* "I started hearing complaints from fellow officers that we had a co-commander at Fort Carson. While General Hudachek rode herd on his subordinates, the wives reported that Mrs. Hudachek did the same on them. The Hudacheks were a devoted couple, and the general had made his wife his partner in running the post. Ann Hudachek served prominently in all the advisory councils he had set up to oversee the commissary, the PX, the childcare center, everything. She obviously had a deep commitment to the welfare of the soldiers under her husband's command and to their families. The rub was the brusque way both Hudacheks went about their roles. I became the lightning rod for these grievances. Finally, I decided, yes, pay the king his shilling, and the queen, too, if necessary. But the situation at Fort Carson had gone too far. I had been watching it for four months and saw morale sagging. I believed that I had a responsibility to act."[34]

Powell went to Hudachek's chief of staff, Col. Tom Blagg, requesting an appointment and informing him what he wanted to see Hudachek about. He was warned, "Colin, . . . don't do it. . . . I'm warning you—you won't help him. And you might hurt yourself." Powell went ahead anyway, and as Blagg had predicted it was not appreciated and it did not go well.[35]

I have given many lectures to junior officers on leadership. Often I have been asked during the question and answer periods, "But what if you stand up for what's right and you're punished for it?" This is what happened to Colin Powell with General Hudachek. Powell commented:

> By May 20, 1982, I had completed my first year at Fort Carson. The man who ten months before had wanted to put my name before the major general selection board called me into his office. "Sit down," Hudachek said. He was a chain-smoker, and the cigarette trembled in his hand as he handed me a two-page document. This was my annual efficiency report. My future hung on these pages. When I finished reading it, I said, "Is this your considered judgment?" He nodded. "You realize the effect it will have?" I said. "This report will probably end my career." "Oh no," Hudachek protested. I was coming along fine, he assured me. And he would be rating me again next year. "The next report will take care of you," he added. Unconvinced, I excused myself, got up, and left.[36]
>
> I went to bed that night with my head in a whirl. This was the worst professional judgment passed on me in twenty-four years in the Army. Bernie Rogers had warned me at charm school that 50 percent of us were not going to make two stars. I now knew which half I fell into. At GOMO, the General Officer Management Office in the Pentagon, young lieutenant colonels who move generals around would look at this report and think, this walk-on-water soldier had finally been punctured. Powell turned out to be just a political general. Can't hack it in the field. Shy Meyer would see the report and shake his head; Colin's been away from the troops too long. And the next promotion board would look at an unblemished record until now, and wonder, what happened to this guy? I slept poorly that night.[37]

I discussed this with Gen. Shy Meyer, who was chief of staff of the army at the time. He informed me that he heard about Powell's problem with Hudachek and proceeded to pull him out from the division and place him in a two-star job, thus saving his career.[38]

One of the first issues that Powell had with President Bill Clinton concerned gays in the military. "It was perhaps one of the most difficult times in my military life," Powell said when he came in with a decidedly different view on this issue than the one held by the president and commander in chief.

> All the powers said, well, this is what the president wants to do. What's your view? I said, "My view is the same view that I gave to the previous president. If this president wishes to move in this direction, then he will give us an order to do so. But if he asks me my advice, it must be the same advice I gave to George Bush last week." That caused all kinds of hell to break loose, but I was . . . accused of being a disloyal general, and that I was essentially disloyal to the president. Well, you can imagine how that feels when people say those things about you. I caught hell during that period and as I subsequently said to people, "Look, if the president had decided on the day that he took over a change of policy, I would have executed that. He didn't. He asked me my advice and I gave it to him. And it would have been the height of disloyalty for me to have changed my advice over a period of two days because the commander in chief changed."[39]

I then commented, "It was in the papers that you were threatening to resign. Did you or any of the other chiefs?" He responded:

> No. I had a lot of generals writing to say you have to resign over this. And I said no. I never considered resigning over anything. Because I'm not commander in chief; he is. And my inspiration comes from Marshall. Marshall, in 1947 or '48, when he argued vociferously against recognizing Israel and when he lost it, when Truman said we're going to do it, some thought Marshall should resign.[40]

In my interview with Gen. John M. Shalikashvili, chairman of the Joint Chiefs of Staff from 1993 to 1997, we were discussing MacArthur's standing up to President Roosevelt when MacArthur was chief of staff. "I've not had any dramatic moments like when

MacArthur was chief of staff. On the other hand, I think that each one of us who served in very senior positions, have had moments when he found himself in disagreement with senior political leaders, perhaps even with the commander-in-chief. It's at moments like that one has to stand up and be counted. During my four years as chairman these moments were never as dramatic as those in which MacArthur was involved but they involved such issues, for instance, as whether the administration was sufficiently resourcing the military. I remember when I first testified before Congress that we were some twenty billion dollars underfunded in our acquisition accounts and what a stir that caused.

"There were also a number of times there were disagreements over other issues, such as the proper task for our forces in places like Bosnia, or over particular arms control proposals. But in each case, as the discussion went on you could sense that you owed the country and the president that you stick by your guns and give your best military advise, not the most popular advise. In the end the president always made it crystal clear that he wanted my best judgement even if that didn't coincide with the judgement of his other advisors or even his own. In turn you have to be sure that you have done your homework and that your advise is in fact the very best advise you can give, After all, your country might have to live with your recommendation and lives may depend on it. In this regard, I am very proud of the fellow members of the Joint Chiefs who served with me and how well they handled the many tough issues that often confronted them. They were always willing to stand up for what they believed to have been right."[41]

Air force general David C. Jones, chairman of the Joint Chiefs from 1978 to 1982, provides an example of one of our military officer's refusal to be a "yes man" in his campaign for reorganization of the Joint Chiefs of Staff. It was a crusade on Jones's part that resulted in the most significant change in our military organization since World War II. It was a change that the aforementioned chairmen Crowe, Powell, and Shalikashvili, benefited from, as well as our whole military establishment.

Jones's concern went back many years in his career. "My first exposure to the joint system," he told me, "came while I was aide to

General Curtis LeMay. LeMay told me that my first responsibility as aide was to learn, and he included me in almost all of his meetings, even those with the Joint Chiefs of Staff. There was a sharp contrast between the cumbersome procedures in the joint system and the very fast-moving, highly efficient operations at SAC. My reaction was that someone should do something about the joint system, never realizing I would one day be involved."

His concern deepened with the joint system during his short tour in Vietnam with what he considered the misuse of airpower, a problem that was never adequately addressed. The problem then was not only President Johnson's poring over target lists. Several years later, in the summer of 1974 when General Jones became air force chief of staff, he commented, "I felt the many long JCS meetings were an intrusion on my time. I must say it bored me to go down there to the tank, to sit there. I was a good soldier, and I would go when I was in town . . . but my heart wasn't in it. I believe my colleagues agreed with me, but we couldn't come to an agreement on how to change."

There were two particular "war" activities that emphasized the need for change. Jones commented that when he was vice air force commander in Vietnam: "I saw how the joint system really couldn't come to grips with what was going on. We fought at least six different air wars: the navy war in the north, the air force war in the north, the strategic one, the air force war in the south, the Vietnamese war, the army helicopters . . .

"Secondly, there was the April 25, 1980, abortive, and embarrassing failure of the military raid, code named Operation Eagle Claw, to rescue fifty-three American hostages from our embassy in Teheran held captive in Iran. The attempt to rescue them was aborted when only three of the helicopters were operational at the point of rendezvous."

The change that Jones advocated was ultimately implemented through the Goldwater-Nichols Department of Defense Reorganization Act of 1986.

Jones wanted to reform the organization in his first two-year term as chairman, and do it internally working with the service chiefs, but he soon realized that the military service could not reorganize itself. It had to come from the outside: A service chief, as David Jones had been, was "first the chief of his service. History had shown that a chief who does not fight tooth and nail for his own service may soon lose his effectiveness."

Jones knew he would upset the other services, that there would be a "holy" war over the Pentagon's established "turf," that there would be personal attacks from retired military officers as well as active members. He broke ranks with his Pentagon colleagues, knowing that the "military brotherhood" wouldn't like his suggested changes, that he was a turncoat, that the military services were not likely to give up any of their influence. It was unusual within the U.S. military for the "brotherhood" to be critical of senior officers, but the tradition was abandoned in the efforts of the opposition to change to tear down Jones and destroy his reform campaign. In addition, the civilian component of the Department of Defense felt its "empire" threatened in effectiveness because of the high turnover of the political appointees, resulting in a lack of continuity and expertise. This also applied to the military members of the Joint Staff, who average at most two-and-a-half-year tours.

Jones, in leading the fight for change, carefully followed the rules about the appropriate relationship between the military and the civilian authority. He made it clear to the Senate Armed Forces Committee and then Secretary of Defense Harold Brown that he was going to "press for reorganization of the joint system during the next two years. He [Brown] was very supportive and offered to help in any way he could."

With Reagan's election as president, his secretary of defense was Casper Weinberger. When Jones alerted Weinberger, "He responded that he looked forward to receiving my recommendations." When Jones raised the subject later, Weinberger stated that he did not want to address reorganization, for many would conclude that the joint system was all screwed up, and that would impact negatively on the budget. Jones commented that we were screwed up, that many on the hill knew it, and credit would be given if the subject were addressed. Jones commented: "Although Cap was very courteous whenever the subject was raised, I was never able to persuade him."

To accomplish the change, Jones realized that as chairman he was the logical one to seek the changes, particularly because his tenure as a member of the Joint Chiefs for eight years was longer than that of anyone in its forty-year history. It would be a weak argument that he was trying to build an empire for himself, because he had only a few months left as chairman. It was obvious that strengthening the role of the chairman would apply to his successor, not him. He concluded that the change had to come from the Congress and that the press had to be engaged in the process to keep the momentum going and put pressure on Congress to support changes.

To the press Jones said, "During my few remaining months in office, I am striving to make substantial changes in the organization of the Joint Chiefs of Staff. . . . Frankly, I am trying to build support for needed change. I would appreciate any help you could give."

The *New York Times*, in an editorial, wrote: "Rarely have military officers, bred in the tradition of keeping their own counsel except when asked by properly contributed civilian authority, undertaken so public a campaign for change."

As Jones expressed his position: "Although I recognize the very strong and persistent headwinds, I could not leave office in good conscience this summer without making a major effort to illuminate the real issues once more and hopefully wrest some substantial change."[42]

Since its enactment, the Goldwater-Nichols Act, brilliantly negotiated by General Jones, has been heralded as "perhaps the most important defense legislation since World War II," as "the most significant changes in the . . . organizational structure of the Department of Defense since 1949 . . . ," and by the late Les Aspin, former chairman of the House Armed Forces Committee and secretary of defense, as "one of the landmarks of American history. It is probably the greatest single change in the history of the American military since the Continental Congress created the Continental Army in 1775."

The careers of all the generals in this study are marred by experiences when they were not "yes men" and didn't tolerate such men on their staff. It was a turning point in Marshall's career when, as a captain, he "tossed aside caution" and challenged Pershing, telling them "there's something to be said" and that he was wrong. Marshall's colleagues told him he would be "fired right off," but he wasn't. Instead, he went on to become Pershing's operations officer and rose to the rank of colonel within a year.

Marshall challenged Roosevelt in his first cabinet meeting by telling the president, "I don't agree with you at all." As they left the

White House, the secretary of the treasury told Marshall, "Well, it's been nice knowing you." In less than a year, Marshall was selected by Roosevelt to be army chief of staff. Marshall told the president he wanted the right to say what he thought, which "would often be unpleasing." As secretary of state, he told his deputy, Dean Acheson, "I shall expect of you the most complete frankness, particularly about myself."

When Roosevelt wanted to make drastic cuts in the army budget in 1933, MacArthur, then army chief of staff, stood up to the president in no uncertain terms. Roosevelt told him, "You must not talk that way to the president." MacArthur reflected, "I felt my army career was at an end." It wasn't.

When Gen. J. Lawton Collins was told that he was going to be chief of staff in 1949, he asked Gen. Wade Haislip to be his deputy. Haislip responded, "Why do you want me? You and I haven't agreed on anything in thirty years." Collins replied, "That's exactly why I want you."

When Marshall struck out at then brigadier general Eisenhower and told him that men on his staff would not be promoted, Ike gave it right back to him: "I don't give a damn about your promotion and your power to promote me." Eisenhower said, "From that day on he started promoting me."

General David C. Jones had the character to speak up before the Senate Armed Forces Committee, challenging Secretary of Defense McNamara. As a result, he was taken off the promotion list for brigadier general. But the air force would not let that terminate his career, and Jones went on to become chief of staff and chairman of the Joint Chiefs.

General Schwarzkopf refused an idiotic order from an engineer brigadier general who had never been in operational warfare and didn't know what he was doing. Schwarzkopf told the general, "I'm sorry, but I cannot obey your order." He was saved by his brigade commander, Col. Joe Clemons, hero of Pork Chop Hill in Korea. Schwarzkopf's career went on, but Clemons's career was ended by that incident.

Brigadier General Colin Powell stood up to his division commander, Maj. Gen. John W. Hudachek, and Hudachek gave him a bad efficiency report. Powell told him, "This report will probably end my career." It didn't, because then army chief of staff Shy Meyer pulled him out of the division and put him in a two-star slot, thus saving his career.

Admiral Crowe spoke his mind to his boss, Admiral Long, and was told by a friend: "Nobody talks to Bob Long that way." Crowe thought he was finished. He wasn't. He went on to become chairman of the Joint Chiefs.

Shy Meyer challenged the Senate Armed Forces Committee, telling it that we had a "hollow army." He was ready to submit his resignation. He didn't have to, and his straightforward comment resulted in the necessary funds to assist the army to catch up.

General Jones challenged the organization of the Joint Chiefs, for which his brother officers of the other services were severely critical of him. He was successful with the passage of the Goldwater-Nicholos Act, which Les Aspin, former secretary of defense, called "probably the greatest single change in the history of the American military since the Continental Congress created the Continental Army in 1775."

A successful military leader in our republic must have subordinates with the character to introduce controversial input into decision making and to carry the decision to a conclusion, even if disagreeing with it. The top military leader must have the character to accept challenge, even though, as Crowe said, sometimes a "no man . . . upsets me," and Twining commented, "It sure takes the ego out of you."

Notes

1. Omar N. Bradley, *A Soldier's Story* (New York: Henry Holt and Company, 1951), 20.

2. Forrest C. Pogue, *George C. Marshall, Education of a General* (New York: Viking Press, 1963), 152–53.

3. Ibid.

4. Leonard Mosley, *Marshall: Hero for Our Times* (New York: Hearst Books, 1982), 121.

5. Ibid., 122.

6. Pogue, *George C. Marshall*, 330.

7. Letter from Maj. Gen. Paul L. Ransom, USA (Ret.), to Edgar F. Puryear, Jr., dated September 4, 1962.

8. Letter from Maj. Gen. Charles H. Corlett, USA (Ret.), to Edgar F. Puryear, Jr., dated July 31, 1962.

9. Stimson diary, September 15, 1941.

10. Personal interview with Gen. Joseph T. McNarney, USAF (Ret.), and Edgar F. Puryear, Jr., August 22, 1962.

11. Dean Acheson, *Present at the Creation* (New York: W. W. Norton, 1969), 213.

12. Douglas MacArthur, *Reminiscences* (New York: McGraw-Hill, 1964), 100.

13. Ibid., 101.

14. William F. Halsey and J. Bryan, III, *Admiral Halsey's Story* (New York: Whittesey House, 1947), 138–39.

15. Ibid., 132–33.

16. J. Lawton Collins, *Lightning Joe: An Autobiography* (Baton Rouge: Louisiana University Press, 1979), 339–40.

17. Ibid., 343–44.

18. Ibid., 344.

19. Personal interview with Gen. Wade Haislip, USA (Ret.), and Edgar F. Puryear, Jr., September 12, 1962.

20. Personal interview with Lt. Gen. James H. Doolittle, USAF (Ret.), and Edgar F. Puryear, Jr., February 7, 1977.

21. Personal interview with Gen. Carl A. "Tooey" Spaatz, USAF (Ret.), and Edgar F. Puryear, Jr., September 19, 1962.

22. Personal interview with Gen. Nathan F. Twining, USAF (Ret.), and Edgar F. Puryear, Jr., March 3, 1977.

23. Personal interview with Gen. Bruce K. Holloway, USAF (Ret.), and Edgar F. Puryear, Jr., July 7, 1978.

24. Ibid.

25. Personal interview with Gen. Edwin W. Rawlings, USAF (Ret.), and Edgar F. Puryear, Jr., February 10, 1977.

26. Personal interview with Maj. Gen. Chaplin Meade, USAF (Ret.), and Edgar F. Puryear, Jr., April 1, 1981.

27. Personal interview with Gen. Charles Gabriel, USAF (Ret.), and Edgar F. Puryear, Jr., July 17, 1986.

28. Personal interview with Gen. Larry Welch, USAF, and Edgar F. Puryear, Jr., February 19, 1987.

29. H. Norman Schwarzkopf, *It Doesn't Take a Hero* (New York: Bantam Books, 1992), 127.

30. Ibid.

31. Ibid., 167–68.

32. Personal interview with Gen. H. Norman Schwarzkopf and Edgar F. Puryear, Jr., October 27, 1995.

33. Personal interview with Adm. William J. Crowe, Jr., USN (Ret.), and Edgar F. Puryear, Jr., May 16, 1997.

34. Colin Powell, *My American Journey* (New York: Random House, 1995), 267.

35. Ibid., 267–68.

36. Ibid., 270.

37. Ibid., 271–72.

38. Personal interview with Gen. Edward C. Meyer, USA (Ret.), and Edgar F. Puryear, Jr., July 14, 1997.

39. Personal interview with Gen. Colin L. Powell and Edgar F. Puryear, Jr., October 16, 1997.

40. Ibid.

41. Personal interview with Gen. John M. Shalikashvili, USAF (Ret.) and Edgar F. Puryear, Jr., June 4, 1997.

42. Personal interview with Gen. David C. Jones, USAF (Ret.), and Edgar F. Puryear, Jr., January 20, 1998.

Chapter 5: Books: The Importance of Reading

Education has for its object the formation of character.
—Herbert Spencer

There is no history: There is only biography.
—Ralph Waldo Emerson

In 1940, Dwight D. Eisenhower was a colonel stationed at Fort Hood, in Texas, serving as chief of staff to Maj. Gen. Walter Krueger, commander of the Third Army. Eisenhower was called to Washington to meet with army chief of staff George C. Marshall. He did not look forward to the call because he was afraid it would take him back to Washington and staff work, away from service with the troops, which he had wanted for years.

At this conference, Marshall asked Eisenhower for his thoughts about how Japan's challenging the U.S. presence in the Pacific should be met, particularly in regards to the Philippine Islands, which were then still a U.S. territory. The observation was made by one of Ike's biographers that, "The question shook Eisenhower. He knew he had developed a reputation in the Army as an idea man. But he realized [that Marshall] and his War Plans Division were not bereft of ideas of their own. He was obviously to be tested for a job, probably at the War Department itself."

Eisenhower as an idea man raises significant points. I asked him, "How does one develop as a decision maker? Is it a God-given talent, or can it be developed, and if so, how does one grow and improve?"[1]

His response was twofold. First, he stressed the importance of being around people who were making decisions. He certainly had that experience in his career. He had worked for Douglas MacArthur on two occasions in Washington and Manila and for Marshall as chief of staff. Second, he stressed the importance of books, particularly history and biography.

In his book *At Ease: Stories I Tell My Friends* is a chapter entitled The Key to the Closet. Judging from his remarkable career, the chapter might well have been called The Key to Success. In this chapter he reflected: "My first reading love was ancient history. At an early age, I developed an interest in the human record and I became particularly fond of Greek and Roman accounts. These subjects were so engrossing that I frequently was guilty of neglecting all others. . . . Out of that closet and out of those books has come an odd result. Even to this day there are many unrelated bits of information about Greece and Rome that stick in my memory. Some are dates. I have a sort of fixation that causes me to interrupt a conversation when the speaker is one year off, or a hundred, in dating an event like Arbela; and often I put aside a book, until then interesting enough, when the author is less than scrupulous about chronology.

"In any case, the battles of Marathon, Zama, Salamis, and Cannae became as familiar to me as the games (and battles) I enjoyed with my brothers and friends in the schoolyard. In later years, the movies taught children that the bad guy was the one in the black hat. Such people as Hannibal, Caesar, Pericles, Socrates, Themistocles, Miltiades, and Leonidas were my white hats, my heroes. Xerxes, Darius, Alcibiades, Brutus, and Nero wore black ones. White or black, their names and those battles were fresh news, as I could never seem to get it into my head that all these things had happened two thousand years earlier—or that possibly I would be better advised to pay attention to current rather than ancient affairs. Among all the figures of antiquity, Hannibal was my favorite.

"Since those early years, history of all kinds, and certainly political and military, has always intrigued me mightily. When a historical novel is well written and documented, I am apt to spend the whole evening in its reading. The campaigns of the more modern leaders—Frederick, Napoleon, Gustavus Adolphus, and all of our prominent American soldiers and statesmen—I found absorbing.

"When I got around to the Americans, Washington was my hero. I never tired of reading about his exploits at Princeton, at Trenton, and particularly in Valley Forge. I conceived almost a violent hatred of Conway and his cabal, and could not imagine anyone so stupid and so unpatriotic as to have wanted to remove Washington from command of the American Army. The qualities that excited my admiration were Washington's stamina and patience in adversity, first, and then his indomitable courage, daring, and capacity for self-sacrifice."[2]

Eisenhower's reference to Washington was interesting because certainly George Washington was also a reader. At the time of his death, he had a library of more than nine hundred books, a significant number for that day. Washington very early developed a habit of reading, ordering new books from London by the trunk load. The selection of the books read and studied was important in his becoming knowledgeable in military affairs, English history, and agriculture. He even read the popular English novels of the period, such as *Tom Jones*.[3]

It is noteworthy that a recent biography of George Washington entitled *Founding Father: Rediscovering George Washington* (1996) has a chapter entitled Ideas, which discusses at length Washington's education. The author, Richard Brookheiser, quoted Thomas Jefferson, who said of Washington, "His time was employed in the action chiefly, reading in agriculture and English history."[4]

Washington was not a college graduate, although most of his contemporaries were so educated, such as Thomas Jefferson at William and Mary and John Adams at Harvard. Although there were twenty-four college graduates at the Constitutional Convention, it was the largely self-educated Washington who was selected to preside.

His reading included the controversial literature of the time, particularly pamphlets that discussed the issues of the day. Biographer Brookheiser commented: "Though Washington's experience as Commander in Chief disposed him in favor of a stronger national government, reading showed him the way. During the debate over the Constitution, he read, besides the *Federalist*, the essays of half a dozen other polemicists, pro and con, and cited them in the first draft of his Inaugural Address." Washington encouraged the idea that newspapers be free of charge. Visitors to Mount Vernon during his retirement years found that he subscribed to ten newspapers.[5]

Where do ideas come from?

In its entry on Benjamin Franklin, the *Encyclopaedia Britannica* reveals: "Next to George Washington, he is possibly the most famous 18th century American." Franklin, whose father was a soap and candle maker, was the tenth of seventeen children. Despite his modest start, by the age of fifty young Ben Franklin had amassed a small fortune and proceeded to devote himself to a life of public service. Among his many contributions were his role in writing the Declaration of Independence, securing financial and military aid from France during the American Revolution, negotiating a treaty with Great Britain that recognized the thirteen colonies as a sovereign nation, and framing the Constitution.

Although Franklin's public service contributions were significant, including service as a colonel in the Pennsylvania militia, he also made his mark as an inventor. Where do ideas flourish? From reading and reflecting, Franklin developed the Franklin stove, still in use today. He conceived of the lightning rod and was well known in Europe for his research in electrical experiments and theories. He invented bifocal glasses. In Philadelphia, his residence for most of his life, he organized the first volunteer fire department (at every meeting, members were required to bring their own buckets of sand). He started the first public library, the first hospital, and Philadelphia's first academic academy (now the University of Pennsylvania). Suggesting how to get ahead in life, he wrote *Poor Richard's Almanac,* which was a widely recognized "best seller" and contributed to his fortune.

Catherine Drinker Bowen, author of ten biographies, wrote in 1974 of Franklin: "In an era when the fomenting and support of the revolution are claimed by youth as their special attributes, it is significant to recall that two hundred years ago the person feared by the crowned heads of England and many parts of Europe as the most dangerous man in America was Benjamin Franklin—age sixty-eight to eighty."[6]

What is surprising is that with all his extraordinary achievements, Franklin's schooling ended at the age of ten, and that was limited to only one year of formal education and one year with a tutor. Where did his ideas originate and how did he prepare himself for such significant positions of responsibility? The answer was that he loved to read.

His autobiography provides considerable insight into the importance of reading. It had always been a part of his life; he wrote, "I do not remember when I could not read." Indeed, his friends thought he would make a great scholar and encouraged him. "From my infancy, I was passionately fond of reading, and all the money that came into my hands was ever laid out for books"[7] His father's library was limited to books in polemic divinity, "most of which I read. I have often regretted that, at a time when I had such a thirst for knowledge, more proper books had not fallen my way."[8]

As a youth, Franklin became an apprentice printer. "I now had access to better books . . . often I sat in my chamber reading the greatest part of the night when the book was borrowed in the evening and to be returned in the morning, lest it should be missed or wanted."[9]

He developed his writing skill by copying the style of other writers, which, he says, "encouraged me to think I might possibly in time come to be a tolerable English writer, of which I was extremely ambitious. My time for these exercises and for reading was at night, after work or before it began in the morning, or on Sundays, when I contrived to be in the printing house alone. . . ."[10]

In spring 1724, Franklin sailed for England and continued his interest in books. "While I lodged in Little Britain," he wrote in his autobiography, "I made acquaintance with one Wilcox, a bookseller, whose shop was next door. He had an immense collection of second-hand books. Circulating libraries were not then in use; but we agreed that on certain reasonable terms, which I have now forgotten, I might take, read, and return all of his books. This I esteemed a great advantage, and I made as much use as I could."[11]

Returning to Philadelphia from England, Franklin formed a group of twelve who met once a week, had dinner, and discussed books assigned for the evening. He persuaded the members to "club" their books to a common library convenient to the entire group so "each had the use and advantage of using the books of all the other members, which was nearly as beneficial as if each owned the whole." It didn't work out, so he "set forth my first project of a public nature, that for a subscription library," which, he commented, "was the mother of all North American subscription libraries. . . . These libraries have improved the general conversation of the Americans, made the common tradesman and farmers as intelligent as most gentlemen from other countries, and perhaps have contributed to some degree to the stand so generally made throughout the colonies in defense of their privileges."[12] This was the beginning of free public libraries in this country.

Franklin further reflected, "This library afforded me the means of improvement by constant study, for which I set apart an hour or two each day, and thus repaired in some degree the loss of the learned education my father once intended for me. Reading was the only amusement I allowed myself. I spent no time in tavern games, or frolics of any kind, and my industry in my business continued as indefatigable as it was necessary."[13]

In the history of our country, one of America's most remarkable soldiers was Arthur MacArthur, father of General of the Army Douglas MacArthur. At age eighteen, the elder MacArthur won the Medal of Honor in the Civil War and was, at nineteen, the youngest full colonel in the Southern or Northern forces.

After the Spanish-American War, Arthur MacArthur, now a lieutenant general, was appointed military governor of the Philippine Islands. When William Howard Taft was later sent as civilian governor, there was considerable friction between the two. Governing the Philippines after the war was controversial indeed, because the whole matter of the United States having a territory was in question. This resulted in a Senate investigation, with extensive party confrontation between Republicans and Democrats over the matter.

Because of his role as military governor, MacArthur was an obvious choice to be a witness. In the 1902 hearing, his breadth and knowledge were great. He testified on political theory and the principles of democracy. When he was asked if the United States should have annexed the Philippines, he showed vision by speaking eruditely on the political, economic, and military reasons for the importance of the islands. He thought the Philippines had great potential as a market of U.S. goods, as a strategic base in the Far East to increase trade with China and to help protect Hawaii, and as a political base to spread democracy. He said, "It is the stepping stone to a commanding influence—political, commercial, and military supremacy in the East."[14] With no more than a high school education, he was a self-made man. His education derived from a lifetime of serious study through independent reading.

On February 8, 1904, the Japanese navy attacked the Russian Pacific fleet at Ports Arthur and Dairen in Manchuria, resulting in war. President Theodore Roosevelt, prior to offering his "good offices" to bring about peace in 1905, sent Arthur MacArthur to travel to Japan and Russia to study the war. MacArthur's observations to Roosevelt were invaluable, as his biographer, Kenneth Ray Young, wrote: "For thirty years, he had read nearly every book published on East Asia, and his deep interest in China and Japan had been reinforced by experience in the Philippines." Indeed, as early as 1882, he tried to obtain an assignment as the military attaché to Peking.[15]

During his study of the situation in Asia, Arthur MacArthur had as an aide his son, Lt. Douglas MacArthur. Douglas was ordered by his father "to purchase every book he could find on the countries they visited, and in the evenings, they read, talked and analyzed the experiences. The general insisted that Douglas keep meticulous records, and each day his reading list grew. By the end of the trip, the MacArthurs had read dozens of books on the countries they visited."[16]

Throughout his military career, Douglas MacArthur sought to live up to his father's brilliant contributions as a soldier; Arthur's example was a significant factor in Douglas's development. After the Civil War, Arthur MacArthur was stationed primarily in the western territories. One biographer said that he was "a great reader of other men's books, and sends for them by the trunkful. It is not light fare."[17]

What did he read? An efficiency report, filed in the adjutant general's office the year after the closing of the frontier, noted that Arthur had pursued investigations in political economy, the colonial and revolutionary period in American history, a comparison of American and English constitutions, an extensive investigation into the civilizations and institutions of China, and the works of Gibbon, Macaulay, Samuel Johnson, Thomas Mathers, David Ricardo, John Stuart Mill, Henry Carey, Walter Bagenot, Thomas Leslie, and William Jevons.

After 1905, the two MacArthurs' reading list continued to grow. They had a voracious appetite for books—Greek and Roman history, the history and culture of China, and whatever they could find of value on each country. Their trip lasted eight months, during which they traveled 20,000 miles.[18]

Douglas MacArthur wrote in his memoirs that the Asian tour was "without a doubt the most important factor in preparation for my entire life . . . the strength and weakness of the colonial system, how it brought law and order but failed to develop the masses along the lines of education and political economy."[19] This was to become an important foundation for a general who would eventually be responsible for the occupation of Japan and the establishment of democracy there after World War II.

At his father's death, Douglas MacArthur inherited more than four thousand books. Throughout his life, he followed a rigid schedule of reading, selecting difficult books covering a wide range of subjects.

On June 12, 1919, sixteen years after graduating from West Point, Douglas MacArthur was appointed superintendent of his alma mater. There he integrated into the curriculum studies in history and biography inspired by his extensive reading. He found West Point in a state of disorder and confusion. The four-year course had been shortened during World War I because of the pressing need for officers. There was now a need for a new generation of officers for the future requirements of the army. The army chief of staff, Gen. Peyton March, informed MacArthur that "West Point is 40 years behind the times." Reflected MacArthur, "West Point would have to be revitalized, the curriculum reestablished."[20]

What was wrong? What changes were needed? MacArthur summarized them.

"Conditions with respect to the course of study were chaotic, educational qualifications for admission were drastically lowered, the morale of the cadet body was low." There were no upperclassmen, thus no cadet officers to serve as examples, and "the old West Point could not be recognized as it appeared in June 1919. It had gone, it had to be replaced."[21]

He removed the cadets to a regular encampment for the summer period. He wanted the cadets in direct contact with actual service conditions. He wanted to change a life that was "cloistered, almost to a monastic extent." He required each cadet to participate in major sports.[22]

Although these changes were needed, clearly most important was MacArthur's decision to expand the curriculum with more courses on international relations, history, and economics, to help establish a more worldly intellectual foundation.

William Manchester wrote in *American Caesar* that while Douglas MacArthur was stationed in the Philippines in the 1930s, his wife Jean "was forever giving him biographies of Confederate generals, among them Douglas S. Freeman's four-volume life of Lee, G. F. R. Henderson's two volumes on Stonewall Jackson and J. A. Wythe's *Nathan Bedford Forrest.*" "A speed reader," commented Manchester, "MacArthur could get through three books a day."[23]

After leaving the Philippines, as ordered by President Franklin D. Roosevelt in 1942, MacArthur moved to Australia to organize Allied forces for retaking the territory invaded and occupied by the Japanese. One biographer wrote, "MacArthur spent long evenings in the bungalow's library. An earlier tenant had been highly literate; the shelves were packed with books in several languages. . . . Phrases from this cultural smorgasbord would find their way into the articulate communiqué he dictated . . . each morning. He can quote Shakespeare, the Bible, Napoleon, Mark Twain, and Lincoln in expounding a single idea, and Johnston reported that he drew . . . on . . . a statement by Plato, or sometimes on a passage from Scripture."[24]

An officer who served him described MacArthur's tour as chief of staff: "He worked long hours at his office and seemed content to spend most of his evenings at his quarters at Fort Myer across the Potomac. Always a prodigious reader and student of history, he would relax with a book in his library (reading the books his father bequeathed to him). . . ."[25]

Reading played a vital role in the character development of Marshall, Eisenhower, Washington, Franklin, and MacArthur. This passion for reading and the positive effect it had on these great leaders was also shared by the men who led soldiers on both sides of the American Civil War, as well as the army and Army Air Corps during World War II.

It is worthwhile to look at some of the key leaders of the Civil War to see the impact that reading had on their development. Reading and study were vital in establishing a reputation in the early military career of Maj. Gen. George B. McClellan, selected by President Abraham Lincoln to command the Army of the Potomac in 1862. McClellan graduated from the U.S. Military Academy in 1846, ranking number two in a class of fifty-nine cadets. He was assigned to the Corps of Engineers, the most elite branch in the army.

After graduation, and being stationed at West Point, McClellan spent a significant part of his education with an extracurricular organization known as Mahan's Napoleon Club. The club was open to the faculty and other officers with a keen interest in studying their profession. It frequently met to discuss the papers written by members of the Napoleonic campaigns. McClellan wrote a paper on Napoleon's campaign into Russia in 1812. It was cited as a superb study by his group.

In June 1851, he was reassigned to an undemanding Army Corps of Engineers project on the Delaware River, where he began to study German. In March 1855, he was selected to go to Europe to study the Crimean War. Two other officers went with him, Majors Richard Delafield and Alfred Mordecai.

During the ensuing six months of studying French, British, German, and Russian installations and fortifications, McClellan visited Waterloo and saw the famous battlefield. After studying it thoroughly, he wrote back to a friend, "I can now almost imagine that I was a spectator of the great drama."

After the men returned, Secretary of War Jefferson Davis told McClellan to write his report on cavalry and engineering aspects of the war. Major Mordecai was to report on ordnance and Major Delafield on fortifications. McClellan brought back with him two hundred books. The topics ranged from field rations to veterinary medicine.

McClellan learned a great deal from this experience, and it clearly established his reputation as a student—indeed an expert—in the art of war in the minds of state governors and officials in Washington looking for leadership after the Civil War started.

In 1861, a reviewer wrote of McClellan's report: "A prime interest attaches to his work, because unconsciously the author had given us in advance his repertory of instruments and principles. From the written word we may anticipate the brilliant achievement. . . . To this point, the written word, the years of study and reading were put into effective use to leading an army into battle."

I must emphasize with McClellan's example that reading alone cannot ensure success as a military leader. He was a student of military history, but critics of his command record would wonder why he failed to profit from the works he studied. An accomplished student of war, he was a failure as a field commander. McClellan's problem was a lack of character. Jackson biographer Byron Farwell wrote, "Jackson considered a military education important, but he believed that 'something more is required to make a general' and among the qualities necessary, he listed 'judgment, nerve and force of character.'"[26]

General Robert E. Lee was a serious reader and successful field general. As a first classman (senior) at West Point, Lee and some other classmates were made acting assistant professors to tutor cadets having difficulty with mathematics. Although Lee was compensated for the time spent tutoring, his grades began to fall. To bring back his class standing, he had to curtail this employment, although he later had time to resume his independent reading. From January 26, 1828, through May 24, 1828, he borrowed fifty-two books from the library, indicating a wide area of interests: the works of Rousseau, Machiavelli's *Art of War*, biographies, and treatises on Napoleon.

While Lee was superintendent at West Point, he again had access to the best military library of the day. During his two years and seven months there, he read forty-eight books, fifteen of which were military biography, history, and the science of war. Seven of these were on Napoleon and his Russian campaign.

Ikenrode and Conrad's biography of Confederate general James Longstreet observes, "Seldom has a man more completely illustrated his character than did Longstreet by his deeds and words— more by deeds than his words. Longstreet had given little thought to the art of war, he was no reader of books like Jackson, the student. His idea of the theory of war was, as it might be expressed, casually picked up, . . . Longstreet did not read books." The authors further elaborated, "Longstreet was not a student of war, not a deep thinker in the subject of war, and when placed in positions demanding knowledge and initiative, he failed. Not having studied strategic combinations in all circumstances, he did not know what to do."[27]

General Thomas J. "Stonewall" Jackson was indeed a reader. His biographer James I. Robertson, Jr. wrote: "Jackson became enthralled as well by bookstores. He spent hours examining volumes on the shelves. Determined to become a soldier in every possible way, he began on historical narratives and military biographies. Ancient history and treatises on the campaigns of Napoleon Bonaparte were his favorites. On occasion, Jackson would secure a contemporary periodical to feel the pulse of national events."[28]

I wrote to the Virginia Historical Society to determine the books that Jackson had in his library. The collection included the *Life of Andrew Jackson,* which contained "anecdotes illustrative of his character," as well as biographies on Cromwell and Henry Clay, many treatises on Napoleon and George Washington, and numerous books on religion and scientific subjects.[29]

General Ulysses S. Grant in his memoirs wrote of his West Point years: "I did not take hold of my studies with avidity, in fact, I rarely ever read over a lesson the second time during my entire cadetship. I could not sit in my room doing nothing. There is a fine library connected with the Academy from which cadets can get books to read in their quarters. I devoted more time to these than to books relating to the course of studies. Much of the time, I am sorry to say, was devoted to novels, but not those of a trashy sort."[30] Grant's biographer, William S. McFeely, wrote: "Here was the characteristic balance of boldness and conventionality. Grant credited himself with the intellectual initiative and then, as quickly, apologized for it. Those books mattered to him; he felt it important to record his debt to them. They were good books, and reading them was fun."[31]

General William Tecumseh Sherman's interest and love of books and reading began at age nine. His father, Charles R. Sherman, died, leaving a widow and eleven children, one of them "Cump" (Sherman's childhood nickname), who had to be farmed out to various family members and friends. Fortunately, nine-year-old Cump had only to move next door to live with the family of Thomas Ewing, a successful lawyer who imparted a love of books and reading to him. Sherman biographer John F. Fitzgerald wrote: "Books became his companions. He read everything he could get his hands on. . . ." Ewing insisted that his wife gather all the children together and have Cump read to them from the nine volumes of S. G. Goodrich's Peter Parley books. These concentrated on geography, history, and morality and opened up the world for him. Maria Ewing encouraged Cump to read every night before going to bed.[32]

Ewing's library was described as "unrivaled in the area." This reading developed Sherman's lifelong interest in geography. Said biographer Marszalek, "[Sherman's] reverence for the American Union was no doubt stimulated by these books."[33]

In July 1846, Captain Sherman was ordered to California aboard the naval vessel USS *Lexington*. He was a member of Company E of the 3d Artillery, whose role was not defined as they left port. The *Lexington* was at sea for six months, and Sherman read all the books on the ship.

Once he was out of the army, in April 1859, Sherman accepted the position as superintendent of the new Louisiana Military School, which today is Louisiana State University. One of his first missions there was to place great emphasis on reading. He traveled to New York to buy several thousand volumes for the school library, four hundred of which were on history and geography.

Sherman loved books all his life. In his retirement years, he read considerably. His large personal library included the twelve volumes of the *Dispatches of Wellington,* the plays of Shakespeare, and the three-volume work by Buckle entitled *History of the United States,* as well as books by Walter Scott, Charles Dickens, and Washington Irving.

There was probably no single person who made more decisions in World War II than Gen. George C. Marshall. He considered reading important to his professional life and a factor in sound decision making.

"In the home life, I realize today," Marshall commented, "I got a great deal of benefit from reading. My father read aloud, very well, and liked to do it, strange to say. My mother read to me a great many things like *Ivanhoe* and all that series of books. But her eyes went bad on her and she couldn't read much anymore. Then my father liked to read and we all liked to listen. He read a great many things. I can recall some of them. I remember the Saracinesca series—*Sant Ilano* and *Don Orsino* by our writer, F. Marion Crawford [an American novelist], who lived in Rome. I remember the Fenimore Cooper stories that he read to us, and particularly the famous stories by Sir Arthur Conan Doyle."[34]

In an interview, Marshall described some of the less-than-serious books he read as a boy: "In those days there were large, thin paper Novels—the Nick Carter series, the Frank Merriwell series, the Old South series. We were forbidden from reading all but the Frank Merriwell series and those were highly recommended. . . . In order to read the Nick Carter series, which was very much like Jesse James at his best, we would retire to the spring house."[35]

Reading got Marshall into trouble as a young child when he was employed at St. Peter's Episcopal Church. "I pumped the organ. The place for the pumper was in a very narrow region in the rear of the organ and the pump was just a handle like the tiller of a boat. The pumping was not difficult, except you had to be there. But there was a long period of waiting during the sermon. One of those mornings, I was occupying this period of waiting with a five-cent novel of that day about Nick Carter. Just in the most exciting portion . . . my attention was called to the organ by the thump, thump which the organist, Miss Fanny Howe, could make from the keyboard. And I realized that she had started to play at the end of the sermon and no music was coming out. . . . She was not only displeased but rather outraged. . . . She relieved me from my duty with the organ."[36]

In high school, Marshall was an average student in mathematics, spelling, and grammar, but he commented, "If it was history, that was all right. I could star in history. Benjamin Franklin and Robert E. Lee were my personal heroes."

In an interview with Forrest Pogue on March 6, 1957, Marshall reflected on reading as a cadet at the Virginia Military Institute: "Of the books that I read at that time, it was pretty much anything I could get my hands on, particularly the last year and a half. I didn't discover until about then that my roommate Nicholson—he and his brothers were orphans and they owned the *Times-Picayune,* which was just merely the Picayune paper of New Orleans—he made a casual remark one day that they got all these books to review and they sold them for five cents apiece. So we immediately got him to contact a friend of his on the paper and he, the friend, would send us a barrel of books at a time. You will find on the register there the record of books contributed to the library by Nicholson. That's the way it came about. I was a very rapid reader and Peyton was a rapid reader and Nicholson was a very slow reader. Peyton and I just read through the barrel."[37]

In an interview, General Eisenhower discussed in detail with me the importance of reading in his development as a professional soldier. "I was not a particularly good student at West Point. They had a course at West Point called Military History that was different from what it is now. One of the things we studied was the Battle of Gettysburg. The first thing we were required to do was memorize the name of every general officer or acting general officer. You had to know what he was commanding. Then they gave you the situation or the position of each of the commands at such and such an hour on such and such a day. I always hated memorizing, although I have a pretty good memory. But this wasn't the kind of thing that interested me, so I didn't pay any attention to my history and I almost got found [flunked]. I despised it the way it was taught."[38]

Despite being injured in football as a cadet, Eisenhower was commissioned in the army. "Then I made up my mind that if I was going to have a military career, I was going to have a good one. I don't mean to say I stopped having fun. I guess I was just as frolicking as anyone, in my way. But when I put myself down to study, I wasn't doing anything else. I was searching new plans, new ideas. I was very impatient about the idea of trench warfare and why we didn't break away from it. I read everything I could on trench warfare. I didn't get into that war at all; so I just accepted the training end of it because they said I had such special ability as a trainer. This was cold comfort to a young officer."[39]

He continued: "There was no question that Fox Conner got me started in better methods of preparing myself. I was studying back in 1915, '16, '17, '18, '19, but I met him and I went with him in '21.

He was the one who gave me a systematic plan of study. He had just been in the war as the operations officer of the AEF [Allied Expeditionary Force]. He was a smart, patient man, and he decided that I ought to amount to something, so he was going to see if I would."[40]

Conner gave Major Eisenhower historical books to read, then asked him questions about them. He set aside for Eisenhower a room in his quarters in Panama as a study. He placed maps on the wall to study world strategy. He had Ike teach classes to the post officers. They were constant companions in the jungles of Panama, where at night, sitting by the campfire, Conner would quiz Ike on the books assigned to him to read. Eisenhower wrote the field orders and letters and accomplished all the other administrative matters.[41]

It was a unique experience for a young man to receive the tutelage of one of the most brilliant officers in the army. Of all the training Eisenhower received, perhaps the most valuable was the result of Conner's understanding that the key to the next world war, a fact he considered was written into the Treaty of Versailles, would be Allied command. Twenty years before the event, Eisenhower began the study of Allied unity; this was, of course, where he performed his greatest service in World War II.

George Patton came out of World War I with the most tank combat experience of any soldier in the U.S. Army. Eisenhower, although serving in a stateside tank training unit, never had overseas duty in World War I. After the war he was assigned to Camp Meade, in Maryland, where he met Patton. Together they read, studied, and discussed their profession, then started a tactical and technical school, balancing the practical with theoretical. Ike reflected, "Those of us who had not been abroad during the war badgered George and the others who had taken part in battle into giving us detailed accounts of plans and operations. We began to evolve what we thought to be a new and better tank doctrine."[42]

"Indeed," Ike wrote of the experience with Patton, "both of us were students of current military doctrine. Part of our passion was a belief in tanks, a belief derided at the time by others." They believed that tanks should have a "more valuable and more spectacular role," expounding their theories and refining their tactical ideas.[43]

Their reward for such study of their profession was a reaction that would discourage men of lesser character. Ike commented: "Both of us began articles for the military journals; he for the Cavalry, I for the Infantry. Then I was called before the Chief of Infantry (a major general)!

"I was told that my ideas were not only wrong, but dangerous, and that henceforth I would keep them to myself. Particularly, I was not to publish anything incompatible with solid infantry doctrine. If I did, I would be hauled before a court-martial.

"George, I think, was given the same message. This was a blow. One effect was to bring George and me even closer. We spent a great deal of time together, riding through our respective commands during the day, and talking, studying, and blowing off steam at night. With George's temper and my own capacity for something more than irritation, there was surely more steam around the Officers Quarters than at the post laundry."[44]

Ike informed me that the same chief of infantry attempted to destroy his career by preventing his receiving orders to attend the advanced infantry course. This meant that he would never be assigned to the Command and General Staff School at Fort Leavenworth, and thus would never rise higher in rank than major (as I will discuss later). Conner stepped in to change this, however.

Eisenhower's love of books and reading continued throughout his career. After Eisenhower returned to Washington as plans officer for General Marshall, he and Mamie established residence in the Wardman Park Hotel. Their grandson David Eisenhower wrote about Ike's love of books, pointing out that in their apartment, "[Mamie] displayed their bound set of Harvard classics, purchased in the early 1930s, in a bookcase next to several framed French prints acquired when they had lived in Paris on the Rue d'Auteil twelve years earlier."[45]

Patton, one of the most outstanding field commanders of World War II, agreed with Eisenhower on his distaste for memorizing the names of generals and dates, but they both believed in reading and studying history and biography.

Leadership of people in wartime is unchanging. Patton told his son on the eve of D day, June 6, 1944: "To be a successful soldier you must know history. Read it objectively, dates and even minute details of tactics are useless. What you must know is how man reacts. Weapons change, but the men who use them change not at all. To win battles you do not beat weapons, you beat the soul of every man."[46]

The editor of *The Patton Papers*, Martin Blumenson, made this observation on Patton's study of history: "It was useless to study warfare before 1870, for the lessons before that date were no longer relevant and practical. To Patton, history moved in cycles; therefore, styles in warfare reoccurred. Without perspective a painting was valueless; and so it was with things military. Ancient tactics were hardly to be copied, but professionals had to be familiar with them and with the reason for their adoption. For the basic nature of man had changed but little during the course of recorded history.

"Starting with 2500 B.C., Patton classified wars after the types of armies involved, that is, mass or professional. He ran through the Egyptians, Syrians, Greeks, Macedonians, Romans, Africans, Goths, Byzantines, Franks, Vikings, Mongols, Swiss, Turks, British, French, Spanish, Dutch, Germans, and Americans—ending with the Boer War. From these historical examples, he extracted certain lessons. For example, professionals fought better in protracted operations, in campaigns where supply was difficult, and in wars where discipline was more important than emotional inspiration."[47]

An avid reader, Omar N. Bradley in his autobiography described his father, John Smith Bradley, a teacher in a one-room schoolhouse in Missouri, as "a curious blend of frontiersman, sportsman, farmer and intellectual. [He] . . . was an omnivorous reader and lover of books. Everywhere he taught, he encouraged his students to read and created small libraries for them."[48]

The father's love of reading was passed down to his son, who recalled: "I idolized him. He succeeded very quickly in inculcating in me a love of books. After I could read fairly well, I devoured books such as Sir Walter Scott's *Ivanhoe*, Kipling's *Jungle Books*, and the like. I was particularly fascinated by history—tales of the French and Indian Wars, the Revolutionary and Civil Wars. I would act out many of the battles on the living room rug, using dominoes to build forts and empty .22 cartridges to represent lines of soldiers. I made 'heavy artillery' from hollow elderberry reeds or brass tubing and would bombard the domino forts with navy beans. In any mock wars, the Americans always won."[49]

After graduating from West Point in 1915, Bradley reported to Fort George Wright, in Spokane, Washington, where he continued his interest in books and reading. Second Lieutenant Edwin Forrest Harding, U.S. Military Academy, 1909, was also stationed there. Bradley reflected: "Forrest Harding was a serious student of history, a fine writer and a compulsive teacher. Soon after we arrived, Forrest organized an unofficial weekly gathering in his home to which he invited about six lieutenants on the post. For several hours under his guidance we would discuss small unit tactics, squads and platoon in attack on a variety of terrain and so on. These meetings were immensely stimulating and educational, often turning into broader discussions of military history. No single person in my early Army career had a more salutary influence on me than Forrest Harding. He instilled in me a genuine desire to thoroughly learn my profession."[50]

Like Eisenhower, Bradley did not see combat in World War I and thought he was therefore "professionally ruined." At Fort Grant in 1918, his battalion, because of many discharges, became seriously understaffed and was therefore quite small. He described the months following the armistice as a "bitterly cold, inactive winter, reading a great deal . . ."[51]

Bradley commented on his tour of duty between 1920 and 1924: "In those years, I began to seriously read and study military history and biography, learning a great deal from the mistakes of my predecessors. I took a particularly keen interest in one Civil War general, William T. Sherman, who despite his infamous reputation in the South was probably the ablest general the Union produced."[52]

I asked Bradley how one developed the feel or sixth sense needed for decision making. In answering, he emphasized the importance of reading and studying. "You first study the theoretical handling of troops; you study the principles of war and principles of tactics and how certain leaders applied them. You are never going to meet with that exact situation, but when you know all these principles and how they were applied in the past, then when a situation faces you, you apply those principles to your present situation and hope you come up with a good solution. I think the study of military history, and what the great leaders did, is very, very important for any young officer in developing this quality."[53]

Captain J. Lawton Collins was assigned to Fort Benning during the tenure of Marshall as deputy commandant of the Infantry School in the early 1930s. Marshall had significant influence on the young officers assigned to the faculty, as Collins recounts: "Colonel Marshall seemed to take special interest in Charlie Bolte and me. Additional tasks were frequently given to one or the other of us, for inquiry and oral report. We became members of an informal study group comprising most of the officers named above, reinforced from time to time by Doctor Stayer, Major Harold R. Bull, Major Bradford G. Chynowth, a brilliant member of the Infantry Board, and others, which met occasionally in an evening at Colonel Marshall's quarters. Monitored by 'Doc' Cook, one or two of the group would report on a book or subject for inquiry assigned at the previous meeting by Marshall or Cook. Subjects were seldom of a direct military nature, but ranged from geopolitics to economics, psychology, or sociology with reference to their effect on military problems. A lively discussion always followed."[54]

Collins's thirst for reading started while he was a cadet at West Point, but his interests were much broader than the strict study of military subjects: "I was one of those rare cadets who enjoyed West Point, or at least admitted his enjoyment. The academy exceeded my expectations, especially the toughness of the curriculum. I entered with the aspiration of graduating near the top of my class and joining the Corps of Engineers. But I soon realized that I would have to give up all other interests and concentrate all my time on studies if I was to have a chance of making top ten in the class. The studies then were mostly technical, whereas my bent was toward the humanities. The academic schedule was not as crowded as now, and cadets had more time in the winter months to read and reflect. I spent many hours in the library reading Swinburne, Masefield, Lafcadio Hearn, Ibsen, and other poets and playwrights. I had been introduced to them by Lucius H. Hi, a Yale man, and the only civilian professor at the Point. As head of the Department of English, he was a refreshing influence."[55]

* * *

The most remarkable team in the Allied effort of World War II was that of Eisenhower and Gen. Walter Bedell "Beetle" Smith, who became chief of staff. Smith had only a high school education, but throughout his career he was an avid reader. It was this self-education that made him so invaluable. As soon as it was announced that Ike was to be the commander for the invasion of France, he wanted Smith.

The relationship was superbly summed up by Smith's biographer: "From the beginning, Ike and Beetle composed a near perfect blend of personalities. Eisenhower's strength lay in human qualities: his modesty, common sense, optimism, and good humor. He had the power to draw people toward him. Eisenhower's smile won the immediate trust and loyalty of others. This contrasted with Smith's calculating detached professionalism. A high-strung man who lived on his nerves, Smith's goal-oriented devotion to duty drove the allied staff. A taskmaster to his subordinates, he showed the subtle skills of a diplomat in his relations with the British. He sacrificed personal considerations and used any method to achieve his end."[56]

But why was Smith so valuable with little formal education? During the delay from June 26, 1942, until his actual arrival in London on September 7, 1942, Smith was offered command of a division. He gave it serious thought but decided to join Ike in London. Again, selflessness was a clear part of his character; he gave up the rewards of command. To prepare for his responsibilities as Ike's chief of staff, he proceeded during the summer of 1942 to bury himself in books that described staff duties, theoretical and historical accounts of chiefs of staff, covering the history of warfare throughout the centuries in all parts of the world. This professional reading was a pattern of Smith's career and was essential for his preparation for the responsibilities that he would perform so well.

Although this is primarily a study of American generals, I would like to include Winston S. Churchill. He attended high school at the prestigious prep school Harrow but was not a strong student. He was never able to matriculate at Oxford but went to Sandhurst, the British equivalent to West Point, an institution for educating career professional soldiers.

In his memoir, *My Early Life,* Churchill describes his experience at Sandhurst: "I had a new start. Discipline was strict and the hours of study and parade were long. . . . I was deeply interested in my work, especially tactics and fortification. My father instructed his bookseller Mr. Bain to send me any books I might require for my studies. So I ordered Hamley's *Operation of War,* Prince Kraft's *Letters on Infantry, Cavalry and Artillery,* Maine's *Infantry Fire Tactics,* together with a number of histories dealing with the American Civil, Franco-German and Russo-Turkish Wars, which were then our latest and best specimens of wars."[57]

He continues by confessing that after Sandhurst: "I had always liked history at school. . . . I resolved to read history, philosophy, economics and things like that; and I wrote to my mother asking for such books as I had heard of on these topics. She responded with alacrity, and every month the mail brought me a substantial package of what I thought were standard works. In history I decided to begin with Gibbon. Someone had told me that my father had read Gibbon with delight; that he knew whole pages of it by heart, and that it had greatly affected his style of speech and writing. So without more ado I set out upon the eight volumes of Dean Milman's edition of Gibbon's *Decline and Fall of the Roman Empire.* I was immediately dominated both by the story and the style. All through the long glistening middle hours of the Indian day, from when we quitted stables till the evening shadows proclaimed the hour of Polo, I devoured Gibbon. I rode triumphantly through it from end to end and enjoyed it all. I scribbled all my opinions on the margins of the pages, and very soon found myself a vehement partisan of the author against the disparagement of his pompous-pious editor. I was not even estranged by his naughty footnotes. On the other hand, the Dean's apologies and disclaimers roused my ire. So pleased was I with the *Decline and Fall* that I began at once to read Gibbon's autobiography."

Later when Churchill was stationed as a young officer in the Bangalore, he continued his passion for reading. "From November to May I read for four or five hours every day history or philosophy. Plato's *Republic*—it appeared he was for all practical purposes the same as Socrates; *The Politics of Aristotle,* edited by Mr. Weldon himself; Schopenhauer *On Pessimism;* Malthus *On Population;* Darwin's

Origin of Species; all interspersed with other books of lesser standing. It was a curious education." His love of history and biography continued throughout his life.[58]

The first chief of staff of the separate air force, Gen. Carl "Tooey" Spaatz, was an avid reader. He was a student officer in 1925 at the Air Service Tactical School at Langley Field, in Virginia. One objective of the army school system was to relieve the officers from the burden of their normal duties and give them the opportunity to study, think, and reflect. Spaatz's diary reveals that he read widely and did not limit it to strictly professional matters: "May 10, 1925: Am reading Huneker's *Steeplejack;* May 18, 1925: Finished Don Marquis' *The Dark Hour;* May 25, 1925: Literature by Arthur Schnitzler . . . *Monsieur Lamblin* by George Ancey presents a character which is difficult to visualize as an actuality."

Most meaningful was the comment, "Read *Steeplejack* until noon—quotation: 'But to pass our interval between two eternities raking in gold is simply absurd to me . . . ,' henceforth, I am to acquire sufficient gold to cease any worry about old age. It may be ridiculous for an aviator to worry about old age, but I do, coupled with apprehension that some day I may quit my army career, either through my own volition or otherwise."

In 1957, Gen. Thomas D. White became air force chief of staff. A brilliant soldier-statesman, he served at a critical time for the air force, with the Cold War going on. He was fluent in seven languages, including Chinese and Russian.

I asked White about his career and preparation for higher responsibility. He commented on the importance of his reading: "My last year in Panama I was aide-de-camp to General John M. Palmer, who was one of the great scholars of the old army. He wrote a number of books and was coauthor of a work that related to the National Defense Act of 1920, the big reorganization act after World War I. He was the author of *Washington, Lincoln, Wilson: Three War Statesmen,* another on General von Steuben, *America in Arms,* and *Statesmanship or War.* General Palmer had a great influence in my life because he was such a student of history."[59]

White tried for years to be assigned to China and finally received orders for language training there. He left San Francisco for Peking on June 10, 1927. He kept a diary of his trip across the Pacific and his China tour and continued his study of languages. "There are two Capuchin monks aboard going to Guam for sixteen years. Rumor has it, they are from Spain. . . . I have been practicing Spanish with them. I am surprised to find how quickly I forget, yet I can nearly say everything without thinking so at one time. I guess I know the language very well." He later wrote in his diary on June 15, 1927: "I spent most of the time, so far, reading, also brushing up on Russian, which sounds foolish, I do know. But it is the most interesting language. Especially if we go to Peking by way of Fusan and Mukden. I find that I can read a good deal of Russian and my eight months of it at Georgetown have given me the pronunciations correctly, so certainly no harm is done in studying it if I want to, so long as it doesn't interfere with my later study of Chinese. People used to laugh at me, I am sure, when I studied Chinese for recreation at West Point and elsewhere, but I take pleasure in thumbing my nose at all of them now—I haven't seen anyone who wasn't green with envy at the idea of going to China as I am."

White also spent a good deal of time reading. He wrote on June 18, 1927: "I am reading *An Outline of Chinese History* which is the latest book on China and is very interesting indeed. I also have enough big books to last me for three or four voyages, like this one, including *The Story of Philosophy, Napoleon* by Emil Ludwig, *The Royal Road to Romance,* etc., etc."

White's knowledge of international relations was to be a large factor in his selection as chief of staff and, most importantly, in his exceptional performance in that position.

White really worked hard at it. "I have had my nose in a book," he wrote on January 27, 1930, "all the time as I am working to catch up the work I lost out while I had the bad foot. Also I want to finish my aero dictionary (in Chinese), which I am working on before Major Magruder is relieved as military attaché. I have to complete it before I go away." He also was publishing in the professional journals. "Just got the May number of the 'U.S. Air Services' with my article 'Acrobatics on Paper, or How to Write a Chinese Dictionary.'"

During White's visits to Manila, he stayed with Joseph Smith, a West Point classmate. Smith, who retired from the air force as a lieu-

tenant general, later remembered that White, in his last year in China, "was permitted to roam around and do what he wanted. . . . He used to tell me he'd take a rickshaw boy and go into the country as much as two weeks at a time, just traveling around, living with people, talking Chinese, and learning the way of those people. He knew a lot about their art and their culture. He was very interested in that sort of thing. . . . His main objective was to learn how to speak the different dialects of their language."[60]

Lieutenant General Louis E. Byers, U.S. Army (Ret.), told me about White: "While [he was] on duty as a language officer in Peking, his courage, imagination, and willingness to undertake the unusual caused him to ask Nelson Magruder, U.S. military attaché in China, for permission to visit the battlefront during the early Japanese thrust into Manchuria. The clarity, accuracy, and objectivity of Tom White's reports were such that they were sought throughout the War Department. From this time on, he became a marked man."[61]

An insight into his thirst for learning and his interest in international affairs was provided by his writing home as a young lieutenant in 1926: "As for Christmas presents for me, I think I'd rather have a subscription to the magazine *Foreign Affairs* than almost anything I can think of."

On his study of languages he commented: "Have been doing a good deal of studying lately as well as some writing. You will be surprised to know that I can read all of the first thirty pages of my Chinese lesson book. . . . I can now write the Chinese script—which is supposed to be very hard. I really enjoy such things, and it seems to come easy to me. I can read Spanish, Portuguese, some French and Italian, and a little Chinese, which isn't bad for twenty-one years, counting that I have had to do other studies most of my life.

"When I was at Bolling Field I went to night school at Georgetown, but I don't think I stuck with any of [the subjects] very much except the language courses. I took both Chinese and Russian, but I put aside any ideas of foreign service, because in those days, for sure, one had to have a private fortune to get to the top, though I never have been particularly conscious of that."

When the United States recognized the Soviet Union, the first U.S. ambassador appointed to Moscow in 1933 was William C. Bullitt.

President Roosevelt told Ambassador Bullitt that he could appoint anyone he wanted to his staff. Bullitt insisted that he be permitted to have an airplane of his own so he could fly wherever he desired within the Soviet Union. The Kremlin approved, and the newspapers referred to him as Moscow's first "flying ambassador." He selected Thomas D. White, who was the first, last, and only American to receive a Soviet pilot's license.

Commented White: "I suppose you could say I tried to prepare myself for the day when we would recognize the Soviet Union. I studied Russian at Georgetown and that paid off. When I was selected to go to the Soviet Union as air attaché, I can't say I did anything to set it up, other than the fact that I had studied Russian and some people knew it. It was a complete surprise to me when I was named. I was sent for by General MacArthur when I was a lieutenant at Bolling Field and General MacArthur was the chief of staff. I couldn't figure that one out. General MacArthur told me that he was sending me to Moscow. I didn't ask anybody for that assignment, but I had made application for more foreign duty."[62]

The tour in the Soviet Union was a broadening experience for the future chief of staff of the air force. He learned about communism as it was practiced in the Soviet Union, and about the nature of the people and government officials.

He continued his habit of reading and frequented the local bookstores. He wrote in his diary: "Random note—People in bookstore seem surly and unfriendly. Maybe have read more anti-capitalistic propaganda. I am always taken for a German. Not complimentary, I understand!" He obtained a Russian middle-school geography book, which he described as "very useful."

General Matthew B. Ridgway succeeded Eighth Army commander Gen. Walter H. Walker after he was killed in an accident during the Korean War late in 1950. Ridgway performed brilliantly, turning around a series of defeats. He was a serious reader. In an interview he commented that as a cadet at West Point: "I did a prodigious amount of reading up there, which probably detracted from my class standing but paid off much greater dividends in the long run. I read a tremendous amount from my yearling year on—almost all on biography and military history. Books such as Hamilton's *A Scrapbook of an Officer.* He was the military attaché of Great Britain with the Japanese in Manchuria. Incidentally—of course, I couldn't possibly foresee this—but forty years later as commander in Korea some of these things he had written about then came back vividly. Probably indirectly, and without my being aware of it, they were helpful: for instance, his description of the stoicism and physical endurance and acceptance of deprivation of the Japanese soldier on the march there in the bitter winter weather. I could look back on that winter in trying to tell our people that these hardships in Korea that you are enduring are no more than other troops of other nations have endured in years past and you can do it, too."[63]

The role of consideration in successful leadership will be discussed in a later chapter, but a foundation for its importance is presented by Ridgway, something he learned through his reading: "I want to mention this, as I just did to somebody here not long ago, speaking about consideration for your men. I also mentioned the great amount of reading I did outside of my curriculum at West Point when I was a cadet. There are a series of books written by Germans. They were written toward the end of the eighteenth century, one on *Letters on Artillery, Letters on Infantry, Letters on Cavalry*. . . . The one *Letters on Infantry* is still fixed strongly in my mind with the principle. Hohenlohe, I think, was the last name of the author. But anyway, *Letters on Infantry* you have, no doubt, got in the War College Library. Now this man came from a noble German family and yet his regard for his men is due the greatest credit to any company commander of that day. He advised that the unit commander should learn the background of the recruit's family (well-to-do, shoemaker, butcher, whatever he might be) . . . , should learn the man's problems at home if he had any. Just wonderful insights. Now this is just absolutely contrary to what you would have thought to be the normal behavior of the higher ranking Prussian-type officer."[64]

Ridgway was asked if this was out of character for the stereotype of the Prussian officer. "Yes," he responded, "but that is what he did. Books like that made a tremendous impression on me and had a very strong influence in my own career from the time I reported for duty in the 3d Infantry. It was a great book."[65]

He stated that his emphasis was on reading biography and military history. "My father had exposed me to a great deal of it. He cultivated a strong love of reading. I was a very small kid and he made me read aloud to him. Books like *Intellectual Development of Europe* and *The Conflicts between Science and Religion.* I read those things out loud to him and all of Victor Hugo's books, things of that sort. And, of course, you didn't have television or radio then, so you read. It was in those days at these little army posts, where there wasn't much to do, that a great deal of a boy's spare time, mine anyway, went into reading. A great deal of it."[66]

Ridgway gave emphasis to the importance of reading to one's professional growth, commenting that while assigned as an instructor at West Point: "I was studying everything I could out of the library on things, but these classes were of utmost importance to me. You learned so many things that these officers had in their personal combat experiences in handling men. You learned the pitfalls of those who had failed, and this, combined with your reading, provided the major sources for your fruitful leadership later on. A man by himself can have but a very limited personal experience. So you've got to draw on the experience of others, both in reading and in talking to men who have made their names in combat, who have demonstrated superior leadership. I just get them in the evenings and talk, not delivering lectures, but just sit down in your own homes, where they just ramble on. It is just a priceless opportunity."[67]

What role did reading have in the formation of the leadership of some of the more recent senior military leaders?

On May 16, 1997, in the U.S. Embassy in London, I interviewed Adm. William J. Crowe, Jr., former chairman of the Joint Chiefs of Staff, on the significance of reading. Crowe was serving in London as our ambassador. I mentioned that Douglas MacArthur's father, at his death, had a library of more than four thousand books. Crowe responded, "I have that many books in my library." I asked him when his interest in reading began.

He responded: "Clearly with my father. My family was curiously divided. I was an only child and my mother shaped my personality and father shaped my intellectual interest. He was an attorney and a voracious reader—also very Anglophile. He came over here when I was here in '64 and '65 to visit. It was the only time he ever visited me. I took him to the wax museum and he went down that row of monarchs, didn't look at any of the tags and named every one of them! An Oklahoma lawyer! He lived English history. He had a large library and was very partial to novels—Sir Walter Scott, Sabitini, the older stories. When I was about nine or ten he would read to me after dinner. I remember the first book he read to me was *Ivanhoe*. We went through it together. He read and I listened. He had a habit, which I subsequently acquired, of reading every night when he went to bed. Sleep experts, of course, tell you that it's not good for you. He read every night and I started doing the same thing."[68]

I asked Crowe what books interested him now.

"Since I've been in England [as a U.S. ambassador], I must have read a hundred books. I've read all of the Patrick O'Brien books, Taylor Frazier books, all kinds of history books. I just read this new biography of Captain Cook, which I thought was marvelous. I've recently read three or four books on Admiral Nelson. I'm reading one now on Calhoun, Clay, and Webster. It's thick going but, gosh, it's interesting. I also just finished *Undaunted Courage*.

"My father also loved oratory. I inherited a whole lot of books on oratory. He was very intellectually oriented. The reason I went to graduate school was because of him. He put a great stress on education."[69]

I asked him what reading had the most impact upon his career and his performance.

"I must say something in response to what you mentioned earlier: The Princeton graduate education experience was a watershed. I had no idea it would be so influential. I don't mean professionally; I mean personally. That the world is not absolute, that everything is not black and white like most naval officers are taught it is, that politics is everywhere. That was pretty good advice. As you know, with the dissertation, its value is not how much you know, it's how much you don't know."[70]

I asked him what books he had in his library.

"I really like biographies. That's the main thing I read. I like history, but I read biography most of all. I spent a long period of my life worrying about the Civil War. I have a statue of Lee on my desk [as the greatest general of the Civil War]. But after reading more about the Civil War, I changed my mind. I think the greatest general of the Civil War was Sherman. I loved reading about Lee, but I must admit that Sherman had the best idea of the Civil War. While he's hated in the South, his idea was not to shoot people but to destroy property. In the march through Georgia up through Virginia, he killed very few people. He destroyed a lot of farms, buildings, and crops, but he didn't kill people. Sherman had been through Shiloh and he said, 'I don't like those kinds of battles.'

"Biography is a lifetime investment. I worry about naval officers who don't read. I also read a great deal about World War II."[71]

Crowe continued: "While in the pre–World War II days, individual independent reading was about the only opportunity, other than service schools or the officers corps. The postwar era sends promising officers to full-time graduate school at some of our most prominent universities.

"Princeton forced me to become more analytical and more tolerant than I had previously been. It challenged me to reassess some of my more conventional and ingrained navy views. It was one of the things that set me somewhat apart from many of my colleagues, that at times made my career so tenuous but also lifted it up. I became more willing to question, to reexamine, to argue for alternatives."[72]

General David C. Jones served under four presidents: Nixon, Ford, Carter, and Reagan. He had only two years of college: one year at Minot State and one year at North Dakota University. What role did reading have in his career?

"I have an insatiable appetite for information. Life is one of constant learning. I read a lot of professional works—military history, leadership—but also about what's going on in the world. Just listening to thirty minutes of news at night is not enough. You need to broaden yourself with in-depth reading. When I realized that race relations were a problem in our air force, I read every book I could get on the subject. With the tremendous material resources the air force had, I continued to spend time each week reading books on leadership.

"To me there are two things you get by reading. Number one,

whatever you learn from it. Second, and equally important, it makes you start thinking more broadly, particularly about leadership. I would strongly encourage reading biographies and memoirs of our top military leaders, but I want to emphasize that I ran into people who read a lot but didn't learn anything. With the foundation of this reading, you need to put yourself into the shoes of the commander, and it's useful to discuss your reading with others. It's a learning process. The reading and discussion help shape values."[73]

In an interview with Gen. Edward C. "Shy" Meyer, chief of staff of the U.S. Army from 1979 to 1983, I asked him if he was a student of military history.

"I read one set of books every year," he responded. "The whole time I was in the military, it was *Lee's Lieutenants*. I read all three volumes annually, and they were the only books I took to Vietnam with me—indeed, the only books I carried with me in every move." I asked him why. "Because if you read through them you begin to understand the elements of leadership. If you analyze the relationship among individuals, which is what leadership is all about, you can see how leaders convince someone to do something. The way Lee interfaced with all his 'lieutenants' was to me the quintessential way that leaders succeed.

"*Lee's Lieutenants* reminded me that my relationship with the individuals—whether in combat on the battlefield, in the Pentagon, or elsewhere—would be important to my own success just as it was at the heart of Lee's success, and the success of the Confederacy, for several years. When some of those lieutenants were gone, the same relationship and the resultant cohesion that existed wasn't there.

"I have read all the biographies and autobiographies of those who were involved in leadership positions, particularly in the military, such as Eisenhower's *Crusade in Europe* or MacArthur's *Reminiscences* and Bradley's *A Soldier's Story* and Forrest Pogue's four volumes on General Marshall. These books are still in my library along with many other military biographies and autobiographies as well as those of successful civilian leaders.

"While in the army, I got up early every morning at 3:30 or 4:00 A.M. and read for my own information. That was my own precious time to read what I wanted to read. Otherwise, I didn't get a chance to read. I jealously guarded that time and didn't think about what was going on in the army. I found that if I didn't set aside time to read, it wouldn't get done. Today, to be a reader, you have to work at it. Today, work is so all-consuming that you must set aside time to read. While the leaders of World War II were developing, there was no television; there was nothing to distract you except reading, polo, and golf."

I suggested that it is a cop-out for those who devote no time to reading to claim the distraction of television or a lengthy workday.

Meyer responded: "Taking the time to read and think is so important to see how other people have reacted in the past to challenges similar to those you face in the present. I selected a segment of Pogue's biography of Marshall relating to mobilization for the army chief of staff principals to read. We sat down and discussed the problems they had in those days [1939], and it turned out they were much the same problems we had in our hollow army."[74]

I suggest that many of today's officers use as an excuse to not read the fact that they have a demanding workload. During World War II, General Marshall as chief of staff worked seven days a week. From 1939 until he retired as chief in 1945, he took in that six-year period only nineteen days of leave. Yet he still found time to read.

In her book *Together,* Mrs. Marshall recalled the planning for the Casablanca Conference: "That fall George was busy furthering the plans that had been discussed at the conference. They were as intricate as the works of a watch, and as delicate; and required understanding, vision, and endless patience. When he came home at night he would often be too tired to talk. I would send to the library for a pile of books and place them at the side of his chaise lounge. My husband has always been an incessant reader and I was hard put to keep him supplied. He would go through a pile of books with the avidity of a swarm of locusts devouring a green field."[75]

General W. L. Creech, U.S. Air Force (Ret.), also provided an example of the necessity to discipline and structure reading. I discuss in chapter 6 General Creech's rapid rise to four stars and the lasting impact he has had on the management style and combat capabilities of the air force. Like the vast majority of the top leaders I have cited, Bill Creech was a voracious reader from his earliest years, despite heavy job demands and a remarkable record as a fighter pilot. As a lieutenant he flew 103 combat missions over North Korea. For six years afterward he was in the demanding jet aerobatics business both as a Thunderbird and a Skyblazer (the U.S. Air Force team in Europe), including four years as team leader. During that period he flew in 557 official air demonstrations in countries around the world. Being a part of either of those elite flying teams is the greatest tribute a fighter pilot can receive from his colleagues.

After a three-year stint as dean of the prestigious U.S. Air Force Fighter Weapons School, he became executive aide to the commander of Tactical Air Command. Following National War College, he served two years as a staff assistant to the secretary of defense; then, as a full colonel, he flew 177 fighter combat missions (in 156 days as a fighter wing deputy for operations, or DO) in Southeast Asia—before reporting to headquarters, Seventh Air Force, in Saigon for six months as Gen. George Brown's assistant deputy for operations. Despite the obvious challenges and time demands inherent in such a string of jobs, Creech still made time for lots of outside reading.

I asked him what role reading played in his development as a leader.

"What I have tried to do in my own life and what I have seen in those who turn out to be the most successful in rising to senior leadership positions is that they never, ever stopped their intellectual growth. One of my favorite quotes is from John Wooden, the famed coach of UCLA, whose team won ten NCAA championships in twelve years. He said, 'It's what you learn after you know it all that counts.' The people who fell short on this were those who didn't look on their college experience as primarily a road to further knowledge, a quest for knowledge. The quest for intellectual growth in one's air force career occurred in a couple of ways: one, through books and the written word; second, to learn about current air force operations, the current challenges, to think and grasp for information that broadens you. Your formal schooling helps in that regard.

"The best intellectual growth comes from being a consummate, ever voracious reader of books of all kinds. Of course, with long duty hours and long TDYs, that's not easy. You must develop the discipline to make yourself read a book a week, or least a book every two weeks. With respect to the choice of reading, I wouldn't attempt to give advice, except that in my own case what I found most valuable were books on human psychology; indeed, this field comprised about seventy-five percent of my reading. I concentrated on issues of motivation—what motivates people to want to excel, what motivates people to want to work, what motivates people to want to come to work in the morning.

"I also studied history. When I read biographies, what interested me was how did people who I chose to read about and wanted to emulate develop their intellectual growth. Were they voracious readers? Were they readers of history? Eisenhower and Patton were renown for being great readers. It must be a lifelong commitment, even an obsession, and you must never stop the process of your intellectual growth. Those are the people in my experience who become the best leaders of others. But it is also necessary to study people by talking to younger airmen, prowling around, getting to understand their fears, hopes, frustrations, and needs.

"I've known people with towering intellects who had probably read three hundred more books than I have who couldn't manage a three-car funeral. They don't understand what makes people tick, and if they don't understand what makes people tick, they don't understand what makes organizations tick. In the final analysis, what's making the organization successful or unsuccessful is its size and commitment and the talent and training and ability of the people in it. That's why I studied psychology."[76]

With the plethora of books and articles currently available, how does one sort out the most meaningful material? In 1987, Gen. Carl Vuono, after his selection as chief of staff of the U.S. Army (which he held until 1991), found a solution. He assembled a small group of army officers and civilians to assist him in reflecting on the important issues facing the army. He called it "Assessments and Initiatives" in recognition of the principal mandate of the group: to make assessments of key issues and offer him options for initiatives that could address those issues in ways that would most benefit the army and the nation. Group names, used by other army chiefs, were considered and rejected, including the "Army Studies Group" and "Staff Group," because conducting academic studies was clearly not the principal focus of this team activity. Nor was the group part of or a replacement for the formal army staff or army Secretariat. This group, which was given the name "The Chief of Staff of the Army's Assessments and Initiatives Group" (abbreviated CAIG), reported solely to Vuono and was enjoined to maintain the strictest confidentiality in its work. Among the principal areas of CAIG work were national security strategy; civil-military relations; relations with the public, the media, Congress, the White House, and the internal army; army training, leader development, modernization, research and development, doctrine, force design and force structure; and maintaining quality in the army from selection of soldiers for enlistment through their reentry into civilian life. The CAIG products included fresh assessments of sensitive issues unburdened by institutional pressures or biases, and options for action that might otherwise not be produced by the formal army staff processes, for institutional or other reasons. In short, the CAIG was an honest broker whose only clients were the chief of staff and the nation.

Vuono used the CAIG as a source of policy initiatives and review. He also used the CAIG to assist him in reaching beyond the army into the areas of research and reflection that his pressing duties denied him. The members of the CAIG, in addition to fulfilling their responsibilities in addressing army issues, researched and produced short peices on topical issues, books, and publications that might otherwise not have come to Vuono's attention. Each week, a compilation of these thought pieces—the "Issues Book"—would be prepared for Vuono's review over the weekend or on trips. The book contained, on average, fifteen to twenty submissions, each one to five pages in length. Often these included a precis of seminal articles or books, sometimes written for publication by members of the CAIG themselves.

Vuono commented to me on the value of the CAIG in fulfilling this aspect of its multifaceted responsibilities. "The Issues Book was a great stimulus to me for a lot of ideas. I would routinely get the book on Friday nights, and I would review it over the weekend or when I traveled. We had a broad range of people working on the book, so there was never any shortage of ideas. The book proved to be a great broadening experience for me; it gave me ideas—ideas that stretched across the breadth of the human experience. It's hard to say that any particular article or book or paper really triggered me into making a specific decision on any issue. But that kind of research and background provided vital elements in the decisional environment. I would never have had the opportunity to get that kind of information on my own—I just couldn't do it with the demands of my schedule and the plethora of books published each year. Sometimes, the Issues Book would focus me on a particular book or article, and I would have the CAIG provide me with the original material. There were books I read—and ideas that I was exposed to—that I never would have picked up had the Issues Book not alerted me to them. It was a very valuable tool for my decision making.[77]

I asked Vuono what role reading had in his career development prior to this. He replied: "Reading had a significant impact on me throughout the years of service. Military history, biographies, stories of leadership all helped shape my thinking and my understanding of the profession of arms. One such book was Field Marshal William Slim's *Defeat in History,* a study of the war in Burma."

I asked Vuono what he got out of the book, and he answered with a single word: "Tenacity. . . . Slim kept at it—he would never accept defeat, despite the conditions, the impossible odds, the arduous nature of the environment itself. He kept at it. That had a lot of resonance with me.

"Another book [that was important to Vuono] was Bradley's autobiography in which he exposed to me his own humanity and his genuine concern for his soldiers. Forrest Pogue's biography on George Marshall had an equally significant impact. Through his words, I came to know this most complex and gifted of twentieth-century leaders. T. R. Fehrenbach's book on Korea became a watchword for me. . . . He poignantly outlined the human tragedy of unpreparedness and the price that the American soldier paid for shortsighted, fiscally governed training and readiness programs in the aftermath of World War II. Indeed, it was Fehrenbach who sharpened for me a phrase that became a motto for my years as the chief of staff: 'No more Task Force Smiths,' a reference to the first ill-prepared battalion formation that was thrown into Korea to stem the Communist advance and was annihilated on the hills overlooking Osan. Never again must the United States send its young men and women in harm's way ill-prepared and ill-equipped to fight and win and to return home safely."[78]

When General Schwarzkopf was offered the position of chief of staff of the army after successfully leading the allied effort to remove Iraq from Kuwait, he refused the opportunity. He told me, "The job went to General Gordon Sullivan, who had exactly the right combination of toughness and fairness."[79]

Sullivan offered his insight into the importance of reading: "Books are an important part of any U.S. Army leader's professional development. There is never enough time to do all the reading we want to do, but I learned early in my career that I could make some time for reading. By doing so, I was able to find relaxation in the midst of challenging assignments, prepare myself to master that day's challenge, and educate myself for the bigger problems hidden in the future.

"Professional journals and periodicals . . . help me stay in touch with changes and viewpoints in our world, our society, and our army. Short journal articles always give me the timely information I need, and they are an important means of discovering authors whose longer works match my interests.

"I always enjoy reading military history. I tell people that history strengthens me. It helps me and, I would hope, others realize that mortal man can overcome the obstacles in his path, transforming his situation through sound decisions and steadfast application of his will. . . .

"My point is: Read to relax, to learn, and to expand your horizons. You will be better for it as you will grow personally and professionally."[80]

I asked Schwarzkopf if he was a reader like MacArthur, Eisenhower, and Bradley. "Yes, but probably not to the degree of the others you're speaking of, because of time constraints. I just denuded myself of my library [he had just retired]; I gave the books to local schools, but a lot of them had inscriptions written. It was embarrassing because I had to cut the pages out of them with the inscriptions because someone might steal theirs from a library. I gave away a couple thousand books, easily. Every time we moved it was always a terrible thing because we were always having to pay excess weight charges. We had as many as forty-five book boxes."[81]

I asked him what role reading had in the development of his leadership. "You either learn from history or you are doomed to repeat it. I became very interested in military history at West Point. They had this course entitled The History of Military Art. I loved that course. I have kept my History of Military Art books over the years. When I left Vietnam, as my farewell present to Colonel Truong, just appointed General Truong, I sent back to West Point and got a set of West Point atlases and left them for him.

"I have been fascinated with the leadership of people like Lee, Grant, Sherman, Patton—obviously, and Bradley. I have all their books. I started reading and collecting these books as a lieutenant and captain. My father had a complete set of the Harvard classics published back in the twenties. When he died, I said I wanted these books and they became part of my library."[82]

I asked if he had read the Harvard classics series. "Oh, yeah, and I had another set of books entitled *Modern Eloquence,* a series that ended with the 1920s. They were speeches given throughout history by famous people. It wasn't just history that I read; because I will confess to you that I also love poetry. As a young man at West Point, I spent hours reading poetry books."

I asked him who his favorite poets were. "At the time I was a romantic, so all the Cavalier poets were my favorites—Lovelace and people like that. I loved Browning, I loved Shakespeare. Some of the things Shakespeare did were absolutely wonderful. Also the works of Keats, Shelley, Wordsworth.

"Part of one's success is sensitivity and caring for other people. I am a hopeless romantic. I can watch some dramatic movie and sit there and tears will stream down my face although I know full well it is a conjured tale. I feel things. I feel passion; I feel pain on the part of other people. This goes back to intuition and how I can feel the emotions of other people."[83]

The interest in reading came later for Gen. Colin Powell. He told me, "It was only after Leavenworth [the Command and General Staff

College at Fort Leavenworth, in Kansas] and the National War College that I really started to understand the importance of reading. I read about Marshall and Eisenhower; to get immersed in these books was an influence in my life. The first book I read was Janowski's *The Professional Soldier*, then four volumes of Pogue's biography of General of the Army George C. Marshall, and particularly *The Armed Forces Officer* by S. L. A. "Slam" Marshall."[84]

General John M. Shalikashvili, chairman of the Joint Chiefs of Staff from 1993 to 1997, was sixteen years old when he came here from Poland. I was amused when he told me that he learned English from watching John Wayne westerns. He later became a serious student of the military. "I remember," he said, "when I first became interested in military affairs I tried to read all I could get my hands on about Napoleon. After I came to this country, we were getting ready to celebrate the centennial of the Civil War, and I read everything I could about the Civil War. Then I studied the books on World War II. I read Eisenhower's book *Crusade in Europe* several times. I was fascinated with Douglas MacArthur's memoir *Reminiscences*. It was interesting to compare that work with Manchester's book on MacArthur, *American Caesar*."[85]

Shalikashvili encouraged reading among young officers. "I recall how frustrated I would get when I was a battalion commander, I would worry about lieutenants—how difficult it was to get them to read a book about military history. You could always order them to read, but I wanted them to become enthused with military history. I remember how delighted I was one day when by chance I asked a lieutenant to read *Killer Angels* and to give me a report on it. He did and was just bubbling over that book. From then on I used that book to get young officers started on reading, so they would hopefully fall in love with reading military history."[86]

It was clear that Eisenhower's reading history developed role models for him, as it did with the other generals discussed in this chapter, particularly qualities that were so much a part of Ike's character: stamina and patience in adversity, indomitable courage, daring and capacity for self-sacrifice. All of these were part of his success as a leader faced with crushing responsibilities as a general in charge of the greatest armada in the history of war.

For those who aspire to future positions of challenge and re-sponsibility, reading biographies is essential. Life is short, and in life we learn and grow from personal experiences. But because life is short, people are limited to their own experiences. With biographies, we learn and grow more rapidly by benefiting from the experiences of others, people who have made a mark.

Over the last thirty-five years, I have observed that those generals who were avid readers had superior depth and perception. Their reading helped to develop their character and leadership qualities. Their major interest was biography and history, but many were in-terested in the works of Socrates, Plato, Aristotle, and Shakespeare. As youths they all read adventure novels of authors such as Sir Wal-ter Scott, Rudyard Kipling, and James Fenimore Cooper, who sparked their interest in the adventures of a military career. Their sensitivity is illustrated by these "warriors" who loved poetry. The sixth sense they possessed, their intuition, was honed and enhanced through the ideas and character of other leaders.

In our democracy we take for granted the unlimited opportunity we have to read books. In 1997, a student from formerly Commu-nist Bulgaria arrived in the United States to study. In an award-win-ning essay, Krassimira J. Zourkova wrote: "I still wonder whether growing up under communism in Bulgaria was something I should regret or something I should be thankful for. I tell my American friends how in second grade my diploma came with a compulsory enrollment in the children's sub-division of the Communist party, and about my grandfather who was expelled from medical school because he was 'politically unreliable.' Yet, what I never managed to get across is the positive side: this special, intangible appreciation of life—this awe for the ordinary things—that communism brought into my childhood.

"I remember the surprised look on my roommate's face when she saw me sliding my hand up and down the cover of one of my text-books, as if caressing it. She laughed and asked me whether I was daydreaming. In fact, I had been thinking about the book itself, be-cause I was opening it for the first time. This initial encounter with a book, from the first touch of its smooth cover to the brief crack of the glue as one opens the front page and presses the leafs down, was a moment which had turned almost into a ritual—long ago, when I would come home from school, and on the rare, 'lucky' nights as I called them, I would find a book which my father, after hunting for it for days, had left on the table to surprise me. In those days, it was almost impossible even to find the books for purchase. Often I had to wait in line for hours, and then, when the store opened and the crowd rushed in I would have to snatch as many books as possible (hoping the title I was looking for happened to be among them) before the shelves got swept shining—empty within minutes.

"For me, learning to feel the special individual significance of any given book took growing up in the years when books were at the same time a rare commodity, an unattainable luxury, and a small, romantic, everyday dream. So, when my friends ask me what it was like back in those years, I tell them to go into our University library, and to find, on one of the thousands of shelves, a book with folded pages, with stains on the paper, and with someone's careless, red-ink notes over the text. I tell them that if upon seeing all that, they feel a strange, inexplicable ball of anger roll up in their throat—they will have known."[87]

There is a message here of value to the young military officer on the importance of reading and building a professional library in citing the influence it had on the leaders discussed. William Lyon Phelps, a professor at Yale University for more than forty years and owner of a library of more than six thousand books, made a radio broadcast on April 6, 1933, on the importance of reading and building one's own library. Part of this speech is worthy of quoting here because it focuses on the value of reading: "The habit of reading is one of the greatest resources of mankind; and we enjoy reading books that belong to us much more than if they are borrowed. A borrowed book is like a guest in the house; it must be treated with punctiliousness, with a certain considerate formality. You must see that it sustains no damage; it must not suffer while under your roof. You cannot leave it carelessly, you cannot mark it, you cannot turn down the pages, and you cannot use it familiarly. And then, someday, although this is seldom done, you really ought to return it.

"But your own books belong to you; you treat them with that affectionate intimacy that annihilates formality. Books are for use, not for show; you should own no book that you are afraid to mark up or afraid to place on the table, wide open and face down. A good reason for marking favorite passages in books is that this practice enables you to remember easily the significant sayings, to refer to them quickly, and then in later years, it is like visiting a forest where you once blazed a trail. You have the pleasure of going over the old ground, and recalling both the intellectual scenery and your own earlier self.

"Everyone should begin collecting a private library in youth; the instinct of private property, which is fundamental in human beings, can here be cultivated with every advantage and no evils. One should have one's own bookshelves, which should not have doors, glass windows, or keys; they should be free and accessible to the hand as well as to the eye. The best of mural decorations is books; they are more varied in color and appearance than any wallpaper, they are more attractive in design, and they have the prime advantage of being separate personalities, so that if you sit alone in the room in the firelight, you are surrounded with intimate friends. The knowledge that they are there in plain view is both stimulating and refreshing. You do not have to read them all.

"There are, of course, no friends like living, breathing, corporeal men and women; my devotion to reading has never made me a recluse. How could it? Books are of the people, by the people, for the people. Literature is the immortal part of history; it is the best and most enduring part of personality. But book friends have this advantage over living friends, you can enjoy the most truly aristocratic society in the world whenever you want it. The great dead are beyond our physical reach, and the great living are usually almost as inaccessible: as for our personal friends and acquaintances, we cannot always see them. Perchance they are asleep, or away on a journey. But in a private library, you can at any moment converse with Socrates or Shakespeare or Carlyle or Dumas or Dickens or Shaw or Barrie or Galsworthy. And there is no doubt that in these books you see these men at their best. They wrote for you. They 'laid themselves out,' they did their ultimate best to entertain you, to make a favorable impression. You are as necessary to them as an audience is to an actor, only instead of seeing them masked, you look into their inmost heart of hearts."

Notes

1. Personal interview with General of the Army Dwight D. Eisenhower, May 2, 1963.

2. Dwight D. Eisenhower, *At Ease* (Garden City, N.Y.: Doubleday, 1967), 39–41.

3. Richard Brookheiser, *Founding Father: Rediscovering George Washington* (New York: The Free Press, 1996), 139.

4. Ibid., 137.

5. Ibid., 140.

6. Catherine Drinker Bowen, *The Most Dangerous Man in America* (Boston: Little, Brown, 1974), ix.

7. Benjamin Franklin, *The Autobiography of Benjamin Franklin* (New York: Barnes and Noble, 1994), 13.

8. Ibid.

9. Ibid., 15.

10. Ibid., 18.

11. Ibid., 89.

12. Ibid., 113–14.

13. Ibid., 121–22.

14. Kenneth Ray Young, *The General's General* (Boulder, Colo.: Westview Press, 1994), 302.

15. Ibid., 312.

16. Ibid., 323.

17. William Manchester, *American Caesar* (Boston: Little, Brown, 1978), 23.

18. Young, *The General's General,* 323.

19. Douglas MacArthur, *Reminiscences* (New York: McGraw-Hill, 1964), 31.

20. Ibid., 79–80.

21. Ibid., 80.

22. Ibid., 80–81.

23. Manchester, *American Caesar,* 177.

24. Ibid., 324.

25. Ibid., 145.

26. James I. Robertson, Jr., *Stonewall Jackson: The Man, The Soldier, The Legend* (New York: MacMillan Publishing USA, 1997), 484.

27. H. J. Eckenrode and Bryan Conrad, *James Longstreet: Lee's War Horse* (Chapel Hill and London: The University of North Carolina Press, 1936), 363.

28. Robertson, *op. cit.* 84.

29. Correspondence with Virginia Historical Society and Edgar F. Puryear, Jr., July 12, 1998.

30. Ulysses S. Grant, *Personal Memoirs of U. S. Grant* (New York: Charles L. Webster & Company, 1885) 38–39.

31. William S. McFeely, *Grant: A Biography* (New York: W. W. Norton & Company, 1981), 16–17.

32. John F. Marszalek, *Sherman: A Soldier's Passion for Order* (New York: The Free Press, 1993), 11.

33. Ibid.

34. George C. Marshall, *Interviews and Reminiscence for Forrest C. Pogue* (Lexington, Va.: George C. Marshall Research Foundation, 1991), 67.

35. Ibid., 58.

36. Ibid., 54–55.

37. Ibid., 95–96.

38. Eisenhower interview, May 2, 1963.

39. Ibid.

40. Ibid.

41. Ibid.

42. Eisenhower, *At Ease*, 169.

43. Ibid.

44. Ibid., 173.

45. David Eisenhower, *Eisenhower: At War 1943–1945* (London: Collins, 1986), 57.

46. Letter from Gen. George S. Patton, Jr., to Cadet George S. Patton, III, dated June 6, 1944.

47. Martin Blumenson, ed., *The Patton Papers* (Boston: Houghton Mifflin Company, 1972), 890.

48. Omar N. Bradley, *A General's Life* (New York: Simon and Schuster, 1983), 17.

49. Ibid., 17–19.

50. Ibid., 38.

51. Ibid., 47.

52. Ibid., 53–54.

53. Personal interview with General of the Army Omar N. Bradley and Edgar F. Puryear, Jr., February 15, 1963.

54. J. Lawton Collins, *Lightning Joe: An Autobiography* (Baton Rouge: Louisiana State University Press, 1979), 51.

55. Ibid., 6.

56. D. K. R. Crosswell, *The Chief of Staff: The Military Career of Walter B. Smith* (New York: Greenwood Press, 1991), 110.

57. Winston Churchill, *My Early Life* (Suffolk, England: St. Edmundsbury Press Limited, 1989), 57.

58. Ibid., 123–35.

59. Personal interview with Gen. Thomas D. White, USAF (Ret.), and Edgar F. Puryear, Jr., April 30, 1963.

60. Personal interview with Lt. Gen. Joseph Smith, USAF (Ret.), and Edgar F. Puryear, Jr., July 6, 1977.

61. Personal interview with Lt. Gen. Louis E. Byers, USA (Ret.), October 14, 1977.

62. White interview.

63. Interview with Gen. Matthew Ridgway, USA (Ret.), and Lt. Col. John M. Beair, November 24, 1971.

64. Ibid.

65. Ibid.

66. Ibid.

67. Ibid.

68. Personal interview with Adm. William J. Crowe, Jr., USN (Ret.), and Edgar F. Puryear, Jr., May 16, 1997.

69. Ibid.

70. Ibid.

71. Ibid.

72. Ibid.

73. Interview with Gen. David C. Jones, USAF (Ret.), and Edgar F. Puryear, Jr., June 12, 1984.

74. Interview with Gen. Edward C. "Shy" Meyer, USA (Ret.), and Edgar F. Puryear, Jr., July 17, 1997.

75. Katherine Tupper Marshall, *Together* (New York: Tupper and Love, Inc., 1946), 97.

76. Personal interview with Gen. W. L. Creech, USAF (Ret.), and Edgar F. Puryear, Jr., December 20, 1998.

77. Interview with Gen. Carl Vuono, USA (Ret.), and Edgar F. Puryear, Jr., April 14, 1997.

78. Ibid.

79. H. Norman Schwarzkopf, *It Doesn't Take A Hero* (New York: Bantam Books, 1992), 493.

80. Personal interview with Gen. Gordon R. Sullivan, USA (Ret.), and Edgar F. Puryear, Jr., April 20, 1999.

81. Personal interview with Gen. H. Norman Schwarzkopf USA (Ret.), and Edgar F. Puryear, Jr., October 27, 1995.

82. Ibid.

83. Ibid.

84. Personal interview with Gen. Colin Powell, USA (Ret.), and Edgar F. Puryear, Jr., October 16, 1997.

85. Personal interview with Gen. John M. Shalikashvili, USA (Ret.), and Edgar F. Puryear, Jr., June 4, 1997.

86. Ibid.

87. From an article by Krassimira J. Zourkova, an undergraduate student at Princeton University, a publication for alumni and friends of Princeton University, spring 1997.

Chapter 6: Mentorship: Guidance, Counseling, Advice, Teaching, and Door Opening

How does one develop as a decision-maker? Be around people making decisions.
> —General of the Army Dwight D. Eisenhower

The first duty of a leader is to create more leaders.
> —General W. L. Creech, USAF (Ret.)

In answering my inquiry on how to develop as a decision maker, General Eisenhower commented, "Be around people making decisions. Those officers who achieved the top positions of leadership were around decision makers, who served as their mentors." Several years ago I was a scheduled speaker at the Air Force Squadron Officers' School (SOS) at Maxwell Air Force Base, in Alabama. The school, intended for lieutenants and captains, is the only company-grade course for all branches of the air force. In contrast, the army has company-grade schools for officers at the various branch schools, such as infantry and armor.

The speaker just before me was an air force general who advised members of the class that to get ahead, each needed to get a "sponsor" and to "hitch your wagon to a star." This comment concerned me, because he clearly gave the impression to the class of some five hundred young officers that success depends upon whom you know rather than job performance and what you know. This was upsetting to the students, who during the break expressed their disillusionment.

For the younger generation coming along, it is important to answer the question of how one gets ahead and succeeds in the military. In response to that question, this chapter develops mentorship in the careers of some of the twentieth century's most successful army and air force generals. In my interviews with more than a hundred four-star generals, I asked each man whether he thought his success was the result of having a sponsor. Not one of the generals who achieved four-star rank believed that his promotions or assignments were because of whom he knew, the way he parted or cut his hair, his school, his family, or his golf game. They all believed that their success was based on dedicated service to the country. In turn, however, their superior job performance led to impressing the people in their career who could mentor them.

A most perceptive insight into sponsorship was provided to me by retired general Edward C. "Shy" Meyer. He preferred the term *mentor* to *sponsor.* Mentorship has the perception of meritocracy rather than politics, which is so often associated with the word *sponsorship.*

"First of all," Meyer commented, "you have to define what the components of mentorship are. One component is in the area of guidance, counseling, advice, and teaching. How did you learn from that individual? Why did that individual take time to teach you? What guidance, counseling, and advice did you receive? That's one facet of mentorship. The second facet is door opening; it's providing opportunity for an individual. The more I've thought about mentoring in practical terms, the more I realize I believe it involves teaching and door opening. And that's different from your normal relationship with your boss or your commander. Your boss or your commander can handle you as a competent, capable individual and tell you what to do but without taking the time to teach, advise, or counsel. Also he can do it without feeling the obligation to open doors for you."[1]

What Meyer meant by opening doors was providing the opportunities for assignments that might assist in professional growth. This usually resulted in getting the toughest and most demanding jobs and working longer hours than most of a person's contemporaries. A mentor was someone who took the time to guide, counsel, advise, and teach and prepare one for increased responsibility, and thus higher rank.

The career of Gen. George C. Marshall furnishes a superb example of mentorship. He served as an aide and was on the staff of three generals: Gen. J. Franklin Bell, chief of staff of the army from 1906 to 1910; Maj. Gen. Hunter Liggett; and Gen. John J. Pershing, commander of the American Expeditionary Force (AEF) for World War I (1917–18) and chief of staff of the army (1920–24). Each man provided Marshall with extensive guidance, counseling, advice, and teaching. They were also excellent role models as exceptional combat leaders who received rapid promotions, Bell in the Philippines and Pershing in Cuba in the Spanish-American War.

Marshall's first meaningful mentor was General Bell, whose early career was unpromising. An 1878 graduate of West Point, he spent his first twenty years of service as a lieutenant, twelve of them as a second lieutenant. The future did not seem bright for him. He got his chance during the war in 1898, when he was assigned as a major of engineers to the Philippine expedition force. His performance in the Philippines was one of the most brilliant displays of courage in American history; for it, he was decorated with the Medal of Honor.

In 1906, he became army chief of staff, a position he held until 1910. He achieved this when he was not quite fifty, just eight years after discarding his lieutenant's bars. Although General Bell established a great record as a fighting commander, his lasting contribution was made during his tour as commandant at Fort Leavenworth (1903–06). It was there that the first tie began between Bell and Marshall. Bell's goal was to create a school to turn out fully competent professional soldiers, the intellectual center of the army.

When Bell became commandant at Leavenworth, he insisted that regimental commanders select only the best-qualified officers to attend this first course, which started in 1906. Marshall was selected, although he was only a junior first lieutenant. There were fifty-four in the entering class, most older and more experienced than Marshall.

Marshall wrote of this experience: "It was the hardest work I ever did in my life. . . . I learned a thoroughness which (later) stood me in good stead through all the clamor and push and excitement [and] lack of time. . . ." He also said of this year of study, "I finally got into the habit of study, which I never really had before. . . ."[2] Marshall graduated number one in his class, a significant achievement; this class standing at Leavenworth was to follow him throughout the rest of his career.

As chief of staff of the army, Bell came from Washington to make the graduation address. Graduating number one, Marshall obviously came to Bell's attention in a lasting way. Bell, a man with a brilliant war record, intellect, and vision, appealed to young officers such as Marshall.[3]

In 1913, Marshall was assigned to the Philippines for a three-year tour as aide-de-camp to Gen. Hunter Liggett. Marshall's first connection with Liggett was at Leavenworth when Liggett was commanding a battalion of the 13th Infantry and Marshall was an instructor. After class, Liggett met often with Marshall to discuss lessons that Marshall was teaching. During these meetings Liggett was impressed by Marshall.[4] In the Philippines Liggett spent many hours with Marshall taking him on inspections, having him take notes on what needed improvement. Often he sent Marshall out on his own to check field exercises.[5]

After his tour as chief of staff, General Bell was assigned to command the Philippine Department. Marshall was fortunate, early in his Philippine tour, to make a favorable impression upon Maj. Johnson Hagood, a member of Bell's staff. Hagood heard about a wager having to do with military fundamentals made between Marshall and a fellow officer. Hagood asked Marshall if it were true, and Marshall admitted that it was. Hagood remarked: "It taught me something. The lesson I learned, and I never failed to apply it during the rest of my career, was that the great thing in training soldiers is to get at the essentials, and when you're inspecting, to look for the essentials."[6]

In 1913, Marshall became adjutant to now Lt. Col. Johnson Hagood at Fort Douglas, in Utah. In Marshall's efficiency report, to answer the question "Would you like to have him under your command?" Hagood wrote, "Yes, but I would prefer to serve under his command." Hagood called Marshall a "military genius" and recommended that he be made a "brigadier general in the regular army, and every day [that] this is postponed is a loss to the Army and the nation.... [He] has had the training and experience, and possesses the ability to command large bodies of troops in the field." This efficiency report, dated December 31, 1916, was endorsed by Brig. Gen. Hunter Liggett and reviewed by Major General Bell. Hagood went on to become chief of staff of U.S. Services of Supply in France in World War I. In 1934, while Marshall was a colonel, Hagood, now corps commander, urged Secretary of War George Dern to promote Marshall to brigadier general.[7]

Marshall's achievements, which had come to General Bell's attention over the years, peaked when he became commanding general of the western department. Bell selected Marshall as his new aide. That duty, with a man of Bell's caliber, was challenging and instructive.

As army commander of the western United States, Bell was concerned with the border trouble that erupted in 1916 between the United States and Mexico. The field commander of U.S. forces on the Mexican border was Brig. Gen. John J. Pershing, another officer who was destined to play a significant role as a mentor in Marshall's life.

Marshall first met Pershing while serving as Bell's aide and soon became Pershing's most valuable staff officer in World War I. At first, he was in a different assignment in France. A maneuver in October 1917 went poorly, producing critical comments from Pershing. Much to Pershing's surprise, Marshall pointed out that the difficult maneuver was called with only one day's notice when it should have had two weeks' planning. (This account is developed in more detail in chapter 4, on "yes men.") Pershing, who was not in the habit of hearing young officers even talk to him, was reported to have said only, "Yes, you're quite right," as he stalked away. Shortly thereafter, Marshall was moved up to the operations and planning staff of Pershing's First Army under Hunter Liggett.

Marshall handled every challenge effectively and soon became one of General Pershing's most trusted subordinates as operations officer. In May 1919, Marshall became Pershing's aide, then continued to serve Pershing during his tour as army chief of staff from July 1921 to September 1924.

Pershing himself was mentored during his military career. Certainly a strong factor was a meeting in January 1897 between New York police commissioner Theodore Roosevelt and then Captain Pershing. It was the beginning of a lasting friendship that gained strength while they served together in Cuba, with Roosevelt leading his Rough Riders from the battlefields to the White House. There is no doubt that this close association with Pershing aided Marshall. He commented to him, "My five years with you will always remain the unique experience of my life." Marshall's career reached an impasse when MacArthur was chief of staff of the army from 1930 to 1935, when Marshall was not promoted to brigadier general. MacArthur even reassigned Marshall from troop command to be senior instructor for the Illinois National Guard, an assignment Marshall disliked. He asked for reconsideration for the first and only time in his career. It was denied.

Nevertheless, Pershing was still mentoring Marshall. He even took the matter of promotion to the president. The results speak for themselves. In Roosevelt's correspondence is the following note:

The White House
May 24, 1935

Memorandum for the Secretary of War:
General Pershing asks very strongly that Colonel George C. Marshall (Infantry) be promoted to Brigadier.
Can we put him on the list of next promotions? He is fifty-four years old.
F.D.R.

Marshall was promoted in 1936.

When Gen. Malin Craig was about to retire as army chief of staff, Pershing went to President Roosevelt and said: "Mr. President, you have a man [Marshall] over there in the War Plans Division who has just come here. Why don't you send for him and look him over? I think he will be a great help."

Marshall, a brigadier general far down on the list of general officers, was selected by Roosevelt to be the chief of staff of the U.S. Army in 1939.

General MacArthur had the most unusual mentorship of any of the generals in this study. He was born into the army, and his father, Arthur MacArthur, became his most important mentor. The senior MacArthur was an inspiration for any young man. For Douglas it was not surprising that the army would also be his life. Thirty years after his father's death, he commented, "Whenever I perform a mission and I think I have done it well, I feel that I can [stand] up squarely to my dad and say, 'Governor, how about it.'" A classmate at West Point commented that MacArthur "often wondered if he could ever become as great as his father." The classmate also said that Douglas spoke of his father with affection and pride and felt it his duty to be the general's worthy successor.[8]

Kenneth Ray Young, in his biography on Arthur MacArthur, *The General's General*, wrote: "Douglas's success in the army can partially be attributed to his father's influence. D. Clayton James suggests that Arthur MacArthur's 'most significant legacy to his son was the talented gathering of young officers who served under him in the Philippines. . . . These officers did not forget . . . when General MacArthur's son served under them in future years. Talented as he was, Douglas would enjoy a meteoric rise due in no small measure to the special interest of officers who were beholden to his father.' The name MacArthur meant something to them, and when Douglas's name appeared on the promotion lists, he always had a number of mentors to aid and abet his career because they felt an obligation to his father."[9]

Pershing also was a mentor for Douglas MacArthur. MacArthur was one of the few officers whose World War I grade was not reduced. Just before the end of Pershing's tenure as chief of staff, MacArthur's mother wrote asking him to consider promoting her son. Ten days before the end of Pershing's tenure as chief of staff, MacArthur was promoted to major general. Was it favoritism or meritocracy? The *New York Times* commented on the promotion: "He will be the youngest Major General on the active list of the army. He is considered one of the ablest and brightest of the younger officers of the regular army, and with good health he stands a splendid chance of some day becoming head of the army."[10] This was an excellent prediction. In 1930, Douglas MacArthur was selected by President Herbert Hoover as chief of staff.

Dwight Eisenhower graduated sixty-first out of 164 from his class at the military academy. This group who finished in 1915 later was to be called "The Class the Stars Fell On," because of the 164 graduates; fifty-eight members earned one or more stars by the end of World War II. Why was Eisenhower to be the most successful of his classmates? Why was he selected as supreme commander during World War II? How did mentorship affect his career?

The answers to these questions are not simple; but undoubtedly, the most singularly important factor was his selection for duty in the War Plans Division in the army general staff in December 1941.

Eisenhower's first assignment after graduation from West Point was to Fort Sam Houston, in San Antonio, Texas. It was there that he met a slender, attractive young lady with dark brown hair and violet eyes. Her name was Mamie Geneva Doud, and he later married her. His introduction to this young lady was through three young lieutenants, Leonard T. Gerow, Wade H. Haislip, and Walton H. Walker. The men were to become lifelong friends, and two of them were destined to play roles in Eisenhower's remarkable career.

The most important of these was Gerow, a 1911 graduate of the Virginia Military Institute. He and Eisenhower were to be assigned together again, at Command and General Staff School at Fort Leavenworth, in Kansas, where Eisenhower was first in the graduating class of 1926.

In 1940 Gerow, now a brigadier general, was head of one of the most important departments in the U.S. Army general staff, the War Plans Division (WPD). On November 18, 1940, Gerow sent a brief radiogram to Eisenhower, then on the IX Corps staff at Fort Lewis, in Washington, telling him of a pending assignment and asking if he had objections to this job.

Eisenhower had serious objections, which he detailed in a long letter to his friend, citing his lack of troop and command duty, feeling that he needed more such experience if his overall potential were to be achieved, and asking that the project be reconsidered. His plea paid off, and Gerow postponed Ike's transfer to Washington. Eisenhower wanted a field command more than anything else in the world. His answer could have been the most fateful decision of his life and would certainly have great bearing on his future career. If he accepted Gerow's offer, it would probably mean the end of any opportunity to get command, and spending another world war as a stateside officer. The next day he wrote to Gerow, who acceded to Ike's request to remain with the troops.

Colonel Eisenhower remained at Fort Lewis until he received other orders on June 24, 1941, assigning him to headquarters, Third Army, San Antonio, Texas, then commanded by Gen. Walter Krueger. It was to be a short tour for Eisenhower; he was to be called again for the plans job, the second time by General Marshall himself. This time he was not given the chance to refuse. A week after Pearl Harbor, Eisenhower was in Washington as assistant to General

Gerow. Gerow played a role in Eisenhower's selection, but so did other personalities.

Another influential person in Ike's selection to the War Plans Division was Gen. Mark Clark, his close friend. Not long after the Louisiana war maneuvers of 1941, Clark related that General Marshall told Clark that he intended to make some changes in the staff in Washington. Marshall asked Clark, "I wish you would give me a list of ten names of officers you know pretty well and whom you would recommend to be Chief of Operations Division of the War Department General Staff." Clark answered: "I'll be glad to do that, but there would be only one name on the list. If you have to have ten names, I'll just put nine ditto marks below it."

"Who is this officer of whom you think so highly?" asked General Marshall.

"Ike Eisenhower," answered Clark.

"I've never met him," Marshall said, but he quickly added that he knew of Ike's brilliant record. General Clark noted that "not long thereafter, Eisenhower was ordered to Washington. . . ."[11]

Another officer who played a part in Ike's selection was Walter Krueger. "Toward the end of the Louisiana Maneuvers, when General Marshall asked me whom I regarded as best fitted to head the War Plans Division which I had headed several years before, I named Eisenhower, though I was loath to lose him."[12]

It was a combination of factors, rather than any single one, that resulted in Ike's selection. But once he arrived, it was his performance that helped his rise up the ladder of responsibility, although it would be naive to deny that there was a certain element of luck involved in his success.

When I interviewed Eisenhower, I asked him why he thought he was selected for the position in 1941. "I think Gerow and Mark Clark and possibly Wade Haislip suggested me, pointing out that I had come out number one in the Leavenworth class, which was very competitive. I think Marshall rather respected the Leavenworth training."[13] More than any other individual, the man responsible for Ike's achievement at Leavenworth was a tough, dedicated, and brilliant soldier by the name of Fox Conner. Their relationship is detailed in chapter 5.

"General Conner," Eisenhower said, "made up his mind at Panama he was going to give me ground work in making tactical decisions. Every day, instead of having the usual general orders, the special orders to handle our command, he made me write the field orders. I wrote the field orders every single day for three years for everything we did. Having done this, the writing of field orders just became second nature to me."[14]

Writing field orders was one of the requirements at Leavenworth. Another area of emphasis was war problems. Eisenhower had his first exposure to this type of problem in 1919 at Fort Meade in association with Patton. "George Patton and I were great friends. He was getting prepared for Leavenworth and had sent for the back [former] problems. Then he said to me, 'Let's you and I solve these together.' He was eight years senior to me, and Leavenworth was still years ahead in my career, but I worked the problems with him. We began to solve them, and I found that as long as you didn't have any pressure on you, they seemed very easy. I liked them and got a lot of fun out of it. We'd go to his house or my house and the two of us would sit down, and while our wives talked for the evening, we would work the problems. Then I would open up another pamphlet, find the answer, and we'd grade ourselves. Later, I used to send for these when I was teaching classes."[15]

Had it not been for Fox Conner, Eisenhower might never have had the opportunity to attend Command and Staff School. Because of a dispute with the chief of infantry over the use of tanks, the then Major Eisenhower was apparently going to miss the chance to attend Leavenworth. Conner, who appreciated the value of the school, decided to intervene. He had Eisenhower transferred to the adjutant general's department. The adjutant general had a quota of two openings a year for Leavenworth, and as a favor to Conner he gave Eisenhower one of those slots in 1924.

Not long after Eisenhower's arrival on the army staff as deputy of the operations division, he replaced his boss and good friend Leonard Gerow. General Marshall explained: "When I brought him to head the Operations Division after Pearl Harbor, I put him in the place of a good officer [Gerow] who had been in that job two years. I felt he was growing stale from overwork, and I don't like to keep any man on a job so long that his ideas and forethought go no further than mine. When I find an officer isn't fresh, he doesn't add much to my fund of knowledge, and worst of all, doesn't contribute to the ideas and enterprising push that are so essential to winning the war. General Eisenhower had a refreshing approach to problems. He was most helpful."[16]

In any profession, the men at the top want men around them who have ideas and imagination and can supplement and contribute to and mature their own thinking. Eisenhower performed this function.

The next significant step in Eisenhower's rise was responsibility for drawing up a plan for joint Allied operations in Europe. He was given this task in April and by June had completed the staff work on the project. He took the report, entitled "Directive for the Commanding General, European Theater of Operations," to General Marshall and suggested that he read it in detail. Marshall replied: "I certainly do want to read it. You may be the man who executes it. If that's the case, when can you leave?"[17]

Less than a week later, Ike had his orders and left for London to assume command of the European theater of operations (ETO). It is history that Ike moved from the ETO position to command the Allied invasions of North Africa and Sicily, and he became the supreme commander for the invasion of France.

Eisenhower's career illustrates that having the ability to lead is not enough; there must be an opportunity to demonstrate that ability to an influential superior. A combination of mentorship, luck, and years of preparation and hard work gave Eisenhower the chance for significant leadership, which he ably discharged.

George Patton started on the road to success as quickly as possible for any young U.S. Army officer, and his mentorship was key. Soon after his graduation in 1909, he became aide to Gen. Leonard Wood, army chief of staff from 1910 to 1914. This assignment was of great importance in light of Wood's personality.

Serving as Wood's aide had a definite impact upon Patton. Wood's greatest influence, however, was indirect, because it was through his aide's position that Patton made what was perhaps the most important friendship and contact of his life. The president at this time was

Howard Taft, and his secretary of war was Henry L. Stimson. Patton was selected to be Stimson's escort for many official functions at Fort Myer. It was no coincidence that Patton then became one of Stimson's aides. Patton knew that Stimson was an avid horseman, and they took many rides together. Stimson quickly became attached to Patton, who exemplified the code of the officer and gentleman, which Stimson himself followed. Patton had the necessary social graces, was professionally knowledgeable, and was dedicated to serving his country. A friendship was started that grew stronger through the years and later affected Patton's career.

Patton was unique by having participated in every significant peacetime event available to an army officer. The first of these was the border skirmish between the United States and Mexico, precipitated by the bandit Pancho Villa. When Villa moved across the border and raided Columbus, New Mexico, President Wilson decided to take decisive action. He ordered General Pershing to take a contingent of troops to follow Villa into Mexico, capture him, and put a stop to his activities.

At the time, Patton was stationed with the 8th Cavalry at Fort Bliss, in Texas, near the border tower of El Paso, and was living next door to Pershing. The troops at Fort Bliss were anxious to get into action to avenge the deeds of Villa, but only a small group was chosen. When Patton learned that the 8th Cavalry was not selected for the expedition, he was terribly dejected. Rather than accept the inevitable, he decided to do something about it. He parked himself on a chair outside Pershing's office for almost forty continuous hours. Finally the aloof Pershing noticed him and asked him what he was doing there.

Patton answered, "I have been waiting for a chance to speak with you, sir."

"Well, you've got it. What do you want?"

"I want to go to Mexico with you, as your aide, sir."

"I have already chosen my two aides."

"You can use a third one, sir, and if you take me I promise you will never regret it."

"There's no use staying around here any longer. Go back to your quarters. You may hear from me."[18]

* * *

In a few days Patton did hear from him. His "modest insistence of his own excellence," as his fellow officers described it, and his determination to fight impressed the general sufficiently that he decided to take Patton along. Pershing did not regret his decision. Patton distinguished himself in service to the general and managed to work in a couple of daring episodes as well.

In 1917, the United States entered World War I. General Pershing was selected to command the American Expeditionary Force (AEF). Remembering Patton's outstanding work in Mexico, Pershing asked him to command his headquarters company. Patton jumped at the chance to get to France and also be promoted to captain. Within a year he rose to full colonel.

Patton attended the French Tank School at Champs Lieu and later set up a tank school to train American soldiers. He also managed to attend the French General Staff College at Langres, where he was pleased to be able to renew his friendship with Henry Stimson, who was also attending as a reserve army lieutenant colonel.

When Patton got into action, he proved again to be a most courageous soldier and won the Distinguished Service Cross for heroism in action. He also received the Distinguished Service Medal "for exceptional, meritorious, and distinguished services" in organizing and directing the tank center.

Patton never forgot the chances Pershing gave him in the Mexico conflict and in France. Before he sailed from the United States for action in North Africa in 1942, he went to see Pershing, saying, "I can't tell you where I'm going, but I couldn't go without coming to ask you for your blessing." The old general replied, "You shall have it. Kneel down." After the blessing, Patton stood at attention and snapped a salute to his mentor. It is reported that Pershing rose from his chair and "twenty years dropped from his shoulders as, standing erect, he returned the salute."[19]

When the United States prepared to send forces overseas in World War II, Patton, among our few experienced tank battlefield commanders, was one of the first officers considered for action in North Africa. The importance of the long and close friendship between Patton and Eisenhower played a role in his selection, as did the influence of Henry Stimson. Later when Patton's deplorable behavior, such as the slapping incident in Sicily, caused an uproar, Eisenhower and Stimson stood by him. They felt that the country and the army needed Patton to continue as commander.[20]

I later discuss mentorship relating to all the post–World War II generals who became chiefs of staff or served as chairmen of the Joint Chiefs of Staff, but first there are several air force generals who are worthy of mention, such as Curtis LeMay, who made significant contributions to airpower and the defense of the nation. LeMay was commander of Strategic Air Command from 1948 through 1957, vice chief of staff from 1957 through 1961, and chief of staff of the air force from 1961 to 1965.

LeMay had a mentor. In one in-depth interview with him, I asked if there was any person who significantly affected his career. He replied: "During my thirty-five years of service, I've been fortunate in coming in contact with practically all of the leaders of the air force during that period, and we've had a great number of very good ones. All of them, of course, have made an impact not only on me but on everyone else in the air force at the time. If I had to single out anyone, I would say Robin Olds made the greatest impact on me, or at least he made the first impact that really got me started.

"I first came into contact with him when I was ordered into the 2d Bomb Group in 1937. Up until that time, I had been a squadron officer without any great responsibility, [just] the normal responsibilities a squadron officer pilot had. Working for him, for the first time I began to get an insight as to what leadership meant and the great amount of work that had to be done to build a first-class air force that all of our great leaders at that time had visualized and were trying to build. This is the first time I ever got the overall picture, the true picture of what we were all trying to do, and how we had to go about doing it, and the great amount of work that had to be done.

"I remember being temporarily detailed to a group operations office to fill in for a regular operations officer who was ill. During the period of two weeks I served over there, I think I learned more than I had all the years I'd been in the air force up until that time. I guess it was probably a chain of circumstances that brought this about. The operations officer's desk was down near the main entrance to the building, so the first lesson I learned was that I had better be at my desk in the morning before Colonel Olds came to work. He usually stopped at the desk, and every morning he gave me about two weeks' work, so I fell rapidly behind in the period I was over there. But I learned a lot, not only from there but all the time I served under Colonel Olds in the 2d Bomb Group. It was quite an experience."[21]

LeMay learned the important role of mentorship observing the British Royal Air Force (RAF) during his World War II experience in Europe. He commented: "Early in the war I met an old man over in England, Lord Trenchard. He had commanded the British Expeditionary Air Corps in Europe in World War I. He was responsible for getting the first independent Air Force in the world, the Royal Air Force. I guess he must have been pretty close to eighty then, but he was still a fine old man. He put on a uniform and spent all the time he could where he could walk to get around American air bases and British air bases to see what the troops were doing, just to talk to them a little bit. Tell them a couple of stories. After a couple of talks with him, it dawned on me that Portal, Tedder and the guys who were really running the RAF had been his aides at sometime or other. So I remarked on this coincidence, how it happened.

"He said, 'Well, it was no coincidence. Nobody wants to be a dog robber for an air marshal very long. What I did was pick out some of the smartest guys I could find, keep them with me for a short period of time, and let them see what problems I had to deal with and how I went about solving them. Being smart guys to start with, they learned something. And they retained it and went on and did well when they got more important jobs. . . .'

"I thought that was a pretty good idea. So I tried to do that, because I didn't have the freedom of getting people and determining their assignments as Trenchard had. To some extent I did pretty well. A couple of my guys became four-star generals . . . three others [became] major generals. One exceptionally good one was killed in action in Vietnam or he'd have been up there, too. I did pretty well. Of course, I picked out some smart guys to start with. I tried to give them some training—the kind of problems that you get and how you go about solving them. Getting an answer, hopefully the right one."[22]

* * *

An example of LeMay's mentorship is Gen. David C. Jones. I discussed this with Jones, and he told me: "I was assigned to Omaha and in the ops plan division, and was told I was nominated to be one of the individuals to be considered an aide to General LeMay. The main interview that took place was where all four of us who were nominated had dinner at LeMay's quarters. I was a fairly new lieutenant colonel. After dinner, we had a discussion. A couple of days later I was notified that I was the new aide to LeMay.

"When I went in to report to him, the only thing said was, and these were the key words, 'Your first priority is to learn and the second is to serve and don't ever mix those two up.' That was the total guidance I got in taking over the job. He didn't want an aide wandering around getting him drinks and doing the typical 'horse-holding' business. He figured an aide could be exposed to the big issues. Looking back, he was preparing me to move up to a higher job rather than just being the typical social aide.

"LeMay told me it was a one-year assignment as his aide. Nearly three years later I asked, 'Is my one year up?' He smiled but didn't say anything. I left him when he went to Washington to be the air force vice chief in 1957. I was to go back to a flying assignment, but LeMay said, 'Go to maintenance. You need some experience in logistics.' I went out to be the head maintenance guy at Castle Air Force Base, B-52s and C-135s. It was a great move. It gave me a much better understanding of logistics and maintenance. I had thousands of airmen working for me. Normally commanders under the centralized system had few enlisted men working for them. Thus, the learning continued after I left him as aide. It was a risk since in operational flying I could have moved up quickly to wing commander, but I realized, as General LeMay advised, I could learn a great deal more in maintenance.

"I went to the War College in 1959 and graduated in 1960 and became . . . the advocate of the B-70. This aircraft was very controversial. Normally, major generals and lieutenant generals go over to brief Congress, but LeMay sent me as a junior colonel to go over to lead the fight for the B-70. It was a good experience for me. I was exposed to Secretary of Defense McNamara, and also Harold Brown (who went on to become secretary of defense under President Carter), and to Congress. It was part of the broad experience LeMay wanted me to have, part of the mentoring. I also got to understand about how to operate in the Pentagon as an action officer, and it helped me a great deal when I became chief.

"I never felt I was a fair-haired boy, that someone was looking after me all the time. I didn't think that [LeMay] in any way showed any favoritism. It was up to me to perform. I don't want anyone thinking I had a guardian angel."

Jones had another mentor in Gen. Walter Sweeney. "When Sweeney was commander of Tactical Air Command," said Jones, "he offered me a fighter wing. I had never been in fighters in my life. I could have become a wing commander in B-52s with an almost guarantee of a promotion. It was a risk for me, particularly since it was a case of activating a fighter wing, which is a lot tougher than just running a wing. That was a risky thing to go into the fighter business.

"LeMay also told me, 'When anybody is in my office, you be in there; wherever I go, you go with me.' On one occasion, I got thrown out of McNamara's office when I went in with LeMay. On another occasion, Secretary of State John Foster Dulles visited Omaha when I was LeMay's aide. There were only three of us in the room. I didn't participate in the discussion—I was there to learn."[23]

A final impact on Jones was Secretary of Defense James Schlesinger when he was commander of U.S. forces in Europe. Schlesinger was scheduled for a brief visit of several hours, but it extended to many days. During his visit, Jones personally gave him all the air force briefings. Schlesinger later told me that this was his first impression of Jones's exceptional leadership ability and vision and was the beginning of his support for him to succeed George Brown as air force chief.

A superb example of General Meyer's definition of mentorship—which included guidance, counseling, advice, teaching, learning from the individual, taking time to teach, and providing challenging assignments for professional growth—is illustrated in the career of Gen. George Brown, air force chief of staff from 1973 to 1974 and chairman of the Joint Chiefs of Staff from 1974 to 1975.

Brown had a remarkably rapid rise during World War II, from second lieutenant to full colonel in less than two years. One might conclude that with such a fast start, it was inevitable that he would rise to four-star general officer rank. There were, however, two other contemporaries who had meteoric rises during World War II to full colonel at a young age, but none achieved the success that Brown did.

General Jacob Smart described Brown's success in an interview. "There was a deliberate effort on the part of some senior air force people to assist in his development and advancement. One of them was Ennis Whitehead, a superb person with many qualities of leadership, both positive and negative. He once told me that he recognized George Brown as a man of unusual capacity and had encouraged his growth, recommending George's assignment to positions that would further broaden him."[24]

Whitehead himself commented on June 9, 1950, in his endorsement to Brown's effectiveness report, "Of all colonels of fifteen years of service or less, I rate Brown number one. In my judgment, he is the most competent officer of a similar length of service whom I have ever known."

Upon completion of the War College in June 1957, then Colonel Brown was selected by Gen. Thomas D. White, air force chief of staff, as his executive officer. I asked General Brown why he was selected for that position. He replied: "I wasn't aware that I had ever met him, but I had worked with and been associated quite closely with General Jacob Smart, his assistant vice chief of staff. I think that he arranged for my selection, although he has never said anything to me about it. The only time I ever laid eyes on General White before I went to work for him was when he came to the National War College to speak and I was just one in the class. When we were about to receive orders, I said something to General Smart about what he thought the future might hold, and he said, 'Why?' I said. 'Well, I've got property here in this area, a house that I need to dispose of. If I'm not going to stay in this town, I'd just as soon get out.' He said, 'Don't worry, you're going to be staying right here.' I think those two worked this thing out together.

"It says a lot for General White that he'd take me on, because I knew nothing about the Pentagon or how to get anything done there. Usually a senior officer is pretty selfish about who he has on his immediate staff. He wants them to help him. It was not the normal thing to have somebody who you can help. I think—and I don't want to sound conceited about this—they believed that they could bring me in as the chief's executive and push me on to other things that would benefit the air force."[25]

Brown's close friend, who also worked for the chief, was Gen. Robert J. Dixon. I asked him, "Would you say that General White had an impact on Brown's development?" Dixon replied: "There is no doubt about that. You couldn't be around White without being impressed and learning. At that stage, colonels like ourselves were like sponges—worse than sponges, like vacuum cleaners. We'd sweep it all up wherever we could get it. There wasn't a minute of the day that a million impressions didn't hit us, not only with General White but with other senior people, too. My impressions of people from those days are the most vivid because they were formative days. Our minds were wide open. Washington was an exciting town, and we had exciting jobs.

"General White had a very firm grip on what he did and didn't do, on what he wanted and didn't want. He had a gentle style, but there was a lot of steel in his gloves. I never saw anything but the glove. General White had a conviction, shared by George Brown, that the open warfare of 'Let's bring the matter to a head and get the damned thing settled' was not the way to go about doing things. To some extent, White was criticized for that by others who were more direct. However, he believed in persuasion. George learned from that. It was his nature and approach, too. Both George and General White had tempers; George had a temper that could really flare on occasions. But, given a preference, George would prefer to conduct things in a gentlemanly fashion. George also thought that General White was an eye-opener in terms of being able to see long-range issues, being willing to let the short-range gain go and be happy with the long-range victory. General White's view on the importance of outer space to the nation, to the air force, was an example of a long-range view. It's very trivial now, since everybody knows that space is important, but then, nobody appreciated it. I think the kind of vision that General White had taught George, as he taught me, was a new way of looking at things."[26]

One of the most challenging assignments in Brown's career development was as the military assistant to the secretary of defense from June 1959 through August 1963, particularly the last two years while serving under Secretary of Defense McNamara. To say that Mc-Namara was controversial and disliked by many military officers at the time would be an understatement, but Brown's service with him was remarkable and well appreciated by McNamara.

Upon completion of his tour as commander of the Seventh Air Force and as deputy commander for air operations of Military Air-lift Command Vietnam (MACV), Brown, in September 1970, became commander of Air Force System Command.

I asked Brown why he thought he became chief of staff of the air force. He replied: "Oh, I never thought about it. I have no idea. Perhaps I was the best choice among my contemporaries. I started out in bombardment . . . and I got into everything else except Lo-gistics Command and Systems Command. I'd been in Vietnam a year when Ryan visited us. He was then vice chief and had been nominated to be chief. He told me that I was going to follow him as chief of staff."[27]

"[He told me that] before he became chief, and I said, 'Jack, look, don't say that, because you don't have to make a decision now. Keep your options open.' He said, 'No, your selection is obvious, assum-ing you don't stub your toe, and your health is all right. But I want you to know now, because I want you to start thinking about it, and to think in such a way that you prepare yourself mentally for it.'

"Considering the jobs I had held and the exposure I had gained, it appeared quite evident that I was being prepared, although I had never thought about it until he mentioned it; it had never occurred to me. But I had been executive to the chief of staff and executive to the secretary of defense for four years. Then I went to MAC [Mil-itary Airlift Command], MATS [Materiel Air Transport Command], the Joint Task Force, and here as assistant to the chairman of the JCS [Joint Chiefs of Staff] for two years, and finally to Vietnam. So I knew the game around this town pretty well, on the Hill and in the Pen-tagon, and at State, and the National Security Council from my ex-perience here with the chairman. And I'd been on the Policy Plan-ning Board at State, where I was thrown in with a lot of people in high government positions today, like national security adviser Brzezinski.

"But I really don't know what caused Jack Ryan to do it. Anyway, I said, 'Don't even talk that way; that's silly.' Then, when I finished in Vietnam, I wanted to go to Europe, because I figured it was time David Burchinal left and then that job would be open. We were in Washington, D.C., for a conference, and Jack Ryan got me in a corner and said, 'You're coming home and you're going to Systems Command.' I replied, 'I don't know a damn thing about Systems Command.' And he said, 'That's precisely why you're going.'"[28]

I discussed Brown's Systems Command assignment with General Ryan. He explained: "I visited George Brown quite often at Seventh Air Force and was very impressed with what he was doing there. He was thorough, he knew what was going on, and he was able to influence his Army superiors. His assessment of application of force was extremely good. He could pull the F-4 outfits from Da Nang and Cam Ranh Bay off in country and move them out of the country without causing a big uproar in MACV. He stood up for his convictions without antagonizing people.

"So we pulled him back when he finished his tour in Vietnam, and I put him in charge of Systems Command, because I thought it needed an operational type. I thought it might be wise to bring some new blood in, and a top-notch man at that. And, of course, I was also thinking of my successor. Brown was logical, and I felt it would do him good to get some Systems Command experience, because weapons acquisition is one of the big jobs that the chief of staff has. This assignment would let him learn that side of the job and still be in the Washington area. So I told George I would recommend him to be my successor sometime in the fall of 1972."[29]

The undersecretary of the air force at the time of Brown's selection as commander of Systems Command was John McLucas. He told me: "We all agreed that George was the right man to be the next air force chief of staff, and that the Systems Command would provide the best background he could get for the job. General John Ryan, immediately after he was nominated for air force chief of staff, informed George Brown that he was his choice to succeed him as chief. Although this was four years before Brown was selected, George was being groomed long before this."[30]

A more current example of mentorship is Gen. Edward Meyer. His mentorship is particularly interesting because he was only a lieutenant general when he was jumped over fifty-seven other generals senior to him to become chief of staff of the army in 1979. He was a 1951 graduate of West Point.

As a major, Meyer was assigned to Supreme Headquarters Allied Powers Europe (SHAPE) from 1961 to 1963. He told me of this experience.

I'd say the individual who had the greatest impact on me was General Jim Moore when he was chief of staff of SHAPE. I was his aide and assistant executive officer. The story of how you get there gets to be important and it also relates back to how I got the job as his aide. It goes back also to relationships that have a big impact on how people get ahead. One of my classmates, Lou Michael, had been his aide for a couple of years and I had moved over to France. I lived in Orleans and had a very good job—a job that I enjoyed—in the G-1 section of the communications zone. I had a chance to go play golf when I was home; we liked it there, and we had good friends down there.

About that time I got a call saying, "General Moore is looking for an aide this summer. Would you like to do it?" And I said, "Well, let me talk to Carol and I'll call back." I was up at Oberammergau at a school and I said, "Screw it, I'm not going to go up to SHAPE and deal up there. I'll just stay here and enjoy what I'm doing." I had a good boss and good people to work with.

I got a call from Lou Michael. "Well, what have you decided?" and I said, "I've decided not to do it." As soon as I said that, he said, "Wait a minute." Then General Quinn, who had been my battle group commander with the 101st Airborne Division and now worked directly for General Moore, the chief of staff, got on the phone and said, "You get your ass up here. You need to come up here. It's an important job for you." I reluctantly said, "Yes, sir."

This highlights the fact that life is never simple. There are always people involved whom you've served under who therefore have an opinion of you—good or bad—and want you to go on to another position.[31]

Meyer worked for General Moore for a couple of years as his aide and assistant executive officer. It was a period during which he learned about an area of the army he hadn't been exposed to—staff work and international operations. For two years he was intimately involved in every piece of staff work that was developed, because they permitted him to work on challenges not normally available to a young major. He traveled with General Moore, so he got the opportunity to sit in on discussions that his boss had with heads of state and other armed forces. In addition, he was able to deal with Gen. Lauris Norstad, SHAPE commander, on a personal basis. Meyer told me: "General Moore's function was principally one of providing the opportunities, to provide the guidance when I screwed up—because I did—of teaching me by example. We would have one-on-one discussions on broad issues on which he and I would disagree. He knew that he was getting the views of someone who wasn't in World War II, talking to a young punk about issues of broad international interest."[32]

Through his work at SHAPE, Meyer was associated with two other officers, each of whom went on to the grade of lieutenant general before retirement. Meyer commented: "Charlie Corcoran and Woodie Woodward were both at SHAPE headquarters. Corcoran was in the nuclear weapons business and General Woodward was in the force development business. Both of them were superb action officers, but when I came back to the United States, they were in the office of the chief of staff of the army, Gen. Harold K. Johnson."

Meyer reflected on this opportunity: "I think when you talk about mentoring, you have to think of the people who took the time to provide guidance, took the time to teach, took the time to counsel when you needed counseling—and that's ass-chewing as well as backpatting. They played an important role in opening doors. For example, I went to the Armed Forces Staff College and when I finished there, two of the officers who had worked for General Moore at SHAPE brought me in to work at the office of the chief of the Coordination Staff and Analysis Group."[33]

These relationships provided Meyer the opportunity to work in the office of the chief of staff as a major and lieutenant colonel and to associate with Generals Abrams, Johnson, and Wheeler. Meyer also dealt directly with all of the general officer deputies. His responsibility in the Coordination Staff and Analysis Group was to look into the organization to make sure that what the chief said was really understood, so that action officers on the staff didn't waste a lot of time developing erroneous papers. Meyer watched the infighting within the army staff for greater authority. All of this education came from General Moore's mentoring.

Meyer had the opportunity to work for a group of people who had grown up in a staff environment to which he had never been exposed. For the first time, he had to deal with congressmen, prepare senior people for hearings, and assist in preparing retired General of the Army Omar N. Bradley for his briefing for a hearing on pay issues for Congress. So Meyer had a good opportunity to watch and observe the workings of the office of the chief of staff, and its main function.

Meyer's next service was with the troops in combat when he served from 1965 to 1966 under Maj. Gen. Harry Kinnard, division commander of the 1st Air Cavalry Division, the airmobile division going to Vietnam.

Meyer told me: "General Kinnard brought together people and gave everyone the opportunity to come up with ideas. His greatness was in his willingness to turn things over to people. I remember one time, after we got to Vietnam, I said to him, 'Here we are in this division, and we never get a division operations order.' He said to me, 'Shy, if you had the kind of commanders I have, how much time would you spend on a division operations order?' Everybody knew what he wanted; he gave broad guidance and everybody knew exactly what to do, and that was the way he operated. It was a marvelous learning experience for me. He taught me the importance of making sure all of your subordinates know exactly what is going on, and that you give them the authority to do the things they are supposed to do. He gave you a job and left you alone to do it. That permeated the whole division."

Meyer's assignment as a brigadier general was to the 82d Airborne

Division. He had been selected for promotion to brigadier general but had not been promoted yet. A number of classmates there were also colonels. He said: "I had a call from General George Blanchard, who said to me, 'Will you come down and be the assistant division commander?'"

Meyer had just gotten back from Vietnam and was at the Brookings Institution, where he was to be for a year. But they let him go early in order to take this command, so he was there for only about six months.

Meyer explained further: "When George Blanchard was commander of VII Corps in Europe, I served under him also in the 3d Infantry Division, so I worked for someone I knew who knew me. He did exactly the same things over there that he had done so well with the 82d Division."

The 82d Airborne was the all-American division, the pride and joy of everybody. Just before Meyer arrived, they had been ordered to go to Jordan. There were a lot of problems between the Israelis and other countries and nations, but the 82d was able to produce only one brigade, so there was a lot of concern about getting the division in shape. Blanchard was a good motivator, having many ideas every day about how to get people excited. He brought the senior leadership to get the battalion commanders working together. He had bubbling enthusiasm in everything he did. Blanchard taught Meyer the importance of working closely with the men, to consider the impact on soldiers in everything he did. They began programs on leadership, extending to the noncommissioned officers (NCOs). They had the first class in the army on race relations and the first real focus on drugs in a division.

In Vietnam, Meyer served under Gen. Mike Davison, who was field force commander, actually the equivalent of a corps commander. Davison's predecessor had spent most of his time dealing with charts and data. Davison was out flying to every firebase, dealing with operations, knowing what was happening on a daily basis. Meyer had the job, as chief of staff of the 1st Cavalry, of knowing what was going on during the Cambodian incursion.[34]

Then he was back to the Pentagon. "I was a three-star as deputy of operations," he said, "and General Dutch Kerwin was vice chief of staff. He was the one I went to for help and guidance anytime I had very serious problems with the army staff and the Joint Staff. He was always there.

"You always need someone who is a mentor to you. I believe mentoring is important, that General Moore and others who did that had the greatest impact on my life. Dutch Kerwin was that sort. Some senior people expect you to come in and give them all the answers. Dutch Kerwin really helped when I had problems. I could sit down and talk to him about these problems and he helped me solve them. A lot of bosses want finished products, but sometimes it's better to sit down and go over all the details with an experienced and wise person, and Dutch Kerwin always took the bitter bite off the challenge."

Why was Meyer selected to become army chief of staff? Why was he jumped over fifty-seven more senior generals? He explained:

I was on orders to go to Heidelberg in 1979 to be commander in chief of our army forces in Europe. My orders were already published. We had already sent off one household shipment and the packers were there to get the rest. I already knew who the next chief of staff of the army was going to be.

I got a call on Friday afternoon from Secretary of Defense Harold Brown saying, "The president would like to talk to you tomorrow morning." That was a Saturday morning. I said, "Gee, Harold, I'm sorry, but I'm going up to my dad's eightieth birthday." We were going to celebrate his birthday up in St. Marys, Pennsylvania, before I left for Europe, and all my brothers and sisters were coming in for the event. He said, "Well, I think it's important to go over and see the president." I said, "Well, I allow as how you're right." He didn't tell me what it was about.

So I went over to see the president. I thought he wanted to talk to me about what a great choice he'd made in sending me off to Heidelberg. I was going to reinforce that and tell him about all the great things I was going to do in Europe. He started to talk about the Far East, Korea, and a lot of areas like that. Then he said to me, "What are your ambitions?" I thought, here I am, a young punk fifty years old and I've been selected for four-star rank and I'm going off to command in Europe. I said, "Well, I'll tell you, Mr. President"—and this is a true story—"when I was a young lieutenant down in Fort Benning, I used to walk along Baltzel Avenue, across from the golf course, and I decided that I'd like to live in one of the big houses on Baltzel and train young infantrymen down at the infantry school." And he said, "That's not what I had in mind, General. What are your ambitions? What do you hope to do when you come back from Heidelberg?" I said, "I really hadn't thought about it. I'd like to go into the training business or something like that." And the president said, "Well, what about being chief of staff?" I told him I never really wanted to be chief of staff. And he said, "Well, what if you were to be chief of staff right now?" Then I gave him all the reasons why I should not be chief of staff right now—you know, age and a whole host of reasons like that. And he said, "Well, I'll call you back next week."

So I got back in my car and drove up to St. Marys for my dad's birthday celebration, and after that I came back through to Carlisle Barracks. I got in on Sunday night and was going through all this mental trauma of "what if?" I had to come here in my role as DCSOPS [deputy chief of staff for operations] to look over the new curriculum and a few other things before driving back to Washington on Monday night. And while here, I got this call from Harold Brown saying, "The president says you're going to be chief of staff." That's a very big mantle to have thrown on very narrow shoulders all of a sudden, and you wonder what you can do. Fortunately, between Carlisle and Washington, there's Mother Seton's in Emmitsburg and Mount St. Mary's up the side of the hill, so I stopped in there and went up into the grotto and walked around awhile and I thought about that. And it sort of came to me—okay, look, if they're going to tell me to do it, I'll go ahead and do it, but I'm not going to do it alone, and I'm going to share all that I can with a whole bunch of other people. As long as everybody does his share, even I can look good doing it. So, that's sort of the basic philosophy I've tried to apply as far as my overall leadership's concerned.

I had to go back, and then I wasn't allowed to tell my wife. The next day the packers were continuing their job when I called and told her I wasn't going to Europe, and she had to stop packing. There's still a bit of sensitivity there in the family.[35]

When it was announced that Meyer was to be chief of staff, one of his fellow generals commented: "He was bound to be Chief of Staff one day. More than most soldiers, he has had the perfect combination of assignments in the Army. He's had command and staff jobs, he's been in Europe, Korea, and Vietnam, he's worked at the Pentagon, he knows Capitol Hill. He's had a perfectly balanced career."[36]

Whereas General Eisenhower, when asked how one develops as a decision maker, stated, "Be around people making decisions," General Meyer's career provides a more recent example of exposure to key decision makers. When one reviews Meyer's career, the people he worked for, one can see the importance of what he prefers to call mentorship.

Even as army chief of staff, Meyer continued to have a mentor. "Dave Jones," he reflected, "was chairman of the Joint Chiefs of Staff when I was chief of staff of the army and when I was DCSOPS. So I was with Dave Jones for seven years."

What impact did Jones have? "Dave Jones was the consummate insider," said Meyer. "He understood the way the Pentagon worked, the interface workings between the Pentagon and Congress, better than anybody I watched. Watching him deal, I learned a lot. I also shared with him some of the same frustrations he had with the inability of the staff to be able to provide short-term needs of a chairman. Some of his techniques encouraged what I call 'ad hocracy,' in which he created ad hoc groups to deal with certain issues. I followed that technique, developing a high-technology division and other particularly revolutionary ideas. I found that in the Pentagon, the staff system is very structured, and it doesn't break down easily. That's the prime lesson I learned from Dave Jones. He knew how to get things done in the Pentagon."[37]

General Meyer was succeeded as U.S. Army chief of staff by Gen. John A. Wickham, Jr., who served from 1983 to 1987. Meyer was a mentor for Wickham. As a lieutenant colonel in Vietnam, Wickham was severely wounded and was recovering in Walter Reed Hospital in Washington when Meyer was working on the Joint Staff. He brought Wickham to the attention of his boss and requested he be assigned to the Joint Staff while he was recovering. This was a significant turning point in his career.

General Wickham made the following comment regarding mentorship in his career: "I had very little mentoring that I look back on. I would have liked to have had more. I would have liked to have had senior officers call me in and say here are the good things you're doing [or] here are the bad things you're doing, and here's how you can grow.

"What has transpired in the army, I guess, in the past ten years or so has been an evolution of emphasis on the leader to lead, to have a moral obligation to mentor and counsel those who are coming along. I've talked with literally tens of thousands of soldiers and officers in my years as chief and I did a lot of videotapes that were shown to virtually everybody in the army, active and reserves. Many of those tapes focused on the issue of mentoring and counseling young leaders, that this was an obligation to transfer your experience and that the kind of positive leadership we're looking for is not the negative dictatorial leadership that we sometimes have associated with the past. (The hard-drinking, foul-mouthed, profane leaders that were harsh in dealing with subordinates. Like the zero defects mentality.) We tried to purge that from the army and to foster positive, inspirational, example-setting leadership. That goes hand in glove with the mentoring.

"Another illustration: In my responsibilities as army chief of staff—I think all the service chiefs had the same responsibility—they are responsible, among their other duties, for managing the general officer corps. You basically have a battalion of generals, 412, and the army chief makes all of the assignments. He develops the stable of upward mobile opportunity for the more capable people. I guess I spent, on the average, twenty to twenty-five percent of my time just managing the general officer structure. And I needed all the help I could get in doing that. Therefore, I went out to solicit views, peer ratings, peer views of brigadier generals and major generals to determine how people were viewed from below. It was very revealing. It was another factor in making decisions about assignments, because

I would find out whether some individuals were ruthless with subordinates. In that case, I would obviously be reluctant to give an individual like that a position of responsibility over soldiers and young leaders.

"In all of my oral guidance to promotion boards—the promotion boards to select brigadier generals and promotion boards to select two-stars from the one-stars—one of the points I made was we need to be concerned about selecting leaders who set the positive example of leadership, who transfer knowledge and who do well at mentoring.

"So I give all these little snippets to give you a sense of how the culture has changed over the years in the way of developing solid leadership qualities and thorough leadership training throughout the army, because we all recognize, absent of wars, we're going to lose combat experience. I'd had no combat experience before I went in to command an infantry battalion in Vietnam."[38]

The majority of the leaders I have mentioned who were beneficiaries of ample mentoring from one or more of their bosses in turn adopted a similar mentoring style with subordinates of their own—hence, the ripples that such mentoring can provide.

Perhaps one of the most instructive examples of that principle in action is the case of Gen. W. L. Creech, who commanded the Tactical Air Command (TAC) for six and a half years, from May 1, 1978, to November 1, 1984. In chapter 5, I discuss Creech's "rapid rise to four stars." In fact, when he was given his fourth star in May 1978, he had reached that rank faster than anyone who entered the U.S. Army Air Force–U.S. Air Force (USAAF-USAF) after 1938. Those who entered in the 1930s who were later to make four stars had their promotions greatly accelerated, of course, by the unique demands of World War II. That rapid rise was due to successful mentors from whom Bill Creech had greatly profited, and also from his outstanding performance in a long string of high-profile jobs. As you will see, his performance as TAC's commander fully justified that accelerated promotion to four stars.

Before commenting on the excellent mentoring system that Creech developed, I should first outline some of its highly beneficial and long-lasting effects. For example, Gen. Chuck Horner, the overall air commander in Operation Desert Storm, had this to say about the impact of Creech's mentoring upon the air force's extraordinary performance there: "I want everyone to know of the monumental contribution made by General Bill Creech to the success of our air campaign in the Gulf War. I was in the Tactical Air Command both before and after he brought us fresh ideas on how to organize and lead in the late seventies and early eighties, and I can tell you that the difference it made—to our spirit and our capabilities—was like night and day. He untiringly taught all of us, over and over, what to me were three essential points. *The first:* The critical importance of decentralization in the way you organize, to ensure a maximum of flexibility, responsiveness, and feelings of ownership. *The second:* The absolute necessity of getting leadership and commitment from everyone—and I do mean everyone. *The third:* The power of quality in everything that you do.

"A few days after the war was over I was visiting one of our bases. The wing commander and I were visiting with the people who had performed so brilliantly, basking in the glow of our success, and reminiscing about the events that contributed to it. As we talked more and more about how it had all been put together, the wing commander turned to me and put it in these words: 'You know, General Horner, after all that General Creech did for us, we couldn't miss.' I strongly echo his sentiments. The American people gave us unashamed and unwavering support, and General Bill Creech gave us the organization and training that made the success of our crusade possible. I can't thank him enough for that."[39]

Please note the phrase "He untiringly taught all of us . . ." That, indeed, goes to the heart of the mentoring system that Creech put in motion upon assuming command of TAC.

In my interview with him regarding that system, he gave special credit to one of those who had mentored him: "I want to give credit where credit is due in developing my own concepts of mentoring. In serving thirty-five years as an officer in the air force, I served under some twenty-five different bosses. Some were outstanding, some were mediocre, and some were poor leaders. You can learn from the latter, too, of course. Primarily you learn what not to do. Only four of those bosses went out of their way to provide any special mentoring—or leadership training, if you prefer—to those of us who worked for them. And far and away the best of those four was General Dave Jones, whom I first worked for when he was the CINC of United States Air Forces in Europe [USAFE].

"At his commanders' conferences, he painstakingly taught leadership skills to the wing commanders, drawing on his own experiences over the years, and he would take several days in doing so. I was especially impressed by the insights he provided us on the effective management of aircraft maintenance, one of our greatest challenges then and now. He was especially knowledgeable in that area, thanks to the foresight of his principal mentor, General Curtis LeMay, who had sent him to a maintenance leadership job after he had served several years as LeMay's aide. Dave Jones was highly effective in passing that hard-won knowledge on to us. Subsequently, when I served as his deputy for operations and intelligence at headquarters, USAFE, he provided lots of one-on-one mentoring that helped me greatly both then and over the years. It was those examples that I used as a baseline in setting up the mentoring system in TAC.

"That mentoring system in TAC actually had three parts: selection, mentoring, and grooming. Each of those are very important; indeed, they feed one upon the other, and if you're weak in any of the three, the system will fall well short of what's needed."[40]

Why was this mentoring system that Chuck Horner had praised so highly effective? The empirical evidence says it was. Indeed, it produced some twenty-one four-star generals, including several chiefs of staff and a vice chairman of the JCS. These "TAC graduates," as some called them, went on to command at one time or another virtually all of the major commands in the U.S. Air Force that called for four-star commanders, including the Strategic Air Command, Air Education and Training Command, Air Force Materiel Command, and Air Force Mobility Command, as well as the three "Tactical Air Forces"—that is, TAC, USAFE, and PACAF (Pacific Air Force). And all of that out of a command that represented only 22 percent of the total manpower strength of the U.S. Air Force. Make no mistake, however, TAC was a huge and sprawling organization with 105 operating locations, 180,000 people (counting gained guard and reserve units over which TAC exercised cognizance), and some 4,500 aircraft (more than twice all the U.S. airlines combined).

Referring back to General Chuck Horner's comment about Bill Creech's teaching, over and over, "the critical importance of decentralization in the way you organize to ensure a maximum in flexibility, responsiveness, and feelings of ownership," that is precisely what Creech did with TAC upon taking over as commander. His massive reorganization not only was abundantly successful, producing an 80 percent improvement in productivity and vast improvements in everything from reenlistment rates to combat capability, but it ran directly counter to the McNamara-era emphasis on centralization that had been the air force's eagerly embraced and perpetuated management style for those many intervening years. Again, Gen. Dave Jones played a pivotal role.

Bill Creech explains it this way: "Although General Jones had grown up in SAC, he was as annoyed with the highly centralized style of management as I was. And when he selected me to command TAC commencing May 1, 1978, I told him I was going to rip up that old centralized way and start afresh. All he said in response was, 'Go to it.' Later, as air force chief and chairman for an eight-year span, he served as occasional 'top cover' for me when the Washington bureaucrats, who were aghast at what we were doing, chose to interfere in a major way. But typical of the Jones style, he left me to fight the vast majority of those battles alone, and there were battles aplenty. His previous mentoring provided all the armor, and all the chutzpah, I needed."[41]

In this same vein, instructive passages on this transformation are found in the book *Beyond the Wild Blue: A History of the U.S. Air Force 1947–1997*. Written by Walter J. Boyne, it was released coincident with the independent air force's fiftieth anniversary (and later was a basis for a four-hour miniseries on the History Channel). Boyne served many years as director of the National Air and Space Museum in Washington and also has written fifteen aviation-related books.

Boyne had this to say about what his research revealed: "One has only to look at the great ossified bureaucracies around the world to realize how difficult it is to reverse the course of rigid, centralized bureaucratic control. On rare occasions a turnaround occurs. . . . Often there is a single person who becomes identified with the change of direction. So it was with the air force. Identification of the man responsible emerged in the course of a number of in-depth interviews with four-star officers. . . . All were candid and forthcoming about their own careers in the air force and in assessing the contributions of others. Each one, quite independently and usually in a different context, attributed the remarkable turnaround in air force management style, with a consequent increase in proficiency, efficiency, and improved quality of life, to one man: General Bill Creech. Jones ranks him with General LeMay as one of the two most influential men in his long air force experience."[42]

Renowned management guru Tom Peters, after studying the "TAC Turnaround" in great depth, had this to say: "Bill Creech led perhaps the most impressive 'corporate' revolution we've witnessed in this century."

And that new style eventually spread throughout the air force, by the unavoidably obvious success of the new approach as well as by the "TAC graduates" taking it elsewhere—further proving the effectiveness of the new style over the old ways. But that wasn't all that was behind Chuck Horner's glowing assessment of this period of change on the eventual air force success in the Gulf War. That same period saw in TAC the development of a host of new combat tactics; a massive foray into precision munitions; the fielding of an array of new combat systems, including A-10s, F-15s, F-16s, the F-117 Stealth fighter, and the F-15E night fighter; plus new and improved munitions to attack surface-to-air missile (SAM) sites and sheltered aircraft, as well as the precision-radar platforms of the airborne warning and control system (AWACS) for the air battle and Joint Stars for the ground battle. Those systems provided vastly improved situation awareness for battle managers.

The following is an illustration of the Creech-led seminal change in combat tactics: "The profound change of course at TAC was not confined to managerial methods. Creech was a warrior who found TAC's tactics encumbered with what he called 'go-low disease'—the perceived need to fly at minimum height to avoid enemy surface-to-air missiles. Creech argued that the buildup in enemy anti-aircraft artillery (AAA) made the go-low approach dangerous, and that new methods were needed. He decreed that taking out the SAMs was the first order of business—that the enemy defenses should be nullified and rolled back so that follow-on aircraft would have the flexibility to operate at high or low altitude in hostile territory, depending upon the nature of enemy defenses.

"The new tactics were drummed into TAC in practice in the rigorous air force red flag training at Nellis Air Force Base and with the complementary [flag] training programs Creech had devised. The payoff for the realistic training came in the Persian Gulf War, where USAF casualties were remarkably low. Those coalition partners who stayed with the go-low philosophy suffered heavily as a result of their unwillingness to change tactics."[43]

And that's precisely how Chuck Horner chose to fight the Gulf War. The U.S. Air Force fighter forces, over forty-three days of intense day-and-night combat, lost only thirteen fighters and suffered only three pilot deaths. Creech points out that the British, who tried the go-low tactics in the early days of the war, lost 10 percent of their force of Tornado fighters. If the U.S. Air Force fighter loss rate had been equivalent to that of the British, the air force would have lost some 160 fighters, not thirteen.

Creech summed up Horner's success in these terms: "Never in the history of large-scale armed conflict has there been so much damage inflicted on the one side, with so little damage incurred by the other. Clearly we had readied ourselves to fight the 'next war' not the 'last one'—the latter a charge hurled at us by our many vociferous critics over the years. That same crowd also said the systems we were fielding 'were too complicated to work in combat.' Chuck Horner, and the brave men and women in Operation Desert Storm, proved them dead wrong."[44]

But would all of this have mattered if Creech had not developed a mentoring system to help ensure that the new thinking would be devoutly embraced, and then perpetuated, by the many others that followed along behind him? It's highly doubtful that it would have. So, what were the essential features of the mentoring system that Creech devised?

Here is how he described it to me: "It had the three parts I described to you earlier: selection, mentoring, and grooming. I spent an inordinate amount of time in the selection process—as did the numbered air force commanders—studying the records and interviewing those who aspired to lead our wings and our air divisions.

The more time I spent on that, I found, the less time I spent cleaning up after field mistakes.

"With respect to mentoring, we took a very broad view of who was to get it. Our mentoring involved all of those who were incumbents in or were logical aspirants for wing commander or higher jobs. We met four times a year in three-day special interactive sessions that I conducted personally. We didn't talk in those sessions about recent happenings. We talked about leadership and how best to go about it in the various areas that required top leadership involvement and teaching. Keeping in mind, of course, my oft-stated dictum that 'The first duty of a leader is to create more leaders,' I said that we were not expecting them to be one-person bands. To the contrary, we emphasized that they should be using the same mentoring techniques with their subordinates. I learned that from all the times in which bosses I had worked for went away to commanders' conferences and came back with nary a word about what had gone on there. They treated knowledge as power when withheld to themselves when, in fact, knowledge has power only to the extent it is shared with others. That's especially true in a military outfit, and we were very mindful of that.

"As a related matter, we had separate one-week training sessions for those same individuals that taught them the things they didn't know. And there was a lot they didn't know. A centralized system, which had been the air force practice for years, provides a very narrow education in its functional silos. For example, most of those with the greatest potential for senior responsibility in a 'fly and fight' organization knew a lot about operations but very little about other critically important activities like maintenance, supply, and base support—with everything in the latter discipline from infrastructure upkeep to air police to dining halls to budgeting. I taught several of those 'other discipline' classes myself. That demonstrated that I had taken the initiative over the years to educate myself on those various matters, and [it] sent a signal that the attendees were expected to do no less. That training paid big dividends in building our new culture, and our success. Some say the top boss is too busy for that sort of involvement. Nonsense. That's where it all starts, and that's also where it ends if you're not very good at all of that."[45]

In our discussion, I asked General Creech why he separated grooming from mentoring when, in my usage of the term, the latter encompasses the former. He responded: "I separated the two in both my thinking and my actions because I looked on them as recognizably different, albeit related, activities. In a sense it could be argued that our extensive, widespread mentoring also 'groomed' commanders for higher rank. But, also, there was further grooming required for those who were especially talented and especially well suited for the highest ranks—as that judgment had emerged from seeing them in action with bullet-biting responsibilities.

"Said another way, in a large outfit—and TAC had 105 operating locations, 33 wings, and 10 air divisions—the mentoring should be for the many, not just for the few, and the special grooming should be for the few, not for the many. Those at the rank of colonel and above whom we saw as having the potential for the most senior air force positions were groomed by moving them from job to job and by making those jobs as diverse as possible. Most of what we do in the leadership business is not rocket science, though some would have you believe it is. It's really a case of the human science, and some are good at that, some are not. Those who are can take diverse jobs with which they are unfamiliar and soon make positive contributions.

"Accordingly, those we had singled out for grooming for three- and four-star rank had no less than four different jobs, and for some as many as six, during my six and a half years at the helm of TAC. A way to think of it is this: When you mentor, you are passing along the benefit of your experience. If you groom leaders by moving them from job to job, you are enriching their own experience, and they thereby profit from facing leadership challenges in many different settings.

"Moreover, there was a major side benefit. As a result of that approach to grooming, it came as no surprise to me later when the TAC people started dominating the air force's most senior leadership positions. Their broad-based grooming gave them an appreciable advantage, and it showed in the promotion lists."[46]

As a side note, after General Creech retired from the air force, he joined the business world and has been in heavy demand ever since as an adviser to some of America's most illustrious corporations. He wrote a best-selling book entitled *The Five Pillars of TQM:*

How to Make Total Quality Management Work For You. He decided to write the book as Desert Storm was unfolding in early 1991, when he contrasted what he was seeing in the business world (along with various leadership and organizational inadequacies) with how extremely well the U.S. Air Force was doing in the Gulf War air combat. His book is currently in its eleventh printing in seven foreign languages. Among other business-world plaudits, *INC.* magazine picked Creech for its "Dream Team of the Decade," a six-member team winnowed from a long list of successful U.S. business leaders. The magazine dubbed those six selected leaders as most able "to meet the challenges of the nineties and beyond."

This discussion started with the premise that effective mentoring can produce beneficial ripples as those same techniques are passed on from generation to generation. To test the lasting power of the Creech approach, we can turn to a recent example. Lieutenant General Hal Hornburg is the commander of the Ninth Air Force of Air Combat Command (formerly TAC) and is dual hatted as the air component commander of United States Central Command (CENT-COM). Hornburg served as a wing commander during the Gulf War under the tutelage of Gen. Chuck Horner. Recently, Hornburg commanded the forces that participated in Operation Desert Fox, a four-day series of strikes against Iraq.

After that operation was over, Hornburg wrote the following letter to Bill Creech, dated December 24, 1998:

> Dear General Creech,
> After Operation Desert Fox, I sent an e-mail to General Horner saying "thanks for showing us how." His response was: "Don't be surprised, we were Creech trained." As you know, all missions were flown at night—no losses, pretty good results— again largely thanks to you. Only wish more people knew. Lots of wives will welcome home husbands, and kids their Dads, because of you. On their behalf I thank you.
>
> Most sincerely,
> /s/ Hal Hornburg[47]

General Creech had earlier received a letter from Gen. Merrill A. McPeak, then air force chief of staff:

> 16 January 1991
> Dear General Creech,
> Just back from the Middle East where I had the opportunity to inspect the theater Air Force we have built there from scratch. You would be very proud of our young men and women.
> We are about to harvest the results of years of hard work and leadership by you and a handful of other great airmen. We will do well. But we need to recognize that we are beholden to you, because you really built this magnificent Air Force we have to-day.
>
> Warm regards,
> Merrill A. McPeak, General USAF
> Chief of Staff[18]

That's certainly a nice tribute to the staying power of General Creech's own approach to mentoring. But it also helps to prove the premise, demonstrated throughout these pages, that effective mentoring long has been, and long will remain, a critically important part of creating first-class military leaders. It takes lots of extra effort and close attention by those who choose that path, but it has a very high payoff that can last for years and years. Bill Creech sums up the mentoring business quite well with his admonition with which I began this chapter: "The first duty of a leader is to create more leaders."

When interviewing Admiral Crowe, I asked him, "Who were the personalities in your career who you felt had some role in your success?" He responded: "A peculiar thing happened in the mentors who enabled me to advance my education, a strong factor in my career. When I came back to the navy from Princeton, of course, the navy has a strong antiintellectual bias. I don't think my degree from Princeton helped me very much at all to make flag officer, because the prejudice against education was pretty strong, but after I made flag officer, the navy used to brag about it all the time. [Admiral

Crowe has a Ph.D.] It opened up vistas for me that would not have happened otherwise.

"The 'doctor,' of course, was important, but also the education. My education began to really tell when I was a flag officer. I had learned things at Princeton that were appropriate to what I was doing, much more so than before I received flag rank.

"What in particular did I learn? Well, the way the political system works, the way it works in Washington. Many things surprise military officers who go there for the first time, but these things didn't surprise me at all because I had studied them. My first job as a captain after Princeton was in the East Asia section in the CNO's office, a political-military job. I was the officer in charge of the Pueblo repatriation program. That's when I first came to Admiral Moorer's notice; he was the CNO. Throughout a period of a year, I had been in and out of his office so much, done so much, that from then on I was on his radarscope. (I'm not sure how heavily I was on his radarscope.) In that same post, a rear admiral came in by the name of 'Blackie' Wenel, who subsequently got promoted to three stars. He was a special assistant to Moorer when he was chairman. Then he was promoted to four stars and ended up his career as the NATO guy, our rep on the military committee. Then he retired. . . .

"Wenel became a strong sponsor of mine. He was very supportive of me. Also during the Pueblo thing, I became friendly with the vice CNO by the name of Bernard Clarey, who was subsequently head of the selection board that selected me for flag rank.

"There's a very interesting story there. I had a rather strange career pattern which most people wouldn't have given a dime for my having a shot at admiral. I was put in the Micronesia negotiations at Zumwalt's behest. When I came back, I didn't know it but I was slated for the command of a cruiser. Zumwalt canceled it and sent me to the Micronesia status negotiations. Wenel was incensed, and he made sure Zumwalt knew what he was doing. Zumwalt filed a fitness report on me because of that; it said anybody can go command a cruiser, but this guy is one of ten thousand who can do this Micronesia status job.

"Clarey became a very strong supporter of mine, which subsequently became extremely important. When the time came for consideration of my promotion to admiral, Clarey was the chairman of the board. On the first deliberation, I was not selected, didn't make the cut. So Clarey called the board back and pulled my name out and made a speech on my behalf. 'I would like for you to reconsider Captain Crowe. He has not had the sea experience most of you officers would like, but look at what he has done. This man is a very potential candidate for chairman.' In any event, of course, he was head of the board, and they reexamined, and I made the cut.

"That year, Zumwalt had written a letter to the promotion board stating we got to have some iconoclast in this navy, and he strongly recommended that the board try and get out of their normal pattern, which was not easy for a board to do. That they should look at people with unusual records and unusual capabilities, and I think Clarey fell back on that. That was the board's charter and he used that to get me back on the list. Once the board did that, they gave the chairman of the board quite a bit of latitude. I was selected. They usually let him have one or two names. In any event, Clarey was a good friend of mine.

"Wenel was very instrumental in my career. I was considered sort of a political military type. I had the problem of trying to get a command. Where the hell would I go to command? Surface people wouldn't want me in a fleet, nor the aviation or submarine people. The Persian Gulf, while small, was a distinct command and I had the theory it was more of a political command. I went to see a classmate by the name of Worth Bagby, who was at VC, and I said I would like to have command of the Middle East Force. Not many people ever said that about the Middle East Force (I think that I was the only one who ever said that). He said, 'Why do you want to do that?' I said it's exotic, another part of the world, and it's right down my alley. He said, 'What do you mean?' I said there are a lot of political things, and that's what I do. I said if you will tell me you'll send me there, I'll learn Arabic. He was so fascinated by this that he went to see the CNO [Holloway], who said that's a great idea, but I can't assure him of that. So I didn't learn Arabic, but I did go there. When they finally got around to it, they had seen that the command was going to disappear. So I ended up in the Middle East, and I had a command.

"Now there were four or five other officers, one or two years ahead of me, who were prominent in the political-military business. They were all sort of aiming for the deputy CNO for plans and policy. There I was out in Bahrain, way the hell out of anywhere. While out there, of the three or four competitors I had, one of them died, one of them stepped on the vice CNO's toes and got shuttled off because the vice CNO just didn't like him. Another was working on the chairman's staff group and got caught in a scandal. Luck was very much a factor in this. All of a sudden, when it was time to fill the position of vice CNO for plans and policy, I had done something out in Bahrain. We saved the command. We turned around the decision of the government in that year for the command to continue, which, as time showed, proved to be very important. When they got ready to pick a deputy chief of staff for plans and policy, all my major competitors were gone. At least that's the way it looked to me."[49]

I asked General Powell why he thought he was selected as chairman of the Joint Chiefs of Staff. His immediate response was, "Beats me. I worked very hard. I was very loyal to people who appointed me, people who were under me, and my associates. I developed a reputation as somebody you could trust. I would give you my very, very best. I would always try to do what I thought was right and I let the chips fall where they might. And as I told many people, and people don't believe this when I tell this to them, I said, 'It didn't really make a difference whether I made general in terms of my self-respect and self-esteem. I just loved being in the army.' I wasn't without ambition, but ambition wasn't fueling me."[50]

In 1971, as a major in the infantry, Powell was awarded a White House Fellowship. The objective of the fellowship program was to expose young comers to the federal government at the highest level and to give future U.S. leaders a better understanding of public policy formulation. There were 1,500 applicants; the list was narrowed to 130 to be interviewed. Powell won and was assigned to the Office of Management and Budget (OMB) when Caspar Weinberger was its director, but shortly thereafter Weinberger became secretary of health, education, and welfare. His deputy was Frank Carlucci. Both were to become important to Powell's career, for each went on to become secretary of defense. During Powell's tenure as a White House Fellow, his class traveled to the Soviet Union and Red China.

Powell returned to service with troops and was assigned to the 101st Airborne Division at Fort Campbell, in Kentucky. The division commander was John Wickham. "That's where General Wickham got to know me. We became very, very close and he became a mentor. General Wickham went from Campbell to the director of the Joint Staff. He thought his career was at an end because of the Joint Staff. General Wickham was my principal mentor during my general years until he retired, then Carl Vuono became my mentor when he became chief in 1987."

In 1977, Powell served in the office of the secretary of defense, and over the next three years became senior military assistant to the deputy secretary of defense. In 1983, Powell was assigned as senior military assistant to Secretary of Defense Caspar Weinberger. He later served as deputy national security adviser, with an office next door to Vice President Bush, where "we shared a bathroom," he commented. In President Reagan's administration, Powell was national security adviser.

There had never been a chairman with such extensive exposure to international relations. Powell worked closely as a general officer with Vice President Bush, two secretaries of defense—Weinberger and Carlucci—and President Reagan. "I've known all of them in a political sense and they knew they had a general, a chairman who understood the political world they lived in. I've been characterized as being a political general. My answer to this is, I'm guilty. But I had a pretty good infantry record for twenty years."[51]

But a mentor is not always a senior officer. In the case of General Shalikashvili, it was a sergeant. "When I started out, I wanted to be the best second lieutenant around," he told me. "At the beginning I didn't worry about becoming captain or major, or whatever. As a matter of fact, all my life I tried very hard not to think about what I might eventually become. Rather, I tried to concentrate on becoming the very best of the rank I held at any given moment. When I was first commissioned, I was assigned to Alaska and my platoon sergeant was a Sergeant Grice. Grice devoted his life to making me the best platoon leader around. Our unit was a mortar battery of the First Battle Group of the 9th Infantry. Sergeant Grice would come in in the morning and say, "Sir, I've organized that poncho inspection just like you ordered.' I'd look surprised, but Sergeant Grice would take time to show me just how to conduct such an inspection and what to look for. The next day he might surprise me with something else, but each event was designed to help me become a better platoon leader. He was such a wonderful man. I wish every second lieutenant could have a Sergeant Grice. He is the one who taught me what caring for my men really entailed. From him I learned the importance of knowing all the ins and outs of my job. I learned that when I walked down the gun line and asked the soldiers some questions, that if I didn't know the answers better than the soldiers, they would see through me, whether I really knew what I was talking about or not. By the way, I learned that this is as true for a platoon leader or platoon sergeant as for a four-star general."⁵²

Shalikashvili commented on advising young officers: "And if there is one thing I wish for each and every one of you, it is a Sergeant Grice to teach you about soldiers, about leaders, and the responsibilities and joys of soldiering together. Not everyone is as blessed as I was; not everyone finds his Sergeant Grice and many don't; not because he isn't there, but because unknowingly, and foolishly, they push him away. Don't do that. Look for your Sergeant Grice; NCOs have so very much to teach us."⁵³

I asked General Shalikashvili why he thought he was selected as chairman. "The obvious thing that comes to mind is to say that you don't know, and that there were so many more better qualified. I think part of it is an accident of timing. I happened to have caught the eye of the public and maybe of the leadership in Washington during Operation Provide Comfort, an operation that was running right at the completion of Desert Storm. It had as its objective the humanitarian relief effort to help the Kurds in northern Iraq. Because this operation was a good human interest sort of story, it caught the imagination of the press and so my name came to the forefront. Right after that, I was assigned to Washington as Gen. Colin Powell's assistant, so I got to know the decision makers in Washington, in and out of the Pentagon. And so when the search started for a new American general to be appointed as the next NATO Supreme Allied

Commander in Europe my name appeared on that list and to my surprise I was selected. It so happened that as soon as I arrived in Europe, Bosnia became a hot issue. Consequently my name was attached to many of the actions being worked in Washington and when not so long after I arrived in Europe it came time to replace General Powell my name once again made it on that list. So I guess that I would have to attribute my selection as chairman partly to timing, partly to being at the right place at the right time and to some degree having worked around those who made these decisions."[54]

General Eisenhower answered the question "How does one develop as a decision maker?" by saying, "Be around people making decisions." It is clear that the foregoing selected officers who achieved the highest positions of responsibility were around people making decisions: men who provided them guidance, counseling, advice, and teaching and had roles in giving them an opportunity to perform superbly, to thus impress and succeed. It is also emphatically clear that mentorship doesn't just happen. It must be earned, and the rewards are the toughest jobs, longest hours, and personal sacrifice.

Notes

1. Personal interview with Gen. Edward C. Meyer, USA (Ret.), and Edgar F. Puryear, Jr., July 14, 1997.

2. Forrest C. Pogue, *George C. Marshall: Education of a General* (New York: The Viking Press, 1963), 93.

3. Ibid., 102.

4. Ibid., 107–08.

5. Ibid., 127.

6. Ibid., 121.

7. Ibid., 138.

8. Personal interview with Col. George C. Cochew, USA (Ret.), and Edgar F. Puryear, Jr., December 19, 1962.

9. Kenneth Ray Young, *The General's General* (Boulder, Colo.: Westview Press, 1994), 164.

10. *New York Times,* August 7, 1930.

11. Mark W. Clark, *Calculated Risk* (New York: Harper and Brothers, 1950), 10–11, and personal interview with Edgar F. Puryear, Jr., December 22, 1962.

12. Walter Krueger, *From Down Under to Nippon* (Washington, D.C.: Combat Forces Press, 1993), 4, and personal interview, July 30, 1963.

13. Personal interview with General of the Army Dwight D. Eisenhower and Edgar F. Puryear, Jr., May 2, 1963.

14. Ibid.

15. Ibid.

16. Harry C. Butcher, *My Three Years with Eisenhower* (New York: Simon and Schuster, 1946), 247–48.

17. Kevin McCann, *Man from Abilene* (New York: Doubleday and Company, Inc., 1952), 51.

18. Alden Hatch, *George Patton, General in Spurs* (New York: Julian Messner, Inc., 1950), 53–54.

19. Charles R. Codman, *Drive* (Boston: Little Brown, 1957), 145.

20. Dwight D. Eisenhower, *Crusade in Europe* (New York: Doubleday and Company, Inc., 1948), 102.

21. Personal interview with Gen. Curtis E. LeMay, USAF (Ret.), and Edgar F. Puryear, Jr., August 28, 1975.

22. Ibid.

23. Personal interview with Gen. David C. Jones and Edgar F. Puryear, Jr., January 20, 1998.

24. Personal interview with Gen. Jacob E. Smart, USAF (Ret.), and Edgar F. Puryear, Jr., July 17, 1979.

25. Personal interview with Gen. George S. Brown and Edgar F. Puryear, Jr., September 14, 1977.

26. Personal interview with Gen. Robert E. Dixon, USAF (Ret.), and Edgar F. Puryear, Jr., June 10, 1980.

27. Brown interview.

28. Ibid.

29. Personal interview with Gen. John D. Ryan, USAF (Ret.), and Edgar F. Puryear, Jr., August 9, 1979.

30. Personal interview with former secretary of the air force John L. McLucas and Edgar F. Puryear, Jr., February 21, 1980.

31. Personal interview with Gen. Edward C. Meyer, USA (Ret.), and Edgar F. Puryear, Jr., July 14, 1997.

32. Ibid.

33. Ibid.

34. Ibid.

35. Ibid.

36. *New York Times* (May 3, 1979).

37. Meyer interview.

38. John A. Wickham, *Four Star Leadership*, 185–86, and interview with Edgar F. Puryear Jr.

39. Bill Creech, *The Five Pillars of TQM* (New York: Truman Talley Books/Plume, 1994), 121–22.

40. Personal interview with Gen. W. L. Creech, USAF (Ret.), and Edgar F. Puryear, Jr., December 20, 1998.

41. Ibid.

42. Ibid.

43. Ibid.

44. Ibid.

45. Ibid.

46. Ibid.

47. Letter from Gen. Hal Hornburg, USAF, to Gen. W. L. Creech, USAF (Ret.), dated December 24, 1998.

48. Letter from Gen. Merrill A. McPeak, USAF, to Gen. W. L. Creech, USAF (Ret.), dated January 16, 1991.

49. Personal interview with Adm. William Crowe and Edgar F. Puryear, Jr., May 16, 1997. The discussion has as its source this interview and his book *The Line of Fire*.

50. Personal interview with Gen. Colin L. Powell, USA (Ret.), and Edgar F. Puryear, Jr. The following is based on the interview and his book *My American Journey*.

51. Ibid.

52. Personal interview with Gen. John Shalikashvili and Edgar F. Puryear, Jr., June 4, 1997.

53. Ibid.

54. Ibid.

Chapter 7: Consideration

In every position of command your subordinates will want to know how much you care for them, far more than they will ever care how much you know.

—General John K. Cannon, USAF (Ret.)

I asked this question of more than a hundred four-star generals: "How do you lead men in such a way that they will die for you in combat and work twenty hours a day, in time of peace for weeks and sometimes months if necessary, to resolve a certain crisis or problem?" The answer was unanimous: A leader must first set the example and show his devotion to a life of service to God and country; second, he must show consideration for the people serving with him.

I asked Lt. Gen. Willis D. Critenberger to comment on the leadership of General of the Army George C. Marshall. Critenberger addressed Marshall's consideration for others: "I was a corps commander in Fifth Army in World War II. General Marshall came over for an inspection of the troops in Europe. Upon his return to Washington, within twenty-four hours, someone on his staff called Mrs. Critenberger, who was living in San Antonio. When they got her on the telephone he himself came in and said: 'This is General Marshall, Mrs. Critenberger. I want you to know I saw your husband last night in Italy. He is well and I thought you would like to know.'

"He did this for many of the families of his commanders. This is a factor in his leadership that is in contrast with his rather dignified and serious manner. It was so reassuring for the family of a serviceman to have the head man call up and say, 'I just thought you would like to know he is all right.' That does everything for the morale of the soldier and his family."[1]

Throughout World War II, Marshall contacted the wife, mother, or nearest relative of every senior officer he met on overseas inspection trips and commented on how they were. That it was greatly appreciated can be measured by the Marshall papers, which have many responses from the wives, daughters, and parents expressing their appreciation for his call. He regularly corresponded with the wives of longtime associates such as Bedell Smith, Patton, Mark Clark, and Eisenhower. He believed it made the separation less difficult to bear.

Throughout World War II, Marshall was constantly on top of matters that concerned the welfare of soldiers. He sent military ambassadors throughout the world with the sole mission of listening to gripes and recommending how to remedy them. He gave emphasis to assuring that the soldiers on the front line were taken care of with such things as soft drinks, cigarettes, and candy as well as the ammunition and weapons they needed.

When Marshall went to a combat area, he insisted on going with only the driver, dispensing with the commanding officer, and making inquiries about the welfare of the troops as he drove around. His telephone calls and letters were not limited to the senior officers he visited. I interviewed an enlisted man who served as a driver when Marshall made his first inspection after the invasion on June 12, 1944. Upon Marshall's return, he called the driver's parents to tell them, "I have just seen your son. He was my driver in Europe and I wanted you to know he is doing well."

On a trip to North Africa in 1943, Marshall was surprised to see Maj. Gen. Lucian K. Truscott, who had been in command of an army corps at Anzio. The two had a long talk, and Marshall asked Truscott if he knew that Ike had requested him to serve in the invasion of Europe. Truscott replied that he had not heard of the request. It would have meant an army command for him, but he couldn't be spared from the Italian battle. "He felt," said Truscott, "I should know that Eisenhower had asked for me, and be aware that my services at Anzio had been well understood and were fully appreciated." Truscott had a reputation for being a "soldier's soldier"; but tough as he was, he records his reaction to Marshall's compliment: "I was deeply touched, for there was no call upon General Marshall to tell me this. It was one of those generous and thoughtful things that always distinguished him in dealings with his subordinates."[2]

One World War II veteran of the Bataan death march wrote: "I met General Marshall in person only once. This was the time when he sent his personal plane to San Francisco to transport me wherever the spirit moved, in order to reunite me with the widely scattered members of my immediate family, right after I returned from my prolonged incarceration in a Japanese prison camp. After I had accomplished this mission, I reported to the General at the Pentagon to thank him for his consideration. General Marshall put everything aside, delayed very important appointments, made me feel at home, and devoted a lengthy period of time in a most human approach to my personal situation."[3]

General of the Army Henry H. "Hap" Arnold was also sensitive to the well-being of his subordinate staff officers in Washington during World War II. His concern for his men included personal and professional satisfaction. Any professional officer is anxious, if his country is at war, to go where the action is, to be involved in the fighting. This opportunity passed by Arnold in World War I. "My ambition to take an air outfit to France," he said, "was never realized. In a sense, it remains a disappointment to this day. During World War II, in Washington, I deliberately deprived myself of the aid of a whole series of fine chiefs of staff and valuable top-flight advisors so that these men would not miss out on wartime experience that I never had."[4]

Arnold went on: "Early in 1941, trying to get better information about the war in Europe, we sent officers abroad from all parts of the Air Force organization—combat units, staff, training center, and materiel command. Whether they could be spared or not made no difference. I followed the same procedures during the war because I thought it far more important to give these men a crack at combat operations than to keep them on duty in Washington. I always remembered my own frustrated attempts to get overseas in World War I.

"Officers like Spaatz, Eaker, M. F. Harmon, Stratemeyer, Delos Emmons, and such advisors as George C. Kenney and the late Frank M. Andrews were sent overseas to big commands of their own. Acting Chiefs of the Air Corps and Deputy Chiefs were changed as often, no matter how good they were, but, unfortunately, many good men never had a chance to demonstrate their ability in combat."[5]

Once, Arnold's longtime friend, stationed at Wright Field, needed a good young officer to understudy one of his department heads.

Arnold told this friend, "I'll recommend one who'll be an answer to your prayers. Your gain will be my loss. . . . But this young man is too good to be held to the confines of one squadron. He can benefit the whole Air Corps if you take him with you, but first you must promise me you'll give him a chance. He is not prepossessing in appearance."[6] The man was given his chance and performed brilliantly.

During World War II, Arnold often dropped in on the enlisted men's mess as part of any visit to an installation, even if only to land for refueling. One reporter traveling with him recounted such an incident. Arnold went up to the chow line and said to the man behind the steam table, "Let's taste that." He sampled it and remarked to the man behind the steam table, "I wondered why in the hell the men weren't eating."[7] Then he turned to the base commander, obviously intending that the latter correct the poor-quality meal being served.

He was concerned for feelings as well as for physical comfort. Once Arnold called in a colonel on his staff and instructed him, "Pack your bags. We're going somewhere." The colonel responded, "May I ask where we're going?" Arnold's response was, "You may not."

As it turns out, their destination was an advanced flying school of the Army Air Force. They arrived in time for graduation exercises, which were in progress. Each young man who had earned his wings stepped forward to get his wings and be commissioned. One young man in the crowd was obviously excited, constantly looking up at the visiting colonel who was with Arnold. As the anxious young man came forward, Arnold turned to the colonel and said, "All right, Thomas, step forward and pin the air force wings on your kid."[8]

Between the wars, Gen. "Tooey" Spaatz was commander of a pursuit squadron. It is hard to believe, but in the twenties these fighter pilots had no parachutes. In early June, just before leaving Ellington Field, one of the pilots, Lt. John K. Cannon, was injured in a midair collision. His aircraft had fallen three thousand feet, fracturing his skull, along with many other bones, and causing severe shock. This might have been averted had he been able to bail out, but he had no parachute, because there were none available in the squadron. Spaatz took corrective measures. He learned on arriving at Selfridge that McCook Field in Dayton, Ohio, had parachutes, and he wrote to Maj. Thurman H. Bane: "I am instructing all pilots who take cross-country flights which take them near Dayton to stop over for the purpose of being fitted with a parachute. I understand that you have a number on hand. . . . I am very desirous of having every pilot report there as soon as possible to procure this equipment."[9]

On July 19, 1922, Spaatz received a response from Bane, chief of the engineering division: "Your request is a bit irregular. As you know we are not a supply depot. However, we are very anxious to help you out in this situation and will fix up your pilots as fast as they fly in here until we are ordered to stop by higher authority."[10]

Spaatz had once commented about his World War I flying: "We had no parachutes until after the war, and we weren't bothered with insurance salesmen at all!" He joked about it when it concerned himself, but when it involved his men, he had a different outlook.

Cannon's accident also emphasized the need for better medical support. Captain Eaker once requested an ambulance to take injured flyers to a hospital, to which the army general responded that horse-drawn carts were sufficient for their injured polo players and should fulfill the needs of the air service. But when Spaatz saw Cannon's injuries, he ordered a civilian ambulance to carry Cannon to the hospital. The horse-drawn ambulance ride would have killed him. Spaatz had considerable difficulty in getting the army to pay for his initiative in making this unauthorized expenditure. His justification, written to the commanding officer of the VIII Corps Area, Fort Sam Houston, was that "the nature of the skull and superior maxilla fractures were [sic] such as to require the most careful handling in transportation. The distance from Ellington Field to Camp Logan [to a hospital] is twenty-five miles, and it was feared that to transport Lt. Cannon in any of the ambulances on this post would result in jarring which might prove fatal."[11] Cannon not only survived but rose to the rank of four-star general.

Preparing for future accidents could not be delayed. Spaatz wrote to a friend on June 30, 1922: "I'm calling on you for help. The nature of the work carried on by a pursuit group requires the services of a highly efficient surgeon, and some well-trained nurses."[12] This overture began dealings to establish flight surgeons to fulfill the specialized needs for flying personnel. Spaatz endeared himself to his men because of his actions that reflected his concern for each of them.

Nor did he give up quickly on his men. "I have been thinking," Spaatz wrote to his friend Maj. Frank D. Lackland at Fort Sam Houston on August 22, 1922, "of submitting a report, through channels, about Asp. As far as ordinary routine work is concerned, he is incompetent as an officer; it is difficult to keep him on the job. On the other hand, he has a natural bent for engineering and technical matters; he will work all day and night trying to learn something about a new motor or a new airplane. If he could be placed in some position where he could exercise this natural inclination, I believe he would become a fairly valuable officer. The difficulty has been in deciding whether an officer with these inclinations was valuable enough to the service to keep. . . . I would like a little advice from you in this connection. . . . There is no use in giving up hope until the end [that is, submitting his official report]."[13]

The 1920s were, of course, the days of Prohibition—and of widespread disregard for it. "General Patrick had had reports that there was a liquor problem at Selfridge Field," related Ira Eaker. "He called Spaatz in and asked him if that were the case, and Spaatz responded, 'No sir. We do not have a liquor problem at Selfridge Field. All of my officers are on duty when they are supposed to be on duty and they abide by rules and regulations meticulously.' He went on to say that they did serve liquor in the evenings. 'When we have it—and it's scarce, you know—I don't prohibit liquor on the field because it would be unrealistic. They would simply just go off the base and get into trouble. I keep them on the base. I make it pleasant for them to be at the officers' club and remain in the base.' Patrick told me later that Spaatz's response appealed to him. Spaatz had the courage to disagree with [him]. Spaatz himself was not aware that the conference had gone so well. I remember, too, that when Spaatz came out he said, 'Well, I guess I'll have a new assignment. I'd appreciate it if you'd let me know where it is. I'll be going as soon as you know.'"[14]

General Eisenhower was tremendously considerate of the welfare of his commanders. In December 1942, Gen. Mark W. Clark, deputy for the North African invasion, attended a conference with Eisenhower in Algeria. Eisenhower had to leave hurriedly to fly to Gibraltar. At the airfield there were many newspaper reporters and photographers hoping for a press conference. Time was so short that Eisenhower did not answer any of the reporters' questions. "He did, however," said General Clark, "make one of the friendly and thoughtful gestures that are so typical of him. When the reporters and cameramen were crowding around him, he said he had time for just one thing. Then he fished a star out of his pocket and pinned it on my shoulder. 'I've been waiting for a long time to pin on this third star, Wayne,' he said. 'I hope I pin on the fourth.'"[15]

Ike seldom asked his commanders in the field to report to him, preferring to go to them and saving them the inconvenience of leaving their commands. When he traveled to the front, he always insisted that his temporary headquarters be set up away from the battle commander's headquarters. This ensured that he would not be a burden upon the officers busy with the actual fighting.

There are many acts of thoughtful consideration among these top leaders. "General Vandenberg made a trip to Korea during the Korean conflict, and I traveled with him," recalled Maj. Gen. Richard A. Grussendorf, then his aide. "In General MacArthur's headquarters, the aide asked Collins and Vandenburg to come on in and I found a seat outside General MacArthur's office. I was about to sit down when Van said, 'You come with me,' and so I followed him in. I met General MacArthur, and he was very cordial and accepted the fact that there was a colonel in the room, but Van said, 'I want you to listen to this.' It was very considerate of Van, but I think it was also part of my training—I would better understand messages and JCS papers and so on. Also, [his] thoughtfulness: It wasn't just a 'come on in with me and meet the big man thing so you can tell your grandchildren.'"[16] This also provides an example of mentorship.

Through his career, Gen. Nathan F. Twining was thoughtful and considerate of both officers and enlisted men. A most appreciative account of Twining as an instructor came from Lt. Gen. Elwood R. "Pete" Quesada. Quesada had been recruited from the University of Maryland by the air corps to attend pilot training but primarily to help build up the training school football team. Cadet Quesada elected to take advantage of this opportunity to learn to fly. One of his teammates on the football squad was instructor Twining. Said

Quesada: "I remember Twining more as a football player than I do as an instructor. Twining was a decent, pleasant fellow. He was a first lieutenant then, having been in the army about five years. We got to be good friends on the football team together, and although he was an officer, a rather senior one at that, and I was an enlisted man, he was always extremely friendly to me, which I appreciated and enjoyed. Officers and enlisted men did not mix, but he did make my life very easy.

"What I particularly remember was the fact that I broke my leg playing football, and they wanted me to keep up with the class, so they offered me the chance to take flying instruction during the Christmas holidays when everyone else had gone home or elsewhere for Christmas. They, of course, had to come up with a pilot instructor who was willing to give up his Christmas. Nate Twining volunteered to be my instructor. So for two weeks during the Christmas break I got special instruction. It was a very decent thing for him to have done and I have never forgotten it."[17]

General Lauris Norstad remembered reporting as a new second lieutenant to his first duty station. "My first air force station was at Wheeler Field in Hawaii. I lived at Schofield Barracks, and Nate was the senior officer living in the bachelor officer quarters. I was assigned to his quarters area, and I remember so well how nice he was to me. He introduced me to everyone in the quarters, to the people on the post. He was very considerate, very thoughtful, and very nice. I've always liked him, and I've never forgotten that first contact that I had with him."[18]

In July 1950, Twining became deputy chief of staff for personnel in Washington. In this role, he showed particular interest in the enlisted men, because he realized how tremendous the cost of training was for them in the highly technical air force. If these men left the service after their first enlistment, training would have been a waste of money, so reenlistment rates had to be stepped up. He felt the answer to this was to make air force careers more attractive, with fringe benefits, higher pay, and better housing. He also wanted to instill in servicemen the feeling that their positions were secure and they were respected by the civilian population. His attitude almost became air force dogma. High-ranking officers began to dismiss questions about how big the air force should be with the terse comment, "Numbers are nothing but a racket." They preferred to discuss the problem of how to get airmen to look on the service as a career. One general officer even insisted, "I would take a hundred-wing force if I knew that every man was well trained and steady on his job."

One of Twining's responsibilities at Duncan Field included working with the new flying schools being set up. Major General Daniel E. Hooks said: "I was sent out to one of these schools as a first lieutenant. At that time Nathan F. Twining was a major, and he was an inspector for our area. We used to look forward to his visits, as we knew he would not only tell us where we might be in error but would also show us how to correct our mistakes. He would tell us where other similar schools were running into trouble and how we could avoid such trouble. He was interested in helping us along, not just criticizing. He was expert, open, frank and friendly, and completely honest. We appreciated his help and were always glad to see him."[19]

General Curtis E. LeMay was selected as commander of Strategic Air Command in 1948. The Cold War was beginning, and LeMay was aware of the threat of the Soviet Union. He was incredibly demanding of his people, particularly with the requirement that many bomber aircrews be constantly on alert. They were separated from their families for long periods of time, often months, either in the alert-crew area on their air bases or deployed overseas. No one ever doubted, however, the concern that LeMay had for his airmen.

LeMay told me: "You've got to worry about your people. No one else is going to worry about them if you don't. It's up to the chief of staff to take care of his people, and this is something that takes up quite a bit of his time. I wouldn't attempt to try to single out any one duty as being more challenging than the others. On the other hand, I tried to set up a criterion of keeping foremost in mind the good of the country, and the air force and the armed services second, and then your people. You have to spend a lot of time on your people. Certainly, you can't carry out the complex duties that are charged to the air force now unless you have a good professional team working on those problems, and this means that somebody has to pay attention to the type of people you get, the type of people you keep—

and it's one [field] that requires a great deal of time. One that, I feel, I made some contribution in, but certainly not enough. There's still a lot of work to be done in this field and one that chiefs that follow on behind me will have to spend a lot of time on."[20]

When LeMay took command of Strategic Air Command, a general said to me, "I was director of installations in Headquarters, USAF. General LeMay was a tireless worker to build Strategic Air Command to the superb deterrent force that it is today. He personally directed an all-out effort to improve the lot of the officers and airmen of SAC. He was particularly active in our efforts to improve barracks, BOQ and family quarters. Every time he visited Headquarters, USAF, which was often, he came to see me on this subject, and we had a continuous personal correspondence on it. He contributed immeasurably in what success we obtained. The rank and file in the Air Force recognized and applauded General LeMay's strenuous efforts to improve their personal well-being."[21]

A lead crew for the old B-36 represented an investment of $3 million. But it was not the money that was the telling factor. "We can replace the money," LeMay said, "but it is extremely dubious whether we shall, in a crisis, ever be given enough time to replace the crew."

During LeMay's stint as SAC commander, a plane went down in a tragic crash where the survivors later perished. The lesson to be learned was that you cannot defeat cold, hunger, and isolation by sitting on your hands. This crew of gallant men endured much, but their courage and stubborn cheerfulness was not enough. They should have been taught what to do to survive. "The leader must equip himself mentally and physically to do it," said LeMay, "and he must act."[22]

LeMay did act to correct the situation. The air force lists, active and reserve, as well as the army, were combed for skiers, explorers, mountaineers, trappers, and woodsmen to obtain personnel to set up schools to teach downed aircraft crewmen to survive off the land, whether it be tundra, jungle, desert, or mountains. This saved many men with indispensable training and experience.

LeMay continued: "There are still, perhaps, a few 'realists' around who will shrug off the loss of such crews as merely a part of the normal attrition which afflicts any operating air force. They could not be more mistaken. To the Strategic Air Command, no pilot, no bombardier, no gunner, no crew is expendable.[23]

"SAC's mission is to preserve the peace by presenting to the enemy the constant poised alternative of total retaliation. But our deterrent value in peace, and our destructive potential in war, depend alike upon our readiness to deliver a knockout atomic punch—not in a year or a month or a week, but now. Not with crews we might eventually train, but with the precision teams at our disposal today."[24]

General J. P. Ryan was chief of staff of the air force from 1969 to 1973. I asked him why some leaders in time of war instill in their men the willingness necessary to perform complex and dangerous missions. He responded: "As you well know, people have been trying to find the answer to that one for years. But I think one of the important things is to submerge your own ego. Your success depends upon the fulfillment of the activities of your men. You by yourself are rather helpless really. I think I realized that my success was the result of the efforts of a large number of people under me and I tried to show my respect to them for what they had done for the teams' effort and for their unit and, of course, it built me up.

"I asked them questions. I found out what they were doing. I was interested in what they were doing. You learn a hell of a lot this way also. Every question you ask, you're going to answer it better. I've never seen a man yet who didn't react favorably to someone taking an interest in what he was doing. Many a night, for instance in the old B-50 days when we were changing jugs like they were going out of style, I'd be out there at ten, ten-thirty at night crawling up a ladder standing there beside a man working on it and I'd start asking questions. 'What are you doing?' Of course, I learned. Well, I learned a lot of other things, such things [as] maybe he couldn't get a cup of coffee because the mess hall wasn't open, so I'd take care of him that way. I would even go get the coffee. I saw to it that the mess would have coffee and breakfast throughout the entire night. I was interested in his work and he'd bust his butt for me."[25]

I asked General Ryan how he got extra effort out of people. "By communicating with them. I talked to them, not down to them, because I was interested in what they were doing. And I learned from the questions that I asked them.

"As a brigadier general, for example, I went from division commander to be a staff officer at Omaha where I was director of materiel. On every opportunity that I was out on an inspection trip or on an orientation trip to a base, I spent my time down in maintenance activities—talking to the airmen, talking to the officers, finding out what they were doing, finding out what their problems were."[26]

General George Brown's career was filled with thoughtfulness, consideration, and sensitivity for others. One officer remembered: "Brown had a great sensitivity for the people he led. One of his crew members, Sergeant Treadway, from Montana, was deeply depressed. Brown counseled with him, and Treadway left him and went back to his tent. A little later, the sergeant emerged from his tent fully outfitted in cowboy boots, broad-brimmed hat, and everything else that went with traditional western gear worn in Montana. He then proceeded to parade around the base for an hour or so. This, of course, was against all uniform regulations, but after his hour was up, he returned to his tent and put his uniform back on, a new man. Brown had told him to do this, and it turned out to be very effective therapy."[27]

Brown was at McChord Air Force Base from July 1951 to April 1952. "While at McChord," remembered General Faught, "our families remained at Kelly Air Force Base. This created a serious morale problem for our people. George called the maintenance people and explained to them the number of airplanes we needed in commission to fulfill our daily schedule in flying troops over to Japan and bringing back the wounded. [George] decided that if we could keep the required number of aircraft in commission, we could also operate a shuttle between McChord and Kelly, to enable people to fly back to see their families occasionally. He set up a roster so that about every two and a half weeks, the lowest airman to the highest-ranking officer could take trips to Kelly."[28]

At McChord, Brown commanded a provisional wing that was under another colonel senior to him. "I can't remember his name offhand," said Faught, "but I believe that he felt some jealousy toward George. Brown in the day-to-day routine of carrying out the mission just did what he was told and delivered more than what was asked of him, ignoring the interference of the more senior colonel, who decided he couldn't do anything about Brown. So this colonel tried to take it out on George's subordinate commanders. George had put four of us in for promotion, but that colonel was not going to have any part in us being promoted. He believed that we were simply troop carrier personnel not deserving of promotion. George informed him that he was going to see their boss, General Stowell, personally about the matter. But before that occurred, the commander gave in and agreed to the recommendations for promotion. None of us ever forgot this effort on George's part."[29]

Nor did this go unnoticed with Brown's rating officer, Col. Richard F. Bromily, who wrote, "He is loyal to his people and his organization to a fault."

Another insight shows Brown's consideration. "In our case," said Frank Rogers, "we had a lieutenant colonel named Jim Johnson, who became available and was made our A-4, or director of materiel for our wing. Jim had a real problem in that he had to establish logistic support for the AC&W [aircraft control and warning] sites of the two division headquarters in our area. I recall discussing with George an effectiveness report that he had rendered on Jim. In this discussion he said to me, 'I have put an awful lot of responsibility on Jim to work out these problems. He's been doing it with little or no help.' I then realized that Brown recognized that there were some built-in limitations in everyone.

"The system that provided us with our people was such that not everyone could be a Ph.D. or a Napoleon in battle. One had to have a sort of feeling of compassion, or at least understanding, that some people were just busting their butts and really putting out, yet the results weren't always perfect. These kinds of people had a place in the organization and had to be handled accordingly. I had known Jim for a long time and, although he was an extremely capable man, I think it's fair to say that there were better-qualified directors of materiel in the air force. He was, however, our man, and he was doing the best he could do for our commander. George Brown appreciated his effort and wanted to see his career blossom. He took into consideration all the factors that make up a human being."[30]

Brown's consideration for others was not limited to military personnel. His rapport with the troops, particularly the noncoms and enlisted men, certainly came from his background in the military. He also had a broad knowledge of the importance of all people—the civil service employees as well as the military. At Selfridge Air Force Base, there was a nine-hole golf course that had been there for years. None of the civil service employees there were allowed to play golf on the course; it was reserved strictly for the military. Brown learned about this in the base barbershop soon after he took command. The barber, an avid golfer, said, "I sure would like to get a chance to play the golf course out there once in a while." Brown said nothing then but decided that civilians could play the golf course during the week, but not on Saturday and Sunday when the military were off duty. A large number of civilians began using the course in the mornings before office hours, in the evenings, and for three or four holes on their lunch hours. The fact that they were included as part of the team was extremely important to them. Brown told Colonel White of his decision. "You cannot afford to ignore part of your command and treat them like poor peasants." White commented, "He treated everybody exactly the same way—officers, enlisted men, or civilians."[31]

Some officers tend to forget about the enlisted personnel on occasion, but not George Brown. The two fighter squadrons had permanent brick barracks, each with its own mess hall. Brown commented: "I can't understand why these men on Sunday morning have to get up and walk to the PX to pick up their newspapers and then come back to the mess hall." The mess hall, unfortunately, had the same hours on Sunday as it had throughout the week, although the base was closed and the men were not working. This meant that on Sunday, breakfast was served from 0600 to 0800. Brown said, "None of us living in quarters eat breakfast between six and eight on Sunday. We have a leisurely Sunday morning breakfast and read the papers. Why shouldn't the troops in the barracks have the same thing?" So he changed the mess breakfast hours on Sunday to between 0800 and 1100.

"The troops just loved it," said White. "They could go down to the mess hall anytime between eight and eleven o'clock in the morning in their bathrobes and slippers; they didn't have to put on uniforms.

The newspaper people were instructed to deliver the newspapers to the mess hall rather than to the exchange. The men could pick up their various newspapers and walk through the chow line and say to the cook, 'I'd like a couple of eggs over easy and some bacon and pancakes.' Then they could go over and sit down at the table. Since nothing was precooked, they'd read the paper until their food was ready."[32]

General David C. Jones, former air force chief of staff, brought Maj. Gen. Bob Thompson to work for him as chief of engineering, a two-star job. He started civil engineering management evaluation teams to study everything having to do with services on the bases. General Jones was concerned about this from the billeting office to the BX to the stores and variety that the commissary stocked. Were people treated courteously? Was the service side of the air force providing a service? Frequently the answer was no. The teams didn't have to take a high-handed approach. Jones used to go through their thick reports in detail. Their studies did not just note deficiencies but had positive, constructive suggestions about what to do to improve service to air force people. They provided a lot of cross-fertilization as well as learning from what they saw at the different bases. Jones then would spread this information throughout the entire air force.[33]

Jones's chief of chaplains, Maj. Gen. Henry J. Meade, related: "I remember one time when I was with General Jones on a trip to Japan in late 1977 and early 1978. He was a great jogger and still is. He hardly ever skips a day. Anyway, he was suited up in his morning jogging outfit. We were at Yokota Air Force Base. He came across a place called the American Village, where enlisted people lived just outside the base. He was about as angry at what he saw as I've ever seen him. What he had seen was deplorable. The fact that the enlisted GI had to live in this crap sickened him. That was all he talked about. He talked about it at every stop and he brought it up in PACAF headquarters at Hickam as he was being debriefed. I know that the commander of Yokota walked away pretty badly scarred. But General Jones shook things up to improve the situation. A splendid man. GIs would bring their wives even though they didn't have enough rank to bring their families over. Unauthorized people were living in a foreign establishment and not being able to use the privileges. That really set him off. He certainly changed all that. He was a GI's guy. He really was."³⁴

General Jones was clearly people-oriented. Ironically, some criticized this—some of the senior people—that it was all contrived. "I completely denied that," Chaplain Meade told me. "I feel that at no time was David Jones a charlatan. At no time was he using people-related issues for his own benefit. He had no reason to. He was the chief. He was particularly interested in minorities. He was dead serious about making sure that minorities got their honest shake in the air force. There was no mincing of words there. He introduced these human relations programs in the Pentagon to address racial issues and demanded that all attend. Then he promulgated them worldwide in the air force. Every officer had to attend mandatory human relations conferences several times a year in which minority issues were raised. This drove some people crazy. They hated to go to those things. They thought it was like a Sunday School, that they were being preached to, that it was an insult to their intelligence. Jones wanted these impediments to minorities halted immediately, and this program of his accomplished wonders."³⁵

Colonel Robert H. Baxter, USAF (Ret.), told me: "Another people program of General Jones's was his pressing for a much more active role for retired air force people. He put out the word to all commanders that it was an air force family, and encouraged them to call the retirees out, perhaps semiannually or whatever felt right in the local situation. He wanted to renew their contact with the air force and keep them a part of it to show them that we were interested in them, and to seek their counsel. For example, he would often confer with General LeMay. He listened to General LeMay, realizing that times had changed since LeMay's days. He recommended this as a matter of policy to his commanders, letting the commanders figure out for themselves just how valuable the help was from the retired people and how they should handle it. His thrust was quite simple: 'We want,' he said, 'to do more to invite them out to participate in functions on the base.' It was done for both officers and the enlisted personnel. He had a very active interest in the enlisted men's widows' home. They had a bit of a head start on the officers' home down in San Antonio, which he also supported very strongly."³⁶

General Thompson had this to say: "[Jones] encouraged base commanders, wing commanders, major commanders to include the retired in various functions. If you went to Bolling Air Force Base, for example, or Andrews now, you would find an office manned by retirees several hours each day. There was a publication that covered a fifty-mile radius of the area. General Jones created this. The idea was that retirees with any problem or challenge could call there, talk, visit, and would have the support, or even financial support, from commanders, funds to help them with a particular crisis."

Major General Robert C. Thompson said of Jones: "[He] even showed consideration for the other military services. When General Creighton Abrams, the former Vietnam army commander and army chief of staff, died, General Jones held a ceremony for his widow, Mrs. Abrams, within a few weeks after his funeral. He had not had a great deal of direct contact with General Abrams, but he clearly knew of the rapport that he and General Brown and Abrams had established in Vietnam, which led to increased air force–army cooperation. He just made General Abrams, posthumously, a command pilot, and we mounted a set of command pilot's wings for him, feeling that that would be the most symbolic thing that the air force could give to him. He had a little ceremony with Mrs. Abrams, just in the office. There couldn't have been more than ten people there as he presented the wings to her in a tribute to General Abrams."[37]

One of the most meaningful acts of consideration by General Jones was provided by Chaplain Meade. "On that same trip to Japan, David Jones showed some great personal character. We were briefed during that visit in 1981 on a continuing problem concerning young children born of GIs to native Koreans, the Amerasian situation. There was a Maryknoll priest named Father Al Keane, in Seoul, who was very close to the army's and air force's presence in Korea. He was one of the few able to care for children who were born of an American GI and a Korean. In most cases the father would have left to go home with no marriage involved, abandoning mother and child. Because Korean society rejected this arrangement, the children were outcasts who could never be accepted in local society. Father Keane's purpose was to acquaint the military and the Congress of the enormity of this problem. With voluntary funding he built three or four orphanages to safeguard these youngsters. He became involved in a comprehensive adoption program in which people in the States could adopt these little waifs. If the children weren't adopted when they were young, the hope of adoption later was lost. We briefed General Jones about this. He, as always, threw himself headlong into the program. Mrs. Jones, along with the wife of the American commander in Korea, and I visited several of these Amerasian orphan homes. It tore our hearts out when we went there. Jones invited Father Keane to come back to the States, telling him he would support as much as possible in having this program heard by whichever congressional contacts he had. He did just that.

"Alfred Keane came to the United States in May 1982 to argue for the 'Amerasian Bill' that he had been laboring so hard to get on the floor. It was to come up for debate after testimony was heard. He asked General Jones to testify, which he agreed to do."[38]

Some criticized General Jones within the air force, saying that "the air force was falling to pieces under Jones's leadership, that while he was spending time and money on people programs, people's needs, people's behavior, the air force's fundamental mission was eroding. That's what I kept hearing. Some would say that if, instead of using his time and energy on his human relations program, he had put it to work for him pushing congressmen to vote for more aircraft and defense systems, he might have been more persuasive with the president when he made the decision to scrap the B-1."[39]

But the criticism did not blunt Jones's determination to care for the troops at every level of command. He was an astute observer of the halls of Congress, but he was always a caring commander for the essential role as a humanitarian leader.

Another example of simple human kindness in leadership was obvious when Colonel Schwarzkopf remembered vividly a consideration by his division commander at Fort Lewis.

"I'd been back from the headquarters exercise only two days when Cavazo's executive officer called: 'The general is on his way over to see you. He wants to talk about your maintenance program.' I thought that was odd, because our maintenance program was fine. I hung up the phone, went to the window, and saw a couple of jeeps pull up. With Cavazo were both of his assistant division commanders, a sergeant major, and a couple of other officers. He burst into the office and said loudly, 'Norm, the Army has really screwed it up this time.'

"'Sir?' I said.

"'Would you believe that the United States Army has selected you to be a brigadier general?' He laughed, pulled out the official promotion list that would be published the following day, and pumped my hand. Meanwhile a couple of officers brought in a cake decorated with a big red star. I was moved by the celebration and congratulations—but all I could think of was going home to tell Brenda."

That evening Cavazo went to Schwarzkopf's home to see his new brigadier general and Brenda. Schwarzkopf asked him, "There's one favor I'd like to ask. . . . I'd like to give my brigade the day off tomorrow." Cavazo responded, "Absolutely."

Schwarzkopf continued: "At 6:30 A.M. the entire brigade assembled on the parade ground. I clambered up onto the raised platform that commanders use to direct calisthenics. 'This afternoon, at fourteen hundred hours, the Department of the Army is going to announce that I have been promoted to brigadier general,' I told them. The whole brigade started to *cheer.* I hadn't expected that and got all choked up. Then I said, 'Any commander worth his salt knows that when a good thing happens to him, it happens because of the soldiers under his command. I am proud of this brigade.'"[40]

One would think that in this day, with the prolific literature available on leadership and management, all officers would be aware of the importance of consideration. Unfortunately, that is not the case. A recent example was provided by General Schwarzkopf:

> The most challenging part of my work turned out to be community command, which was unique to Germany. We'd only been in Mainz a month when Brenda got a call from a neighbor, a captain's wife, who'd picked up a young Pfc. hitchhiking. The young man was in tears. She'd asked what was wrong and he'd explained that his wife and baby daughter were due to arrive at the Frankfurt international airport that night and he had no money and no place for them to stay. Brenda called me at work and I immediately got on the phone with the 1st

Brigade commander. "I'll check into it," he said, "but chances are they're nonsponsored dependents."

"What difference does that make?" I asked.

"That means they're not our responsibility."

"Colonel, one of your men is standing by the side of the road in tears because he can't take care of his wife and baby, and you're telling me it's not our responsibility? You get that man's battalion and company commanders on the phone and solve that soldier's problem. Then get back to me and let me know what you've done."[41]

With Schwarzkopf behind it, there were immediate results. They arranged an emergency loan, found his family a hotel room, and helped him rent an apartment. The commissary, medical clinic, and day-care facilities were opened to the nonsponsored dependents, even though privates first class and specialists fourth class were not technically authorized to bring their wives and children. But because the families came anyway, Schwarzkopf saw to it that they were cared for.

Certainly President George Bush was aware of the importance of doing thoughtful things. General Schwarzkopf related that in December 1990 when he was commander of Desert Shield–Desert Storm: "I went back to my room at the Ministry of Defense. Brenda had sent a little Christmas tree with lights. I switched it on, put a cassette of Christmas music on the tape machine, and was nearly asleep when I heard the red phone to Washington ring in my office. It was President Bush. 'I couldn't let this day go by without calling to wish you and all the men and women under your command a Merry Christmas,' he said. 'I know that you are far away from your loved ones, but I want you to know that our thoughts and prayers are with you. You know the course we are on. Our prayers will stay with you during the coming days.' I told him how much we appreciated his call and thanked him on behalf of all Central Command.

"After we hung up I turned on my Christmas music again and listened long into the night until I fell asleep."[42]

Schwarzkopf also realized the importance of teaching his subordinates the role of consideration. While serving in Vietnam, he visited one of the companies of his battalion, but its commander was not there. The company executive officer said he was in the rear visiting wounded soldiers in the hospital, so he waited for him to return to compliment him on looking after his soldiers. The captain never returned, so Schwarzkopf went looking for him. He found him in the mess hall in a nice, clean uniform eating Christmas dinner with some of his officer friends.

> I praised him for visiting his men in the hospital and then asked, "Why didn't you go straight back out to your company?"
>
> "Well, sir, I wanted to have Christmas dinner."
>
> "What about your troops? Don't you understand that it was your responsibility to see that they had their Christmas dinner?"
>
> He frowned. "Sir, as far as I'm concerned . . . ," he began, but then stopped. "Sir, I knew you were bringing them a Christmas meal, and I thought that as long as I was here, I'd take a shower and put on clean clothes and eat my dinner."
>
> "Captain, do you realize what you've just told your troops? You think they don't know that while they're out in the boonies on Christmas Day, their leader is in the rear? If you're not willing to go through the discomfort of spending Christmas with them in the field, how do you expect them to believe you'll be with them when they go into battle?"[43]

Schwarzkopf also showed consideration for the South Vietnamese soldiers while he was in Vietnam. Within a few miles of the Cambodian border there was a heavy firefight resulting in casualties of U.S. and South Vietnamese troops. American helicopters flew in to remove the wounded. Schwarzkopf reflected:

> The Vietnamese soldiers decided to load the corpses on the helicopter for the return flight to Pleiku. "No bodies!" the crew told them, and tried to push the bodies off while the pilot revved his blades. I ran over and climbed on the skid next to the pilot's window. He was a captain. I shouted, "What's going on?"

"We don't take bodies in this helicopter. They get blood and shit all over the flight deck."

"Hey, we've got to get these bodies out of here. If we don't, we have to carry them."

"I don't give a shit. We ain't takin' bodies out." If those had been dead Americans, I knew he wouldn't have thought twice, and that burned me up.

"Let me tell you something, sport. Either you take those bodies or you stay here on the ground because I'm not gonna get off this skid. If you take off, I'm gonna fall off this airplane and die. Are you willing to take responsibility for that? And second, if you try to take off, I'll shoot your ass!" Either he didn't realize I was bluffing, or the fact that I was a major focused his attention: they loaded the bodies on.

Without knowing it, I'd endeared myself forever to the South Vietnamese troops. They saw an American who cared enough about them to climb up on a helicopter skid and make the pilot accept their dead. Word went all the way back to Saigon and up to Brigadier General Du Quoc Dong, the airborne commander. For weeks after I returned to Saigon, American advisors came up and told me they'd heard about the incident from their South Vietnamese counterparts.[44]

General John M. Shalikashvili, another modern officer, told me: "I cannot overstate the importance of character and of caring. I think that people respond best to leaders that are confident because they know what they're doing, because they are men of character, and because it shows that they deeply care for those they lead. I am convinced that the best leaders truly love those they lead. You've asked me why people follow leaders in peacetime. This is different from wartime, because in peacetime soldiers have more time to think things through. There has to be a more conscious effort than in wartime. You have to like people. It is, I submit, more difficult on a day-to-day basis. You may have seen a young lieutenant sitting by the side of his tank eating his C ration. By going over to sit by him and by looking him in the eye, you can see whether he's enjoying being

there or not. You get to know many such men by name and where
they live and what they're doing. And you do this because you in turn
enjoy being with them. How often have you brought a general on
an inspection in the field and you find that there is a tent set up
where the generals and officers sit, as opposed to having the generals sit down and talk with soldiers for a while. That's what the generals enjoy the most and that's what the soldiers will always remember."[45]

How then do you inspire the people you work with to give their
all? First, a leader who is dedicated to serving God and country is an
inspiration and a role model; he has a contagious leadership quality. Second, the hallmark of a leader is one who has respect and admiration for people, which is engendered through caring about
them and showing genuine consideration. This fosters confidence
and loyalty and raises morale. In the commander's personal humanity lies his ultimate strength.

Notes

1. Personal interview with Lt. Gen. Willis D. Critenberger and Edgar F, Puryear, Jr., October 20, 1962

2. Lucian K. Truscott, *Command Mission* (New York: Dutton, 1954), 383, and personal interview, September 11, 1962.

3. Letter from Maj. Gen. A. M. Jones, USA (Ret.), to Edgar F. Puryear, Jr., dated August 10, 1962.

4. Henry J. "Hap" Arnold, *Global Mission* (New York: Harper & Row Publishers, 1949), 48.

5. Ibid.

6. Ibid.

7. *Colliers*, 112 (December 25, 1943), 26.

8. Ibid.

9. Letter from Maj. Carl Spaatz to Maj. Thurman H. Bane, A.S., dated July 13, 1922.

10. Letter from Maj. Thurman H. Bane, A.S., to Maj. Carl Spaatz, dated July 19, 1922.

11. Personal interview with General Carl Spaatz and Edgar F. Puryear, Jr. September 19, 1962.

12. Ibid.

13. Letter from Maj. Carl Spaatz to Maj. Frank D. Lackland, Air Officer, VIII Corps Area, dated August 22, 1922.

14. Personal interview with Lt. Gen. Ira C. Eaker, USAF (Ret.), and Edgar F. Puryear, Jr., October 4, 1977.

15. Mark W. Clark, *Calculated Risk* (New York: Doubleday and Company, Inc., 1948), 122.

16. Personal interview with Maj. Gen. Richard A Grussendorf and Edgar F. Puryear, Jr., July 8, 1978.

17. Personal interview with Lt. Gen. Elwood R. "Pete" Quesada and Edgar F. Puryear, Jr., June 22, 1977.

18. Personal interview with Gen. Lauris Norstad, USAF (Ret.), and Edgar F. Puryear, Jr., August 22, 1977.

19. Personal interview with Maj. Gen. Daniel E. Hooks and Edgar F. Puryear, Jr., January 21, 1976.

20. Personal interview with Gen. Curtis E. LeMay, USAF (Ret.), and Edgar F. Puryear, Jr., August 28, 1975.

21. Letter from Gen. Colbey M. Myers to Edgar F. Puryear, Jr., dated November 30, 1996.

22. Curtis E. LeMay, *The National Geographic Magazine* (May 1953), 565.

23. Ibid.

24. Ibid.

25. Personal interview with Gen. J. P. Ryan, USAF (Ret.), and Edgar F. Puryear, Jr., August 9, 1979.

26. Ibid.

27. Personal interview with Col. Carl Barthel, USAF (Ret.), and Edgar F. Puryear, Jr., August 8, 1979.

28. Personal interview with Maj. Gen. Courtney L. Faught, USAF (Ret.), and Edgar F. Puryear, Jr., August 8, 1979.

29. Ibid.

30. Personal interview with Maj. Gen. Frank Rogers, USAF (Ret.), and Edgar F. Puryear, Jr., August 6, 1979.

31. Personal interview with Brig. Gen. Ernest J. White, USAF (Ret.), and Edgar F. Puryear, Jr., March 8, 1981.

32. Ibid.

33. Personal interview with Col. Robert H. Baxter, USAF (Ret.), and Edgar F. Puryear, Jr., April 19, 1979.

34. Personal interview with Maj. Gen. Henry J. Meade, chaplain, USAF (Ret.), and Edgar F. Puryear, Jr., April 1, 1981.

35. Ibid.

36. Baxter interview.

37. Personal interview with Maj. Gen. Robert C. Thompson, USAF (Ret.), and Edgar F. Puryear, Jr., October 27, 1980.

38. Meade interview.

39. Ibid.

40. H. Norman Schwarzkopf, *It Doesn't Take A Hero* (New York: Bantam Books, 1992), 211.

41. Ibid., 226–27.

42. Ibid., 398.

43. Ibid., 161.

44. Ibid., 115.

45. Personal interview with Gen. John M. Shalikasvili and Edgar F. Puryear, Jr., June 4, 1997.

Chapter 8: Delegation

If your subordinates cannot do [the work] for you, you haven't organized them properly.

—General of the Army George C. Marshall

You must avoid passing on to the commander petty decisions. . . . Get away from the shovel handle and out of the ditch [to] oversee the workmen on the project.

—General of the Air Force Henry H. Arnold

At the Cairo Conference in November 1943, General Eisenhower flew in to attend the Combined Chiefs of Staff meeting at the now famous Mina House Hotel. There he briefed the men on future operations, primarily the plans for the invasion of France, code-named Overlord.

General Marshall was concerned about Ike's tired appearance and suggested that he take a vacation for several days. "If your subordinates cannot do [the work] for you," Marshall told him, "you haven't organized them properly."

Marshall was a superb delegator in his relations with Ike as D-day commander. When Eisenhower went to Europe in 1942, Marshall told him, "You don't need to take or keep any commander in whom you do not have full confidence. So long as he holds a command in your theater, it is evidence to me of your satisfaction with him. The lives of many are at stake; I will not have you operating under any misunderstanding as to your authority, and your duty, to reject or remove any that fails to satisfy you completely."[1] Marshall never violated this rule.

Throughout World War II, Marshall also insisted that the Combined Chiefs (composed of American and British officers) not interfere with Eisenhower's conduct of operations in North Africa, Sicily, Italy, France, and Germany. He objected strenuously whenever the Combined Chiefs attempted to issue orders or advice directed to any field commander.

In January 1945, just prior to the Yalta Conference, top Allied generals met at Malta. The most important item on the meeting's agenda was probably the strategic plan for concluding the war against Germany. The British presented one plan; Eisenhower, represented by his chief of staff General Smith, argued for another. Marshall felt so strongly about Eisenhower's authority as supreme commander that he insisted that Ike's plan be adopted, and he presented an ultimatum to the British members of the combined staff. He informed them that if the British plan were submitted to the prime minister and President Roosevelt, and approved, he would have no choice but to ask for Eisenhower's relief as supreme commander. Such an attitude by the usually restrained and quiet Marshall won the day, and Eisenhower's plan was approved.

After Eisenhower had taken over command in Europe, Marshall attempted to relieve him of things that would distract and wear him down. He instructed Ike not to get involved in politics and, above all, not to waste his precious time and energy defending past actions; he had the future to worry about. When very important persons came to visit him, Marshall instructed him to refrain from arguing or debating with them and to "merely listen politely, 'yes' them if necessary; but, above all [don't waste your] brain power."[2]

In December 1943, after Eisenhower had been selected as supreme commander for the Allied invasion of Europe, he was trying to decide if he should come home for a few days. He had been under a terrific strain and needed a break to restore mental freshness, but how could he leave with the mammoth undertaking before him? General Marshall finally decided for him. On December 30, 1943, Marshall sent a message saying, "Now, come on home and see your wife and trust somebody else for twenty minutes in England."[3]

Marshall's relationship with Eisenhower was typical of his mode of leadership. As chief of staff, he followed a similar approach with all the officers under him. "Army officers are intelligent," General Marshall would say. "Give them the bare tree, let them supply the leaves."[4]

Ike had a policy with his staff, strongly encouraging their input but emphasizing the importance of delegation. He wrote on June 25, 1942, "Staff officers are free to see the chief or the commander at any moment to bring to their attention such matters as necessary or desirable. They are free to solve their own problems wherever possible and not to get into the habit of passing the buck up."[5]

When Eisenhower organized a headquarters, he was careful in the selection of his staff. He told them: "You are hand-picked experts in your fields. I expect you to get your jobs done without supervision. Otherwise, I made a mistake in selection."

He relied on the staff to relieve him of administrative details. His chief of staff during World War II, General Smith, described Eisenhower's ability to delegate authority as "beautiful." Duties were delegated, but there was never any doubt that Eisenhower was boss. In interviews and correspondence, all of his staff officers stated that in one way or another. He was a commander who would listen to all points of view with the ability to analyze a problem, extract its core, and work out a solution. He was so gifted that he could put his finger quickly and accurately on the crux of a situation.[6]

General MacArthur was also a superb delegator and had a policy to meet with as few people as possible. He was always available to the senior members of his staff; the junior members worked through his chief of staff. As Gen. George C. Kenney, his air chief, put it, "It is by avoiding doing too much that General MacArthur gets so much done." He left his mind free of battle planning so he could concentrate on the long-range aspects of the war. Thus, he could instantly exploit each opportunity as it occurred. "I don't do much," he said, "except think a lot, scold a little, pat a man on the back now and then, and try to keep a perspective."[7]

His former chief of staff, Lt. Gen. Stephen J. Chamberlin, said MacArthur was a great leader because "he could place responsibility in subordinates and let them go. Sometimes as a member of his staff I was scared, and I wondered if General MacArthur knew what I was doing. When I got to be his chief of staff, I realized he always knew just what I was doing; but I don't know how he knew."[8]

Once, Gen. George Kenney went into General MacArthur to request permission to fire anyone who was incompetent and to decorate the deserving. He got an immediate go-ahead from him. "You couldn't beat that for cooperation," Kenney recalled. "If General MacArthur ever decides that he has confidence in you, he goes all the way. When anyone backs you up like that, it makes it easy to work your head off for him."[9]

MacArthur was interested in results, and he wanted officers who would get them. Kenney decided shortly after his arrival in Australia to organize all his fighter groups into a single command. To head the new organization he selected a young colonel whose new position would give him the rank of brigadier general. MacArthur approved Kenney's request. When his staff heard of the proposal, an officer remarked, "That kid. Well, I hope he's twenty-one." MacArthur overheard the comment. He turned to his staff officer and said, "We promote them out here for efficiency, not for age." The officer being promoted was thirty-two years old.[10]

General Kenney said of his many years with MacArthur, "I found myself admiring him as a general, liking him as a man, and inspired by his innate gift for leadership. MacArthur leads—he does not drive. People who work for him drive themselves to carry out his wishes. They feel that they must not let 'the Old Man' down. You never feel that he has given you a direct order to do something, but at the same time his positive way of expressing himself never leaves you in doubt. I do not remember ever having been given a direct order by MacArthur during the whole time I worked for him, but I always knew exactly what he wanted done and knew he expected me to do it."[11]

During MacArthur's tenure as army chief of staff from 1930 to 1935, it was admirable that he did not delegate to others the really difficult and dirty jobs, those sure to be severely criticized. The United States has often seen a march of veterans on the nation's capital, usually during a period of depression. In the 1930s, there was again a World War I veterans' march, hoping to persuade Congress to pay them a $25 billion bonus.

As the group grew in size, it grew in boldness. Soon the Washington police could not control recalcitrant elements of the bonus marchers. There was also grave concern that an epidemic could spread from the shacks they were inhabiting on the Anacostia River. The marchers had inadequate sanitation, food, and shelter.

Finally President Hoover was forced to take action and gave the following orders to MacArthur: "You will have the United States troops proceed immediately to the scene of disorder. Cooperate fully with the District of Columbia police force which is now in charge. Surround the affected area and clear it without delay. Turn over all prisoners to the civil authorities. In your orders insist that any women and children who may be in the affected area be accorded every consideration and kindness. Use all humanity consistent with the due execution of this order."[12]

With tear gas, the back end of sabers, and the threat of bayonets, the bonus marchers were driven from the city by seven hundred army troops. Those with cars were given fuel to head them on their way. As they left the city, their shacks were burned to the ground.

MacArthur's role in this unfortunate action was personally taking command. He knew that the American public would resent chasing veterans away from their nation's capital, regardless of provocation. He could easily have avoided responsibility by assigning the task to some subordinate commander. It was typical of MacArthur that he never ordered others to do what he was not willing to do himself. As he told a fellow officer, "If the President gives me orders to act, I would not give this distasteful and disagreeable job to any other officer of the United States Army."[13]

General of the Army Henry H. "Hap" Arnold, chief of the U.S. Army Air Force from 1938 to 1946, emphasized that a commander should not attempt to make all of the decisions. It would be too overwhelming. One must delegate the more petty decisions. He commented to one of his officers, "Keep the commander informed of the state of the command at all times, but you must avoid passing up to the commander petty decisions and a mess of infinitesimal detail."

Although Arnold was a man of great drive and energy, he stressed that a commander should not try to do everything. "Until his staff is thoroughly trained," he said, "he will supervise all the duties himself, but it is more than one man can undertake and he will be wise, indeed, if he early ensures the adequate training of these assistants and then delegates to them the responsibility, retaining supervisory power."[14]

When an officer is a squadron or group commander in the air force, there are many details he can take care of personally, and one may tend to attempt to run these things with a minimum of delegation. But a commander at any level must learn to control his organization from a detached point of view. As he goes up in rank, he can no longer concern himself with petty details or even work with his hands. "He must get away," said Arnold, "from the shovel handle and out of the ditch so that he can oversee all the workmen on the project."[15]

One reason for Arnold's successful leadership was his ability to choose good people, then delegate full authority to them, with only general directives. Brigadier General Clarence P. Cain remembered his early years of leadership: "I served under General Arnold as supply officer during the time in the 1920s when the air service delivered the air mail for the U.S. Postal Service. General Arnold picked specialists for key jobs and then left them alone. He would back his subordinates to the hilt. He never forgot a favor. But if he took a dislike to an individual he could be mighty tough."[16]

A specific example that another officer remembered was that of Maj. Gen. Rush P. Lincoln: "When I was ordered to Australia, General Arnold showed his confidence in me by giving me only one order: 'Rush, go out there and take action to stop the Japs. Something is wrong out there and you correct it.'"[17]

I asked Gen. Carl A. Spaatz how Arnold found the people to whom he could delegate. He responded: "All the money that was spent for national defense between World War I and World War II went to the navy, which was sunk at Pearl Harbor. We were just a small smattering of people in the air corps—four hundred, five hundred officers, and some of them were not too good. That's what we had with which to expand to two or three million people for the war." I asked if Arnold had chosen his staff well. He said, "I would say he picked his staff very well from what he had to pick from. . . . He took the resources he had and put them to the best advantage."[18]

It was surprising, however, that with all his vision Arnold was reluctant to quickly advance some of the brilliant younger officers early in World War II. Because of the large increase in the size of the air force, General Marshall suggested that Arnold select a few relatively junior air corps officers to be jumped in rank, thus preparing younger talent for effective leadership. Arnold replied that if he promoted these officers, he did not believe he could sustain the morale of the World War I flyers among the senior colonels. Many of these had been reduced from wartime rank in 1919 and had served as long as seventeen years as lieutenants. Jump-promoting "youngsters" in their thirties, he thought, would shatter the morale of the older, more experienced group. Marshall, therefore, proceeded on his own, immediately promoting Lt. Col. Laurence S. Kuter, age thirty-six, to the rank of brigadier general. Kuter had been a lieutenant colonel for only about three weeks when this promotion was made. Arnold was then instructed to place the thirty-six-year-old Kuter in a high position on his staff and be less concerned about the morale of the older officers and more concerned with providing incentives for the younger ones.

One of Arnold's West Point classmates, Maj. Gen. H. B. Hayden, who was also with him in both world wars, commented on Arnold's leadership. "He was able to turn over to other men, his subordinates, their definite jobs and leave them alone. . . . If they did not do their jobs on time, they were replaced by other men. He learned to keep good discipline and looked after his men."[19]

Arnold's key plans officer during World War II, Gen. Orville A. Anderson, said of Arnold that he gave "almost total leeway. I never went to Hap's office. Now, there were times when I wanted to brief him and say, 'Here's a big issue coming up,' and I wanted to let him know what the issue is. But as his planner, until he says, 'Now you've gone berserk,' I'm supposed to do what I think Hap would do if he had the same opportunity to read as deeply into the problem as I had. In other words, as long as I think I have logic and reason to support the stand that I take . . . I'm not afraid of Hap or anybody else."[20]

Arnold's delegation had an amusing side: "According to Smart, one day during World War II, a group of staff officers, including several generals, was in Hap Arnold's office being thoroughly chewed out for something important that had not been done. At noon, the wall clock in the office emitted a loud, deafening buzz, as did all clocks in the Pentagon. Irate at the interruption, General Arnold bellowed, 'Why doesn't somebody do something about that damn clock!' A young, obscure colonel in the group did something. He picked up a heavy, empty inkwell off General Arnold's desk, threw back his arm, took aim, fired, and shattered the clock into fragments, never to buzz again. The young colonel was 'Rosie' O'Donnell. Arnold decided he was someone [to whom] he could delegate considerable responsibility, and he would use his talents extensively. He almost at once became a brigadier general. He rose to four-star general. He might readily have remained a colonel if not for the demonstration that particular day."[21]

General Thomas D. White commented to me: "The first thing that comes to my mind in decision making, which may not be the most important thing, is don't become bogged down in detail. . . . So many of the people who can't make decisions are very often the people who can't see the forest for the trees.

"To avoid getting bogged down, a leader must delegate and then be ready to accept the consequences if the subordinate to whom he delegates makes a mistake. . . . [He] must be able to back him up."[22]

General White, during his tenure as air force chief of staff, in a speech he presented to the wing at the U.S. Air Force Academy in 1957, further elaborated his thoughts on the importance of delegating in decision making: "Leadership," he said, "means many things to many men. I cannot tell you how to become a good leader; that is something you have to find out for yourselves. There is no positive checklist to follow—but you must have the desire." He then quoted Gen. Freiherr von Hammerstein-Equord, the former head of the German War Department and chief of army direction.

"I divide my officers into four classes as follows: The clever, the industrious, the lazy, and the stupid. Each officer always possesses two of these qualities. Those who are clever and industrious I appoint to the general staff. The man who is clever and lazy is destined for high command because he has the nerve to deal with all situations. Use can, under certain circumstances, be made of those who are stupid and lazy. But, whoever is stupid and industrious must be got rid of at once.

"I have always considered General von Hammerstein's observations very interesting; particularly so, when one attempts to analyze the four categories he listed.

"It is quite clear to me why General von Hammerstein wanted clever and industrious officers on his staff. Such men are particularly needed today. Men with imagination and the power to comprehend the essential nature of the problems or situations, and who are not afraid to work, are extremely valuable to a commander.

"But, what did von Hammerstein mean when he said the clever

and lazy man qualified for the highest leadership posts? The cleverness attribute we needn't discuss except to point out that he meant brains and experience—experience because no man would be in a position to be considered for high command had he not already gained considerable experience.

"To me the General used the word 'lazy,' however, in a wholly unusual context. The general didn't mean lazy in the true sense. He meant, without a doubt, the ability to distinguish between the really vital and the less consequential; he meant the attribute of being able to grasp the essentials and to refuse to be cluttered up with the nonessentials. Once the man with such attributes has charted his course based on vital essentials, he delegates the rest to subordinates—subordinates whom he has selected, whom he trusts and in whom he can repose confidence. These men do the 'work' so the high commander can perform the major tasks. Then this clever and so-termed 'lazy' commander accepts full responsibility for his actions. The major decisions are his alone and he accepts the consequences as worked out in detail by competent subordinates. That's what von Hammerstein meant by the 'nerve' to deal with all situations."[23]

General Carl "Tooey" Spaatz was the first chief of staff of the separate air force. I asked him why, in his opinion, he was a successful leader. He responded: "I drink good whiskey and I get other people to do my work."[24] There is more than humor in this thought. He meant he delegated authority to others. His assistant vice chief of staff was Maj. Gen. William F. "Bozo" McKee. In an interview, McKee related Spaatz's policy of delegating decision making:

I'll tell you a significant story about General Spaatz, and then you can see why he was so successful. When General Spaatz was chief of staff, Hoyt S. Vandenburg was vice chief and I was assistant vice chief. By that time I had gotten to know Spaatz quite well. It was a Saturday morning, and Vandenburg was gone. I had three papers that had to be signed by the chief of staff, or at least I thought they had to be signed by the chief of staff. So I took these three papers in to General Spaatz shortly after eleven o'clock that morning. I said to him, "Sir, I've got three papers here that require your signature as chief."

I was a major general at the time, and General Spaatz looked up to me and he said, "Bozo, didn't you just get promoted?"

I said, "Yes, sir."

"Who promoted you?"

"You did, sir."

"Why in the hell do you think I promoted you?"

"Sir, I don't know."

"Well, I'll tell you. I promoted you to sign papers like these. Do any of these papers have to do with war starting tomorrow?"

"No, sir."

"Then you sign them. If you make a mistake, I'll forgive you once. If you make a mistake two times, you're fired. Furthermore, I'm in a hurry because I'm due to meet some friends at eleven forty-five and I've got to go. So you sign these papers."

I went back to the desk and read these papers three more times with great care before I signed them, and that was the last I heard of it. The reason I tell this story is that General Spaatz, when he had confidence in somebody, believed in the world's simplest fundamental of leadership—that is, to give your subordinates authority. Spell it out and then let them discharge it.[25]

This leadership style probably keeps a leader from getting deserved credit, such as the unassuming Spaatz. Curtis LeMay commented, "To me, Spaatz was lazy. I have a suspicion that a lot of Spaatz's success was due to the people he had around him. That very fact, however—to get the people around you to do your work—makes him a good leader. General Spaatz used to brag about the fact that he was lazy and would have everybody else do the work. Spaatz was able to set the goal and say, 'This is what we have to do to get it done without my having to do it myself.'"[26]

Spaatz once said facetiously to Maj. Gen. Robert E. L. Eaton, "I owe my success to two things: I give a man a job, and I never tell him how to do it. He's supposed to know how to do it."

Remarked Brig. Gen. Harold A. Bartron: "General Carl 'Tooey' Spaatz had, in my opinion, more ability to inspire confidence in his commanders than anyone with whom I ever came in contact. He did this by reposing confidence in them.

"The general officer in command of service troops in the Mediterranean theater in World War II had a nervous breakdown and had
to be replaced overnight. General Spaatz selected me for the
job. . . . He took me to one side, and said, 'Bartron, Duncan is sick
and is going to be sent home. You will replace him. This is the toughest job in the theater, he has just broken down. I hope that you, too,
do not break down. You run the job the way you think it should be
run; go anyplace anytime you want to go. Take time off and often
whenever you like. If you're going to be away from your office for
more than three or four days, let me know.'

"In more than a year, during the war, General Spaatz visited me
only once, and in that time it was more of a social visit than otherwise. As he left he said to me, 'Bartron, I know you think it funny I
didn't ask you a lot of questions as to how things are going. I get that
from reports before I make a visit. When I inspect a commander, I
look for only one thing, his frame of mind.' I guess he wanted to
check and see if I was going to crack up."[27]

But in crucial moments Spaatz stayed in touch, as Maj. Gen.
Robert B. Williams remembered:

> On the night of October 13, 1944, the 1st Air Division, which
> I commanded, had been briefed for a full-scale attack on the
> fighter factories around Anklam in northern Germany. About
> 3 A.M. in the morning of October 14, I was in my operations of-
> fice checking the weather at our bases. They were all 0-0 with
> dense fog. An operations officer came over and said General
> Spaatz wanted me on the scrambler phone.
>
> I picked up the telephone, and General Spaatz said to me,
> "Bob, how are things in your area?" I responded to him that we
> were socked in and couldn't see to even taxi. He then said to
> me, "We have the first perfect bombing weather in Northern
> Germany that we have had in many months, and there is no
> telling when we will get another day of weather as good as this."
> I was, of course, aware of the fact. But General Spaatz went on
> to say to me, "However, if you're fogged in and can't take off,
> there is nothing we can do about it. I'll leave it entirely up to
> you."

I told General Spaatz that I would get my division airborne and that we would bomb Anklam with the ones that did not crack up on takeoff. Our pilots did an unbelievable job of getting several hundred B-17s off the fog-bound fields without a single fatal accident. The operation against Anklam was an outstanding success. I mention this because I consider the manner in which General Spaatz handled this situation as an excellent example of fine leadership. If he had ordered us on that mission, I would have tried to convince him that it was impossible. However, when he left it squarely up to me, what else could I do?[28]

General White, as chief of staff, relied on his executive officer, then Col. George S. Brown, to make his workload more bearable. For example, if a paper came in that in Brown's judgment presented too many options to the chief, he had the staff rework the paper and arrive at a better position so that the chief could choose from two options rather than five.

Brown also screened and summarized much of the other paperwork that came through the office. In a normal day, the chief would probably sign anywhere from thirty to fifty staff summary sheets or letters going to the other services or letters external to the air force. Principally, the bulk of the paperwork consisted of staff summary sheets, but many of these were quite thick. Brown read each report and would write a one- or two-sentence precis, such as, "This is not controversial," or "The staff's in full agreement," or "No hidden problems." With Brown's help, White never left a paper in his basket overnight.

On one occasion, General White was scheduled for a speech in San Francisco. After receiving a draft of the speech, White said to Col. Tim Ahern, "You know, this doesn't say anything. You and George Brown sit down and put something in the speech so it says something." At that time, military personnel were often quoted in the press, as they spoke with some authority. The audience was a meeting of NATO parliamentarians. Brown and Ahern decided that White should issue a call to our NATO partners to do more toward their own defense posture. They carefully couched some words to that effect and submitted the speech for necessary clearances. Donald Quarles, the undersecretary, read and approved it. Then it went through the bureaucratic clearance labyrinth of the State Department and the Joint Chiefs and finally was scrutinized by the office of the secretary of defense security review. White gave the speech, and it was picked up and quoted in newspapers in San Francisco, Washington, and New York.

"We got back and were feeling pretty good about the speech," reflected Ahern. "The morning after, the telephone rang. Edith McCaffrey, the chief's secretary, said, 'The president is calling.' It was Eisenhower. At the assistant exec's seat they had a little mike where you could listen to the telephone conversations of the chief. It was foot operated so that there was no click like somebody picking up on the phone. I listened to the conversation. Ike was livid. In his first burst of anger there were no preliminaries with General White. He said, 'What the hell do you think you're doing? What's the idea? What are you trying to pull? Why are you getting everybody excited?' He went on and on.

"General White replied he had gone through all the clearance processes, that it was not something he had unilaterally taken up and spoken off the cuff on. He had touched all the bases. He made no effort to say, 'Well, sorry, no excuse, sir.' He simply said, 'I did all the things I'm expected to do.'"[29]

While Gen. Larry D. Welch was chief of staff of the air force, from 1987 to 1991, I asked him, "What are your thoughts on delegation?"

He responded: "Even as chief of staff, there are times when I'm my own action officer. Right now, I'm the action officer on OERs because I need to be. Other people were working on it, but I'm going to work that action personally and everybody knows it. I'll work it with my DP [deputy for personnel], so the DP doesn't get cut out. The DP has senior action officers helping him do this and we're going to work this together. But the only way you can make that work without destroying the staff is to pick your issues.

"That's what General Creech did. That's what General Dixon did. General Dixon immersed himself in Red Flag. I sat in the office doing captain and major type work. General Creech absolutely immersed himself in the rated course business when we were struggling with how we could produce the numbers of pilots we needed. General Creech was the action officer and tried to teach wing commanders to do that. He said, 'Don't be a one-man band. Don't try to run the wing by yourself. But you pick those issues that you need to immerse yourself in to become the action officer.' I preach that all the time. I went through a period where I wasn't delegating enough, and it kind of grew on me. And the way I recognized it was that I wasn't leaving the kind of talent behind that I ought to leave behind. I found that when I left my job as wing commander, the wing had quite a bit of trouble after I left."[30]

General Welch believed that delegation is key—the most effective way to increase the quality of decision making. He told me: "The first is to be sure decisions are made by people in the best position to make them. And that is almost invariably on a lower level than the bureaucracy tends to allow decisions to be made. Second, pushing decisions down to where they ought to be made has the tremendous advantage of training decision makers at the right level. With centralization, and I don't want to take the negative side, what tends to happen in large bureaucracies is that the decisions are elevated to a higher level based on the assumption that people there are inherently more capable of making these decisions. They are either smarter or they know more or they've had more experience, et cetera.

"I don't believe that to be true. I believe that the smartest decisions are almost always made by the individual who has the most responsibility for implementing a decision. If indeed we require the decision to be made at that level, then we get better decisions in the first instance. Often we are training decision makers, and therefore we have better decision makers at every level.

"As an officer develops in his or her career, he or she should have had appropriate experience at making appropriate decisions at appropriate levels. Decision makers at every level must become aware that they are required to make those decisions. Nothing focuses the attention like having the responsibility for making decisions, and this focused attention in and of itself sharpens people's decision-making skills.

"One day I challenged General Creech, when he was commander of Tactical Air Command, regarding the risks associated with delegation. I asked him, 'Aren't you giving up control of things? Aren't you taking a terrible risk by allowing wing commanders and squadron commanders and flight-line supervisors to make these kinds of decisions?'

"I thought his answer was exactly the right answer. He said, 'Number one, it's not surrendering control.' He said he wasn't controlling the process. He's instead controlling the standards and controlling objectives. But there's no need for senior people to control the processes. You want to control the outcome. You control the outcome by measuring the outcome and controlling the standards. Second, and I believe this very strongly, you reduce the risks of bad decisions by pressing decisions down to the level of the supervisor who actually carries them out. His attention is more focused. He is less likely to be distracted by other considerations that are ineffective. He's a hell of a lot more likely to make a decision work right. So the risk is reduced.

"General Creech would very much provide the values, provide the standards, make it clear that the objectives were, back then, very much hands-off on how you do your job. So that with General Creech, the passing or failing the test was all up to you. He provided the opportunity, the guidance and he'd show what the test was. The movement to the three-star level is probably the real narrow place in the general officer's business, because that's a diligent job. Obviously, the rank goes with the job. I know that in my business, deciding along with all the rest of the four stars, the secretary, et cetera, as to who should fill a three-star position is probably the most difficult in our officers' decisions."[31]

General Brown's success in accomplishing his ends at McChord Air Force Base came from the full support of his subordinates, instilled by his reciprocal loyalty to them. "We always appreciated the fact that he had short staff meetings," Maj. Gen. Courtney Faught said. "He knew what he wanted, said what he wanted, and our job was to go out and do it. What I particularly appreciated was that he was willing to take a gamble at times on the advice he got from his subordinates. The advice wasn't always right, but he would stand up and defend those people to his superiors even though they had sometimes given him a bad steer. I think a big part of George's leadership was that everybody wanted to do whatever he wanted them to do."[32]

"Our staff meetings," wrote Albert Cochrane of Brown's command at Sandia Base, in New Mexico, "were the places where his simple, firm, common-sense leadership really came to light. As a junior officer, I loved his staff meetings—simply because he insisted they be conducted at a level that everyone could understand. He always got down to the basics. If a member of the staff couldn't do that, he simply didn't last. A few Sandia technicians learned that the hard way."[33]

Brown's ability to delegate authority also helped him at Sandia. As Lt. Gen. Howard Lane, USAF (Ret.), stated, "The people who formed JTF-2 were carefully picked by George Brown. He put people together and then exercised his knack of knowing exactly what level of detail he should be involved in and where he should cut it off. He clearly understood that he didn't have all the brains, that he had to depend on his subordinates, and he had confidence in them. He had a broad objective that some people didn't really understand, but he did. I don't really know exactly what his instructions were from higher command, but he had constant interface with the secretary of defense. He gave us broad guidelines and then said, 'Use your imagination.' He didn't want to know all the details. He wanted results."[34]

Commented Col. Ed McGough, USAF (Ret.): "In my judgment, one of his important characteristics was the real confidence he placed in others. He knew the capabilities and limitations of each person and assigned them with a faith that tasks and responsibilities would be completed properly and in a timely manner. He did not harass or continually check for progress. In today's political and military environment, such a practice takes courage. His subordinates and associates respected him for his vote of faith and responded accordingly. No one wanted to let him down."[35]

General Ryan as chief of staff demanded much more detail than Brown. His morning briefings, for example, were complete concerning the Southeast Asian war in the area of close air support. Detailed charts were presented to Ryan, the secretary of defense, and the chairman of the Joint Chiefs of Staff every morning. "When

George Brown had his first staff meeting," recalled Lt. Gen. Joseph Wilson, "I continued giving the same sort of briefing. We got halfway through and Brown just said, 'That's enough. I've fought a number of wars in my life. I've just spent a year and a half to two years in Southeast Asia as Seventh Air Force commander. I don't need all this detail. That's your job as DO [deputy for operations]. If you have a problem, let me know.' He turned you loose to do your job and did not want details. He was quick to see problems.'"[36]

Commented Gen. William Evans, "Brown told me that he didn't want to jam up his mental computer with a lot of details. He made a great point to me one day when I gave him some heavy details by saying, 'Bill, I don't want these details. I know what the issues are. You remember the details and I'll remember you and where to find you, and I'll call you if I need the background.'"[37]

While serving as commander of Systems Command in September 1970, Brown had to select directors for research operations and needed the approval of the air force secretary to finalize the selection. Brown delegated this to one of his generals, who commented, "As part of the preparation for requesting Secretary Packard's authority, Brown asked for a slate of candidates for program directors. He said to me, 'Jerry, I want you to go over and have a chat with Dr. Seamans. I've selected you to run these defense suppression projects and he wants to meet you before we go to Mr. Packard.' General Brown gave me no lengthy instructions on how to handle my first meeting with the Secretary of Defense. Although I had a good record, I was still surprised at how simply and directly I was given the job—without any threats, charters, or detailed instructions. I felt totally responsible for the projects and to him as I headed across the river to see the Secretary. In any event, the Secretary seemed satisfied, and I was announced to Secretary Packard as the program director by Brown at the meeting with Packard."[38]

General Brown was the senior air general in Vietnam and in that capacity never claimed to have all the answers, as described by Major General Keegan. "Where Brown didn't have personal knowledge, he was very careful to get the best use out of his staff. I think, in the long run, this is a more reliable way of achieving the proper direction and conduct of a complicated air war. Brown must be evaluated in a completely different light from all the others, because he had less combat experience in Vietnam. His style and approach in delegating to his staff were different. His understanding of the division of labor, the limitations in span of control that preclude one man doing everything, made for a healthier operational environment; not more effective, perhaps, than it was under Momyer, but I think it was fundamentally healthier."[39]

George Brown always recognized that the people in one's command are the key to its success. Kenneth Tallman (then a colonel), as officer in charge of Colonels' Assignment Branch, was responsible for the assignment of wing commanders to Vietnam. "I had a verbal request from Brown before he left Washington," recalled Tallman. "In essence, it was 'keep the good guys coming.' He was a people man; he believed in delegating authority, and he wanted to have people in whom he could place confidence. He knew there were many such people in the air force, but he didn't know them personally because he hadn't been associated with a command in some time, or with TAC for many years. Because of the nature of the war, TAC had the largest supply of colonels for Southeast Asia, so he felt that this was the area in which I could help him the most.

"There were very few colonels I nominated for jobs in Vietnam who were not accepted by General Brown. I think this was because of our earlier conversation and my assurance to him that I would pick the best people available and make sure they had some recent experience in TAC.

"Brown told me that his most meaningful learning experience as exec to General White was White's emphasis that one had to be able to distinguish the really vital from the less consequential, to be able to grasp the essentials and to refuse to be cluttered up with the nonessentials, and to delegate the rest to subordinates. Subordinates do the work so the commander can direct the major tasks. Brown, from all reports to me by his subordinates, was superb at this, separating the important from the unimportant. He had the ability to pick good people and get more out of them than they ever thought they could produce."[40]

What inspires a person to give that something extra is to be given a job and then be left alone to do it. That was Brown's way; he put a competent man in charge of an operation and let him run it. He left him alone, then periodically went out to see how things were going, always ensuring that the staff was helping that person. He placed trust in his subordinates, and they respected this vote of faith and confidence and responded accordingly. They felt he was working with them, not against them. His philosophy was that you undercut a subordinate when you as a commander got into the detail. Many officers said of Brown's delegation: "You always felt a strong demand that you'd better get on with the job. . . . There was a sense of firmness about him . . . a determination in what he wanted you to do . . . , that he had a mission and he wanted you to get on with it. He led primarily by example, but that did not mean he didn't force a little now and then. Yet he had a manner and a way of being forceful that endeared him to people."

Similarly in Vietnam, Brown's subordinates summarized his view on delegation and told his operations people, "You are going to run the war—the air operations—the planning. If you have any differences with the higher command, I'll support you." Brown told his wing commanders, "If you want me, call me; otherwise I'll see you at commander conferences." Brown never carried a "brick," a two-way radio, thus saying to his people, "I've got wing commanders. I've got assistants. There's a chain of command. If it doesn't work, we're in trouble."

This is what delegation is all about.

When a decision was needed from Brown, a subordinate did not have to be concerned about getting one, and it was well thought out. "But on the other hand," reflected Gen. Bill Evans, "he would delegate. You felt you didn't have to go to him for every small decision." Brown did, however, have a cardinal rule with his subordinates, telling them: "Don't surprise me. If you have problems you can't handle, bring them to me and I'll help you solve them, but don't surprise me, because that I can't stand."[41]

Delegating to subordinates inspires them to give their best. They don't want to disappoint such a leader, to violate his trust in them. The leader keeps aware of what they are doing, for he always moniters what is going on but without getting bogged down in detail.

How far you go up the ladder in the military depends upon your ability to delgate. You certainly come to understand quickly in large units that you can't do it all yourself. You can try, but those who try, fail. General Schwarzkopf told me: "The only reason why [being] battalion commander was so difficult for me in Vietnam was because I had very few subordinates to whom I could delegate authority, because at that time we just weren't getting talent. We didn't get noncommissioned officer talent, we didn't get officer talent. Company commanders, captains, were people who had one year in the army. It was crazy. But you learned, particularly, that you must develop a subordinate and then delegate authority to that subordinate and depend on him. I would always use my staff. I would always use my chief of staff in any command position I was in from the time I was a colonel. I would use my deputy division commander or I would use my chief of staff in the division or my assistant division commanders. I would clearly spell out what their areas of responsibility were and I would expect them to fulfill their jobs. I was the guidance; I'd give an overall concept. I would make sure what the concept was, then I would allow these people to execute it, because if you don't do that, you are doomed to failure."[42]

The concept of delegation has been incorporated into army doctrine and is one of the key elements of a combat operations order. "The commander's intent describes the desired end state. It is a concise expression of the purpose of the operation and must be understood two echelons below the issuing commander. It must clearly state the purpose of the mission. It is the single unifying focus for all subordinate elements. It is not a summary of the concept of the operation. Its purpose is to focus subordinates on the desired end state. Its utility is to focus subordinates on what has to be accomplished in order to achieve success, even when the plan and concept of the operations no longer apply, and to discipline their efforts toward that end."[43]

Simply put, the commander who effectively communicates his vision for an operation and defines the end state of the operation, or what critical missions must be accomplished to achieve success, gives his subordinate leaders the opportunity to exercise their own individual initiative to ensure the success of the operation. Even if the original plan that was developed is no longer viable, subordinate leaders must be able to adapt and modify, then execute a new plan based on the current situation, knowing that they are still working within the framework that the higher commander formulated.

Delegation of authority, but never responsibility, is clearly necessary. You can't do it all yourself and be successful as your responsibilities increase. The commander who effectively communicates his vision for an operation and defines the end state of the operation, or what critical missions must be accomplished to achieve success, gives his subordinate leaders the opportunity to exercise their own individual initiative to ensure the success of the operation. Even if the original plan that was developed is no longer viable, subordinate leaders must be able to adapt and modify, then execute a new plan based on the current situation, knowing that they are still working within the framework the higher commander formulated.

But delegation is more than sparing the energy of the overworked leader. Delegation is a vital part of assisting in the leadership growth of subordinates. Within our military it is a senior officer's obligation to develop the younger generation of officers for future higher command. In addition, one of the most appreciated acts of a leader is to give a person a job to do and leave him alone to do it. This results in the subordinate not only not wanting to let down the trust and confidence in him but instills the desire to give his or her all.

There is a caveat given by General Eisenhower, who told me: "When you delegate something to a subordinate . . . it is absolutely your responsibility, and he must understand this. You as a leader must take complete responsibility for what that subordinate does." This leads into the next chapter, which emphasizes that you must fix the problem, not the blame.

Notes

1. Dwight D. Eisenhower, *Crusade in Europe* (New York: Doubleday and Company, Inc., 1948), 317.

2. Harry C. Butcher, *My Three Years with Eisenhower* (New York: Simon and Schuster, 1946), 277.

3. Ibid., 464.

4. Edgar F. Puryear, Jr., *Nineteen Stars* (Novato, Calif.: Presidio Press, 1971), 81.

5. Robert H. Ferrell, ed., *The Eisenhower Diaries* (New York: W. W. Norton, 1981), 65.

6. Puryear, *Nineteen Stars*, 212.

7. Ibid., 130.

8. Personal interview with Lt. Gen. Stephen J. Chamberlin and Edgar F. Puryear, Jr., July 8, 1962.

9. George C. Kenney, *The MacArthur I Know* (New York: Duell, Sloan and Pearce, 1951), 51–52, and personal interview, February 16, 1963.

10. Ibid., 114.

11. Kenney, *The MacArthur I Know*, 63–64.

12. Douglas MacArthur, *Reminiscences* (New York: McGraw-Hill, 1964), 94.

13. Clark Lee and Richard Henschel, *Douglas MacArthur* (New York: Henry Holt and Company, 1932), 56.

14. Henry H. Arnold and Ira C. Eaker, *Army Flyer* (New York: Harper, 1942), 168.

15. Ibid., 32.

16. Letter from Brig. Gen. Clarence P. Cain to Edgar F. Puryear, Jr., dated June 12, 1962.

17. Personal interview with Maj. Gen. Rush P. Lincoln, October 9, 1962.

18. Personal interview with Gen. Carl A. "Tooey" Spaatz and Edgar F. Puryear, Jr., August 28, 1976.

19. Letter from Maj. Gen. H. B. Hayden, USA (Ret.), to Edgar F. Puryear, Jr., November 27, 1962.

20. Interview by Donald Shaunessey with General Orville A. Anderson, USAF (Ret.), October 1959.

21. Personal interview with Gen. Jacob F. Smart, USAF (Ret.) and Edgar F. Puryear, Jr., July 17, 1979.

22. Personal interview with Gen. Thomas D. White, USAF (Ret.) and Edgar F. Puryear, Jr., April 30, 1963.

23. Speech given by Gen. Thomas D. White, USAF, at the U.S. Air Force Academy, June 7, 1957.

24. Personal interview with General Spaatz and Edgar F. Puryear, Jr., September 19, 1962.

25. Personal interview with Gen. William F. "Bozo" McKee and Edgar F. Puryear, Jr., July 6, 1977.

26. Personal interview with Gen. Curtis E. LeMay, USAF (Ret.), and Edgar F. Puryear, Jr., August 28, 1975.

27. Letter from Maj. Gen. Harold A. Bartron, USAF (Ret.), to Edgar F. Puryear, Jr., dated October 17, 1962.

28. Letter from Maj. Gen. Robert B. Williams, USAF (Ret.), to Edgar F. Puryear, Jr., dated October 31, 1962.

29. Personal interview with Maj. Gen. Tim Ahern, USAF (Ret.), and Edgar F. Puryear, Jr., September 14, 1977.

30. Personal interview with Gen. Larry D. Welch USAF (Ret.), and Edgar F. Puryear, Jr., February 19, 1987.

31. Personal interview with Gen. Larry D. Welch USAF (Ret.), and Edgar F. Puryear, Jr., December 20, 1998.

32. Personal interview with Maj. Gen. Courtney L. Faught, USAF (Ret.), August 6, 1979.

33. Letter from Lt. Col. Albert Cochrane, USAF (Ret.), to Edgar F. Puryear, Jr., dated April 9, 1980.

34. ersonal interview with Lt. Gen. Howard M. Lane, May 16, 1980.

35. Letter from Col. Edward McGough, USAF (Ret.), to Edgar F. Puryear, Jr., dated August 27, 1979.

36. Personal interview with Lt. General Joseph G. Wilson, USAF (Ret.), and Edgar F. Puryear, Jr., August 5, 1981.

37. Personal interview with Gen. William J. Evans, USAF (Ret.), with Edgar F. Puryear, Jr., April 17, 1980.

38. Letter from Maj. Gen. Gerald K. Hendricks, USAF (Ret.), to Edgar F. Puryear, Jr., dated February 14, 1980.

39. Personal interview with Maj. Gen. George F. Keegan, USAF (Ret.), and Edgar F. Puryear, Jr., January 12, 1980.

40. Personal interview with Lt. Gen. Kenneth A. Tallman, USAF (Ret.), and Edgar F. Puryear, Jr., June 18, 1980.

41. Evans interview.

42. Personal interview with Gen. H. Norman Schwarzkopf and Edgar F. Puryear, Jr., October 27, 1995.

43. *Field Manual 100-5, Operations* (Headquarters, Department of the Army, June 1993), 6-6.

Chapter 9: Fix the Problem, Not the Blame

Fix the problem, not the blame.
        —General of the Army George C. Marshall

In an interview with Gen. Dwight D. Eisenhower, he told me, "Leadership consists of nothing but taking responsibility for everything that goes wrong and giving your subordinates credit for everything that goes well." He personally lived by that credo.

General Eisenhower had an awesome responsibility decision on launching the D-day invasion of France on June 6, 1944. After Ike said, "We'll go," he sat at his portable table and wrote a press release for use if the attack failed: "Our landings have failed . . . and I have withdrawn the troops. My decision to attack at this time and place was based upon the best information available. The troops, the air and the Navy did all that bravery and devotion to duty could do. If any blame or fault attaches to the attempt it is mine alone."[1]

I discussed this further with him, and he told me he remembered Lee's statement after the Confederate defeat at Gettysburg. There are many theories on what might have been the cause of that defeat, but Lee blamed no one but himself. In a letter to President Jefferson Davis, Lee wrote, "No blame can be attached to the Army for its failure to accomplish what was projected by me, nor should it be censured for the unreasonable expectations of the public. I am alone to blame." Then on August 8, 1963, Lee offered his resignation to Davis. "The general remedy for the want of success in a military commander is his removal. . . . Success should be risked to secure it. I therefore, in all sincerity, request your Excellency to take measures to supply my place."[2]

On November 5, 1862, President Lincoln relieved McClellan as commander of the Army of the Potomac, frustrated by McClellan's delay in fighting and his lack of success when he did fight. He was replaced with Maj. Gen. Ambrose Burnside, who may have overreacted to Lincoln's and his cabinet's disgust with McClellan's reluctance to fight. His first action against Lee was moving his army of 120,000 soldiers to take Fredericksburg, Virginia. The battle began on December 11, 1862, and lasted through December 13. It was a bloodbath, with 12,600 Union army casualties and only 5,300 Confederate dead and wounded.

Burnside learned several days later that Lincoln was being criticized for requiring him to fight the battle at Fredericksburg against his will and better judgment. To quell this rumor, Burnside asked to see Lincoln. He informed Lincoln that he would publish a letter accepting complete culpability for the defeat of Union forces at Fredericksburg. Lincoln was very pleased, indeed relieved, and accepted his offer. Burnside was the first of Lincoln's generals who was willing to relieve him of the responsibility of a Union defeat.[3]

After Lee surrendered to Grant at Appomattox, Grant wrote in his memoirs of the private conversation between the two of them: "We had there between the lines, sitting on horseback, a very pleasant conversation over half an hour, in the course of which Lee said to me that the South was a big country and that we might have to march over it three or four times before the war entirely ended, but that we would now be able to do it as they could no longer resist us. He expressed it as his earnest hope, however, that we would not be called upon to cause more loss and sacrifice of life; but he could not foretell the result. I then suggested to General Lee that there was not a man in the Confederacy whose influence with the soldiery and the whole people was as great as his, and that if he would now advise the surrender of all the armies I had no doubt his advice would be followed with alacrity. But Lee said that he could not do that without consulting the President first. I knew there was no use to urge him to do anything against his ideas of what was right."[4]

To the very end, Lee recognized civilian control of his army.

A refreshing example of a Confederate officer who was willing to accept blame was Gen. Albert Sidney Johnston. He had an impossible task with an army of only 50,000 men to fight the Union forces in a territory more than five hundred miles wide, stretching from eastern Kentucky across Mississippi and beyond Missouri to Indian territory. As the fighting developed, he lost half his army, most of Tennessee, and all of Kentucky. With these losses he was accused of stupidity, incompetence, corruption, and even treason. He took the blame as he had taken the praise, offering to relinquish his command. He wrote to President Davis: "The test of merit in my profession is success. It is a hard rule, but I think it right. . . . What the people want is a battle and a victory." Davis rejected his resignation.[5]

In March 1864 Grant received orders to report to Washington to receive promotion to lieutenant general, a grade that had previously been held in our history only by George Washington. Typically Grant gave credit to someone else, writing to Sherman that it was "thanks to you and McPherson as the men to whom, above all others, I feel indebted for whatever I have had of success. How far your advice and suggestions have been of assistance, you know. How far your execution of whatever has been given you to do entitles you to the reward I am receiving, you cannot know as well as I do."[6]

Never during the Civil War was there a case of Sherman accepting plaudits, justified or not. At the battle of Shiloh, on April 6 and 7, 1862, the Confederate forces caught the Union forces off guard and almost handed them a humiliating defeat. When Sherman learned what was happening, he immediately jumped in and led the soldiers in throwing back the Confederate forces. He took no credit for the victory, congratulating Grant instead.

While Eisenhower's forces were pushing into Germany, Hitler, on December 16, 1944, against the advice of his generals, launched a surprise counteroffensive against Allied forces in the Ardennes. He threw 250,000 men into the assault, catching the Allies off guard. The Germans were ultimately brought to a standstill, with Patton's Third Army and other troops coming to the rescue.

British general Montgomery proceeded to call a press conference to claim credit for the success of turning back the Germans at Ardennes. His statement was in part: "General Eisenhower placed me in command of the whole Northern front. I employed the whole available power of the British group of Armies; this power was brought into play very gradually and in such a way that it would not interfere with the American lines of communication. Finally it was put in with a bang, and today British divisions are fighting hard on the right flank of First U.S. Army. You have thus a picture of British troops fighting on both sides of American forces who have suffered a hard blow. This is a fine allied picture. The battle has been most interesting; I think possibly one of the most interesting and tricky battles I have ever handled, with great issues at stake. The first thing to be done was to 'head off' the enemy from the tender spots and vital places. Having done that successfully, the next thing was to 'see him off' . . . and make quite certain that he could not get to the places he wanted. . . . He was therefore 'headed off,' and then 'seen off.' He is now being 'written off.'"[7]

This statement was not true, and Montgomery received a bitter response from American generals. He was not responsible for saving American soldiers from disaster as he claimed. The Americans had 70,000 casualties, the British only 500. If anything, Montgomery should have been blamed for failing to react more aggressively after the Germans were stopped, thus permitting most of the Germans to withdraw and escape.

General Bradley was furious over Montgomery's comment, telling Ike that after this statement, "I cannot serve under Montgomery. If he is to be put in command of all ground forces, you must send me home." George Patton agreed with Bradley and also refused to serve under Montgomery.

Previously there had been complaints about Montgomery, but never before were the American generals so bitter toward him; it was so bad that Ike let Churchill know how upset he was. Churchill certainly understood, and to rectify it he made a speech to the House of Commons giving due credit to American forces.

Patton, in leading the Third Army to greatness during World War II, was never reluctant to accept responsibility. He had an image as the flaming warrior, but the man and the image were two different persons. "I was his Chief of Staff," said Gen. John M. Devine, "when he first made Corps Commander. . . . I had not known him before except by reputation, and I was sure we would never get along. I soon discovered that the man and his reputation were miles apart. I developed a great admiration and respect for him."[8]

This change in attitude toward General Patton was not unusual. Contrary to popular belief, he was not at all harsh with commanders unless they made an uncalled-for error or if there was unnecessary loss of life. In Normandy, in late July 1944, the men of the 5th Ar-

mored Division under Maj. Gen. Lunsford E. Oliver were assembled
and ready for action. They received orders from Third Army headquarters to proceed by a road through the Saint-Lô breakthrough
to an area between the Sees and Selune Rivers. The move was to be
made at night, and they were told that the road would be available
for their exclusive use.

But it didn't work out that way. The road was crowded with troops
from other divisions, vehicles of all sorts, and supply convoys. The
division found it difficult to make progress. General Oliver wrote: "I
soon received orders to pull my division off the road and report to
General Patton at his command post. I proceeded to do it with difficulty in the darkness and confusion and with considerable foreboding. I knew our deplorable situation was not my fault, but I was
afraid George would think it was. I knew if he thought I had failed,
our friendship would not save me. George finally assembled his staff,
corps commanders and division commanders, and opened the conference. He began by saying, 'We are in a hell of a mess, and it is my
fault. I wanted to get going and therefore I had my staff issue orders
without taking time to work out necessary schedules, and the result
is this mess. Now we shall just sit tight until the staff can work out
schedules and restore order.'"[9]

When it came to recognition for excellent performance, Patton
believed, as did Eisenhower, that a general officer should "assume
the responsibility for failure, whether he deserves it or not." If things
went well, he should "invariably give the credit for success to others,
whether they deserved it or not." His reasoning was that a general
who took all the blame and gave everyone else all the credit would
get more out of his subordinates.[10]

At a dinner given for several officers at a private gathering, Gen.
Omar Bradley commented on the brilliant maneuvering by Patton's
Third Army during the Battle of the Bulge, and gave Patton high
praise. Patton replied quickly, "All the credit, all of it, one hundred
percent, goes to the Third Army Staff, and in particular to Hap Gay,
Maud Miller, Nixon and Busch."

This type of laudatory credit from Patton was not confined to
small, private groups of military officers who knew the important role
that Patton's leadership had played in his army's success. At a press

conference after the Bulge operation, Patton said the same thing: "The purpose of our initial attack can be stated briefly. We hit the sons-of-bitches on the flank and stopped them cold. Now that may sound like George Patton is a great genius. Actually, he [meaning himself] had damned little to do with it. All he did was to give orders. It was the Staff of this Headquarters and the troops in the line that performed this matchless feat."[11]

General Theodore R. Milton was forever indebted to one officer for demonstrating character. "I think General LeMay had enormous traits of character. He always did what he thought he ought to do, right or wrong. I remember something he did for me during 1943. I led some missions in the Eighth Air Force and when we were making bomb drops on Bremen, they put up some smoke screens that fooled us, and we didn't do a very good job of bombing. We lost a lot of airplanes, and as a result of the poor performance and the loss of aircraft the brass came up from London for the critique of this mission and quite frankly they were looking for a scapegoat. The mission was not a disaster, it just wasn't a very good job, and it was one of the first real tries we had in going into Germany itself. So, anyway, one or two people got up and had a story which no one challenged, but I personally made a mistake in part of my performance in leading this mission, and, being new, I got up and stated what mistake I thought I had made. I started where I thought I went wrong and went on to describe the errors I had made and how I shouldn't have done it, and before I knew it the critiquing officers were all over me.

"Present in the group was then Col. Curtis E. LeMay. And most all of the people around were senior to him, but as he saw these senior officers going after me he got up and said, 'Wait a minute, now.' He then turned to me and said that 'if that's the worst mistake you ever make, Milton, you'll be all right.' What he had done was to let the senior people know that perhaps they had lost their perspective in their effort to look for a scapegoat. Colonel LeMay's comment silenced these people and that ended the inquisition and, indeed, the whole briefing. There was nothing in it for Colonel LeMay. I wasn't even in his group. Colonel LeMay sat there, and listened to what they were doing, and decided that these people were going about it in the wrong way, that I had simply made an honest mistake. . . . We picked up the wrong initial point coming in, and . . . the smoke screen . . . fooled us. . . . I think this was typical of the way Colonel LeMay behaved in his whole career. He was fallible, he made some mistakes now and then, but he always stuck to what he felt was right. I don't think he ever tried to tailor his attitude or behavior to whatever might have been the current fashion. He was his own man."[12]

But there are times when the blame must be fixed.

During the Vietnam War, a serious and alarming allegation was made on March 29, 1969, by former soldier Ron Ridenour when he wrote to several congressmen and high-level government officials that, in March 1968, war crimes occurred in the Vietnam village of My Lai. The charge was that Charlie Company of the American Division's 11th Infantry Brigade massacred numerous Vietnamese civilians, primarily women, children, and old men.

When Gen. William C. Westmoreland, the chief of staff of the army, learned of this, he ordered an immediate investigation. It was necessary in this incident to fix blame. "Almost as deplorable as the events alleged," wrote General Westmoreland, "was the possibility that officers of the 11th Brigade and the American Division had either covered up the incident or failed to make a comprehensive investigation. The developing evidence in the criminal investigation and in indications of command dereliction led Secretary Resor and me to arrange for an additional formal inquiry into the adequacy of the criminal investigation and the possible suppression of information. When I learned that some members of President Nixon's administration wanted to whitewash any possible negligence within the chain of command, I threatened through a White House official to exercise my prerogative as a member of the Joint Chiefs of Staff to go personally to the President and object. I squelched any further pressure for whitewash."[13]

Westmoreland appointed Lt. Gen. Ray Peers to head the board of inquiry. His reasons? "[Because] he had a reputation throughout the Army for objectivity and fairness . . . and had also been a division commander in Vietnam and thus was thoroughly familiar with conditions; he had never had jurisdiction over any activity in Quang Ngai province. Because he had entered the Army through ROTC at the University of California at Los Angeles, there could be no presumption that ties among brother officers from West Point would be involved. As a result of evidence developed by the Peers board, charges were brought against twelve officers, primarily involving dereliction of duty in suppressing information and failing to obey lawful regulations. These included the former American Division commander, General Koster, who at the time of the investigation was Superintendent of the Military Academy. Lest any findings reflect adversely on the Academy, he requested relief from that post. . . . Something had to be remiss in the American Division's chain of command if anything so reprehensible and colossal as the My Lai massacre occurred without some responsible official either knowing or at least suspecting."[14]

General Koster, as commander of the American Division, had ordered an investigation, but Westmoreland believed that he "made a basic error in assigning the investigation to the commander of the responsible unit. As matters developed, Koster was only censured. Peers thought that this proposed action against Koster was "a travesty of justice and would establish a precedent that would be difficult for the Army to live down. . . . I felt the matter should have been adjudicated in a duly appointed court martial, which would have served the best interests of General Koster, the Army and the nation."[15] Field-grade officers were asking why top officers got off with dismissal of charges whereas the lower grades were subjected to courts-martial.

The investigation resulted in charges against four officers and nine enlisted men, ultimately with trials of two officers and three enlisted men. In the criminal proceedings, all but the platoon leader were in one way or another exonerated, but 1st Lt. William L. Cally, Jr., was charged with the murder of more than a hundred civilians. On March 29, 1971, he was convicted personally with the murder of "at least twenty-two."[16] He was sentenced to dismissal from the army and confinement at hard labor for life, but the sentence was later reduced by judicial review to twenty years. After General Westmoreland's retirement, the secretary of the army reduced it to ten years, a decision sustained by President Nixon. Cally was later released on parole.

But what about the division commander of the American Division, General Koster? General Westmoreland was the senior army commander in Vietnam at the time of the atrocity. He did not run from a determination of whether he was at fault; in Westmoreland's own words, "If Cally was guilty, why not also his superiors including Westmoreland?"

Civilians were also distressed. A *New York Times* article by Bob Mac Crate commented on the dismissal charges against General Koster: "I am shocked by the action of the Commanding General of the First Army in dismissing at this time the charges against Major General Koster in advance of the disposition of the charges against officers within his former command. . . . He has done a serious disservice to the Army. What is involved is a failure to recognize the Army's responsibility to the public at large and a failure to affirm the importance to the Army itself of acting in accordance with the rules of international law, the law of war and the principles of our own constitution."[17]

Congressman Samuel S. Stratton, one of the four members of the House Armed Services investigation subcommittee, was even more vociferous in his condemnation of the army's action. In a news release dated January 29, 1971, he said: "The decision of the Army to drop the charges against Major General Koster in the My Lai case is, in my opinion, a grave miscarriage of military justice. To drop the charges against the top officer responsible in this situation raises once again the whole question of military whitewash."

On February 4, 1971, Congressman Stratton made a long and extensively documented speech on the floor of the House in which he was vehement in his charges against the army in the handling of the Koster case. Here are some of his comments, taken from the transcript: "Dropping charges against the highest ranking officer involved, without any public trial or even discussion of the case against him, and doing so at a time when very grave charges involving the same incident against a junior officer in his command [Cally] are still in the process of trial, can only result in serious damage to the reputation of the U.S. Army, the United States, and to the effectiveness of the processes and procedures of military justice in dealing with matters which involve profound national and international concerns.

"The dismissal of these charges is not only bad, but it has been carried out in a manner that purports to absolve the top military and civilian leadership of the Pentagon of all responsibility. . . ."[18]

General Peers's own conclusion was, "I just cannot honestly believe that General Seaman made the decision to drop the charges
against General Koster on his own and without any reference to the
Pentagon. The precise reverse is probably true. The Pentagon must
have decided to let General Koster off the hook, even while subordinates were still being tried on far more serious charges, probably
because they feared that a full public airing of the charges against
Koster and of his incredible mismanagement of his command would
make the Army look very, very bad."[19]

The investigation thoroughly studied whether General Westmoreland should have been guilty and exonerated him. It was certainly not a "whitewash" of Westmoreland. All one has to do is read
General Peers's report to understand that he sought the truth and
showed no favoritism to the army chief of staff. The importance in
the Cally case in fixing the blame was to ensure that this type of incident never happened again.

There is no better challenge to a military officer's character than
in his dealings with the media. In spring 1987, the United States was
having difficulty with Iran, and the Iranians threatened to and indeed did place mines in the Persian Gulf. We met this threat in part
by changing the flags on foreign ships to the U.S. flag; thus any damage to the ship would be an attack against the United States.

Admiral William J. Crowe, Jr., commented: "The Kuwait tanker
Al Rekkab was rechristened the *Bridgeton*. Unfortunately it struck a
moored mine. It meant that Teheran had made the decision to risk
the wrath of the United States. Fortunately, no one was injured in
the explosion and the tanker was able to proceed. However, had it
been one of our destroyer escorts, there might have been the loss
of the ship and many casualties. The media were raking us over the
coals about the *Bridgeton*. Why? The fact we did not have minesweepers in place before escorting the tankers. . . . Our patrolling in advance of the convoy hadn't been all it should have been. . . . I was
not in a position to complain. . . . The media attention to this matter didn't seem to go away. . . . One day I told Weinberger that if he
would let me, I would get hold of the press and kill the story. Weinberger's response was, 'How are you going to do that?' My response
was, 'I plan to tell them we made a mistake when the *Bridgeton* got

mined and that I was the one who made it. We should have had more minesweeping capacity out there and we should have looked at our intelligence data more critically.' Weinberger's face flushed. 'Do not do that,' he said. 'Never, never, never, never admit that you made a mistake. They will never let you forget it!' 'Okay,' I said. And I didn't do it."[20]

But three weeks later Crowe was making a speech in San Diego and an aggressive local reporter got up afterward and asked a long question about the *Bridgeton* mining, clearly to embarrass him. He failed to follow the secretary's advice and took the blame, stating, "Look, let me put this thing to rest right now. We were brand new and we had a lot to learn. I personally made a mistake on the *Bridgeton* mining."

Crowe told me in an interview: "The reporter [he was with the *San Diego Tribune*] gave me a strange look. He may never have heard such a response before. Then he sat down. Afterward he published a story reporting what I had said, and I never heard another word about the *Bridgeton* mining. Honesty often actually *is* the best policy. I always remembered Joseph Stilwell's comment after his defeat in Burma. When he finally hiked out of the jungle and got to India, a truly remarkable achievement, there was a press conference. The correspondent asked, 'What happened?' And Stilwell said, 'We got the hell beat out of us.' The press loved Stilwell. There is a lot to be said for simply saying, 'I was wrong.'

"Of course, whoever does that must take the responsibility on his own shoulders. He cannot say, 'The president made a mistake.' He cannot go around including others in the blame. He cannot even use the word 'we.' He has to say, 'I did it and nobody else.' That is the beginning and the end of the mistake routine, but it has to be used sparingly. Otherwise, before too long, people will begin asking themselves, What in the world is he doing there if all he can do is make mistakes?"[21]

A recent example of a senior general openly accepting blame was provided by General Schwarzkopf, who related an incident in the war against Iraq. He was asked by the Pentagon press chief to hold a news conference for the reporters who were traveling with the secretary. He replied, "That's crazy. I'm gonna be busy with Cheney and Powell." As a compromise he was asked to produce in his place "someone in authority." He decided upon army lieutenant general Cal Waller, who had been in the theater for only a month, to stand in for him. It was a disaster for Waller, who, in an effort to be forthcoming, informed the press conference in response to a reporter's question on Central Command's readiness that our ground forces would not be fully prepared to attack possibly until mid-February. Unfortunately this contradicted the president's position of putting pressure on Iraq in advance of the United Nations deadline.

Schwarzkopf was concerned about what might happen to Waller.

> Waller knew he'd screwed up and came to me the first thing in the morning to say so. I felt responsible for having gotten him into this mess and worried he'd be punished. Early in Desert Shield, Cheney had fired General Mike Dugan, the Air Force chief of staff, for giving reporters classified information. So when Cheney and Powell arrived at headquarters an hour later, I asked them into my office.
>
> "General Waller feels terrible about this flap he's created. But I'm the one to blame, for throwing him into a press conference when he's so new to the theater," I said.
>
> To my surprise, Cheney and Powell responded that they weren't that concerned about his remarks. Cheney even quipped, "It's not always bad to send the enemy mixed signals."[22]

Acceptance of responsibility was also a part of the character of Gen. Colin Powell, chairman of the Joint Chiefs of Staff during the war with Iraq. As D day approached in the allied move to force Iraq out of Kuwait, a key decision they made was whether to bomb Iraq's biological installations. The British equivalent of the chairman, Sir David Craig, was concerned, saying to Powell while the decision was pending, "Bit risky that, eh?"

Yes, it was, said Powell, who went on to state: "The bombing would probably destroy the disease agents present. It might also release the killer germs." Powell was concerned that the bombing might endanger the civilian population as well as all the military forces. It was understood by the allies that it could be terrifying, and that we could not retaliate in kind because the allies had signed treaties banning biological warfare. Powell made the decision to bomb, commenting, "As far as bombing biological arsenals and the attendant risk of unleashing rather than preventing a catastrophe, I told Sir David Craig, 'If it heads south, just blame me.'"[23]

All of the chiefs and chairmen I interviewed were in agreement with Eisenhower's comment on "taking responsibility for everything that goes wrong and giving credit for everything that goes well." General David C. Jones, in one of my interviews with him, said, "You can accomplish anything if you don't care who gets the credit. A quiet reflective credit is appropriate. I never appreciated somebody who would come to me, unsolicited, just to make points. I could always tell when someone was trying to snow me, and I would never rely on that kind of person."[24]

General Shalikashvili remarked to me in an interview, "I think it is the saddest thing to see someone with great talent, who could be anything, if he just quit worrying about getting credit."[25]

A special tribute needs to be made to former air force chief of staff Ronald Fogleman. In 1996, nineteen U.S. airmen were killed in the bombing of one of our barracks in Saudi Arabia. The secretary of defense, William Cohen, was insistent that the one-star air force general be punished for not doing enough to prevent this. But General Fogleman opposed making the brigadier a scapegoat, so he retired before his four-year tenure was up. Richard J. Newman wrote in *U.S. News & World Report:* "Yet Fogleman's departure expresses a principle that is broader and in a way more patriotic than standing up for what one believes in: the importance of the military's deference to its civilian masters. He has reinforced that idea at a time when growing military influence in matters of state has caused concern that it is acting beyond the limits of its authority. Military officers have recently become 'more willing to play the political game,' says historian Richard Kohn, to get their way on budgets, security strategies, and other important issues."[26]

There is one final point that emphasizes the importance of accepting blame: General Eisenhower's philosophy about the political aspects of his job was a factor in his military success. He told President Roosevelt in Casablanca during their discussions of his handling of the Darlan affair in December 1943: "I believe in a theater commander doing these things without referring them back to his home Government and then waiting for approval. If a mere general makes a mistake, he can be repudiated and kicked out and disgraced. But a government cannot repudiate and kick out and disgrace itself—not, at any rate, in wartime." In other words, the general was the "fall guy" if a mistake was made; it was a part of the job.[27]

General Grant made the same observation: "In time of war the President, being by the Constitution Commander-in-Chief of the Army and Navy, is responsible for the selection of commanders. He should not be embarrassed in making his selections. In having been selected, my responsibility ended with my doing the best I knew how. If I had sought the place, or obtained it through personal or political influence, my belief is that I would have feared to undertake any plan of my own conception, and would probably have awaited direct orders from my distant superiors. Persons obtaining important commands by application or political influence are apt to keep a written record of complaints and predictions of defeat, which are shown in case of disaster. Somebody must be responsible for their failures.

"With all the pressure brought to bear upon them, both President Lincoln and General Halleck stood by me to the end of the campaign. I had never met Mr. Lincoln, but his support was constant."[28]

Willingness to take the blame is part of a leader's character. There is no better way to focus on the importance of accepting the blame than Patton's statement as described by Major General Devine: "We are in a hell of a mess, and it is my fault." And Devine's reaction, "I developed a great admiration and respect for him," illustrates the impact of this part of a leader's character.

Notes

1. David Eisenhower, *Eisenhower: At War 1943–1945* (London: Collins, 1986), 252.

2. Letter from Gen. R. E. Lee to President Jefferson Davis, dated July 31, 1863.

3. Henry W. Raymond, ed., *"Excerpts from the Journal of Henry J. Raymond," Scribner's Monthly*, XIX, 1879, 421.

4. U. S. Grant, *Personal Memoirs* (New York: Charles L. Webster & Company, 1886), 497.

5. William Preston Johnson, *The Life of General Albert Sidney Johnson* (New York: D. Appleton and Company, 1878), 514.

6. B. H. Liddell Hart, *Sherman: The Genius of the Civil War* (London: Eyre and Spottswoode, 1933), 238–39.

7. Montgomery papers, Imperial War Museum, reel 8.

8. Letter from Maj. Gen. John M. Devine, USA (Ret.), to Edgar F. Puryear, Jr., dated October 9, 1962.

9. Letter from Maj. Gen. Lunsford E. Oliver, USA (Ret.), to Edgar F. Puryear, Jr., dated October 9, 1962.

10. George S. Patton, Jr., *War As I Knew It* (Boston: Houghton Mifflen Company, 1947), 355.

11. Robert S. Allen, *Lucky Forward* (New York: Vanguard Press, 1947), 280.

12. Letter from Gen. Theodore R. Milton, USAF (Ret.), to Edgar F. Puryear, Jr., dated April 9, 1976.

13. William C. Westmoreland, *A Soldier Reports* (New York: Doubleday & Company, Inc., 1976), 375.

14. Ibid., 376.

15. W. R. Peers, *The My Lai Inquiry* (New York: W. W. Norton & Company, 1979), 223.

16. Westmoreland, *A Soldier Reports*, 377.

17. Peers, *The My Lai Inquiry*, 224.

18. Ibid.

19. Ibid., 225.

20. Personal interview with Adm. William J. Crowe, Jr. USN (Ret.), and Edgar F. Puryear, Jr., May 16, 1997; J. Crowe, Jr., *The Line of Fire* (New York: Simon & Schuster, 1993), 193.

21. Ibid.

22. H. Norman Schwarzkopf, *It Doesn't Take a Hero* (New York: Bantam Books, 1992), 394–95.

23. Colin L. Powell, *My American Journey* (New York: Random House, 1995), 504.

24. Personal interview with Gen. David C. Jones, USAF (Ret.), and Edgar F. Puryear, Jr., June 12, 1984.

25. Personal interview with Gen. John Shalikashvili and Edgar F. Puryear, Jr., June 4, 1997.

26. Richard J. Newman, *U.S. News & World Report* (August 11, 1997): 5.

27. Robert E. Sherwood, *Roosevelt and Hopkins* (New York: Harper and Brothers, 1948), 651.

28. Grant, *Personal Memoirs,* 305.

Chapter 10: Reflective Descriptions of Character

General U. S. Grant: Before the Civil War

Prior to the Civil War, Grant failed at everything he did. While stationed in San Francisco, he made efforts to supplement his army income in many ways, such as selling ice; buying cattle, hogs, and horses to sell to immigrants; planting potatoes; advancing funds for a store; and opening a billiard parlor. All these ventures failed.

Grant was extremely lonely while stationed at Fort Humboldt, near San Francisco, without his family, and he began drinking heavily. This sad account is given by one of his biographers: "Melancholy, silent, gloomy, inattentive to what went on around him, solitary, he got the reputation of a souse.

"Perhaps it gave him courage, for he went on with a final new business project, a billiard room in Frisco, which did not pan out. He drank some more. Lieutenant Colonel Buchanan might have dealt with the problem differently had he liked Grant. But when Grant showed up drunk for paymaster duty, Buchanan told him to fill out an unsigned resignation. Another binge and Grant would sign that resignation, Buchanan said.

"For a time he stayed sober. Then at a party, an officer's wife urged him to have a little punch. He took some. The next day, the entire post knew he had become completely done in, and knew also what must be in prospect as he trudged across the dismal parade ground to Buchanan's office. Buchanan took out the unsigned resignation and asked Grant what he thought his proper course was now. He signed. It was April 11, 1854. For fifteen years he had worn cadet gray and Army blue. Now he was a civilian."[1]

After leaving the service, Grant tried farming, but that failed. He was even reduced to selling firewood on the street. In the winter of 1858–59, he moved his family to St. Louis to work with one of his wife's cousins, Harry Boggs, in the business of collecting rent. It was a nasty business for which he was not fit. He and Boggs quarreled often.

"At thirty-seven," wrote one biographer, "Grant had to go back and admit that he was still a failure. The boy who could not bargain for a horse had become a man who could not bring in a crop of potatoes or collect a batch of bills. It was humiliating."[2]

Why, with all these failures, was he so successful as a military leader? The answer lies in his character. I was amused when I asked this question of General Schwarzkopf, who responded, "I would have failed too selling firewood, farming, clerking in a store, and bill collecting."[3]

Generals Sherman and Grant: Character and Professional Rapport

Bruce Catton, in his classic work on the Union army entitled *The Army of the Potomac*, commented: "The generals of that army, the good ones and the bad ones alike, were intensely jealous of fame and distinction." He pointed out that the problems among the Union generals clearly reflected deficiencies in their character that reduced their effectiveness. The book is replete with quotes that illustrate this: "To McClellan that seemed obvious [the allegation that General Pope's handling of the Army of the Potomac was with great neglect and carelessness]. He did not admire General Pope, either as a man or as a soldier. . . ." And "Major General Samuel D. Sturgis, in a meeting with a Colonel Herman Haupt over a railroad's ownership and a scheduling controversy, commented to Haupt, 'I don't care for John Pope one pinch of owl dung.'" On the morale of the Union army, he said that "Bickerings and blundering had sapped its power [speaking of the Army of the Potomac]." He also said that Maj. Gen. "Fighting Joe" Hooker "never got along with any of his superior officers." Of Maj. Gen. Phillip Kearny: "He hated McClellan and he hated Pope. . . ." Of Fitz John Porter toward Pope: "He had nothing but contempt for Pope and he expressed his contempt for Pope both verbally and in writing, a fact which later had tragic results." Of Maj. Gen. John Hutch: "[He] had a score to settle with Pope, whom he hated . . . because Pope gave him an angry dressing down, relieved him of command, and sent him . . . to a lower rank and Hutch felt that he had been unfairly treated. Now he had a chance to get even."

There were many other comments descriptive of jealousy regarding the Union generals. That is not to say that there were not differences among generals in the Army of Northern Virginia, but Lee's character and leadership overcame most of the problems as they surfaced.[4]

The Union generals Grant and Sherman offered a significant contrast. They had exceptional rapport. In my opinion, the rapport was rooted in the character of these two men. While Grant was tied down in Virginia by Lee, Sherman was receiving marvelous and well-publicized accolades on his push through Georgia. His conquest of Atlanta was one factor that saved Lincoln from defeat in the 1864 election. Because of Grant's apparent lack of aggressiveness at this time and Sherman's success, there was considerable discussion among the politicians of Washington to promote Sherman to the rank of lieutenant general. He would have no part of it: He sought no credit or aggrandizement. There was no greater testimonial to Sherman's character than his move to dismiss this idea. On January 22, 1865, Sherman wrote to his brother, John Sherman, a United States senator from Ohio: "I wrote to you that I deem it unwise to make another Lieutenant General, or to create the rank of General. Let the law stand as now. I will accept no commission that would tend to create a rivalry with Grant. I want him to hold what he earned and got." Sherman's selflessness then came through: "I have all the rank I want . . . and it makes no difference to me whether that be Major General or Field Marshal. . . . I have commanded one hundred thousand men in battle, and on the march, successfully and without confusion, and that is enough for my reputation. Now, I want rest and peace. . . ."[5]

Sherman also addressed the issue head-on with Grant, writing to him: "I have been told that Congress meditates a bill to make another lieutenant general for me. I have written to John Sherman to stop it. . . . It would be mischievous, for there are enough rascals who would try to sow differences between us, whereas you and I are now in perfect understanding. . . . I should emphatically decline any commission calculated to bring us into rivalry. . . . I doubt if men in Congress fully realize that you and I are honest in our profession of want and of ambition. I know I feel none, and today will gladly surrender my position and influence to any who is better able to wield the power. The flurry attending my recent successes will soon blow over and give place to new developments."[6]

Sherman, knowing what the bureaucracy in Washington was like, had great foreboding when Grant was called there to have Lincoln bestow on him his new rank of lieutenant general and commander of the Union army. Sherman wrote to his brother, John, a U.S. senator: "Give Grant all the support you can. He is subjected to the disgusting and dangerous process of being lionized. . . . Grant is as good a leader as we can find. He has honesty, simplicity of character, singleness of purpose, and no hope to usurp civil power. His character, more than his genius, will reconcile armies and attach the people."[7]

Further evidence of the remarkable rapport between the two is a letter from Grant to Sherman dated February 7, 1865, wherein Grant stated: "No one would be more pleased at your advancement than I, and if you should be placed in my position, and I am put subordinate, it would not change our personal relations in the least. I would make the same exertions to do all in my power to make our cause win."[8]

The most despicable act was performed by a jealous Major General Halleck, the senior general at the time during the war after Vicksburg when he made Grant his "second in command," which in reality was a nothing position. This meant that Grant was left in isolation with no responsibilities. Halleck ignored him and gave him nothing to do. Halleck's other lackey generals, intimidated by him, slighted Grant and spread unfavorable and untrue stories about him, which were circulated to the press, thus spreading gossip among the troops. Grant suffered terribly but said nothing. Among the generals, the exception was Sherman, whose star was now rising as rapidly as Grant's was descending but whose loyalty and devotion to Grant was special. Had Sherman been self-seeking, he could have capitalized on the situation, but he did not.

Grant eventually became so despondent that Halleck might have achieved what he wanted—to be rid of the man of whom he was so jealous. Grant considered asking for permission to return to his home, which would have, in essence, been his resignation. Sherman heard of this and immediately rode to Grant's camp to ask if it were true, to which Grant responded, "Sherman, you know that I am in the way here. I have stood it as long as I can, and can endure it no longer." Sherman asked if he had business plans. Grant responded, "Not a bit." They discussed it at length, and Sherman persuaded Grant to give his word to reconsider his decision. He did, and the rest of his military success is history. What a special relationship there was between these two great leaders, a relationship based principally on Sherman's character.[9]

Generals Lee and Jackson: Character and Professional Rapport

One of the most remarkable illustrations of Lee's character was provided by the early developments in organizing the Confederate army in 1861. When the Virginia Convention met, Lee ended up junior on the promotion list to some of those already commissioned in the Confederate army, all before Lee was known to be available. The vice president of the Confederacy, Stephens, was concerned that Lee would be upset and slighted by being placed in a more junior position to those already selected. He went to Lee to explain, and later reflected on how he responded: "He at once said that no personal interest of his should, for a single moment, stand in the way of the interests of the state; but that he was willing to take any position—even the rank of a private soldier—in which he could best serve the common cause; and that his rank should, not for a moment, bar [the desired makeup of the army] . . . He was not the man to seek a place for himself, either directly or indirectly."[10]

Lee possessed excellent nerve and had composure mixed with optimism throughout the war. He never got excited. Never during the Civil War, for example, was there any problem or friction in the personal relationship between Lee and Jackson. From the beginning until the end of their relationship, there was never an incident that disturbed Lee. Jackson's Valley campaign and success is one of the most studied accomplishments in military history. Jackson had been opposed in every campaign by an army larger than his. These victories happened at a critical time for the South; they excited—indeed, electrified—the Confederacy and won the hearts of the people. Jackson's attack on General McClellan's right at Chickahominy was his next successful battle. He lead the movement northward, defeated the Union army at Cedar Mountain, then led the Confederate forces against the rear of Major General Pope's proceeding to Manassas, where he held off the Union force until Lee could get there; he then played an important role in that battle. When Lee moved into Maryland, Jackson fell upon the arsenal at Harper's Ferry and seized it. He then moved to join Lee at Sharpsburg, resulting in a draw rather than a defeat for the South. Then there was Jackson's great Chancellorsville victory.

There was never any indication throughout the war that Lee was envious of Jackson's wide acclaim, the admiration of Southerners, and the respect that Union generals gave him. Lee always was genuinely and sincerely pleased with the praise that Jackson received. Even when accolades were directed to himself, particularly after the battle of Chancellorsville, Lee was always the first one to give credit and tribute to Jackson.

Jackson's feelings for Lee were a mixture of love and admiration. What in Lee's makeup elicited such feelings? When one considers Jackson's character, it is clear that Lee had to be not only a soldier, superb in military strategy and tactics, but also a good and deeply religious God-fearing man. Early in Lee's career in the Civil War, he received criticism. If someone criticized Lee in Jackson's presence, it resulted in a quick and even angry response. Once a colleague commented that Lee was "slow." Jackson took him to task, stating: "General Lee is not 'slow.' No one knows the weight upon his heart—his great responsibilities. He is Commander-in-Chief, and he knows that if an army is lost, it cannot be replaced. No! There may be some persons whose good opinion of me may make them attach some weight to my views, and, if you ever hear that said of General Lee, I beg you will contradict it by name. I have known General Lee for five-and-twenty years. He is cautious. He ought to be. But he is not 'slow.' Lee is a phenomenon. He is the only man whom I would follow blindfolded."[11]

Certainly Jackson was competent to evaluate Lee's leadership. Whatever Lee advised him was the best that could be recommended or performed. Jackson would yield to Lee's opinions readily and cheerfully. He revered Lee, looked up to him, never found fault or contradicted him except when he received Lee's letter of congratulations after Chancellorsville, giving him the credit. To that Jackson rebutted, "General Lee is very kind; but he should give the glory to God."[12]

Lee returned Jackson's affection and admiration, conferring with and confiding in him more closely than any other officer. There was never an issue between them on who was the superior or who the subordinate.

Lee had the utmost confidence in Jackson, which was best summed up when, in Fredericksburg, Lee said to a staff officer who was delivering orders for Lee, "Say to General Jackson that he knows just as well what to do with the enemy as I do." There is no more appreciative act of leadership that endears a soldier to his leader than to give him a job to do, then leave him alone to do it.[13]

During the battle of Chancellorsville, Major General Hooker's corps threatened the destruction of the Army of Northern Virginia. There was, because of the threat, talk of retreat. When this was expressed to Jackson, he snapped back, "No sir. We shall not fall back! We shall attack them!"[14]

Jackson had the esteem of his staff and soldiers but not necessarily their affection. Jackson believed in the importance of military education, but to be a general he considered that the qualities of "judgment, nerve and force of character" were necessary. No one could doubt that he personally had force of character. Jackson's leadership success is well summed up by a straggler from Jackson's corps. The Union had unlimited materiel needs, which was obvious to every Confederate soldier. When this straggler, who had had enough of fighting, was approached by a Union force, he surrendered willingly. He looked with awe at his captors' full packs and commented: "You uns is like pack mules—we uns is like race horses. All Old Jackson gave us was a musket, a hundred rounds, and a gum blanket, and he druv us like hell."[15]

General Dwight D. Eisenhower: The Challenge to Allied Leadership

Perhaps the best testimonial of the character of General Eisenhower was his toleration of British field marshal Montgomery of Alamein, to some the outstanding British field general of World War II. To others, Montgomery was an egotistical, arrogant, publicity-seeking officer who considered his judgment as leader, strategist, and tactician superior to all others, British and American. He had been difficult before the selection of the Allied commander, but he became increasingly worse when the decision was made that the commander of the Allied invasion was to be American, not British.

The man originally selected to be the supreme commander, British field marshal Lord Alan Brooke, wrote in his diary on May 15, 1944: "The main impression I gathered was that Eisenhower was no real director of thought, plans, energy or direction. Just a coordinator, a good mixer, a champion of inter-Allied cooperation, and in those respects, few can hold the candle to him." In reflecting upon his comment on General Eisenhower, Lord Alan Brooke later said, "If I was asked to review the opinion I expressed that evening of Eisenhower, I should, in the light of later experience, repeat every word of it. A past master in the handling of allies, entirely impartial and consequently trusted by all. A charming personality and good coordinator. But no real commander."[16]

The strength of Ike's character is further illustrated through the absolutely insulting actions and words of Montgomery throughout World War II, which he tolerated and handled in such a way as to maintain Allied unity. There were constant differences between the United States and Great Britain over strategy. One example in particular illustrates Ike's character. Montgomery was convinced that after the invasion of Normandy on June 6, 1944, there should be a single concentrated offensive, which has been referred to as "Montgomery's single thrust idea." But Ike did not agree. Control of Allied strategy was ultimately taken from Montgomery, but not without a series of incidents that were the most trying of Ike's tenure.

On Ike's decision on strategy, which had the strong support of General Marshall, Montgomery commented that he was "completely out of touch with the land battle" and asked for a face-to-face meeting to discuss the strategy. Ike agreed to meet at his own headquarters, but Montgomery, because he was so "busy" and so filled with his own importance, insisted that Ike come to him. This was arrogant and insulting. Although Ike had severely injured his knee and was in great pain, he flew to Brussels on September 10, 1944, to meet with Montgomery, to perpetuate Allied unity. His injury was so bad that he could not leave the plane, so they had to confer there.

To add further insult to injury, Montgomery insisted that, during the discussion, Ike's chief of staff, Smith, not be present but that his own chief of staff should. For the sake of harmony Ike agreed, and Montgomery proceeded to criticize and ridicule Ike's strategy. Montgomery's intelligence chief, Brig. Gen. Bill Wilkows, commented, "Patience and tolerance by Ike made Monty overstep himself." It got so bad that Ike informed Montgomery "Steady, Monty! You can't speak to me like that. I'm your boss."[17]

Montgomery suggested a plan, given the code name Market Garden. This was imaginative strategy to have the British 1st Airborne Division, along with the U.S. 82d and 101st Airborne Divisions, seize a bridgehead across the Rhine River to Arnhem to obtain "a foothold opening the door to the German heartland." Although Ike had reservations, the idea had possibilities, so Ike permitted the operation to go ahead.

It was an absolute disaster; it almost destroyed the British airborne division, and the two U.S. airborne divisions suffered heavy causalities. Ike was upset with himself for permitting this and commented, "What this action proved was that the idea of 'one full blooded thrust' to Berlin was silly." But in his arrogance Montgomery would not admit he was wrong. Instead he said the failure was because Ike didn't properly back him with enough airpower, troops, and other support needed.[18]

The situation was perhaps best summed up by biographer Norman Gelb: "Market Garden was more than a botched operation. It suddenly brought the Allied commanders down to earth. Thoughts of a speedy victory over Hitler were dashed by the realization that the Allies had missed the boat, that the enemy had managed to recover from the Normandy rout and was no longer in disarray. Brooke was bitter over what he considered Eisenhower's failure to grasp the fleeting chance to end the war quickly by concentrating the Allied assault as Montgomery had proposed rather than attempting to advance on a thin, broad front. However, Montgomery had, by then, committed another monumental error that made prolongation of the conflict inevitable."[19]

On September 20, 1944, with the Arnhem operation having failed, Ike called a conference at SHAEF headquarters of senior generals to zero in on the best strategy for destroying Germany. Bradley, Patton, and Hodges were present, but Montgomery snubbed Ike by not attending. He sent his chief of staff, Brig. Gen. Francis De Guingand, to represent him. Ike, after the meeting, wrote to Montgomery: "I regard it as a great pity that all of us cannot keep in close touch with each other because I find, without exception, when all of us can get together and look the various features of our problems squarely in the face, the answers usually become obvious."[20]

Montgomery, not getting his way on the single-thrust strategy, was quoted as saying that Ike was "completely out of touch with what was going on and does not really know anything about the business of fighting the Germans." On October 8, 1944, Montgomery went over Ike's head when, during a visit by General Marshall to his headquarters, he proceeded to tell Marshall that there was "a lack of grip and operational direction and control was lacking. Our operations had, in fact, become ragged and disjointed, and we had now got ourselves into a real mess."

This was a mistake. Marshall had never been impressed with Montgomery in his leadership in North Africa and certainly not with his lack of success with his forces in the Normandy invasion. But Marshall, who believed that Ike gave Montgomery too much lead, also held back, later commenting that it was "very hard for me to restrain myself because I didn't think there was any logic in what he said, but overwhelming egotism."[21]

But Montgomery would not let up. He arrogantly wrote to Bedell Smith, Ike's chief of staff, to tell Ike, "The present organization for command within the Allied forces in Western Europe is not satisfactory"[22] and that Ike was not suited for fighting a war. What Montgomery wanted was a single ground commander for the campaign—himself of course.

Montgomery now had pushed Ike too far. Ike rebuked him for the first time, even questioning Montgomery's performance in France. He informed him that he was taking away his assignment to seize the Ruhr and was giving the job to Bradley, with Montgomery acting in support. Most importantly, he informed Montgomery that if this was not satisfactory, "we have an issue that must be settled soon in the interest of future efficiency." Ike informed him that if he believed that his approach would "endanger the success of operations, it is our duty to refer the matter to higher authority for any action they may choose to take, however drastic."[23]

Ike finally reached Montgomery, for the time being. Montgomery knew full well that if there was a showdown with the Combined Chiefs of Staff, he would lose. He responded to Ike's challenge, stating, "You will hear no more on the subject of command from me." More specifically, he wrote to Ike: "I have given you my views and you have given your answer. That ends the matter and I and all of us [at 21st Army Group headquarters] will weigh 100% to do what you want and we will all pull through it without a doubt." He signed the letter, "Your devoted and loyal subordinate, Monty."[24]

Future developments showed Montgomery's hypocrisy, for in November he wrote to Brooke, the British chief of staff, that the system of command was prolonging the war, that Ike's orders had "no relation to the practical necessities of the battle," that Ike had elected "to take direct command of a very large-scale operation and he does not know how to do it." He added, "I think we are drifting into dangerous waters."[25]

Montgomery's conduct, along with his leaks, resulted in the British press saying that Ike was out of his depth as supreme commander. Brooke even carried the issue to Churchill, who took the complaint about Ike to Roosevelt, who informed Churchill that he had complete confidence in Ike. So Montgomery condescendingly wrote to Brooke, "Ike seems determined to show that he is a great general in the field. Let him do so and let us all lend a hand to pull him through."[26]

Montgomery asked Ike for a conference for the first week of December with their respective chiefs of staff present but added they "must not speak." Ike agreed to a conference but refused to bar Smith from talking, informing Montgomery that he would not insult his chief of staff by asking him to remain silent.

There was a meeting on December 7, 1944, with Tedder, Bradley, and Smith in attendance. Montgomery insisted that Patton, who was rapidly moving through France into central Germany and Devers, coming up from the south of France, be "reined in" so that all available resources could be concentrated on his, Montgomery's, drive.

Montgomery refused to acknowledge anyone else's ideas at this meeting. Ike did agree, however, to a thrust along Montgomery's northern route, shifting command of the U.S. Ninth Army to him, but he refused to cut off supplies to Patton and Devers. This decision pleased neither Montgomery nor Bradley.

Bradley even commented later of Ike's decision that "this was a classic Eisenhower compromise that left me distinctly unhappy. It tactfully implied that my 12th Army Group Offensive failed." After the meeting, Montgomery wrote to Brooke, "If we want the war to end within any reasonable period you have to get Eisenhower taken off the land battle. I regret to say that in my opinion he just doesn't know what he is doing."[27]

The situation became so bad that on December 12, 1944, Churchill asked Ike to meet him in London along with Brooke to try to salvage Allied unity. At the meeting Brooke proceeded to very undiplomatically criticize Ike for failing to concentrate the forces as Montgomery wanted. Churchill sided with Ike, which upset Brooke to the point that he contemplated resigning.

The Battle of the Bulge brought the matter to a head. Hitler made a last-ditch effort, against the advice of his own German generals, when on December 16, 1944, the Germans surprised the Allies with a powerful attack on U.S. forces in the Ardennes. Initially it went badly for the Allies. Montgomery proceeded to blame Ike, saying it would never have happened if he, Montgomery, had been the ground force commander.

Montgomery invited Bradley to his headquarters to discuss tactics on December 25, 1944, and started "by lecturing and scolding

[Bradley] like a schoolboy," stating that in his opinion incompetent generalship was responsible for the Ardennes, obviously meaning Ike. Montgomery's arrogance and ego were so great that he had the gall to write Brooke that Bradley agreed with him.

Far from it. Bradley, a man of great character, acting the gentleman, listened, wanting to preserve Allied unity, but wrote of the incident: "Monty was more arrogant and egotistical than I have ever seen him. . . . Never in my life have I been so utterly exasperated. It required every fiber of my strength to restrain myself from an insulting outburst. . . ."

Why was Bradley so patient? He stated further of the incident, "However, to avoid a potentially crippling breakdown in the Allied command, I kept my counsel."[28]

Patton, in a brilliant maneuver, moved to Bastogne in forty-eight hours, saving the day for the Allies and stopping the German offensive. But Montgomery would not even listen to Brooke. Montgomery wrote to Ike on December 29, 1944, listing the mistakes made—in his opinion—by Ike and warning him, "We [will] fail again," unless the command structure he proposed be instituted at once. He added: "[One] commander must have powers to direct and control the operations. You cannot possibly do it yourself, and so you have to nominate someone else."

Ike had finally had it and was going to end Montgomery's arrogance, egotism, and indiscretion. He showed De Guingand a cable he had drafted to send to Marshall, suggesting that Montgomery be replaced. What he was saying in essence was that unless Montgomery was relieved, Ike himself would step down. De Guingand well knew that if that happened, Montgomery would be going home disgraced. He also knew that Ike would win this decision, because Roosevelt and Marshall had made their confidence in him very clear.

De Guingand asked Ike to delay sending the cable for twenty-four hours. De Guingand described Montgomery's reaction: "It was one of the few times that I saw Montgomery really worried and disturbed, for I believe he was genuinely and completely taken by surprise and found it difficult to grasp what I was saying. . . . I don't think I had ever seen him so deflated. It was as if a cloak of loneliness had descended upon him."[29]

De Guingand made it clear to Montgomery that if he did not apologize to Ike, his career was over. Montgomery cabled Ike his regrets: "I understand you are greatly worried by many considerations in these difficult days. I have given you my frank views because I have felt you like this. I am sure there are many factors, which may have a bearing quite beyond anything I realize. Whatever your decision may be, you can rely on me one hundred percent to make it work and I know Brad will do the same."[30]

Although Montgomery had made this promise to Ike before, for the sake of Allied unity Ike accepted this response. Montgomery also said he would advance the turning of his offensive to the north, ending his constant procrastination and delay.

But that did not end it. Montgomery, in a press conference in which he was supposed to mend the rift, proceeded to give the impression that it was his leadership and the British army that saved the day in the Germans' Ardennes offensive. This was outrageous and completely wrong.

Ike informed Churchill that something had to be done to set Montgomery, the British press, and the people straight. Churchill agreed and made a speech to the House of Commons repudiating Montgomery's erroneous comments.[31]

Unquestionably Montgomery's ego, arrogance, and lack of discretion and tact could have destroyed Allied unity had it not been for Ike's strong character, leadership, and patience. It took a remarkable man to control himself, but certainly Ike possessed sufficient character.

Through all of this, Eisenhower had great patience. The best testimonial to his ultimate success was a letter written by Montgomery himself on June 7, 1945:

> Dear Ike:
> Now that we have all signed in Berlin I suppose we shall soon begin to run our own affairs. I would like, before this happens, to say what a privilege and honor it has been to serve under you. I owe much to your wise guidance and kindly forbearance. I know my own faults very well and I do not suppose I am an easy subordinate; I like to go my own way.

But you have kept me on the rails in difficult and stormy times, and have taught me much.

For all this I am very grateful. And I thank you for all you have done for me.

Your very devoted friend,

Monty

Perhaps the best way to close the discussion of Montgomery is with the words of Winston Churchill, who said that he "was magnificent in defeat, and insufferable in victory."

George C. Marshall: Bridging the Gap Between the Military and the State Department

It is clear that our military idolized the leadership and character of General of the Army George C. Marshall. This respect for him was not limited to the military, however. Traditionally, in this century, there has been a lack of rapport, indeed suspicious distrust and sometimes contempt, among military and the State Department personnel. In his memoirs entitled *Witness to History,* Ambassador Charles "Chip" Bohlen, who, along with Ambassador George F. Kennan, was the top adviser and expert on Soviet foreign policy, wrote of Marshall's appointment as secretary of state in January 1947: "There was a great deal of nervousness in the Foreign Service over the appointment of a military man as Secretary of State. Marshall's reputation was unparalleled, but morale was low because Byrnes had tended to ignore the Department of State. There was wide apprehension that the General could impose such rigid discipline and procedures that ideas would never make their way to the top.

"It didn't take [him] long to win over almost every important member of the State Department. He gave a sense of purpose and direction. His personality infected the whole Foreign Service. Under him, as under Herter in later years, the department functioned with as much efficiency as I was to note in my nearly forty years in the Foreign Service. True, Marshall had excellent Under Secretaries—first Dean Acheson, then Robert A. Lovett, Assistant Secretary of War during World War II under Henry L. Stimson. It is also true that Marshall had an easy act to follow, because Byrnes paid little attention to the operations of the department. Under Marshall, all the senior officers were consulted, and when policy was decided, there was no question what it was. There was a greater clarity in the operation of the State Department than I had seen before or have seen since."[32]

George Kennan, in his memoirs, wrote: "This is, I think, as good a place as any to say a word about General Marshall. I knew him only late in life during his final tour of duty in a long life of service to the nation. I was not close to him personally (few people were, I gather), but during the year and eight months of our association in the Department of State, from May 1947 to the end of 1948, I had the only office adjoining his own, and enjoyed the privilege (which I tried never to abuse) of direct entry to him, through our common side door. Officially, then, the association was a fairly close one, and I had many opportunities to observe him in his work as Secretary of State.

"There could be no one whose memory has less need of a eulogy from me than George Marshall. Like everyone else, I admired him, and in a sense, loved him, for the qualities I saw in him, some of them well-known, some less so: for his unshakable integrity; his consistent courtesy and gentlemanliness of conduct; his ironclad sense of duty; his imperturbability—the imperturbability of a good conscience—in the face of harassment, pressures, and criticisms; his deliberateness and conscientiousness of decision; his serene readiness—once a decision had been made—to abide by its consequences, whatever they might be; his lack of petty vanity or ambition; his indifference to the whims and moods of public opinion, particularly as manifested in the mass media; and his impeccable fairness and avoidance of favoritism in the treatment of subordinates."[33]

In January 1947, Dean Rusk (secretary of state in 1961 for President John F. Kennedy) was offered by Secretary of War Robert Patterson the opportunity (after graduating from law school) to join his staff to become the army's chief expert on international law. Marshall, however, when he became secretary in 1947, asked Rusk to become the head of the State Department's Office of Special Political Affairs.

Rusk reflected: "I opted for State, to a great extent, because of

George Marshall. He was the most extraordinary man I ever knew. Winston Churchill called him the 'principal architect of victory' in World War II, and Harry Truman called Marshall 'the greatest living American' shortly thereafter. They both were right.

"Marshall had a strong influence on everyone who served with him. He was a great teacher as well. He taught us about public life, both by personal example and by dropping little homilies about what he expected of us. For example: 'Gentleman, don't sit around waiting for me to tell you what to do. Take some initiative. Tell me what you think I ought to be doing!' He expected everyone to perform their job well, whatever the problems. For example, soon after his appointment, Marshall was at a morning staff meeting with about fifteen of us, and someone complained about poor departmental morale. The general straightened himself up, looked around the table, and declared, 'Gentlemen, enlisted men may be entitled to morale problems, but officers are not. I expect all officers in this department to take care of their own morale.' When word went around the department that there was no shoulder to cry on, morale at State went to the highest point I had ever seen it, before or since.

"Marshall's attitude inspired confidence in his colleagues. The old general would tell us, 'Take heart!'; 'Don't despair!'; 'Don't fight your problems, deal with them!'"[34]

But the State Department personality who offered the best insight was Dean Acheson, who served as Marshall's undersecretary of state and went on to succeed Marshall when he stepped down in 1948: "The moment General Marshall entered a room, everyone in it felt his presence. It was a striking and communicated force. His figure conveyed intensity, which his voice, low, staccato, and incisive, reinforced. It compelled respect. It spread a sense of authority and calm. There was no military glamour about him and nothing of the martinet. Yet, to all of us, he was always 'General Marshall.' The title fitted him as though he had been baptized with it. He always identified himself over the telephone as 'General Marshall speaking.' It seemed wholly right, too. I should never have dreamed of addressing him as 'Mr. Secretary' and I have never heard anyone but Mrs. Marshall call him 'George.' The General expected to be treated with respect and to treat others the same way. This was the basis of his relationships. President Truman has put his finger on another foundation of General Marshall's character. 'Never,' wrote the President, 'did General Marshall think about himself. General Marshall's ego never got between him and his task.'"[35]

The Importance of Loyalty

One of the most important fundamentals of successful leaders is loyalty to subordinates, not always an easy task. This provides further insight into Marshall's character. It was decided in the summer of 1941, before the United States entered World War II, to draw up a war plan to include the production requirements, numbers of men, and objective of our national policy. Although President Roosevelt wanted to keep us out of the war, he certainly was partial to the British as Hitler was overrunning Europe.

Preparation of a staff study on this project was assigned to then Maj. Albert Wedemeyer, a member of the chief of staff's Secretariat. His report declared: "[We] must be prepared to fight Germany directly and defeat her." Wedemeyer concluded that the army and Army Air Corps would need 9 million men and the navy, 1.5 million. The report was top secret. To the shock and surprise of the president, the army hierarchy, and Major Wedemeyer, the report was quoted verbatim in the December 5, 1941, issue of the *Washington Times Herald,* with the page one headline stating, "FDR's WAR PLANS!" It created a furor in Washington and was obviously embarrassing, because we were not at war with Germany.

Wedemeyer came under immediate suspicion. He had a German name, knew many of the top German military officers—having attended one of the German advanced courses during the 1930s—and had developed friendships with top Nazi Party members. A week before the leak, he had met with a lawyer whose father was Sen. Burton K. Wheeler, a fanatical isolationist who alleged that Roosevelt wanted to "plow under every fourth American boy." Wedemeyer recently had made a large deposit to his bank account. There was even an anonymous letter to the secretary of war, claiming, "Wedemeyer thinks and says Hitler is a savior."

The circumstantial evidence seemed overwhelming against Wedemeyer. He was interrogated by the FBI, but the investigation never did determine who leaked the report. It would have been easy for Wedemeyer's superiors to take a position of "we don't want to know this man," to reassign him or send him into exile. But Marshall did not do that. He had great respect for his ability; to quote Wedemeyer, "General Marshall never doubted me." Indeed, several weeks later, Marshall promoted him to lieutenant colonel and made him a member of the newly formed Joint Staff Planners, part of the Joint Chiefs of Staff.

On April 1, 1942, Marshall left Washington on a highly secret mission and took Wedemeyer with him. This is certainly an illustration of loyalty by Marshall, but, even more important, it was an illustration of his character. He stuck by Wedemeyer and was not intimidated by circumstantial evidence, the open criticism of isolationists, and the press. Wedemeyer never forgot this; he went on to become a four-star general, remarking, "I would have died for him after that."[36]

General Colin Powell provided a more current example of loyalty. In May 1991, after the conflict with Iraq was over, there was considerable publicity (in the May 13, 1991, issue of *Newsweek* and, prior to that, in the *Washington Post*) stating that Powell was "the Reluctant Warrior," implying that he was privately opposed to the president on the Gulf War.

In his autobiography, Powell wrote:

My phone was eerily silent [as I was taking] a pounding from the media. . . .

The same morning the story appeared, a White House operator called to say that President Bush was coming on the line. I waited uneasily. "Colin, pay no attention to that nonsense. Don't worry about it, " he said. "Don't let 'em get under your skin."

"Thanks, Mr. President," I said.

"Barb says hello. See ya." Click.

Later that day, at, of all places, a gathering on agricultural policy, reporters hit the President with more questions about me, as depicted in Woodward's book. "Nobody's going to drive

a wedge between [Powell] and me," he said. "I don't care what
kind of book they've got, how many unnamed sources they
have, how many quotes they put in the mouth of somebody
when they weren't there. . . ."

I will never forget this loyalty from the President of the
United States at a time when I needed a friend.[37]

But loyalty does not mean there can be any favoritism. Certainly
a part of character is refusing to show favoritism. The victory that cat-
apulted Grant to prominence was the capture of Fort Donaldson, in
Tennessee. Surrendering the fort was one of his closest friends before the war, Gen. Simon Bolivar Buckner. When Grant was destitute
on returning from disgrace from California after a forced resignation, he was without any funds with which to return home. Buckner
first guaranteed Grant's hotel bill, then raised fifty dollars for him.
When Buckner asked for the terms of surrender of Fort Donaldson,
he was counting on Grant remembering this thoughtfulness, but
Grant's answer was unyielding. His response to Buckner was: "No
terms except an unconditional and immediate surrender can be accepted."

General Marshall received uncountable accolades for his brilliant
World War II leadership, but there was at least one dissenting opinion regarding his treatment of his officers. The wife of one of his senior generals wrote that the chief of staff "was my child's godfather
and spent the night my son was born walking the corridors of the
hospital. I thought he was wonderful, but about his leadership I cannot speak very highly. He later treated my husband terribly and un-
forgivably. . . . He let his tried and true friends down . . . he wrecked
my husband's career, broke his heart, and took the rank of major
general away from him. . . ."[38]

Actually this officer's wife could not have paid General Marshall
a greater compliment. Her husband had made an unforgivable error in judgment during World War II. Though he was one of General Marshall's closest friends, Marshall showed no favoritism. The
officer was reduced to the grade of colonel.

"I cannot afford the luxury of sentiment," General Marshall told
Mrs. Marshall one evening while they were walking. "Mine must be

cold logic. Sentiment is for others." Yet the officers mentored by Marshall never forgot him. Secretary Stimson remarked, "They were all as loyal to him as their leader as if they were here in the Pentagon."[39]

There was a similar incident involving Eisenhower as D-day commander. Major General Henry Jervis Miller, quartermaster general of the Ninth Air Force, was a 1915 classmate of Eisenhower at West Point. At Claridge's Hotel in April 1944, Maj. Gen. Edwin L. Sibert, counterintelligence officer of the European theater of operations, overheard Miller repeat over drinks a complaint that supplies were not getting through from the States and could not until after the invasion in mid-June. Sibert reported the case to Bradley, who forwarded the matter to Ike. Miller requested on the basis of friendship that he be sent back to America at his current grade to await "such action as the fates have in store for me." In his reply, Eisenhower told Miller he regretted "sitting as a judge" in a case involving a friend, but Miller was guilty of a serious breach of security. Ike ordered him reduced to colonel and sent back to the United States.[40]

Resisting the Temptation to Leave the Service

Perhaps the need for character was greater during the years of peace than in time of war. The generals in this comparative study were dedicated men, but they were also human. There were times when they were tempted to leave the service because of slow promotions, poor pay, frequent moves, inadequate equipment for training their men, and other hardships.

Marshall, after he had served as army chief of staff, secretary of state, and secretary of defense, was once asked what the most exciting moment of his life had been. "Being promoted to first lieutenant," he replied. He had spent five years as a second lieutenant. In spite of his outstanding success in various assignments and schools, Marshall at thirty-five years of age was still a first lieutenant in 1915, fourteen years after his graduation from Virginia Military Institute (VMI).

In a mood of despondency that year, he wrote to the superintendent of VMI, Gen. Edward W. Nichols: "The absolute stagnation in promotion in the infantry has caused me to make tentative plans for resigning as soon as business conditions improve. Even in the event of an increase as a result of legislation next winter, the prospects for advancement in the Army are so restricted by law and by the accumulation of large numbers of men nearly the same age all in a single grade, that I do not feel it right to waste all my best years in vain struggle against insurmountable difficulties."[41]

Marshall did not leave the service in 1915 and, upon his return from the Philippines in 1916, he was pleased to be assigned, a second time, as aide-de-camp to a man for whom he had tremendous respect and admiration, Gen. J. Franklin Bell. This challenge, and possible U.S. involvement in World War I, undoubtedly were factors in Marshall's decision to remain in the army.

Because of his brilliant performance in World War I, Marshall came to the attention of several prominent and wealthy businessmen who were serving on Pershing's staff. One of these men in 1919 offered Marshall a starting salary of $20,000 to leave the service and work for the J. P. Morgan financial firm. Marshall turned it down even though he knew he would soon lose his wartime rank of colonel. In 1920, he was reduced to the rank of major and a salary of $3,000 a year. Still, he remained in the service.

In 1947, after Eisenhower had retired as chief of staff of the army to become president of Columbia University, the Eisenhowers bought their first new car. It was delivered to their home; after Ike inspected it, he wrote a check for its full cost, almost wiping out their savings. He took Mamie by the hand and walked with her to the door, saying, "Darling, there's the entire result of thirty-seven years' work since I caught the train out of Abilene."[42]

A man certainly did not stay in the army for money. In a personal interview, I asked Ike if he were ever tempted to leave the army. He responded: "There were three times when I was offered what you might say were attractive opportunities to leave the service. The first was right after World War I. I was right here in this town [Gettysburg]. There was a man whose name, strangely enough, was Patton, who was a manufacturer in Ohio or Indiana—someplace in the Midwest—who wanted me to go with him at double the salary I was getting then as a lieutenant colonel. For a while our army pay looked pretty low. Mamie had quite an influence upon me. I was very disheartened that I hadn't gotten over into the battle, and I thought my army career was ruined. I was fed up. After all the studying and hard work, I wouldn't get into the war. Mamie kidded me a little bit, and we decided to go on in the army."[43]

The next offer came in 1927, when a group of people were forming a new oil company. The man putting up a large part of the money was someone Eisenhower had met only a few times; but the investor said he wouldn't contribute unless Eisenhower agreed to enter the new firm—not as the top man but as one of the executives. The backer wanted Eisenhower because he considered him honest and believed he would watch his money for him. Again, Eisenhower turned down the temptation of more money.[44]

In the Philippines, several men who wanted Eisenhower to enter business with them offered to put $300,000 in escrow in a bank if he would join them. The money was to be used by Eisenhower if things didn't work out.

As the offers came forth, Ike always discussed them with Mamie. "We always said we got this far in the army and we're going to stay with it. The only offer I really considered was the first one because of my disappointment over not getting into the war."[45]

In his book *At Ease: Stories I Tell My Friends,* Eisenhower wrote of his son John's decision to go to West Point: "John must have wondered why I stayed in the Army at all. To give him the less gloomy side of the picture, I said that my Army experience had been wonderfully interesting and it had brought me into contact with men of ability, honor, and a sense of high dedication to their country. I reminded John of the incident in the Philippines, when a group wanted me to leave the Army with an ironclad five-year contract at $60,000 a year. The offer had few temptations. Happy in my work and ready to face, without resentment, the bleak promotional picture, I had long ago refused to bother my head about promotion. Whenever the subject came up among the three of us at home, I said the real satisfaction was for a man who did the best he could. My ambition in the Army was to make everybody I worked for regretful when I was ordered to other duty.

"John decided to go to West Point. I asked him about his reasons. The substance of his answer was: 'It's because of what you told me the other evening. When you talked about the satisfaction you had in an Army career, and the pride you had in being associated with men of character, my mind was made up—right then.' He added, 'if I can say the same thing when I've finished my Army career, I'll care no more about promotions than you did.'"[46]

There was probably only one occasion when General MacArthur ever gave thought to leaving the service. He did not get married until he was a brigadier general at the age of forty-two. His wife was a rich divorcée with two children. After their marriage, Mrs. MacArthur, who was used to the gay, exciting social life of New York and Washington, became bored. She believed her husband to be too brilliant to waste his time in making an army career. She wanted him to leave the army to enter the business world. It reached the point where MacArthur had to decide between the army and his wife. He decided to remain in the army, and the marriage ended in divorce.

George Patton was never really tempted to leave the service. He had independent means, and his wife also had considerable wealth. It was truly remarkable for a man of such opulence to make the service—a life so filled with hardship and frustration—his career. But a soldier's life was what Patton wanted, and that was the life he led.

Service life before World War II involved constant sacrifice; nevertheless, fortunately for the United States, a group of outstanding military leaders was ready when Pearl Harbor was bombed on December 7, 1941. Why did these men remain in the service?

When I asked General of the Army Omar N. Bradley, he replied: "Well, just the fact that I liked military work. I like working with men. I like to teach, and you know [that] most of your service involves teaching your own men or instructing at some service school. I liked the outdoors—and you spent a great deal of time outdoors in the army. There is another angle to it, which was more true then than now. In the old days, you had a rather small army, and you knew practically every officer in the army, either personally or by reputation. You usually lived on the post; you were one big family, the atmosphere was pleasant, and you had a nice group to work with. Your contemporaries spoke the same language. There was the feeling that in serving your country you were accomplishing something. There was always something to be done, something to learn."[47]

General Mark W. Clark, who spent sixteen years as a captain, felt much the same way. "I like working with men, training young people. That's why I took it up after I retired from the army. [When I interviewed him, he was president of the Citadel, a state military school in South Carolina.] I liked the outdoors. I was fond of hiking, riding, and all kinds of outdoor activity. I had been raised on an army post and I liked the life an army officer lived, the fine families you met, the children you associated with, because they were invariably raised in Christian families and they were always well disciplined."[48]

General J. Lawton Collins was a lieutenant for seventeen years. He almost left the army in 1919 to study law. He wrote to a friend, who advised him that he would be "crazy" to leave the service for law, because good lawyers could be hired for $250 a month. "Your natural bent," that friend said, "is military service. You would be crazy to give it up."

Collins decided, because he was stationed in Europe, to postpone resigning for a year. "I evaluated the situation very carefully," he said of his position at the end of that year. "I finally decided that there were three things that appealed to me about military service, which I could never get anywhere else. The first was that I was not competing with my fellow officers for money. I was actually holding down jobs that normally went to more senior people. Even though I was drawing just a captain's pay, I was given the opportunity to do things irrespective of my age and rank, and that appealed to me. The second thing I liked was the people I was associated with. They were men of high caliber, men of integrity. And at no time in my three years of service did anybody ask me to do anything that didn't meet my own standard of conduct."[49]

He continued: "At the same time, I met the girl I later married, and that had considerable influence. I decided then I would stick it out in the service for better or worse, and I gave up any thought of resigning from the army."[50]

At about the same time, Generals Spaatz and Arnold almost left the Army Air Corps to join the embryonic Pan American Airways, but they both stayed. Spaatz remained because he liked the life, his friends, and the flying. "There really wasn't any incentive to stay in the service between World War I and World War II as there is now. There was no apparent threat of war in those days. There was, however, a feeling among most of us who came into the old aviation section, the signal corps, that there was going to be a growth in military aviation. We had confidence that it was going to get its due position, and we decided to stay with it."[51]

Patience was certainly a characteristic of air force generals Arnold, Spaatz, Vandenburg, Twining, and White, men who remained in the service during the periods of slow promotion between World Wars I and II. During the early years of our aviation history, when the first man was killed in a balloon accident (in 1908, Lt. Thomas Selfridge of the field artillery), Arnold was thinking of promotion. He related, "It was a plan that has occupied every second lieutenant since the beginning of armies. I was trying to get to be a first lieutenant. In those days in the regular Army, your chances for remaining a second lieutenant for six or seven years were very good. . . ." Arnold became a second lieutenant on June 14, 1907, and was not promoted to first lieutenant until April 10, 1913.[52]

Arnold became a captain three years later, a major a year after that, then jumped to the grade of colonel (temporary) on August 5, 1917, skipping over the rank of lieutenant colonel. Arnold explained the reason for this jump in his own words, which are an insight into his character. As quoted in chapter 1, he wrote in his memoirs, "Promotion came rapidly in wartime—especially in an Air Force in which only a few relatively junior officers knew how to fly. . . . My wife and I looked at these eagles on my shoulders, and though we were certainly pleased to see them there, they seemed unreal, even embarrassing. Youngsters in those days just didn't get to be colonels."[53] After the war, he was reduced to the rank of captain.

Spaatz was commissioned a second lieutenant of infantry on June 12, 1914. His early promotion situation was better than Arnold's because Spaatz was able to get in on what little action there was going on prior to the United States becoming involved in World War I. In June 1916, he was assigned to Columbus, New Mexico, serving with the 1st Aero Squadron under Pershing in the punitive expedition into Mexico. On July 1, 1916, as a result of this action, he was promoted to first lieutenant. In May 1917, he joined the 3d Aero

Squadron in San Antonio, Texas, and in the same month was promoted to captain.

On November 15, 1917, Spaatz again got into the action; he was assigned to France with the 31st Aero Squadron and served in the American Aviation School at Issoudon continuously until August 30, 1918. During this period, he received a temporary promotion to major. After the war he reverted to the rank of captain, but he was again promoted to major on July 1, 1920. He spent another fifteen years as a major, not receiving his lieutenant colonel's leaf until 1935.

General Vandenburg spent a total of twelve years as a lieutenant, receiving his promotion to captain on August 1, 1935, after having been commissioned a second lieutenant on June 12, 1923. It was another five years after making captain before he became a temporary major.

Thomas D. White started off brilliantly: He graduated from the military academy on July 2, 1920, was commissioned a second lieutenant of infantry, and on the same day was promoted to first lieutenant. Although this was quite a contrast to the slow promotions between the wars, any ego trip would have been short lived, for on December 22, 1922, he was returned to the grade of second lieutenant. He was not promoted to first lieutenant again until August 24, 1925. Then it was ten years before he became a captain; he received that promotion on August 1, 1935, after having served more than fifteen years as a lieutenant.

Perhaps the most significant example was that of Nathan F. Twining. He entered the military academy in June 1917, and because of World War I his class was accelerated. He graduated and was commissioned in November 1918 as a second lieutenant of infantry. He became a first lieutenant on January 1, 1920, but was not promoted to the rank of captain until April 20, 1935, thus spending seventeen years as a lieutenant.

One can see that promotions were extremely slow for our first chiefs of staff of the air force. Their patience and sense of duty were remarkable, for during the years of slow promotion they chose to remain in the service rather than enter more lucrative opportunities in the civilian world.

Arnold, as mentioned earlier, had considered leaving the air

corps to join the embryonic Pan American Airways, having been offered its presidency. But when he was exiled to Fort Riley, because
of his continuous efforts to support Billy Mitchell, he concluded,
"That was the end of my plan to resign and become president of our
newly founded Pan American Airways. I couldn't very well quit the
service under fire."[54]

Spaatz was also offered the opportunity to get in on the early development of Pan American as vice president. I asked him why he
decided to ignore these temptations. He responded: "Well, it's aw-
fully hard to give any reason except that you liked the service. There
was the challenge of developing the air force. Most of us who came
into the old aviation section, the signal corps, believed there was going to be a growth of military aviation, and we had confidence in its
being a dominant force for defense and decided to stay with it. There
is a different situation now, where you have a big military requirement for years to come—as far ahead as anyone can see."[55]

I asked General LeMay why he stayed. He responded: "I had gotten a regular commission in the army. Then I had to make a choice
whether I was going to stay in the service or fly in commercial aviation. I gave it a great deal of thought and I finally decided to stay in
the service—mainly, I think, because I liked it. I liked the people I
was working with. It certainly was the finest group of men that I had
ever come in contact with. They all were highly motivated. They were
all gentlemen in every sense of the word.

"I think I was very much impressed by the fact that I could go down
to the bank and sign my name on a note, deposit it, and write checks
on it without any cosigners or anything of that sort, for any amount
of money commensurate with my salary. This, of course, had been
built up by the integrity and honesty of army officers who had
served before me. This made quite an impression on me, and I sort
of felt I wanted to be a part of it, even though it was perfectly apparent in the early days that the monetary rewards were certainly not
going to be great. I have never regretted the decision. I certainly had
gone much farther than I ever expected to go, much farther, and
I've enjoyed every minute of it. I feel that I've rendered a service to
the country and at the same time it's been a very satisfying experience for me. I've never regretted the decision."[56]

Many of the post–World War II senior officers had rapid promotions during the war, but this did not compensate for the slow promotions of the 1920s and 1930s. This was, however, not the factor influencing most of those serving between World War I and World War II to leave the military. There were other factors that could have brought early retirement or resignation even at the highest level. General J. Lawton Collins reflected in his memoirs: "The question arises periodically as to what a Chief of Staff should do if, in all conscience, he cannot support the budget or other policy decisions of the President or the Secretary of Defense. In such a case, he is entitled by law to appeal directly to the President, over the head of the Secretary, if necessary. I believe that in loyalty to the President as Commander-in-Chief, a Chief of Staff should support the President's programs unless, in a crisis, a chief is convinced that the security of the country is at stake, in which instance he should ask to be relieved. I came close to such a point shortly before the outbreak of the Korean War when I felt impelled to inform Secretary Louis Johnson at an Armed Forces policy meeting that I would be unable to accept any further cuts in the number of active divisions in the Army. If the Korean War had not intervened, I might well have been relieved or forced to resign."[57]

General Shy Meyer explained his position as chief of staff, telling me: "I sat down and made a list of matters, of guidelines you truly believe in, what you were taught as a child, what you were taught at school, with duty, honor, and country as your guide, and you won't step behind that line. I sat down and did this ahead of time and defined what would cause me to resign. I said really there were two areas, one where I was in such violent disagreement with the basic principles of the administration or my boss that I couldn't possibly carry out what he wanted. The other was if there was any moral or ethical challenge they were placing me under that I couldn't carry out, then I would resign."[58]

So many junior officers enter the military excited for a challenging opportunity to serve, but, disillusioned with incompetent senior officers, they become discouraged and leave. General Schwarzkopf, who had that experience, provides an excellent example of how strong character helped overcome such disappointment.

His initial assignment as a lieutenant was with the 101st Airborne. He thought he was with the army's elite outfit but became quickly disillusioned. He commented that most of the senior first lieutenants and captains were "hard-drinking rogues" left over from World War II and Korea. "For the first time in my life I found myself required to answer to men I didn't respect—a dilemma for which I was not prepared." He described his company commander as a "short, fat, lazy, forty-year-old first lieutenant" who had come back to the army because "he couldn't make it on the outside. The 101st was an airborne outfit, but the company commander was afraid to jump. He made excuses to the men that he had the flu or some other excuse and decided to travel on the ground to meet them at the drop zone."

That lieutenant was soon replaced by a captain who also couldn't make it in the civilian world. He was an alcoholic whom Schwarzkopf often had to drive home because he was too drunk to drive or had passed out at the bar. The captain told Schwarzkopf that he hated West Pointers, had him do his work, and proceeded to take credit for it. Not surprisingly, the outfit failed an alert. The captain called the company together and told them: "You sons of bitches. You flunked this alert the other day because you're trying to get me in trouble. . . ." Several enlisted men reported his drinking problem, but the investigating officer informed the captain who the complainers were, causing these dedicated, well-meaning soldiers trouble from their commander.

Lieutenant Schwarzkopf was disgusted, but when he went over the captain's head to report his incompetence, he was warned to back off and remain loyal to the captain "no matter what." Schwarzkopf responded: "Sir, I don't want to talk to you about anything." Then he walked out, saying to himself that the airborne could go to hell. But he stayed despite his disgust, and after five months he was assigned to a battle group staff. "One day I discussed my disillusionment with [his boss] Whelan, who knew exactly what to say to make me stay: 'There are two ways to approach it. Number one is to get out; number two is to stick around. Someday, when you have more rank, fix the problem. But don't forget, if you get out, the bad guys will win.' I didn't want the bad guys to win."[59]

Even in Schwarzkopf's later career, there were occurrences discouraging to a lesser man. He wrote in his memoirs that because of his success in all his assignments, he fully expected to be promoted to colonel two years below the zone. "All autumn everyone had told me they were sure I'd be picked; I'd even gotten feelers from various Army units that wanted me for a colonel's job . . . and I'd secretly let myself look forward to it." He said he was not selected, to his "utter shock. . . . I sat in my office reading and re-reading [the promotion list] in stunned disbelief." But he stayed and was finally promoted.

In Vietnam, Schwarzkopf was serving as the senior adviser to a South Vietnamese outfit when several helicopters arrived at the Vietnamese unit to inspect it. He described the incident in his autobiography:

> Eventually the general and the colonel emerged. The colonel said to him, "Sir, this is Major Schwarzkopf, who was the senior advisor on the ground." The general came over and recoiled a little because I hadn't had a change of clothes in a week and had been handling bodies and stank. Meanwhile, the cameramen had followed and several reporters came up with microphones. "No, no," the general said. "Please get the microphones out of here. I want to talk to this man."
>
> I'm not sure what I expected him to say. Maybe something like, "Are your men all right? How many people did you lose?" or "Good job, we're proud of you." Instead there was an awkward silence, and then he asked, "How's the chow been?"
>
> The chow? For chrissakes, I'd been eating rice and salt and raw jungle turnips that Sergeant Hung had risked his life to get! I was so stunned that all I could say was, "Uh, fine, sir."
>
> "Have you been getting your mail regularly?"
>
> All my mail had been going to my headquarters in Saigon and I assumed it was okay. So I said, "Oh, yes, sir."
>
> "Good, good. Fine job, lad." Lad? And with that he walked off. It was an obvious PR stunt. At that moment I lost any respect I'd ever had for that general. The next night, back in New Jersey, the local TV station called my mother and told her that

her son was going to be on the evening news. She watched the report, and until the day she died, she always spoke glowingly of the wonderful general she'd seen talking to her son in Vietnam and bucking up his morale.[60]

Schwarzkopf, in response to the question of why he stayed in the army, commented, "There's a great reward in writing a concept, being in charge of executing that concept and then seeing the results that come from it, looking back to the organization that you lead and seeing them enjoy the fact that they have succeeded. There's nothing better than leading a bunch of winners and to have a group of people who, through the success of your organization, come to think of themselves as winners and are proud of themselves. They're proud of the organization that you've commanded; they're proud of what they do. That's pretty heady stuff. And then to be able to say, 'I made it happen; the organization made it happen, but I was the catalyst that caused it to come about.' That's good stuff."[61]

The answers given by the other outstanding World War II generals were the same: They liked the life, working with men in the outdoors, teaching, the association with people of integrity, the reward of giving service in a dedicated manner to something that counted. There were surely men who remained in the service during peacetime because it was a soft life, but army life was not a leisurely, lazy life for those men who reached the top. While others played, they were working, studying, and preparing. The real explanation of why they stayed is that these men had character; they possessed the feeling of belonging to something greater than themselves; they believed in the code, "Duty, Honor, Country."

One aspect of character is the answer to the question, "Was he there?" Had it not been for the duty to country concept of Marshall, MacArthur, Eisenhower, and Patton, they would not have been around to accept the top positions of responsibility in World War II. How fortunate our country has been that these men were sufficiently patient with the slow promotions, poor pay, inadequate housing, inadequate money for training, the hardship of many moves, the unhappiness of children uprooted from friends, and many other difficulties. Only a dedicated and selfless person would make such a sacrifice.

The military is always confronted with the demands of duty—duty rosters on the bulletin board, duty details, and the duty to keep one's equipment in good condition. The concept of duty is constantly present in every phase of military life.

But duty is more than a detail roster on the bulletin board. Duty with the men described in this book carried the requirement to do what one ought to do, and when one ought to do it, to the best of one's abilities. It was a matter of doing work well for the sake of all. This is summed up well in the Bible: "Whatever thy hand findeth to do, do it with thy might" (Ecclesiastes 9:10).

There are jobs within the military that are certainly not glamorous, but an officer's duty means doing the day-to-day routine jobs well. No matter how much one may love one's work, there are many aspects of the job that are not easy or pleasant.

Duty is a life not centered on oneself. These men saw their duty, and they did it, which required sacrifice—the loss of personal comforts, money, health, and sometimes their lives. They lost themselves in causes larger than self.

But there are rewards for this sense of duty, for the sacrifice. Their lives were filled with a sense of worth, an immeasurable sense of satisfaction. They were given the opportunity in military service to make the best possible use of their lives.

These men had an aim and purpose in life. Was it because they were ambitious? Ambition is the desire to do or to become better. It may be limitless. It comes from within. There are many ambitions for many different aims. There can be ambition for power, popularity, money, and prestige. Ambition can be good or bad. It moves people to overcome obstacles, but it needs direction and control. When there is direction, it is good. One of the greatest motivations for achievement in history has been ambition. But the motives that induce people to follow a particular ambition are not always the highest, not always noble. Ambition to be powerful, or to make the most money, or to achieve the greatest fame were not the goals of these men. Their aim was to follow the creed of service.

They were selfless men. Selflessness entails sacrifice, surrendering something for a greater cause. The selfish person thinks first of himself, whereas the unselfish thinks first of the welfare of others. These men gave themselves, their time, their health, their wealth, and their energy, all to achieve worthwhile goals. To them, sacrifice was a way of life.

Their sacrifice was personal, measured in long hours at work away from their families, neglecting leisure pursuits, and sometimes even forgetting their health. They did not worry about amassing wealth. Service was sufficient. And, of course, when duty called they were ready to give their lives.

A military career is not the best-paying job, nor is it the most comfortable or easy. Indeed, it is a dangerous profession. What motivates this desire to serve and to sacrifice? Love of one's home and family, of one's community. This causes many men to give up much. But the greatest and highest motive for the daily sacrifice of those who serve is their love of God and country.

Notes

1. Gene Smith, *Lee and Grant: A Dual Biography* (New York: Blue & Grey Press, 1984), 64–65.

2. William S. McFeely, *Grant: A Biography* (New York: W. W. Norton & Company, 1981), 64.

3. Personal interview with Gen. H. Norman Schwarzkopf, USA (Ret.), and Edgar F. Puryear, Jr., August 25, 1995.

4. Bruce Catton, *Mr. Lincoln's Army* (New York: Doubleday & Company, Inc., 1951), 5, 7, 30–32.

5. B. H. Liddell Hart, *Sherman: Soldier, Realist, American* (New York: Frederick A. Praeger, 1958), 354.

6. Ibid.

7. Ibid., 229.

8. Ibid., 380.

9. McFeely, *Grant: A Biography,* 119; Hart, *Sherman: Soldier, Realist, American,* 145.

10. Emory M. Thomas, *Robert E. Lee: A Biography* (New York: W. W. Norton & Company, 1995), 193–94.

11. Frank E. Vandiver, *Mighty Stonewall* (College Station: Texas A&M University Press, 1957), 328–29.

12. Byron Farwell, *Stonewall* (New York: W. W. Norton & Company, 1992), 468.

13. Douglas Southhall Freeman, *Lee's Lieutenant, Volume II* (New York: Charles Schribners Sons, 1943), 674.

14. Farwell, *Stonewall,* 493.

15. Ibid., 201.

16. Arthur Bryant, *Triumph in the West* (London: Collins, 1959), 288.

17. Office of the Chief of the Military History Collection (OCMH), Williams, oral history transcript.

18. Norman Gelb, *Ike & Monty* (New York: William Morrow and Company, Inc., 1994), 360.

19. Ibid., 363.

20. *The Papers of Dwight David Eisenhower: The War Years,* Vol. IV, 2186.

21. Montgomery paper, Imperial War Museum; Forrest Pogue, *George C. Marshall: Organizer for Victory* (New York: Viking, 1973), 475.

22. Omar N. Bradley, *A General's Life* (New York: Simon and Schuster, 1983), 338.

23. Eisenhower papers, 2221.

24. Pre-presidential papers, Principal File, Box 53, Eisenhower Memorial Library.

25. Bryant, *Triumph in the West*, 334.

26. Ibid., 336.

27. Bradley, *A General's Life*, 347.

28. Ibid.

29. Gelb, *Ike & Monty*, 393–94.

30. Ibid., 394.

31. Ibid., 397–98.

32. George E. Bohlen, *Witness to History* (New York: W. W. Norton & Company, Inc., 1973), 259–63.

33. George F. Kennon, *Memoirs, 1925–1950* (Boston: Little Brown, 1967), 347.

34. Dean Rusk, *As I Saw It: A Secretary of State's Memoirs* (London and New York: I. B. Taurus & Co., Ltd., 1991), 108–9.

35. Dean Acheson, *Sketches From Life of Men I Have Known* (New York: Harper & Brothers, 1961), 213.

36. Leonard Mosely, *Marshall: Hero for Our Times* (New York: Hearst Books, 1982), 157–58.

37. Colin Powell, *My American Journey* (New York: Random House, 1995), 535.

38. Edgar F. Puryear, Jr., *Nineteen Stars: A Study in Military Character and Leadership* (Novato, Calif.: Presidio Press, 1971), 78–79.

39. Katherine T. Marshall, *Together* (New York: Tupper and Low, Inc., 1946), 110; Stimson diary, December 31, 1943.

40. David Eisenhower, *Eisenhower: At War 1943–1945* (London: Collins, 1986), 208.

41. Forrest C. Pogue, *George C. Marshall: Education of a General* (New York: The Viking Press, 1963), 129–30.

42. Kevin McCann, *Man From Abilene* (New York: Doubleday and Company, Inc., 1952); Puryear, *Nineteen Stars*, 293.

43. Personal interview with General of the Army Dwight D. Eisenhower and Edgar F. Puryear, Jr., May 2, 1963.

44. Ibid.

45. Ibid.

46. Dwight D. Eisenhower, *At Ease: Stories I Tell to Friends* (New York: Doubleday & Company, Inc., 1967), 241.

47. Personal interview with General of the Army Omar N. Bradley and Edgar F. Puryear, Jr., February 15, 1963.

48. Personal interview with Gen. Mark W. Clark, USA (Ret.), and Edgar F. Puryear, Jr., December 20, 1962.

49. Personal interview with Gen. J. Lawton Collins, USA (Ret.), September 20, 1962.

50. Ibid.

51. Personal interview with Gen. Carl A. Spaatz, USAF (Ret.), and Edgar F. Puryear, Jr., September 12, 1962.

52. Henry H. Arnold, *Global Mission* (New York: Harper, 1949), 15.

53. Ibid., 48.

54. Ibid., 122.

55. Spaatz interview.

56. Personal interview with Curtis E. LeMay, USAF (Ret.), and Edgar F. Puryear, Jr., August 28, 1975.

57. J. Lawton Collins, *Lightening Joe: An Autobiography* (Baton Rouge: Louisiana State University Press, 1971). 440

58. Personal interview with Gen. Edward C. Meyer, USA (Ret.), and Edgar F. Puryear, Jr., July 14, 1997.

59. H. Norman Schwarzkopf, *It Doesn't Take a Hero* (New York: Bantam Books, 1992), 82–83.

60. Ibid., 120–21.

61. Personal interview with Gen. H. Norman Schwarzkopf, USA (Ret.), August 25, 1995.

Chapter 11: The Pattern

There are thousands of articles and books written on leadership, and many different theories on how to lead successfully. One theory is called the quality or trait approach, listing professional knowledge, decision, equity, humanity, loyalty, courage, consideration, integrity, selflessness, and character. But listing these qualities is not enough to describe a successful approach to leadership. These qualities need to be given life and meaning by describing them around the careers of men who have proven themselves as successful leaders in the greatest test of all, war. I have described these qualities in my previous books: *Nineteen Stars: A Study in Military Leadership and Character; Stars in Flight: A Study in Air Force Character and Leadership;* and *General S. Brown: Destined for Stars.* With this study of leadership success, I have added more recent generals, which represents thirty-five years of research—conducting more than a hundred one-on-one personal interviews with four-star generals. In addition, I have corresponded with and interviewed more than a thousand officers of the grade of brigadier general or higher. I have consulted hundreds of biographies, memoirs, and other texts on military leadership. The objective was to determine why these generals thought they were successful leaders. I have concluded that there is a pattern to successful leadership. *American Generalship* develops the consensus of their thoughts on successful leadership.

The most important of these qualities is character. After the surrender of Germany in World War II, Churchill wrote in a letter glowing terms of appreciation for Marshall's leadership and specifically emphasized addressing his "respect and admiration for your character." There are many references in this book emphasizing the importance of character. Woodrow Wilson, in a speech at the University of North Carolina, spoke of Robert E. Lee's "achievement which proceeds from character"; and Lee's peacetime minister refers to "those beautiful traits of character which made him seem even grander in peace than in war."

An additional illustration of character after the war was in a letter in which Lee declined a position that provided a considerable sum of money far above his salary as president of Washington College in Lexington, Virginia: "I am grateful, but I have a self-imposed task which I must accomplish. I have led the young men of the South in battle; I have seen many of them die on the field. I shall devote my remaining energies to training young men to do their duty in life."[1]

When during the Civil War the Northern politicians wanted to promote Sherman to the rank of lieutenant general, a promotion he didn't want; he asked his brother, U.S. senator John Sherman, to stop this promotion, telling him about Grant: "His character, more than his genius, will reconcile armies and attack the people."[2] MacArthur wrote in his memoirs, "General Pershing's fame rests largely on his personal character."[3] When General Eisenhower's son, John, was deliberating on his choice of college and career, he chose West Point, telling his dad, in response to why, that it was his father's comment on his satisfaction with an army career, and the pride he had "being associated with men of character."[4]

The leadership profiles of these generals reveal the qualities they exhibited that they had in common and made them great—the pattern. It includes a selfless desire to serve; to accept the responsibility for decision making, which Eisenhower said is the essence of leadership; to have the "feel" or "sixth sense" in decision making; to not be "yes men" in serving their seniors; to not tolerate a "yes man;" to read widely; to serve under senior officers who selected and mentored them, the reward meaning longer hours, greater challenges, and greater sacrifices for themselves and for their families; to be concerned for and considerate of their people; to realize that the ability to delegate determined how far they would go; and, when problems surfaced, to fix the problem, not the blame. With the combination of these qualities, these men met the requirements of command with great success.

But the most significant quality that permeates throughout all the aforementioned qualities is that they were men of character. Character cannot really be defined; it must be described. This description of character, and its role in successful leadership, is the overall objective of this study.

Throughout this book the selflessness of these great military leaders in the history of the country comes through. Perhaps the most frequently quoted statement from an inaugural address is that of President John F. Kennedy:"And so, my fellow Americans: Ask not what your country can do for you—ask what you can do for your country." Our military understood this concept of selflessness that this quote addressed long before Kennedy's inaugural speech. Henry L. Stimson, secretary of war in 1909–11 and 1939–45, focused on it in a comment in his diary: "I had been accustomed throughout my life to classify all public servants into one or the other of two general categories: one, the men who were thinking what they could do for their jobs, the other, the men who were thinking what the job could do for them." He commented that Marshall was the "most selfless public official whom I have ever known."

The tradition of selflessness for our military began with George Washington and is a rich part of our military heritage. On June 12, 1944, while Marshall was on an inspection for the D-day invasion, Eisenhower, in response to the question for Marshall of the principal quality he looked for in selecting a commander, responded: "Without even thinking, I said 'selflessness.'"[5]

Marshall's selflessness was developed in detail in chapter 1, as was the selflessness of Mitchell, Arnold, and Spaatz, who put their careers at risk for developed airpower, as did Jones in fighting for the B-1, and the army's Shy Meyer in publicly calling attention to our having a "hollow army."

General Eisenhower stated: "Making decisions is of the essence in leadership."[6] It would be impossible to succeed as a leader without the ability to make decisions quickly and well. It is sound judgment in decision making and the "feel" or "sixth sense" that mark great commanders. Their decisions were largely the result of their study, experience, and preparation, which developed a feel for the situation, a kind of intuition as a factor in decision making. To accept these grave responsibilities and survive required character of the highest order.

The military leader is frequently a lonely man, both in war and peace, becoming more so when his decisions bear on life and death. It is an overwhelming responsibility that few people desire and for which considerably fewer are qualified. The decision maker must have the character to accept the responsibility of handling many strains and stresses. He must select staff members and subordinate commanders who are strong and dedicated professionals, whose input is based upon ability and years of experience. He must be able to accept their advice but have the strength to override it when the situation demands. Eisenhower's D-day decision shows his real character in the decision-making process. He received the input of his staff and other commanders, watching the weather on June 5, 1944, and other conditions that could impact on the invasion's success. It was a lonely and desperate time for him. After launching the D-day invasion on June 6, there was nothing he could do but to "pray desperately." His chief of staff, Gen. Walter B. Smith, described the situation: "I never realized the lonliness and isolation of a commander at a time when such a momentous decision has to be taken with full knowledge that failure or success rests on his judgment alone."[7] President Harry S. Truman commented that as commander in chief, "no one can make decisions for him. . . . To be President of the United States is to be lonely, very lonely at times of great decisions."[8]

After making his decision, the commander must cope with criticism and the input of those who want to change it before implementation. As Marshall instructed Kennan when the latter was torn apart by press criticism: "The decision you are talking about had my approval, it was discussed in the Cabinet, and it was approved by the President. The only trouble with you is that you don't have the wisdom and the perspective of a columnist."[9] When Ike was asked how to handle the criticism of the "all-knowing press," he wrote in his diary to "ignore" it.

MacArthur illustrated his character in his decision to launch the landing at Inchon against the advice of all the other top military leaders. He told them that if the operation were to run into trouble, he would immediately withdraw the forces. "The only loss then," he said, "will be my professional reputation."[10]

It required character when President Harry S. Truman fired MacArthur, an American hero in three wars, knowing he would receive considerable criticism for the decision, which indeed he did, with the press and some congressmen and senators even calling for his impeachment. As commander in chief he had the responsibility to prevent the possibility of an expanded war with China and the Soviet Union. Avoiding World War III was more important than the criticism he would and did receive. As he so often said of his role as president, "The buck stops here."

General Schwarzkopf was lonely as the commander of Desert Shield and Desert Storm. "I didn't sleep very well in the Gulf. Even after the plan was locked in concrete, every night I would be in bed and say, 'What have I forgotten? What have we missed? Is there something more we can do . . . ?' I think it takes that kind of driving of yourself as a commander if you care about soldiers."[11]

General Colin Powell, chairman of the Joint Chiefs of Staff, commented, "Command is lonely. . . ." He specifically reflected on the night before the Panama operation. "The last night before the invasion, sitting alone in the dark in the back seat of my car . . . I felt full of foreboding. . . . Had I been right? Had my advice been sound . . . ? Was it all worth it? I went to bed gnawed by self-doubt."[12]

Important for decision making is "feel" or "sixth sense," a quality that all top military leaders have. It was summed up by Eisenhower's comment: "One must never lose touch with the feel of his troops. He can delegate tactical responsibility and avoid interference in the authority of his selected subordinates, but he must maintain the closest kind of factual and spiritual contact with them or . . . he will fail. This contact required frequent visits to the troops themselves."[13] He believed that a unit should, if properly led, function well in the commander's absence. He believed that if he could get soldiers to talk with the brass, they would not be afraid to talk with their sergeants, lieutenants, and captains. This openness would produce meaningful ideas, ingenuity, and initiative, which would increase readiness and performance. Ike believed that the army's business was success in war and that "attention to the individual was the key to success."[14]

I discussed the topic of feel or sixth sense with General John Wickham, US Army (Ret.), former Army Chief of Staff. He said:

> Nothing takes the place of personal reconnaissance. Getting a feel for what's going on with the troops is essential for making proper decisions. I made sure that I was available to the troops, not only when I was Army Chief, but also as a brigade commander. When I was Commanding General, 101st Airborne Division, the division was deployed to Germany. We assembled the troops in different groups, a brigade at a time, thousands of soldiers overall, using PA systems in the field, I would get up on top of a jeep hood and talk to them about why we were there, what our purpose was and the importance of setting the example for all the allied nations who would observe our actions. Of more importance, I stressed the essential significance of demonstrating that our assault capabilities with helicopters was the leading edge of technology in warfare; that if we didn't do it well, the 101st as an assault division would likely be finished. When I brought the division back home, I also followed that procedure every quarter of the year to tell them of my vision for the future for the division. Then I turned it over to them to tell me what the key things on their minds were; what they wanted to talk about.
>
> I got questions from them. The staff would be present and would react to them immediately.
>
> I established at Fort Campbell a "dial info" system so that any soldier could call me on an automated recorded system. Our responsibility was to get an answer back to a soldier who had a question or comment in 24 hours. There were at least 500 calls a week coming in. I read the call and the staff's answer to each of them. It gave me an extraordinary comprehension of what was on the soldiers' minds: their pay and family problems, as well as their duty to their leaders. It also gave me a feel of whether the staff was being responsive enough. If they weren't, I would jack them up. I think that similar systems are in use in other units today. I even had calls from senior NCOs. They would be something like this: "Thank you, dial info, for the opportunity to address these problems that you are solving. I

couldn't solve them on my own." So we were helping the leadership chain by using this system.

General William C. Westmoreland, commander of allied forces during the Vietnam War and former Chief of Staff, U.S. Army, echoed General Wickham's observations to me in an interview: "Regardless of where an officer is in the military hierarchy, he is frequently going to be visiting troops. Regardless of his rank, he cannot be successful if he loses contact with troops in the field.

When General Marshall inspected the troops, he would do so without the commander, accompanied only by a driver. Bradley described Marshall as having the human feel. In just walking the inspection line, he could sense a soldier in trouble, then take action immediately to correct the problem. General LeMay could even sense in preflight inspection if a crew were probably going to be shot down.

Is this feel or sixth sense a God-given talent or can it be developed? All the generals I interviewed believed that it could be developed, although certain qualities may be present from birth. To General Bradley, feel is developed through collecting information, "little bits of it," which go to the brain, where it is stored as knowledge. He explained: "When you are suddenly faced in battle with a situation needing a decision, you can give it. When people would call me on the phone and give me a situation, I would push a button and have an answer right then."[15]

Patton called it "military reaction." He explained: "What success I have had results from the fact that I have always been certain that my military reactions were correct. No one is born with them any more than anyone is born with measles. You can be born with a soul capable of correct military reactions or a body capable of having big muscles, but both qualities must be developed by hard work. . . ."[16]

General J. Lawton Collins said that feel was developed by "working hard and studying as a younger man."[17] General William J. Simpson said it was background and training that helped him "understand situations that came up" and prepared him to "anticipate what might occur," thus makeing sound decisions."[18]

Other comments emphasized education, training, experience, and observation. Being around top decision makers as mentors is vital in developing this feel, because a leader observes and learns through the mentors' experiences as well as his own.

General Matthew Ridgway reflected, "I never made a major decision in combat without visiting the trouble spots."[19] In Korea he visited troops throughout the day, then retired early and started the next day equally early. Schwarzkopf described the remarkable Col. Ngo Quang Truong of the South Vietnamese army, who uncannily had the feel of knowing the position of the enemy, where to direct artillery fire, and when to attack.

Showmanship is an important factor in successful leadership. It is part of feel, particularly what influences the troops favorably. Patton wore his ivory-handled pistols, a shiny helmet with oversized generals stars, stars on his neck collar, stars on his shoulders, a formfitting jacket with brass buttons, a riding crop, whipcord riding breeches, and boots. Ike wore the jacket named the "Ike jacket" and also riding britches, boots, a riding crop, and a smile that Bradley said was worth several divisions. MacArthur had his corncob pipe, cigarette holder, braided cap worn at a rakish angle, open-collar khaki shirt, no tie, no ribbons, and only the round circle of stars of the insignia of a general of the army.

Civil War generals' uniforms varied from the private's uniform that Grant wore to the distinguished, immaculate dress of Lee, who, although a general, wore the rank of colonel. Other examples of showmanship include the careless dress of Sherman; Jackson's wearing of his cherished but worn-out VMI cap; McClellan's trotting along the line on a "great black charger"; McDowell's straw hat; and Custer's long golden curls and cinnamon-scented hair oil. The showmanship varied but always had as its objective the reaching down to the troops.

It is interesting to note the impact of the military uniform of a senior officer upon a junior officer. Grant wrote in his *Memoirs:* "During my first year's encampment, General Scott [then general in chief of the U.S. Army] visited West Point, and reviewed the cadets. With his commanding figure, his quite colossal size and showy uniform,

I thought him the finest specimen of manhood my eyes had ever beheld, and the most to be envied. I could never resemble him in appearance, but I believe I did have a presentiment for a moment that some day I should occupy his place on review though I had no intention then of remaining in the army."[20]

Collins as a young lieutenant commented on his second meeting with Gen. John J. Pershing in 1917 in New Orleans: "Now at Chaumont, James and I joined members of the GHQ staff in the drawing room of the chateau where General Pershing was billeted, waiting for the General to make his appearance. When Pershing had visited us in New Orleans he was dressed informally. He was a handsome man even in mufti, but I was quite unprepared for his dramatic appearance, announced by an orderly, as he stood momentarily at the head of the stairs leading down from his living quarters. He was a stunning, commanding figure in his beribboned uniform, tall and erect, perfectly groomed from his iron-gray head of hair to his polished Peale boots. He had seemingly grown in stature as well as reputation since I had met him in New Orleans two years earlier. He greeted me as kindly as he had then and at once made me feel at ease. But I must have had some feelings of awe at the distinguished company because I can recall nothing of the dinner conversation."[21]

General Marshall's wife, in her book *Together,* described an amusing incident that illustrates how her general's simplicity in dress was so effective: "The Army and Navy Reception was the last of the official affairs given at the White House each season, and by far the most colorful. This year it was the last large reception of President Roosevelt's second term, and the first for George as Chief of Staff. General Craig had insisted on his wearing a special dress uniform, which he had designed for himself while holding the office. The broad sash with gold fringe was too yellow, I thought, and I had labored to tone it down with dye to a soft old-gold shade.

"On February 2nd, the day of the reception, the uniform was laid out—all ready for my husband when he came in. I was in my room, also dressing, when the door was flung open and George stood there in full regalia. 'Look at me!' he said. 'I feel like a musical comedy star. I am not going tonight dressed up like this, nor any other night.' In vain I pleaded that General Craig would be offended, but to no avail, and when we arrived at the reception he was dressed in a plain dark blue dress uniform. I did not realize it then, but his uniform, contrasting with the splendor of that evening, heralded a changing world.

"In the morning newspapers, the only man's uniform mentioned was that of General Marshall. They spoke of his unassuming and military appearance in a plain Army dress uniform of dark blue."[22]

One of the clearest qualities in the pattern is the aversion of leaders in the top positions of responsibility to "yes men." No top executive who hopes to be successful wants sycophants around him. Not being a "yes man" was a turning point in Marshall's career when he stood up to General Pershing at his first meeting with him in 1917. Thereafter, Pershing sought him out for advice and soon made him his chief of operations. When Marshall challenged Roosevelt in his first cabinet meeting with the president, Secretary of the Treasury Henry Morgenthau, and others, told him that his time in Washington with the president was over. Morganthau even told Marshall, "Well, it's been nice knowing you." Marshall's time wasn't over. Roosevelt could not afford a chief who was a "yes man." As chief of staff during World War II, Marshall briefed each newly appointed division commander before he took command that an officer must have the moral courage to report facts, unpleasant as they may be, to the ears of the commander rather than trying to keep bad news from him.

In 1939, when Marshall was selected as chief of staff by President Roosevelt, Marshall said, "I told him I wanted the right to say what I think and it would often be unpleasing. Is that all right?" To Roosevelt, it was, and they both lived up to that promise.[23]

Marshall was tough and could take being challenged. As Secretary of State Marshall told Dean Acheson, "I shall expect of you the most complete frankness, particularly about myself. I have no feelings except those I reserve for Mrs. Marshall."[24]

When Roosevelt wanted to drastically cut the size of the military and reduce pay during the Depression, MacArthur, as chief of staff, faced him with some strong and insubordinate speech. Roosevelt told him, "You must not talk that way to the president." Secretary of War Dern was present, and after leaving the White House told MacArthur, "You've saved the army."[25]

General Nathan F. Twining, the first air force officer to be chairman of the Joint Chiefs, told me: "Another thing about leadership is that you should say what you think," insisting upon being told "the way it is," but that "it sure takes the ego out of you, too."[26] The decision maker has to be tough and have a thick skin. Admiral Crowe, another chairman, said he had an aversion to "yes men" and insisted on being challenged during the decision-making process. "I'm human. Sometimes a 'no man' really upsets me. You have something you want to do and here comes some wise son of a bitch and tells you that's a dumb idea. That gets under your skin. But those are the kind of guys that matter." He added that when you disagree, "You've got to step up. That doesn't come naturally. You have to work at that; you have to work at getting your guts up to speak up."[27]

General Larry Welch summed it up: The air force chiefs would not tolerate "yes men."[28]

In dealing with allies, it can be challenging if one is not a "yes man." The beginning of the end for a dictator is when he surrounds himself with "yes men." General Stilwell stood up to Chiang Kai-shek during World War II. On one occasion, Stillwell wrote: "I made a report to the Big Boy [Chiang]. I told him the truth, and it was like kicking an old lady in the stomach."[29] Ultimately Stilwell was fired by Chiang, but after the war Chiang himself didn't last long. Chapter 4 is replete with the careers and leadership of generals who were not "yes men" and would not tolerate "yes men" under their command.

An important time in the progression of the career of J. Lawton Collins was when he challenged a hostile press in Berlin for its unfair reporting of the problems in the post–World War II occupation of Germany. Collins believed that this confrontation "had a salutary effect on them and our officer corps." When Collins was selected to succeed Ike as chief of staff, he asked Gen. Wade Haislip to be his deputy. Haislip responded, "Why do you want me? You and I haven't agreed on anything in thirty years." Collins replied, "That's exactly why I want you."[30]

But it is clear that one should not disagree just for the sake of establishing the position of not being a "yes man." Jimmy Doolittle got fired by Ike for doing that, telling me in an interview, "I do not believe in being a 'yes man.' I do believe in using tact in getting ideas over."[31] General Charles Gabriel told me, "You don't want 'yes men' on your staff. But you also need to be careful how you say 'no' when you disagree with somebody."[32]

One of the most significant illustrations of not being a "yes man" was the success that Gen. David C. Jones had in the reorganization of the Joint Chiefs of Staff, the Goldwater-Nichols Act, which upset the other services for challenging the Pentagon's and service chiefs' established "turf." Essentially, the act provided for the chairman to be the one reporting to the commander in chief, ending the requirement of the various services chiefs to have a consensus on recommendations. (Often to reach a consensus, recommendations would be so watered down that they were of little value.) The change was heralded by Les Aspin, former secretary of defense, as "one of the landmarks of American history" and by another observer as "perhaps the most important defense legislation since World War II."

How does one lead successfully? If, as Ike said, decision is the essence of leadership, is there something one can do to develop as a decision maker? Reading biography and history is part of the pattern in the successful development of leadership and character of these generals. Eisenhower loved reading so much as a child that he neglected his chores and schoolwork. He commented: "Since those early years, history of all kinds, and certainly political and military, has always intrigued me mightily." He added that the qualities of great leaders "excited" his admiration, particularly "Washington's stamina and patience in adversity, first, and then his indomitable courage, daring, and capacity for self-sacrifice."[33] Ike was also influenced by one of the comments of Marcus Aurelius, the Roman general: "Misfortune nobly borne is good fortune." When Ike was stationed in Panama, his boss, Maj. Gen. Fox Conner, assigned him books, which they often discussed, on the role that Allied leadership would have in the next war.

George Washington, whose formal education ended at age fifteen, had a library, at his death, of more than nine hundred books; he ordered books from London by the "trunkload." Although there were twenty-four college graduates at the Constitutional Convention, Washington—the avid reader, the self-educated man—was selected to preside.

Benjamin Franklin's formal education ended at age ten, and he had only one year of formal education. In his autobiography, he reflected, "From my infancy, I was passionately fond of reading, and all the money that came into my hands was laid out for books. . . . Reading was the only amusement I allowed myself. I spent no time in tavern games, or frolics of any kind. . . ."[34]

General of the Army Omar N. Bradley recalled that his father read to him and inculcated in him a love of books. Bradley told me, "I think the study of military history, and what the great leaders did, is very, very important for any young officer in developing this quality of the feel or sixth sense in successful leadership."[35]

General Marshall, as commandant of the Army Infantry School for five years in the early 1930s, encouraged his young captains and lieutenants to read and invited them into his home to discuss books and their readings.

General Thomas D. White, the separate air force's first soldier-statesman as chief of staff, was aide-de-camp to Gen. John M. Palmer, one of the great scholars of the old army, who assigned White books to read. White attended, on his own time, graduate school at the Georgetown School of Foreign Service, taking courses in international relations and the Russian language. Because of this education, he became the first air attaché to the Soviet Union when the United States recognized it in 1933.

Admiral Crowe is included in this study of generalship because he has so much to offer all of the younger generation of officers. When I asked the size of his personal library, he responded that he had more than four thousand books. He told me: "I really like biographies. That's the main thing I read. I like history, but I read biography most of all. . . . Biography is a lifetime investment."[36]

General David C. Jones, with only two years of college, went on to reach the highest position in military service as chairman of the Joint Chiefs. He was self-educated. He told me: "I have an insatiable appetite for information. Life is one of constant learning. I read a lot of professional works, military history, leadership, but also about what is going on in the world."[37]

Ridgway commented that as a cadet at West Point he was a "prodigious" reader, and that as a combat leader things he had read "came back vividly" and were "helpful." He said that books had a tremendous influence on his career.[38]

General Creech, a brilliant combat fighter pilot, was a voracious reader. He recommended developing discipline to read a book a week, emphasizing the study of human psychology to learn what motivates people. His advice to younger officers was that "reading must be a lifelong commitment, even an obsession."[39]

There are new challenges and demands for the qualification of today's officer. To handle the plethora of books, Gen. Carl Vuono, as army chief of staff, charged his Assessments and Initiatives Group with reviewing the current relevant books and professional articles. They were to provide him short items giving him the main messages and thoughts of these current publications. Often the short comments were so meaningful that he would read the entire book. He set aside time for reflection and reading outside his daily office and travel schedule. He told me that his reading was "a great stimulus for a lot of ideas" and "was a very valuable tool for my decision making."[40]

I asked Gen. Gordon R. Sullivan, who succeeded Vuono as chief, about reading, and he told me he continued to have a group of officers whose sole duty was studying "what's happening, what's not happening, and how can I influence the action?"[41] He told me: "If I am wrestling with a problem and I can't quite sort it out, my inclination is to go to history. . . . I grew up reading. It was a big part of my life. In college I was a history major, and I did a lot of reading there."

General Schwarzkopf told me the importance of reading to him: "You learn from history or you are doomed to repeat it. . . . I have been fascinated with the leadership of Lee, Grant, Sherman, Patton, and obviously, Bradley."[42]

Many of today's young officers say that their schedules are too demanding to allow time and energy for reading along with other distractions such as TV. Taking this position is to me an excuse, indeed, a cop-out. General Shy Meyer, who was jumped over fifty-seven generals to become chief of staff, told me: "While in the army, I got up early every morning at three-thirty or four-thirty and read for my own information. That was my own precious time to read. . . . I jealously guarded that time. . . . I found that if I didn't set aside time to read, it wouldn't get done. Today, to be a reader, you have to work at it."[43]

Mrs. Marshall commented that during World War II, Marshall would come home in the evening too tired to talk. She would send to the library for a pile of books, and he would go through it like a "swarm of locust devouring a green field."[44]

Eisenhower said, "Leadership consists of nothing but taking responsibility for everything that goes wrong and giving your subordinates credit for everything that goes well."[45] I had the opportunity to interview many generals who commanded during the invasion of Europe: Generals William H. Simpson, Ninth Army; Courtney Hodges, First Army; Jacob L. Devers, 6th Army Group; Lucian K. Truscott, 3d Division and VI Corps; and Mark Clark, Fifth Army. I asked each of them questions about their own leadership philosophy and for their comments on the leadership of other generals. Their insights were meaningful in describing the role of character.

To my surprise, the senior generals under Clark were reluctant to talk about him. Finally, Lt. Gen. Willis D. Crittenberger, one of his corps commanders, expressed a particular concern about Clark—that when something went wrong, he would report back to Eisenhower that when he found out who was "at fault" he would remove that individual. This usually meant the termination of that individual's career. Critenberger further elaborated that he considered this a character flaw in Clark, to pass the cause of failure onto someone else instead of accepting the responsibility yourself as the senior officer.[46]

General Marshall would say throughout his career to his subordinate officers, "Fix the problem, not the blame." General Eisenhower had in his pocket a note that he would read to the press in the event of the failure of the June 6, 1994, D-day invasion. It stated: "Our landings have failed. . . . If any blame or fault attaches to the attempt it is mine alone."[47] In my interview with him, he told me that he had remembered Lee's letter to President Jefferson Davis after the Confederate failure at Gettysburg in which he stated, "No blame can be attached to the Army. . . . I am alone to blame."[48]

Major General George B. McClellan, twice relieved by Lincoln as commander of the Army of the Potomac for failing to fight aggressively, not being particularly successful when he did, constantly placed the blame on Lincoln, or the secretary of war, or other cabinet and subordinate commanders, never personally accepting responsibility for things that went wrong.

When Grant was promoted to lieutenant general, he wrote to General Sherman, "I feel indebted [to you] for whatever I have had of success. . . . Your execution of whatever has been given you to do entitles you to the reward I am receiving. . . ."[49]

In late July 1944, the 5th Armored Division under Maj. Gen. Lunsford E. Oliver was carrying out movement orders given him by Patton. He ran into difficulty in moving, which was not his division's fault. He was ordered to Patton's command post, where he was fully expecting a chewing out. Present at this conference was his staff, corps commanders, and division commanders. Patton began the meeting by telling them, "We are in a hell of a mess, and it is my fault."[50] Patton frequently would give credit to others. His position on credit and blame was similar to Ike's. Patton, in his book *War As I Knew It*, wrote that a general officer should "assume the responsibility for failure, whether he deserves it or not." If things went well, he should "invariably give the credit for success to others, whether they deserve it or not."[51]

It is important to remember Ike's point on responsibility: "If a mere general makes a mistake, he can be repudiated and kicked out and disgraced. But a government cannot repudiate and kick out or disgrace itself—not, at any rate, in wartime."[52] When the tanker *Al Rekkab* was sunk by a mine in the Persian Gulf, the press was unmerciful in its criticism because we did not have minesweepers in place escorting the tankers. Admiral Crowe, then in command of the area, wanted to tell the media we made a mistake, but Secretary of Defense Weinberger told Crowe, "Never, never, never, never admit that you made a mistake." But the criticism from the media would not go away. Finally, Crowe, ignoring the secretary's advice, told the press that he "personally made a mistake on the *Bridgeton* mining."[53] That ended the matter.

Mistakes will always be made. Lee's leadership philosophy is still valid today: "When a man makes a mistake, I call him to my tent, and use the authority of my position to make him do the right thing next time."[54] General Sullivan told me, "There is too much trying to make yesterday perfect. Fixing the blame is not going to get you anywhere trying to get perfection. We should reflect when a mistake is made, 'What can we learn from what we have done?'"

During the Gulf War to remove Iraq from Kuwait, Schwarzkopf asked his Army deputy, Maj. Gen. Cal Waller, to stand in for him at a press conference. Waller unknowingly made a statement that contradicted President Bush, and Schwarzkopf feared that Waller would be fired. He wasn't, because Schwarzkopf told Secretary of Defense Cheney, "I'm the one to blame."[55]

When Colin Powell approved bombing a target in Iraq that might release killer germs, he assumed the risk, saying that if things went wrong to "just blame me."[56]

General Eisenhower, in answer to the question "How does one develop as a decision maker?" responded, "Be around people making decisions."[57] This thought ties in with the importance of mentorship, for part of mentorship places a subordinate in contact with people at the top who are making the toughest decisions. Using Gen. Shy Meyer's definition, a mentor is someone who provides "guidance, counseling, advice, and teaching" and, with that, "door opening"— meaning opportunity. The result of door opening and mentorship is that with progress in rank and responsibility one gets the toughest jobs, the longest hours, and the greatest sacrifices in family life.

Marshall was mentored by several influential and able officers, most significantly Pershing. MacArthur's first mentor was his father. Eisenhower had the tutelage of Gen. Fox Conner and served under chief of staff MacArthur for three years, from 1932 to 1935, and in the Philippines from 1935 to 1938. He also served under Marshall as chief of staff from 1939 to 1942. Patton was aide to Secretary of War Stimson from 1909 to 1911 and Gen. Leonard Wood and with Pershing in 1916 during World War I. The many other examples of mentorship in the lives of the generals in this book are developed in chapter 6.

The most meaningful mentorship was the program instituted by General Creech during his tenure as commander of Tactical Air Command for six and a half years. He added selecting and grooming as constructs to mentorship to develop his leadership philosophy that "the duty of a leader is to create leaders."[58] His mentorship program should be the program that all of our services adopt. Proof of its value was the fact that twenty-one colonels who went through it became four-star generals.

Leader development is by no means limited to personal mentoring. General Carl Vuono, chief of staff of the army during Operations Just Cause and Desert Storm, believes that the development of a new generation of leaders—officers and NCOs—was the most critical element in the revitalization of the army from the ashes of Vietnam.

In my interview with Vuono, he told me: "For nearly twenty years, the army painstakingly developed leaders at all levels who were competent in the profession of arms, responsible for themselves and their soldiers, and committed to the defense of the nation. The army's leader development program embraced education within our schooling system—such as the Command and General Staff College at Fort Leavenworth and the Army War College at Carlisle Barracks. But it went beyond our schools. Leader development programs reached into the operational assignments—the commands and staffs to which our leaders were assigned, and to self-development, following the model established by George Marshall during the interwar years. Nor did it stop with our senior leaders, for we found that generals needed to be [introduced to] the art of generalship as much as lieutenants needed to be developed into company-grade officers."

The results of this leader development program, according to Vuono, were most evident to the world in the lightning hundred-hour war that destroyed the Iraqi army in Desert Storm.

A question that has been asked from the beginning of analyzing leadership success is "How do you lead men in such a way that they will put their life on the line for you in a combat situation in time of war, and work twenty hours a day for weeks and sometimes months to resolve a crisis in peacetime?" The generals I interviewed were all in agreement: First, a leader must illustrate devotion and commitment to a life of service; second, a leader must be considerate and concerned about his people.

Important in this study is a basic love of and concern for people. A general can get his subordinates to carry out orders through fear, but men and women will never give their all to such a commander. The real leader is loved by his people because they can sense that the leader has a love for them. This is best portrayed by consideration for the staff, commanders, and soldiers. This quality is an evident hallmark of generals in this study.

Marshall would not treat any officer haughtily or let any other officer do so with an enlisted man. As chief of staff, he showed concern for soldiers' families as well, even to the point of stretching regulations. His telephone calls to the wives of servicemen, and arranging for his staff to meet General Pershing, are but some of the many acts he performed out of consideration for his subordinates.

Douglas MacArthur's concern for his subordinates was legendary. His letters to the families of deceased soldiers in his command were wonderful gestures. The chocolate soda for his army commander, General Eichelberger, that MacArthur had waiting for him after he came out from weeks in the jungle was a small matter that was touching and amazing.

General Eisenhower showed a deep concern for his subordinates—for example, the ceremony at the airport to pin on Mark Clark's third star. He attended his orderly's wedding, introduced General Smith to the king of England, and protected Leigh-Mallory when his recommendations were not followed. These and visits to the troops are but a few of his humane acts.

The rough, go-for-broke Patton was underneath a highly sensitive man, particularly when it concerned the soldiers under his command. Tears came quickly when those close to him were killed or when he visited the wounded in hospitals. His method of go-for-broke fighting was designed to save American lives; his outlook that it took eighteen years to make a soldier and only a few months to manufacture ammunition was typical of his attitude. His appreciation for the cooks, truck drivers, wire stringers, and others in noncombatant jobs developed a winning team.

General LeMay summed it up, telling me: "You've got to worry about your people. No one else is going to worry about them if you don't."[59] There are many other examples in chapter 7. General Hap Arnold sacrificed his own incredibly busy schedule to release talented key people from his staff to permit them combat assignments denied to him in World War I. Vandenburg invited a colonel to sit in on a conference with the legendary MacArthur. Twining gave up his Christmas vacation to permit Quesada to catch up on his flight training. General John P. Ryan took coffee to mechanics working late at night. General Brown allowed a crewman to release his frustration by putting on his cowboy hat and boots. He also provided flights home during temporary duty for his officers and men, and he saw to it that enlisted personnel living in barracks could have a leisurely breakfast on Sundays. General Jones, as chief, sent teams throughout the world checking on the base exchange, commissary, schools, the dependents of enlisted personnel overseas, and he included the retired personnel in air force functions, capitalizing on their wealth of experience.

With the prolific literature available on leadership, one would think that all leaders would understand and appreciate the importance of looking out for their troops, yet such is not always the case. General Schwarzkopf illustrates this by his story of the colonel in Germany who was not concerned about the plight of his soldiers' unsponsored dependents. Consideration and concern are basic. I hope the readers of this book are already giving them the emphasis they need.

Marshall told Eisenhower, "If your subordinates cannot do [the work], you haven't organized them properly." How far one goes in the military and, of course, in business, depends largely upon the leader's ability to delegate. The larger the unit, the more important delegation is. One of the most endearing things a leader can do is to give a subordinate a job and leave him alone to do it, backing him up when needed. Eisenhower himself had an open-door policy with his staff but emphasized that his staff members were free to solve their own problems wherever possible and not get into a habit of passing the buck up to him.

It takes time for a commander to develop a team to whom he can delegate. Arnold commented, "Until [a commander's] staff is thoroughly trained, he will supervise all the duties himself, but it is more than one man can undertake and he will be wise, indeed, if he early ensures the adequate training of these assistants and then delegates to them the responsibility, retaining supervisory power." Air force chief of staff Larry Welch knew the importance of delegation in decision making; he emphasized that one had to "be sure decisions are made by people in the best position to make them. . . . Pushing decisions down to where they ought to be made has the tremendous advantage of training decision makers at the right level."[60]

Ike summed it up in his diary on December 10, 1942, reflecting that he was "called upon day and night to absorb the disappointments and doubts of his subordinates and to force them on to accomplishments. The odd thing about it is that most of these subordinates don't even realize that they should not pour their burdens upon the next supervisor; and that when they receive orders to do something, they relieve their commander of a great load."[61]

Again, the caveat on delegations given by Eisenhower must be emphasized: "You as a leader must take complete responsibility for what that subordinate does."[62] General Gordon R. Sullivan, army chief of staff from 1991 to 1995, also stresses this point in a letter he wrote as chief to his general officers on April 14, 1995, in which he stated: "Our values connect our army to the nation, but also permit senior leaders to delegate authority with the expectation that our subordinates will not simply take action, but that they will take personal responsibility for their actions and that they will act responsibly. . . . Our task as senior leaders is to create the institutional environment that demands from our subordinates not simply action, but responsible action."[63]

One of the most impressive interviews I had with the top World War II army generals was with Lt. Gen. Clarence Huebner. He presented an example of mentoring offered by our democracy and the opportunity in the U.S. Army. Educated in a one-room schoolhouse in Bushton, Nebraska, he had only two years of high school and after that only a business school education. In 1910 he enlisted in the army and served in the enlisted ranks until 1916, when he was, because of the exceptional leadership he demonstrated, commissioned a second lieutenant of infantry. I described earlier how various mentors trained and inspired him to greatness. His final assignment before retirement was commanding general, United States Forces, Europe.

I inquired of Huebner what there was about West Point graduates and his mentors that influenced him to emulate them. His response:

"Their character, and particularly the fact that they embodied the concept of Duty, Honor, and Country, the West Point motto."[64]

This emphasizes the responsibility of West Point graduates and the other service academies who over the years have been the model for many fellow officers and enlisted personnel. Douglas MacArthur wrote in his memoirs: "In the final analysis of the West Point product, character is the most precious component."[65] All the generals I interviewed who graduated from West Point prior to World War II and were on active duty between the two world wars commented on the impact of the Cadet Prayer, recited almost daily in their cadet life, on their character development, particularly the prayer's phrase, "Make us choose the harder right over the easier wrong."

There was something special that I observed in interviewing so many of our top military leaders. Few people have had the opportunity I have had in being able to focus in the interviews on why these great men thought they and other generals were successful leaders when commenting on their own leadership and that of their contemporaries. I got a warm and wonderful feeling of their strength, their integrity, the fact that they lived the West Point motto of "Duty, Honor, Country." But one of the air force generals, "Doc" Strother, a West Point graduate, told me: "We received our character training in our homes." I guess it's a case of diamonds in and diamonds out, with their training and association with other men of character accentuating this character building.

They were selfless, loved their country, and forfeited many more lucrative opportunities to serve. They loved their profession and were proud of it, and more importantly they loved soldiering and their soldiers. To be called a soldier, in the army or in the air force, is the finest compliment you can attribute to any professional military officer. Bradley's memoir was entitled *Soldier*, Ridgway's was *A Soldier's Story*, and Westmoreland's was *A Soldier Reports*. These titles reflect the feeling that three of our country's greatest military leaders had for their soldiers.

The generals studied in *American Generalship* truly loved their profession and they loved their soldiers. Ike spent many years in staff work and was extremely pleased to be assigned just before World War II to Third Army stationed at Fort Hood, in Texas. On July 1, 1940, he wrote his classmate Bradley, who like Ike did not see combat in World War I: "I'm having the time of my life. Like everyone else in the army, we're up to our necks in work and in problems, big and little. But this work is fun! . . . I could not conceive of a better job."[66]

In December 1941, Ike received orders to report to the War Plans Division. His initial reaction was: "This message was a hard blow. During the First World War, every one of my frantic efforts to get to the scene of action had been defeated. . . . I hoped in any new war to stay with the troops. Being ordered to a city where I had already served a total of eight years would mean, I thought, a virtual repetition in World War I. Heavyhearted, I telephoned my wife to pack a bag, and within the hour I was headed for the War Department."[67]

Ike's frame of mind and love of the troops were illustrated in a thought in his diary only several weeks after his arrival in Washington. Writing on January 4, 1942, he said: "Tempers are short. There are lots of amateur strategists on the job, and primadonnas [sic] everywhere. I'd give anything to be back in the field."

More recent generals also had deep regrets about leaving troop duty. General Shalikashvili was informed he was to be supreme Allied commander in Europe, and told me of the assignment: "I didn't want that, [I wanted] to spend more time with the soldiers." Similarly, Shy Meyer and Carl Vuono had reservations about becoming chief of staff, the top army position. They lamented that it took them away from serving with soldiers, which they said was "fun."

Often in military service you find officers who are counting the days until they can retire. Obviously those officers are not enjoying their profession and don't make the contribution that the dedicated professional does. They are not having fun. A comment made in a speech by air force general George S. Brown to a group of ROTC students just before his retirement says it all: "In looking at you and the future you have before you in the military, I wish I could do it all over again."

Character permeates throughout each of the descriptions of the leadership of the generals of this book. But character doesn't just develop in the heat of battle or a time of crisis. It develops from the consistent application of moral values and ethical behavior throughout one's military career. The importance of character goes all the way back to the philosopher Aristotle, who emphasized that character is a habit, daily selecting right from wrong. Character is developed during peacetime and must be a part of a general's makeup in both peace and war.

The lives and careers of the generals in this study reveal a pattern for success available to every officer—indeed, to every person. Success, to the limits of one's innate abilities, is available to all those who dedicate themselves to their careers, who are willing to work long and hard to prepare themselves, who recognize and develop that high character necessary to leadership, who love their fellow man and show their concern for his well-being, and who can communicate with others in a manner that inspires confidence and devotion to duty.

Notes

1. Charles Bracelen Flood, *Lee: The Last Years* (Boston: Houghton Mifflin Company, 1981), 175.

2. B. H. Liddell Hart, *Sherman: The Genius of the Civil War* (London: Eyre and Spotteswood, 1933), 240.

3. Douglas MacArthur, *Reminiscences* (New York: McGraw-Hill Book Company, 1964), 350.

4. Dwight D. Eisenhower, *At Ease* (New York: Doubleday & Company, Inc., 1967), 241.

5. Personal interview with General of the Army Dwight D. Eisenhower, USA, and Edgar F. Puryear, Jr., May 2, 1963.

6. Ibid.

7. Walter B. Smith, *Eisenhower's Six Great Decisions* (New York: Longmans, Green, 1956), 55.

8. Harry S. Truman, *Year of Decisions* (Garden City, N.Y.: Doubleday & Company, Inc., 1955), ix.

9. George F. Keenan, *Memoirs 1925–1950* (Boston: Little, Brown, 1972), 346–47.

10. MacArthur, *Reminiscences,* 350.

11. Personal interview with Gen. H. Norman Schwarzkopf, USA (Ret.) and Edgar F. Puryear, Jr., October 27, 1995.

12. Colin Powell, *My American Journey* (New York: Random House, 1995), 427.

13. Dwight D. Eisenhower, *Crusade in Europe* (New York: Doubleday and Company, Inc., 1948), 213–14.

14. Ibid., 313–14.

15. Personal interview with General of the Army Omar N. Bradley and Edgar F. Puryear, Jr., February 15, 1963.

16. Letter from Gen. George S. Patton, Jr., USA, to his son Cadet George S. Patton, IV, dated June 6, 1944.

17. Personal interview with Gen. J. Lawton Collins USA (Ret.) and Edgar F. Puryear, Jr., September 20, 1962.

18. Person interview with William H. Simpson USA (Ret.) and Edgar F. Puryear, Jr., September 20, 1962.

19. Interview with Gen. Matthew Ridgway, USA (Ret.), and Lt. John M. Beair, November 24, 1971.

20. Ulysses S. Grant, *Personal Memoirs of U. S. Grant, Volume 1* (New York: Charles L. Webster & Company, 1885), 41–42.

21. Lawton J. Collins, *Lightning Joe: An Autiobiography* (Baton Rouge and London: Louisiana State University Press, 1979), 26–27.

22. Katherine T. Marshall, *Together* (New York: Tupper and Low, Inc., 1946), 65–66.

23. Forrest C. Pogue, *George C. Marshall: Education of a General* (New York: Viking Press, 1963), 330.

24. Dean Acheson, *Present at the Creation* (New York: W. W. Norton, 1969), 213.

25. MacArthur, *Reminiscences,* 100–101.

26. Personal interview with Nathan F. Twining, USAF (Ret.), and Edgar F. Puryear, Jr., March 3, 1977.

27. Personal interview with Adm. William J. Crowe, Jr., USN (Ret.), and Edgar F. Puryear, Jr., May 16, 1997.

28. Personal interview with Gen. Larry Welch, USAF (Ret.), and Edgar F. Puryear, Jr., February 19, 1987.

29. Letter from Gen. Joseph W. Stilwell to his wife, dated June 7, 1942.

30. Personal interview with Gen. Wade Haislip, USA (Ret.), and Edgar F. Puryear, Jr., September 12, 1962.

31. Personal interview with Lt. Gen. James H. Doolittle, USAF (Ret.), and Edgar F. Puryear, Jr., February 7, 1977.

32. Personal interview with Gen. Charles Gabriel, USAF (Ret.), and Edgar F. Puryear, Jr., July 17, 1986.

33. Eisenhower, *At Ease,* 39–41.

34. Benjamin Franklin, *The Autobiography of Benjamin Franklin* (New York: Barnes and Noble, 1994), 13.

35. Bradley interview.

36. Personal interview with Adm. William J. Crowe, Jr., USN (Ret.), and Edgar F. Puryear, Jr., May 16, 1997.

37. Personal interview with Gen. David C. Jones, USAF (Ret.), and Edgar F. Puryear, Jr., January 10, 1997.

38. Personal Interview with Gen. Matthew Ridgway, USA (Ret.), and Lt. Col. John M. Belair, November 24, 1971.

39. Personal interview with Gen. W. L. Creech, USAF (Ret.), and Edgar F. Puryear, Jr., December 20, 1998.

40. Personal interview with Gen. Carl Vuono, USA (Ret.), and Edgar F. Puryear, Jr., April 14, 1997.

41. Personal interview with Gen. Gordon R. Sullivan, USA (Ret.), and Edgar F. Puryear, Jr., April 2, 1999.

42. Personal interview with Gen. H. Norman Schwarzkopf, USA (Ret.), and Edgar F. Puryear, Jr., October 27, 1995.

43. Personal interview with Gen. Edward C. Meyer, USA (Ret.), and Edgar F. Puryear, Jr., July 14, 1997.

44. Marshall, *Together*, 97.

45. Eisenhower interview.

46. Personal interview with Lt. Gen. Willis D. Crittenberger, USA (Ret.), and Edgar F. Puryear, Jr., October 20, 1962.

47. David Eisenhower, *Eisenhower at War, 1943–1945* (London: Collins, 1986), 252.

48. Letter from Gen. Robert E. Lee to President Jefferson Davis, dated July 31, 1863.

49. Hart, *Sherman: The Genius of the Civil War*, 238–39.

50. Letter from Maj. Gen. Lunsford E. Oliver, USA (Ret.), to Edgar F. Puryear, Jr., dated October 9, 1962.

51. George S. Patton, Jr., *War As I Knew It* (Boston: Houghton-Mifflin Company, 1947), 355.

52. Robert E. Sherwood, *Roosevelt and Hopkins* (New York: Harper and Brothers, 1948), 651.

53. Crowe interview.

54. Flood, *Lee: The Last Years*, 20.

55. Schwarzkopf interview.

56. Powell, *My American Journey*, 504.

57. Eisenhower interview.

58. Creech interview.

59. . Personal interview with Gen. Curtis E. LeMay, USAF (Ret.), and Edgar F. Puryear, Jr., August 28, 1975.

60. Welch interview, February 19, 1987.

61. Eisenhower interview.

62. Ibid.

63. Sullivan interview.

64. Personal interview with Gen. Clarence Ralph Huebner and Edgar F. Puryear, Jr., October 30, 1962.

65. MacArthur, *Reminiscences.*

66. Letter from Col. Dwight D. Eisenhower, USA, to Col. Omar N. Bradley, July 1, 1940.

67. Eisenhower, *Crusade in Europe*, 14.

Index

Index

Index

Pope, General, 302–303, 306
Porter, Fitz John, 302–303
Powell, Colin, 68–73, 131–34,
 138, 179–80, 229–32, 295–97,
 319–20, 342, 354
Poz, Robert, 72

Quarles, Donald, 273
Quesada, Elwood R. "Pete",
 242–43
Quezon, President, 9–10
Quinn, General, 209

Ramsay, Admiral, 48–49
Rawlings, Edwin W., 125
Reagan, Ronald, 136, 171, 230
Reed, Joseph, 13
Reinhart, Major General, 99
Revolutionary War, 13–14
Ridenour, Ron, 291
Ridgway, Matthew B., 90–91,
 104, 167–69, 345, 350, 359
Robertson, Senator, 33–34
Rodgers, John, 25
Rogers, Frank, 248
Roosevelt, Franklin D., 17–20,
 22–23, 50–51, 55, 59, 110–11,
 114–15, 119, 133, 137–38,
 150, 167, 193, 262, 297–98,
 311, 318, 346–47
Roosevelt, Theodore, 148, 192
Rusk,Dean, 59, 316–17
Russo-Japanese War (1905),
 148
Ryan, Jack, 207–208, 246–47,
 276, 357

Saudi Arabia, 297
Schlesinger, James, 204
Schwarzkopf, Norman, 66–68,

93–96, 127–29, 138, 178–79,
 253–56, 280, 295–96, 329–32,
 342, 345, 351, 354, 357
Scott, General, 345–46
Scowcroft, Brent, 72
SHAEF, 13, 78, 80, 310
Shalikashvili, John M., 88, 104,
 133–34, 180, 230–31, 257–58,
 297, 361
SHAPE , 11, 13, 209–10
Shenandoah, 25–26
Sherman, Forrest, 61
Sherman, John, 3, 303–304, 339
Sherman, William Tecumseh, 3,
 17, 153–54, 160, 171, 179,
 287, 303–305, 345, 351, 353
Sibert, Edwin L., 321
Sibert, William L., 108–109
Sicily, 201
Simpson, William H., 6, 85–86,
 103, 344, 352
Singlaub, John, 65
Smart, Jacob, 205
Smith, Joseph, 165–66
Smith, Walter Bedell, 45, 55–56,
 162, 237, 262–63, 309–10,
 312, 341, 356
Soviet Union, 50–51, 57,
 166–67, 244, 342, 350
Spaatz, Carl, 5, 24, 28, 31–32,
 39–40, 81, 87, 123–24, 164,
 239–41, 266, 269–72, 325–28,
 340
Spanish-American War, 147
Stalin, Josef, 19
Stennis, John C., 35
Stilwell, Joseph W., 118–20, 295,
 348
Stimson, Henry L., 1, 7, 17,
 19–24, 112, 199–201, 315,